PERSONAL VISIONS

PERSONAL VISIONS

Conversations with Contemporary Film Directors

by Mario Falsetto

SILMAN-JAMES PRESS   LOS ANGELES

First Edition

10 9 8 7 6 5 4 3 2 1

Library of Congress Cataloging-in-Publication Data

Falsetto, Mario.
Personal visions : conversations with contemporary
film directors / by Mario Falsetto.
p. cm.
1. Motion picture producers and directors—Interviews. I. Title.
PN1998.2.F35 2000   791.43'023'0922—dc21   00-040052

ISBN 1-879505-51-7 (alk. paper)

Cover design by Wade Lageose

Printed in the United States of America.

SILMAN-JAMES PRESS
1181 Angelo Drive
Beverly Hills, CA 90210

To Carole

CONTENTS

Author's Note

The first interview for *Personal Visions: Conversations with Contemporary Film Directors* took place in July 1997. My final conversation was in December 1998. Once a filmmaker consented to an interview, I set about reading everything of substance I could find on that director. Then I carefully analyzed each of their films and prepared my questions. Within that eighteen-month period, I made several trips to London, New York, Toronto, Dublin, and Los Angeles from my home in Montreal to meet with directors for what was always a fruitful, lively conversation. Without exception, each director was incredibly generous with their time.

After each interview was transcribed, I began the process of editing the conversations into a coherent shape. Then, I sent each interview back to the filmmaker for their input and corrections. We then went back and forth with the edited transcript until each director was satisfied with its final shape. In the end, it was incredibly valuable to have each director go through the interview and provide further input, since this allowed them an opportunity to clarify or rethink some of their original responses.

ACKNOWLEDGMENTS

First and foremost, I'd like to thank all the filmmakers who made this book possible. Without question, it was their generosity of spirit and cooperation that kept my own enthusiasm fired up during the three years I devoted to this project. At Concordia University in Montreal, I'd like to single out Dean Christopher Jackson for his help and encouragement. In addition, I received several research grants from the Faculty of Fine Arts at Concordia University that were hugely helpful in defraying some of my project-related expenses. Various research assistants helped with tape transcription, fact checking, and other kinds of assistance on the manuscript, and I'd like to thank them here: Eric Bourassa, Brian Crane, Leah Hendriks, Douglas Hildebrand, Kristian Moën, Sandra "Sam" Macdonald, Scott Preston, Krzysztof Rucinski, and Giovanni Spezzacatena. Without their enormous contributions, I'd still be at the keyboard. To my agent, Christy Fletcher, a special note of thanks. She was an early supporter of *Personal Visions* and never wavered in her faith in the project. My editors, Jim Fox and Tara Lawrence, were as sympathetic and helpful as any author has a right to expect. Finally, Carole Zucker, my greatest supporter and sharpest critic, once again deserves more thanks than I could possibly communicate here. She also read through each interview and offered astute advice that was enormously helpful. I could always count on Carole's unwavering encouragement to remind me of the worth of this project, and to keep a cool head. *Personal Visions* is dedicated to her with the greatest love and affection.

INTRODUCTION

One of the most distinctive features of contemporary American cinema, and perhaps *the* film story of the last twenty years, is the extraordinary explosion of independent cinema. This has inevitably produced a new generation of filmmakers engaged in groundbreaking work, often outside the major Hollywood studios. Internationally, there is no precisely comparable situation, since most non-American films are produced independently, but in the last two decades a new generation of international filmmakers has also emerged ready to take up the mantle of earlier generations. *Personal Visions: Conversations With Contemporary Film Directors* was conceived as a contribution to a better understanding of these new film artists. I was also hoping to provide a forum for artists who I believe have made, or are set to make, a significant mark in the world of film.

In the United States, the very definition of what constitutes an independent film is, at best, ambiguous. The corporate complexity of the contemporary entertainment industry is such that many independent film companies are, in fact, owned by the majors. For example, Miramax is part of the Disney empire; Fine Line and New Line are owned by Time-Warner; October Films has been absorbed by Universal/MCA. And those majors themselves often constitute part of a much larger conglomerate—a development that can be traced back at least to the "corporatization" of Hollywood in the sixties. The structure of the entertainment industry is truly labyrinthian and the conditions under which most films are made are as varied as the films themselves. Studio films, with their emphasis on special effects and formulaic scripts and situations, are less likely to be groundbreaking, but imagination and originality abound in the world of film, both in independently produced work, and in films that emanate from major studios. Whether, in today's filmmaking climate, films can truly carry the independent label or not, it is an undeniable fact that personal filmmaking is flourishing. Many filmmakers of intelligence and conviction are producing remarkable work, a fact I discovered again and again while engaged on this project.

Few people have a real understanding of what it takes to get a feature film made and released. What specifically do film directors do to construct a film? How does a film get from idea to finished product? How do film directors interact with other creative personnel such as actors, set designers, cinematographers and editors? What do directors have to say about their creative work? What is the relationship of the independent filmmaker to the major Hollywood studios? *Personal Visions* seeks to answer these and many other questions about the process of making films.

Why should we be interested in what film directors have to say? In the production of a film, no individual is as close to every aspect of the creative process as the director, or can comment on it with the same insight. A film director is often involved in every stage of the creative process, from its conception through the script stage, the shooting, and postproduction. Who better to interpret the possible meanings of a film than its director? Who is more qualified to examine the intricacies of creation than the individual most intimately involved in all aspects of production?

I began this project in the summer of 1996. Although I had a good grasp of contemporary filmmaking through my twenty years of teaching film, and from seeing large numbers of films each year, I felt the need to research films and filmmakers I had not kept up with, or whose work I simply did not know well. I spent about a year doing preliminary research and thinking about who I wanted to contact. Once I had done that, reality set in and the project took on a life of its own. The precise mix of people included in this book is the result of many factors, some within my control and others the happy outcome of unforeseen circumstances. Anyone who has ever undertaken a project like this will understand that such an enterprise is in constant transformation and its final shape cannot easily be predicted. I spoke with more individuals than are ultimately included here, but I am satisfied that the seventeen interviews in *Personal Visions* represent a singular cross-section of talented, adventurous artists who offer remarkable insight into their films, the workings of the film industry and the role of the film director in the creative process of making films.

Despite the communal nature of filmmaking—obviously many creative individuals contribute—there is an undeniable "auteur" bias to the interviews. As Neil Jordan says, "You only know what you know, don't you?" We cannot change where we come from or our own personal history. In most cases, I was attracted to the personal, auteur filmmaker rather than the studio hired hand. I was always, throughout my life, profoundly affected by many of the great auteurs of the 1960s and 1970s such as Kubrick, Scorsese, Coppola, Fellini, Cassavetes, and many others, and this interest of mine undoubtedly influenced my choice of filmmaker for this project. Most of the people I spoke with initiate their films, work on the scripts, are involved in the editing and sound work: in short, are bound up with the project from its earliest stages until the film is released in cinemas. And often, as in the case of some of the first-time filmmakers I spoke with, they can spend several years promoting the film at festivals and on its international release.

One issue that remains constant about the film industry—whether the films are produced independently or through the major studios— is the difficulty most filmmakers have financing their films. As Alan Rudolph says of the term independent, "There's no such a thing. Everybody is dependent on money; it's just a label now." John McNaughton states, "Two of the independents I worked for went bankrupt, and the films were hardly seen. . . . In many ways, I would rather work for a studio than an independent. They're going to be there next year. They're going to be there to distribute your picture." Richard Linklater claims that "Some people are groping for definitions of independent and they just don't exist. I would say independent is private financing and having absolutely no interference."

But if interference is part of the definition of what constitutes an independent film, then companies such as Miramax offer little comfort. Michael Radford's recent experience on *B. Monkey*, financed by Miramax, is a case in point. He states, "I think what happens is you get companies like Miramax who base their reputations on pushing art movies and then they grow, find a niche market and start to get instantly more conventional. To the point where *B. Monkey*, an elliptical, strange movie with a real elegance to it—probably the best movie I've made—just got completely cut to ribbons. It's twenty-five minutes shorter and the soundtrack is completely different." In today's filmmaking climate, however, you comply or face having your name removed from the film. How many film directors are prepared to see that happen on something that has occupied several years of their life? *Personal Visions* undoubtedly focuses on filmmakers working outside the mainstream, although some of the directors have clear connections to the Hollywood industry. I originally conceived of the book as a project devoted to U.S. independent film directors, but it seemed to evolve organically. As it proceeded, it became clear that filmmakers from other countries should be included. This was partly due to the fact that I live and work in Canada, and partly because the American film industry has such a strong hold around the world that we simply need to hear other international voices. There were filmmakers such as Atom Egoyan, Neil Jordan and Terence Davies whom I had always wanted to talk to, and this seemed like the perfect opportunity to get in touch with them. The collection thus includes individuals from the U.S., Canada, Britain, Ireland, and New Zealand. I am convinced that all of the filmmakers in this collection possess a unique, personal vision about the world that can only be communicated through the medium of film. I have tended to stay away from film directors who have spoken at length about their work over the years. I wanted to speak to individuals who I felt had not had sufficient opportunity to discuss their entire career in one interview, as well as filmmakers who have only recently emerged. I liked the idea of discovering newer artists who I think will be around a decade from now with flourishing careers. Each interview presents background information on the director, and what factors led to their decision to make films. The conversations focus on the creative output of the director in a dialogue that attempts to cover, as much as possible, their entire career up to the time of our conversation. Thus, Neil Jordan and I had a full discussion of his recent masterpiece, *The Butcher Boy*; John McNaughton discusses his personal diary film *Condo Painting*, as well as *Wild Things* and *Lansky*; Alan Rudolph talks about *Breakfast of Champions*; and Nicholas Hytner briefly discusses his ideas on filming the musical *Chicago*, which had yet to go into production when we spoke.

All the discussions examine, to a lesser or greater extent, the director's interaction with other creative personnel. How specifically do directors work with actors, for example, to help shape the characterizations we finally see on the screen, or with the cinematographer and set designer? What difficulties were encountered in the process of making the films? If the film is an adaptation from literature, what issues did they grapple with in moving from one medium to another? But ultimately, the focus of each interview is always the films. The conversations generally end with each director's feelings about the different stages of making a film and a discussion of the current state of filmmaking.

Speaking to these highly talented individuals, and the process of shaping the interviews, has inevitably changed my perception of films and what film directors do. Apart from the pure pleasure of meeting such notably creative individuals, I made many discoveries. One of the most surprising was to hear over and over how physically taxing it is to make a film, and just how emotionally grueling the process can be. As Michael Tolkin says, "I had no idea how exhausting it is to be a director." This sentiment was echoed by John McNaughton, who stated, "The toughest part for me is the actual day-to-day on the set because you're just so at the mercy of things you can't control. The weather, the sun, somebody with the camera truck runs into a lamp pole, the actors, whatever." Benjamin Ross says he "never anticipated that it would be so hard" to make a film. Many of the directors were just coming off the end of production and their weariness was all too evident as we spoke. There was also a huge range of responses about which aspect of the filmmaking process each finds more stimulating. Some directors, like Michael Radford, are in love with the actual shoot itself. For others, that is the least enjoyable part of making a film.

Another important discovery was how all-consuming making a film can be for a director. We assume that a writer or painter is driven to make art, but rarely do we think that a film director has a similar commitment. As Richard Linklater says about making *Slacker*, "I would dream the film. It was just my whole life for those months we were shooting."

It is true that most current films do not set out to reinvent film grammar, or astonish audiences with a radically new vision. In my own experience, the startling discovery of a new Antonioni, Fellini or Kubrick film was a mind-bending experience, after which you could never look at films, or the world, in the same way. We now live in a different era, and the role that cinema plays in our lives has changed. But films like *The Butcher Boy* or *The Long Day Closes* or *The Sweet Hereafter* are genuinely audacious works of art. And they offer clear evidence that originality in film is still a real commodity and that enough films which truly matter still get made. It gives me enough confidence to believe that our collective cinematic future will not be a bleak one, that individuals of uncommon intelligence and commitment will continue to make films which can illuminate the way we live and help us understand who we are. It is my hope that after reading this collection, the reader will share that view. It is also my belief that film artists will continue to find distinctive ways to explore the medium and tell their stories. As Michael Tolkin says, "The human story always needs to be told."

MICHAEL ALMEREYDA

Michael Almereyda spent much of the 1980s writing scripts for films that would eventually be made by other directors (*Cherry 2000*) or working on drafts of films whose final form would alter radically from what he had originally envisioned (Wenders' *Until the End of the World* and Paul Verhoeven's *Total Recall*.) He also wrote several unproduced scripts for such key filmmakers as David Lynch and Tim Burton. Although Almereyda does not regret this experience, he acknowledges that his own directing career was probably held back. As he says, "I wish I'd made three or four times as many films by now. It feels like I'm just getting started."

Almereyda's first feature was the little seen *Twister*, his imaginative adaptation of Mary Robison's highly acclaimed novel *Oh!* The film carefully mixes drama and comedy, and features a deliciously wild, eccentric performance by Crispin Glover, one of America's most outrageous and inventive actors. Although the film itself is a solid achievement, and proved that Almereyda was born to make movies, the experience of making it was painful and very nearly stopped his career in its tracks. It was only Almereyda's discovery of a cheap "toy" camera, the PXL 2000 made for children by the Fisher-Price toy company and now discontinued, that allowed him to channel his creativity into small, personal films which—so far—run the gamut from quirky, romantic comedy (*Another Girl, Another Planet*), to literary adaptation (*The Rocking Horse Winner*) and personal documentary (*At Sundance*). This work has been interspersed between his feature films as a way to keep making films while he awaits financing for his own features, but it has also produced uniquely satisfying films which make no apologies for their "low-tech" look and do not aspire to any other form but the Pixelvision format.

When Almereyda finally got around to directing his second feature—the contemporary vampire film *Nadja* produced by David Lynch—he was able to realize his ambitions with a commercial film. Although made for only half a million dollars, *Nadja* is one of the most original genre films of the last decade. The film incorporates extensive Pixelvision cinematography to render the subjective feelings of the vampire characters, adding a layer of expressionist imagery and originality to a film that, at times, feels like it may be veering off into camp or pretension, but never does. This is in part thanks to a very funny performance by Peter Fonda, who "wakes the movie up whenever he's on screen," in the words of the director. The film is "drastically, self-consciously postmodern, in that it feeds off, drains blood from, all kinds of other vampire movies." This self-consciously poetic style may have limited the film's commercial appeal, but on an aesthetic level it is an unalloyed success and a sensitive, beautiful updating of the horror genre to the dark streets of contemporary New York City.

Almereyda's most recent work includes a contemporary mummy movie (*The Eternal*) starring Christopher Walken, and an updating of *Hamlet* with Ethan Hawke and Sam Shepard. Almereyda is clearly determined to make more films, and we should count ourselves lucky, because he is one of the most intelligent, imaginative contemporary filmmakers. I spoke to Michael Almereyda in New York City.

Almereyda

Let's start with your background and where you grew up. What were the cultural influences of your formative years?

I was born and raised in Kansas and when I was twelve my family moved to Orange County, California. In many ways, that cultural leap determined who I have become. I have fond memories of Kansas, and not so fond memories of Southern California. I've always been mystified by Southern California and I imagine it's something I'll get back to in my movies at some point, because it seems—and it seemed at the time—like a really apocalyptic place, even though it's so casual and sunstruck. There were so many TV stations that movies became unavoidable. So even though I'd been really interested in drawing and painting when I was a kid, movies became too seductive to resist.

Were there any people that were particularly important to you growing up: artists, writers, filmmakers, painters?

The first real artist I ever met who had an impact on me was Manny Farber. He had moved to San Diego from New York, and, when I was fifteen or sixteen, screened a Fassbinder film at the Orange Coast Community College. He showed up an hour late because he got lost on the freeway. He started talking and the projectionist screened the film while he was talking. It was about one or one-thirty in the morning when the film was over, and he was taking questions. I had just read his book, *Negative Space*, by chance, and was also very interested in James Agee, and asked him about Agee. Probably out of sheer exhaustion, he said, "Come to San Diego someday, and I'll tell you about him." And I did. It's not like I was a student of Manny Farber, but he and his wife were very kind to me for a few years before I went off to college, and that influence was very powerful.

Were you seeing a lot of films at that time?

It was the late seventies, and that was a good time. When I went to college, it was the crest of the New German Cinema and those films were really incredible to me. And *Days of Heaven* came out and I watched it a few times at one go; Nicolas Roeg was important. I was a teenager and those films were the ones that galvanized me the most. Before that, on TV, I saw a lot of classic American movies.

You went to Harvard, but did you study film there?

No. I sat in on a lot of film classes, mainly just to watch the movies. Before that, I dropped out of high school, more or less, and attended the University of California at Irvine through an advanced placement program, and saw a lot of movies there.

What were you studying at Harvard?

Art history, mainly. But I took classes in a lot of things and I audited a lot. I was never really interested in—or very good at—prescribed studies in schematic education. I never figured it out and I just dropped out. I have a habit of doing that.

You didn't get your degree?

No. But, it was a wonderful place to be at the time. I wanted, with some urgency, to make movies. I had no idea it would take so long and be so hard.

Were you seeing any experimental film at that time?

Not much, I'm still pretty blind to experimental films. I feel that my real instincts and strengths have to do with stories. At the same time, the few experimental films I did see, I won't ever shake off. I'd love to see Peter Kubelka's *Our Trip to Africa* again. They showed three of his movies at Harvard. They proved you could do something with nothing. And I was very fond of Bruce Conner.

You didn't make any films at Harvard though?

No.

When did you start thinking about making a film?

I had this mistaken idea that the most direct access to directing was through writing, and I inadvertently became a writer. People of a certain generation who made movies usually had a background in theater or writing. I wasn't the most social creature, so it took a lot of learning for me to start negotiating my way through the world of people rather than imagining and writing things.

Were you writing fiction?

I was writing a bit of fiction—stories—and I dropped out of Harvard to finish a screenplay about Nikola Tesla, the turn-of-the-century inventor of modern electricity. My orientation had to do with big-budget spectacles, the kind of movies Fritz Lang made before he came to America. I had mad dreams of doing movies on that scale.

You mean films like *Metropolis* and *Spies*?

Exactly. I wrote a couple of scripts like that. The Tesla script was like a science-fiction movie set in the past. It couldn't have been done cheaply. And the story was nothing if not ambitious. I did a lot of research.

Did you stay around Boston?

I moved to New York, finished the Tesla script, went to Los Angeles, and got an agent very quickly; a pretty elevated literary agent. I got work almost instantly and moved back to New York. I had a screenwriting career for a while. Then I moved to LA, thinking that would be a more immediate way to get access to directing. It was frustrating and I felt thwarted, but I did have a kind of luck. When I look back, I feel bewildered to picture my twenties burned up writing scripts for other people, scripts which were mostly unproduced.

I've seen some of them. Was *Cherry 2000* your script?

Yes, based on a story by Lloyd Fonvielle. That was a rough ride. I wrote it in '84 and, on the strength of that script, was briefly considered a hot Hollywood screenwriter. It took a while for the movie to come out and it had only a ghostly relation to the script. The movie was miscast, a bit of a mess, and dead on arrival.

That was before your first short film, the one you directed with Dennis Hopper.

I took the money from that writing job and made the short while Hopper had a break from filming *Blue Velvet*. The short was an update of a story from Mikhail Lermontov's *A Hero of our Time*, a psychological adventure story, one of the first. Lermontov was a poet killed in a duel when he was twenty-six. It was very romantic material, but I flattened it out and made it a film noir set in Los Angeles.

You made it contemporary?

Yes, it was all updated. Godard and Wim Wenders were definite influences on that film. After Dennis read the script and said he'd do the movie, he recommended me to Wim and I ended up writing the first draft of *Until the End of the World*. This was in 1986-87. That, too, turned out drastically different than I'd imagined. Along the way, I was given an education that I really didn't want, about why it wasn't right or interesting for me to be a screenwriter for other people, even though they are people who are heroes to me. I've written scripts for Wenders, David Lynch, Tim Burton, but it's my day job.

What did you write for David Lynch?

A version of *Fantomas*, reworked from David's first draft. But it'll probably never be made: the rights are incredibly tangled.

When you made this short film with Dennis Hopper, what was the experience like? Did it teach you a lot about making films?

It did, but it took a long time to finish because it was done in 35mm, and postproduction was unavoidably expensive. It's easier to shoot a film than to finish it, and I ran out of money. I did get a job and ended up going to Australia to doctor the script of *Total Recall* for Bruce Beresford. "The first twenty pages are basically all right," he said. "The real trouble begins on Mars."

Paul Verhoeven eventually directed it, of course, but the finished movie feels closer to my script than *Cherry 2000* feels to its script. Some of my dialogue is floating around on Mars, including Schwarzenegger's corny last lines.

When you made the short film, did you know much about directing actors?

No. I wasn't necessarily good at it, but I don't think I was bad at it either. I think it's just a matter of paying attention to who's in the room with you, and that's the only guideline I've ever had about dealing with actors. You respect them for who they are. I'm good at casting, and that's a huge part of filmmaking. I don't want to be too modest or act like I'm not interested in acting. I think the best actors refine and explore who they are, but don't necessarily transform themselves. You have to imagine the details of behavior in the context of the story.

Let's talk about *Twister*. What initially attracted you to Mary Robison's novel, *Oh!*?

Mary Robison is a wonderful writer, completely underrated. *Oh!* is about an eccentric family, but I think all families are eccentric. That's the point of the novel and the film. The book is mainly a chronicle of a desperate, stop-start courtship, played out against a sideshow of family politics. It's about the way people who live under the same roof can be like prisoners of war. It centers on a young woman's outrage at being born into a household where all crucial connections are missing.

Did that script come easily?

I wrote it really quickly. It's a fusion of ideas and gags mostly from the novel. I invented some scenes like the William Burroughs sequence, because I had met Burroughs a few years before and wanted to put him in the movie. There were certain connections to my childhood and my sense of Kansas. The novel is set in Ohio where Mary is from. I had learned from these other extravagant scripts that movies are about people, not about special effects. I had a good stack of scripts that had shown an evolution, but it was an odd place to land for a first film after having imagined directing all these spectacles. That's just the way things happen.

Was the shoot difficult?

It was extremely difficult, largely because I naively hired a cameraman [Renato Berta] who didn't speak English. The producer promptly hired himself to be on-set translator, and from this arrangement you can triangulate all kinds of confusion, miscommunication, a sense of breakdown, and betrayal. It was a travesty, and in various ways—good, but mostly bad—all this fraught feeling, a sense of real craziness, rubbed off on the actors and on the movie as a whole.

Did you feel that your inexperience as a director worked against you in making that film?

Completely. It was more my inexperience in the world, strangely enough. I don't think I was incompetent as a technician or a craftsman. I think I knew what shots I wanted and how to get them. There were power struggles and egos on the set, but I've learned something more about that since then. It's a huge part of directing, either an assumed part or an unadmitted part.

I was so bitterly betrayed by some people that I've only lately begun to realize that *Twister* is probably better than I think and closer to my original intentions than I imagined. But at the time, especially in terms of sound work and music, it veered way off course for me. The power struggle tilted way out of my control. And for the music, I just showed up and there was the music. It felt hugely compromised. It was a cut that I worked out in a kind of constricted way with the producer. But it was very hard, not satisfying, and very hard to recover from. On top of all that, the film wasn't really released, not as any reflection on the quality of the film, but because Vestron went out of business. They took fifteen movies with them,and they all went straight to video. Only three prints were made of the film. It was rescued by a smaller distributor called Grey Cat, and they showed it around the country. It starting getting good reviews almost across the board but it never really had a life; it had sort of an after-life. I'm proud of the actors, though. They did *great* work.

In spite of this convoluted production history, a lot of wonderful stuff survives in *Twister*. It's such an offbeat, almost surrealistic view of middle America.

It seemed to me to be about communication or about miscommunication, about the way people don't connect. At the time, I was really interested in scaling down from these enormous, inhuman projects, and recognizing that the everyday could be extraordinary. So the surrealist slant was just looking at ordinary things in a way that recognizes what's special and uncanny about them.

Did you have any cinematic models for this film?

Wenders was a big hero for a long time. Those early films, like *Alice in the Cities* and *Kings of the Road*, seem miraculous to me. They balance rigor with improvisation, and they allowed people to be themselves, and yet are really charged and fine tuned. There's a tension there, a tenderness about people, and at the same time there's a strong aesthetic operating. They're emphatically beautiful movies. Over time, I'd begun to feel that I wanted my films to be rougher, looser and wilder, but those are still some of my favorite movies, and, at the time, a huge influence.

Another big influence was Renoir, who was the master of making films with groups of people and balancing inner and outer realities. I recently read an obituary that Orson Welles wrote on Renoir. He quoted Renoir saying something like, "For anyone who cares about creating something in movies, the real issue is the conflict between exterior reality and inner non-reality." I take issue with that phrase "nonreality," because it can be just as real as exterior reality. The whole point is how to balance them in a movie and how to feel the tension and balance between the two.

In a conversation I had with Neil Jordan, he quoted Kubrick saying how films have to hide what they're about, that you can never make them too explicit.

I agree, often I make mistakes from reading the wrong kinds of literature, which have decodeable symbols, whereas the *real* subject of the film might be hiding from you. It's a funny idea to come from Neil Jordan, because he's very literary.

But he works with subtext a lot too.

Even that kind of subtext, in Kubrick's work, the meaning might reside in the camera movement. And for Neil Jordan, and a lot of us, it's in some thematic strand or motif woven into the film, whether it's a pop song or a reference the character makes or a relationship. I think for Kubrick, and the Italian cinema as well, the subtext's more physical. I respect that actually, and I aspire to it.

Did you rehearse a lot with the actors.

Not a lot, a little bit. We talked enough for everyone to feel grounded. I like to keep things fresh.

Can you talk about Crispin Glover's performance? It's one of the more stylized performances in any film I've ever seen.

It's fantastic. We met on the set of *River's Edge*, and I chased him to be in the film, a year of talking and coaxing. That meant we had a bit of an unbalanced relationship going on. He knew how badly I wanted him to be in the film, but he never seemed to realize how much I believed in him. I think it's part of his temperament to fight with directors, to be very private and imperious about his decisions. But I liked how he interpreted the part, because the way the part was framed—as wild as Crispin's performance is, as stylized and expressionistic—it defined the character as an eccentric among eccentrics, and I figured it would be balanced by the naturalism of the other performances. Some people thought the movie was out of control, but there was no intention in the different kinds of acting, the different kinds of behavior. The point being that movies can acknowledge these behavioral differences between people, can show in precise terms that life isn't one thing, one narrow wavelength, especially within a family, which is the subject of the movie.

The acting doesn't seem out of control at all. It seems very controlled.

Crispin's performance *was* hugely controlled. He would do the same type of things, these wacky things, exactly the same over and over, and if you tried to get him to change or suggested something for a camera move or an angle, it would really unnerve him. It gave me great respect for him in many ways. What he was doing was really calibrated.

Did he conceive of the character as a dandy?

That came from the book. The character was always wearing extreme getups; the wardrobe was clearly very important, but it was Crispin who came up with the Carnaby Street look. Carol Wood, the costume designer, took the idea and ran with it. It was inspired. Crispin was also very fastidious about his hair, which required as much preparation and attention as the tresses of any of the female cast members, and the concern for "elegance," as he called it, extended to the treatment of the huge family portrait that his character was supposed to paint. At a certain point Crispin determined that the painting—a wonderful, wall-length group portrait, painted by a friend of mine—wasn't "elegant" enough and he threatened to tear it up on camera. I cut the scene rather than see the painting destroyed. At any rate, this gives you an idea of the level of conviction and commitment in Crispin's performance.

Did the other actors have any problem with his performance being on such a different key than theirs?

No, I think everyone respected him. Some people felt that he was in his own world, but that's the character. And the one character he really connected to was his sister, Maureen [Suzy Amis], who Crispin surreptitiously worked out his character had an incestuous fixation on, although it was pretty transparent. It wasn't something I needed to talk with him about. I thought it was great. There was such a mixed dynamic between people who were experienced, people who were secure, people who were confused that it served the movie because we became like a family. One review at the time said that the cast was assembled like specimens in a zoo. I didn't feel that clinical about it, but I did feel that it was well cast and a good mix of people.

The physical world is very alive in the film.

I wanted there to be so much more. One of my bitter complaints was that we didn't have second unit, which is fairly rare in a movie.

It's interesting that when the film begins, the characters are fairly irritating. Everybody seems either weird or unpleasant. But as the film goes along, you end up having a great deal of sympathy for them.

That's good. That's why it took so many tries before the movie got made. That's the nature of families too. If you went to a family gathering, at first you'd feel that everyone's a gargoyle, everyone's grotesque. Once you are *in* the family, you get used to it.

You have that scene in the film toward the end where Chris [Dylan McDermott] is flipping the TV channels with the remote control. There's even a Bill Viola segment in the series of images on the TV screen. Was the intent to illustrate that what we take as normal can also feel exotic and strange?

The whole movie, you might say, is meant to illustrate that. But the use of the Bill Viola image was meant to be more specific. I imagined that the characters, in the last scene, had survived this emotional whirlwind and they were huddled together on this couch like shipwreck survivors on a raft. They're floating into an uncertain future, surrounded by flotsam and jetsam, the cultural debris that TV broadcasts every second of the day. The idea was that within this debris there's occasionally something worth holding on to, that saves us. It was important to have an image that seemed pure. So I went for that simple mirage-like moment from Bill Viola, a stretch of desert sand, the sound of amplified wind, with the hope that it was like a breath, a powerful and soothing image, solid land seen from a lifeboat.

That's actually an amazing shot of those four people on the couch. You look at Crispin Glover and his facial expression is so amazingly strange. So basically the film didn't have a life when it was released?

No. And I don't think you'll find it at Blockbuster Video. It has afflicted my whole career. I haven't quite gotten over it. I'm not in mourning about it anymore, but it's been a very puzzling thing. I've written so many more scripts, and I have so many more ideas for movies, that I feel like I've only covered a corner of the map of what I hope to do.

What did you want the film to be? How did you conceive it?

I had envisioned a more cunning use of sound, more like Jacques Tati where the sound is very natural but selective, and so precise it's no longer naturalistic, similar to other aspects of the film in its rhythms and in the acting. That ideal was just something I wasn't in a position to enforce. And the score, like I said, was just slapped on to the movie.

What about cutting the picture?

The cut was a fight, a struggle and a compromise. But the footage was spare enough that it wasn't fatal. It was very hard for me to live with for a long time. I just moved on and was able to prove to myself that I could make a movie, but I was really knocked around. It's a matter of power: it's the dynamic. I remember taking some solace at the time reading about the first film that Bergman directed. He'd go home and vomit.

Another Girl, Another Planet, **your first Pixelvision film, was made after** *Twister.* **How long did that take to make?**

No time at all, a month between writing the script and shooting it. It was shot in a week. How's this for a product endorsement: "The great rescue operation of my life came with discovering the Pixel 2000 camera." And it's true. I was feeling thwarted and disappointed on many fronts. Then saw Sadie Benning's work, got hold of a camera for $45, wrote a script for it, and slapped it together with a group of people living within a five-block radius of the apartment where we shot it.

Tell me how this camera works.

It records sound *and* picture to a standard audio cassette. But I tend to channel the Pixelvision output onto other decks, other formats. That way you get a clearer image, and the sound is recorded separately and better. *Another Girl* was recorded onto a Beta deck. More recently I've been working with an 8mm portable "clamshell" deck, which allows you to take the camera outside. It's the same little deck and monitor that cops use to watch ballgames in their patrol cars.

Why didn't you use a standard video camera?

I hated video and I'm still not really enamored of it. The flatness, the gassy color, the lack of resolution. Pixelvision is more rarefied and raw. It's hard to make an uninteresting shot with it. The irony is that this cheap, kid's camera has allowed me to make twice as many movies as I would have otherwise, and they're probably my best movies. I consider them movies because they're blown up to film, they're shot just like a movie. There's a clapper, we say "Action," we record sound separately.

What are the limitations?

The depth of field is incredibly limited, and you wouldn't want to make *War and Peace* in Pixelvision. Well, you could, but it would be severely stylized. There's no lens to speak of, just a plastic disk shielding a "photo receptor" attached to a small circuit board.

Still, it seems to go against the aesthetic of the beautiful filmic image that the film industry valorizes.

Sure. I valorize it too. It's keyed to spectacle, and to glamour, and it's hugely seductive. But there's more than one way to skin a cat, and to me Pixelvision has a kind of inverted beauty. A more raw, intimate beauty, like Robert Frank and Bill Brandt and a whole school of rough-and-ready photographers. There's a way of catching reality that may be more intimate, more capable of expressing and receiving spontaneous gestures. In movies, lately, this style tends to get short shrift, but it covers a whole poetic/documentary tradition that includes Jean Vigo, the Italian neo-realists, John Cassavetes, Godard, early Jim Jarmusch. It's not, come to think of it, a typical American style, is it?

There's a lot of humor in *Another Girl, Another Planet*.

I hope so. I'm always amazed when people don't get it.

It's a very moving story as well. The acting is uniformly quite good. What are some of the differences directing actors in that form as opposed to 35mm?

The camera is no bigger than this glass of beer. So people can relax in a way, but the camera has to be very close. At first it's unnerving, then it's easier for actors to relax. There's less of a sense of commotion, and the focus is more intimate because there aren't as many people standing around, which makes it a medium particularly sensitive to actors. The crew is usually five or six people, and it's a good way to work. Cassavetes got away with that same dynamic using 16mm. I aspire to that sense of transparency, where it feels improvised but it isn't.

Did you actually get an elephant in the apartment in that film?

Yeah, didn't you notice? For a while I told people that it was the cameraman in an elephant suit. But no one believed me.

How did you find Elina Löwensohn?

She used to wait tables at a restaurant a few blocks away.

Was she involved in acting?

She had studied acting at New York University. At the time, I wanted to put her in a movie based on a Dostoevsky novel, *The Possessed*, and she was actually doing a play based on the same novel. There had been a lot of coincidences when I met her. She hadn't done the Hal Hartley stuff yet. It took awhile for us to get money. Actually, I didn't have money, I just had the PXL camera.

Can that kind of film get distributed?

The inhibiting factor on it, which I feel unrepentant about, is the music.

The videotape says "temporary music."

That was just to ward off anyone who might be tempted to sue me. The music budget would have been quite steep if we had paid for the music. It was a reaction to *Twister*, where very little of the music that I wanted, or liked, got into the movie. I feel it's a way of saying this is the music I want, this is the music that's meaningful and appropriate.

Is there music from a Fellini film in there?

It's *Fellini's Casanova*, which is a great movie. It's very underrated, and it's thematically appropriate for *Another Girl, Another Planet*.

The film exists as a commercial video. I've seen it in London.

Yeah, they decided to be brave and just say, "the hell with it." Every once in a while I get a statement of how many they've sold, which is about three a year. But it was liberating because the film was done completely on my own terms. I produced it and was in control of everything. It's probably the most satisfying experience, even though I wanted and hoped for more. It was well received on the festival circuit and won an award or two. It didn't really have a commercial life, and I didn't expect it to, because I'd always imagined that two months later I'd be making another 35mm movie and everything would change. But it turned out again to be another struggle to get a movie made. I wrote a script about Edgar Allan Poe that interested David Lynch, but we couldn't get money for it. Then, I wrote what I imagined to be an exploitation film that turned into *Nadja*. We lost money about three days before shooting was to commence. David bravely paid for the whole film himself. I don't know in the history of movies of a filmmaker paying for another filmmaker's movie. It's an amazing kind of generosity.

He was already set to produce wasn't he?

Yes, as executive producer. It was a risk for him, but it turned out okay. He got his money back, and formed a healthy alliance with October Films. But it was scary for a while and very awkward.

When did it change in your mind from being an exploitation film to more of an art film?

I use the term loosely because I don't know if I have the instincts to really make an exploitation film. I like popular culture and I want to be a part of it, but that can't be forced. An exemplary career is Tim Burton's. His films are the kind I imagined myself making when I was in my twenties: art films that happen to be hugely popular.

Personal, yet accessible and imaginative. That's a good aspiration. I'm interested in this relationship of *Nadja* to other vampire films. How precisely does it relate to earlier films in the genre?

It is drastically, self-consciously postmodern, in that it feeds off, drains blood from, all kinds of other vampire movies. It works from a shared pool of references, some more conspicuous than others, which makes, I hope, for something freshly undead, a mix of old and new, quotation and invention. Movies, like life, take place in a perpetual present, but we're always moving in the shadow of previous experience, history, memory. Why not admit that?

It's hard for me to believe in the conventional horror movie aspects, to have conviction about them. I always viewed the film metaphorically, which may not be the best place to start. Probably best to find subjects you have complete, un-ironic conviction about. All the same, I'm still interested in tackling genre stories where the characters are iconographic, and suddenly you turn the corner and they're three dimensional. Hitchcock did that all the time. In the fifties, especially, you'd have these apparently flat, cardboard embodiments of American virtue, and then you'd see Jimmy Stewart or Doris Day have a nervous breakdown. It was frightening.

Why did you decide to use a voice-over?

The voice-over comes from Andre Breton's novel *Nadja*, my creeping literary tendencies crawling into view. In the novel, the guy who keeps meeting Nadja is Breton himself, and he's constantly abstracting or rhapsodizing or poetizing the reality he is describing. In many ways, he's filtering her voice, her madness, and so it seemed appropriate to take his voice. I wish more of that book were in the movie. It was more of a reference than a source.

How do you see the film in relationship to the surrealist movement?

I hope it shares a bit of a blood line. I think surrealism and horror movies are closely aligned. Cocteau is the obvious intersection. In many ways, *Nadja* was a kind of paper cut-out. It was done very quickly and cheaply. The budget was under half a million dollars; Pixelvision was a self-conscious way to keep costs down. I'm proud that it doesn't look like it was made for that little money. But it was really scraped together and, in that sense, it had a surrealistic aesthetic. There was a sense of just finding things, the idea of the found object. Galaxy Craze is a kind of found object.

Had she acted before?

She'd been in a scene cut from a Woody Allen movie, but she had [and has] all but dropped out of acting. She really considers herself a writer and in fact has written a novel, due out soon, which blurs the fact that she's a talented actress, not a zombie walking through a zombie role. The real Galaxy Craze is pretty lively.

Why did you shoot in black and white?

I was adamant about that and part of it was to connect to the Pixelvision, to give it a sense of the nocturnal world where things were caught between waking and dreaming. Also, to connect to this history of horror movies that I really respected, and wanted to refer to, wanted to acknowledge. And it's cheaper. Again, practical considerations can't be denied. It just so happened that Abel Ferrara had the same idea with *The Addiction*.

Were you aware of each other's film?

No, he actually shot after we did, and is very fond of blaming me for copying him. But I like his movie. His obsessions lead him in a different direction, but the two films complement each other. I was kind of amused when they got lumped together.

His is more straight-out existential than yours.

I like to smile through my existentialism. I always thought of *Nadja* as a comedy too, because it has a lot of the structure of a comedy. It ends with a wedding—the classic definition of a comedy—and it's about rebirth and regeneration.

Although not too many classical comedies end on a note of incest! The stylistic logic of using the Pixelvision is interesting to me. It's clearly not just Nadja's point of view.

It was more of an emotional embodiment. Whenever she or her brother would be excited, distraught, or heat up in some way, you would enter that world. Maybe it wasn't quite as rigorous or consistent as it should have been, but I didn't want it to be too schematic.

Were there different styles of performance operating in that film?

Again, everything I've done includes a wild-card performance, and it's not a coincidence that some people say that Crispin is coloring outside the lines or that Peter Fonda is way over the top because, in fact, the script accommodates that.

Do you think Fonda's over the top?

No, not at all. He's working at a different pace. He's more angular. There's a different energy or a different pulse in the performance.

Some people accused him of being over the top and others credit him with being the best thing in the movie. I think he wakes the movie up whenever he's on screen. It was intentional to keep a variety of rhythms flowing through.

Do you think he's giving an ironic performance?

Well, there are different levels of irony. Comedy never works if you're smirking all the time. Buster Keaton is my biggest hero and that's the kind of purity of expression that I'd hope to someday match a frame of. That's the great lesson of how to do comedy.

You mean with a straight face?

Yeah.

Nadja marries her brother at the end of the film, doesn't she?

You noticed that?

I thought that was a good touch to have her marry her brother. Is that what she means when she says that the family is everything?

She's a bit of a narcissist.

Fonda seems to be dressed like he's in a Hammer movie.

There are references shooting all over the place; the film is a big nest of references.

Was it difficult to strike the right tone for that film?

Some people would say I didn't, but I wanted it to be all over the place. I wanted it to be like a Donald Barthleme story, a collage. Again, that was a surrealist aesthetic. I wanted it to refer to Hammer horror movies, and Cocteau, and Breton and Peter Fonda's Corman movies. I also felt that it was fair to integrate all of these things because, to me, life in New York, life in America, is that mixture of high and low.

Can you talk a bit about using the city? How you incorporated New York City at night into your vision?

I hope it can speak for itself. The city is notably beautiful. It was an abstracted view. Often reviews said it was about vampires in the East Village, but we rarely shot in the East Village. It is *the* city, the modern city, the enchanted night world, the city that accommodates and embodies the unconscious.

I was reminded of David Salle's comment in your Pixelvision film *At Sundance* **where he talks about how** *Blue Velvet* **galvanized the amalgam of art aesthetics and the narrative film tradition for a generation. You're continuing that in some ways.**

I don't know that I'm continuing it, I'm just swimming in the same current, and David Lynch is someone I admire and consider a friend. I think we're too close, we have too much in common, for me to think of him as an influence. It's kind of curious that way. I don't study his movies, and I don't feel they've had a direct influence. I feel we've been influenced by similar things. I have similar feelings about being alive, and coming from the Midwest. When *Twister* came out, when the reviews were bad, they would routinely compare me, in a negative way, to Lynch and *Twin Peaks*. In fact, *Twister* was made before *Twin Peaks* ever came out. But it's a similar sensibility.

Is that a made-up language the vampires speak in the film?

It's a direct transcription from Romanian. Elina is Romanian, and she transcribed the dialogue directly.

At times, you're using a kind of long take style in the film, and at other times, the montage is very apparent; you also use a lot of superimpositions. Can you talk about some of these aesthetic choices?

Again, it's a collage and it seemed like it was important to get a rhythm that had variety. It was more instinctive than anything else.

How carefully did you work it out?

I storyboard everything. I can draw pretty well, and there's very rarely a shot that doesn't come from a picture: a sketch, a photograph, a painting. The cameraman's always making fun of me because I'm always looking around for some scrap of paper. The frame is very specific. I think with *Nadja*, my sense of self-criticism tells me it was a little too airless even though that's the style. I wanted something more limber. There was this conflict between naturalism and stylization, and stylization wrestled the movie to the ground in a few places. It's been criticized for that, and probably rightly. But it was always a stylized movie: there was no getting around it. The ideal model was *Alphaville*, which is so magically a mix of cartoon aesthetics and profound poetry.

You said somewhere that you've made a serious commitment to working in genre.

That was a little while back, after *Nadja*, which I was hoping to follow up with a beach movie called *Satellite Beach*. But I couldn't get money for it, and instead succumbed to an offer to make a mummy movie for Trimark. The idea of doing Val Lewton-type movies, "literate" horror films, was exciting to me, the idea of putting things in these movies that are keyed to life—casting non-actors, tossing in music I like, making references that are distinctly outside the conventions of the genre. But I think I hit a wall. It's hard to enter genre territory without finding yourself sealed off from real experience.

The idea of trying to re-invigorate a genre, and make it contemporary, is interesting to me.

Sure. Exactly. When Rembrandt painted a story from the Bible, he gave people contemporary clothes. Godard has made genre films but never set a movie in any time but the present. He'll tell the story of Mary and Jesus and it's in utterly contemporary terms or he'll do a science-fiction film in which the future is recognizably the present. I can still imagine doing genre films, and period films—I have the scripts for them—but my real interest is grounded in the present, here and now.

When I say contemporary, it isn't just setting these films in the present and having them wear modern clothes. It's making them relevant to a contemporary audience.

And you don't think they are?

I think they are. But I think it's hard because, for me, a lot of genre films aren't very successful anymore.

I think it has more to do with scripting, with characters, and with valuing the idea of an inner life. I keep swerving back to visual art. You could have a dozen paintings of still lifes, arrangements of fruit on a tabletop, and only one of them will be by Chardin. And the Chardin will be the only one you want to look at, will have more gravity, more emotion, more intensity than a crucifixion by another painter. In other words, all genres are created equal, and you bring to bear whatever skill and feeling you have. You hope to light a fire that way. It's all kindling. Some stories are richer. I think it's a misplaced, old-fashioned idea that *Citizen Kane* is necessarily a better film than *Touch of Evil* because *Touch of Evil* is in a trashy genre.

I agree. It's interesting that Lucy's [Galaxy Craze] first taste of blood is her own menstrual blood.

It's always amazed me that that part of a woman's life has always been one of the most forbidden things in movies, literature, and popular culture. It's just so buried. Half the population is made up of women and a large part of the other half lives with women. It's just so unadmitted. It's weird to me. I'm glad that's in *Nadja*.

There's a scene where Nadja is floating on the pavement in the foreground of the shot, and in rear-screen projection, you have this action in the background. Did you see that primarily as referencing earlier cinema or trying to create a poetic moment?

It's all those things and more. In some ways it encapsulates the feelings that are at the core of the film, not being able to catch up with the thing you're pursuing. The faster you run, the farther away it gets.

The character of Nadja herself is very ethereal. She's there, but not there.

I wish I had pushed that more.

What regrets do you have about the film?

I don't know how appropriate it is for me to go on about my regrets. It's not the best part of my character. I'd just rather smile and go on.

I think you should be proud of *Nadja*. It's quite an original film. Did it do well, commercially?

It did adequately, but it didn't catch fire in any real way. I think what's key in movies, as you must know from talking to other directors, is if you score one hit you're allowed a certain latitude. People can always say, well, he or she made money once. You can survive for a few pictures that way. I don't really know what the trick is. This is part of my innocence about the world. I wish I knew more about how you conjure money.

Why did you make *At Sundance*?

It was my way of surviving the festival. It was also a way of meeting other directors. An odd thing about Sundance is that the directors are usually too busy dealing with media representatives to actually talk amongst themselves. I'm proud of *At Sundance* because it was intended as a sort of time capsule. Again, it was in a tradition, very much a response to Wim Wenders' movie *Room 666* made in Cannes in the early 1980s, and I think it succeeds as such.

Had you worked out the structure for the movie in advance?

No, like a lot of other documentaries, we discovered it as we went along. I wrote the narration afterwards.

Did you know who you were going to talk to?

We talked to every filmmaker who would come into the room. We cut about fifteen people out just because of the dynamic we discovered in the editing. Some people repeated points. It was very instinctive. I don't regret the cuts, but it was tricky.

Were there people in the film that surprised you with their comments?

Sure, yeah. Were you surprised by anyone?

I found many of them fascinating. I've heard Atom Egoyan's comments about "brain-movies" before. In fact, I heard similar ideas from Stan Brakhage in the mid-seventies. I liked what Atom had to say. I also liked Richard Linklater and Ethan Hawke and Todd Haynes and John Turturro and many others. Larry Gross was interesting, although I haven't seen his film.

He came very prepared. He had thought about it. Most people were too busy running the treadmill to actually think much about the question we posed ["Are you optimistic about the future of movies?"].

Did you come away from that trip optimistic?

Nadja was completely scorned. Perhaps because it had been shown at the Toronto Film Festival, there was no sense of anticipation or impact.

Was talking to the other filmmakers a positive experience?

Very much. I liked meeting them. Personally, I would never participate in a movie like that. But it gave me a way of answering the question by giving a group portrait. And obviously no one wanted to say "I'm pessimistic," even though, as some people continued talking, you could see them getting depressed. Everyone tried to be upbeat because everyone's being a salesman, a pitchman.

Your presence is felt in the film.

I'm curious about that. I don't know.

As a diary film, I think you're certainly there.

It was very much a collaboration with Amy Hobby.

Do you see any kind of future for this form?

Just my own. I did *The Rocking Horse Winner* when I couldn't have made a movie otherwise. It's a way of moving. Now I've got a digital video camera and I've been shooting a longer piece with it. I'm not sure how it'll turn out. It's a lot better than writing scripts which never see the light of day.

Do you see yourself in any sort of experimental tradition?

Maybe I'm deluded, but I really imagine that I'm cut out for the mainstream, and that I've been side-tracked. Maybe the more abstract and experimental, personal impulses will catch up with me later.

Do you consider yourself an independent filmmaker?

Scorsese once said, "I'm an American filmmaker, which means by definition I'm a Hollywood filmmaker." I think that still makes sense for American filmmakers of a certain level of ambition and for a long time it made sense to me. The films that frame and influence you the most are the films you grow up with, even if you try to strip away things you consider tired and false. That is, the system you enter, and fight or befriend, is the same system that is now ruled by Spielberg and Lucas. The fact is, over the years, whether working with a toy camera or financing films without recourse to a studio deal, I've crossed into another country. For a while, that felt like a failure, but maybe it's liberating, maybe it's a blessing, and maybe it's where I belong: the curious, unbalanced, floating world of independent filmmaking.

After *The Eternal* and the digital video film you're now making, do you have any plans?

My next movie is a version of *Hamlet* set in New York, straight Shakespeare but in a modern context and setting, with Ethan Hawke, Sam Shepard, Bill Murray, and Kyle MacLaughlin. It's being shot in Super 16mm, very low-budget, to insure I keep final cut. As you can guess from the cast, I'm still keen on the idea of wading into the mainstream. I want the movie to be personal and intimate, but I'm hoping it's accessible. My whole perspective, again, comes from art history, the long view, which allows that all this stuff to flow into one wide, deep stream. High and low, it's all part of the moment, this particular place and time.

Would you work in Hollywood?

Sure. But I'd insist on final cut, and I'd be unlikely to get it until or unless I scored some sort of hit with a so-called independent film.

With *The Eternal*, despite assurances and a window of good will, I found myself at odds with the people who gave me money, who courted and hired me to make the movie. I was in the editing room for a full year, trying to accommodate some very confused worries and whims. It was a bit like being a taxi driver for someone who doesn't know where they want to go. Actually, the stakes were higher. It was more like piloting a plane for someone who doesn't like flying, is afraid of heights, but doesn't want to land. It was nerve-racking, ridiculous, impossible. The plane didn't crash, I'm still in one piece, the movie is finished and may even be released. But I had flashbacks of *Twister*, and, just possibly, I learned a lesson.

Do you ever feel depressed about the state of the industry?

It's hard to be aware of the world, read a newspaper and not be depressed about the state of everything. Why limit your depression to the movie business? But I'd rather not be self-pitying. I'll be very curious to see what sort of book you come up with, because if people are honest, their lives and careers are never quite what they want them to be. I wish I'd made three or four times as many films by now. It feels like I'm just getting started. And for that reason, you know, I can't afford to be depressed. I refuse.

Is it still possible to do personal or eccentric or poetic work these days, with the industry the way it is?

I think there's a lot of good work being done now.

I personally get discouraged when I see the machine that Hollywood filmmaking can be at work.

It's always been there. Shortly after movies became movies, and the producers put their names on the doors and the studio gates, it was steered and controlled by commerce.

I agree to some extent. But I've always felt that the movies, even at their most crass, were about human beings or emotion, and even on the flimsiest level, about art, and who we are, all those things. Now I don't know if I feel that anymore. I think it has something

to do with the sensational aspect of movies, and the fact that a lot of people in the film business come from fields like advertising. Movies to me have changed although, as you say, there's still a lot of good work out there.

There have always been blockbusters and spectacles. When it first came out, *Metropolis* was a spectacle.

It was a spectacle, but it was also about important human issues.

At the time, it was run down as being shallow and superficial and merely about spectacle.

What is the most difficult thing about being a director?

Dennis Hopper said that the only thing more difficult than making a movie is not making a movie. From what I can tell, filmmaking is addictive, and the inability to do the job properly, or at all, carries a junkie's pathetic sense of anguish. But why dwell on the difficulty? Filmmaking is a privilege, particularly if you can manage to work steadily with a community of friends, if your films and your life have a sort of continuity. That's what I aspire to. That's the story with the filmmakers that have meant the most to me. It's not about being autocratic, forcing your will on people, illustrating a grand vision. It's about finding a community of friends, speaking to the moment.

I like what you wrote in your unpublished notes on the making of *Twister*, **the final paragraph.**

It's rhetoric, sort of the written equivalent of a helicopter shot.

Yes, but do you mind if I quote it for the end of this interview?

Go right ahead.

> When you enter into this work of making movies, or writing them, or even watching them with more than casual attention, it's possible to consider each movie a renewed image of the world. Miserable reality given a new gloss, the facts of our lives stirred and broken so that the best, most complicated moments might be fixed on the screen

with a heightened, replenished value. How else can we justify the degree of dumb labor that goes into conjuring these images, as concrete as architectural constructions, and as insubstantial as dreams? In a good or great movie, the grain of lived experience is enlarged, and given back to the world. We sit in the dark, privileged witnesses, at once enthralled and awake, and we are simultaneously swept away and carried home.

—Michael Almereyda

ANNA CAMPION

Anna Campion comes from one of the most renowned theatrical families in New Zealand. Her parents trained at the Old Vic in London and started the first professional theater group in New Zealand. Her passionate, artistic background was important to her later formation as a writer-filmmaker, although it took her some time to finally sort out the specific form her artistic impulses would eventually take. Anna began her filmmaking career later than her more famous sister Jane, having spent time on the stage in her homeland as an actress before settling in London in the early 1970s. After several detours, including several years' painting, Anna finally ended up studying filmmaking at the Royal College of Art in the mid-eighties. She went on to make several short films, including one called *The Audition*, which starred her mother and sister, and another film made for Channel Four entitled *Broken Skin*, featuring Miranda Richardson. Both films are poetic mood pieces, very much concerned with the emotional life of their characters. They are elusive narratives, blurring the distinction between fiction and non-fiction in the case of *The Audition*, and in *Broken Skin*, navigating between the realms of reality and dream.

Campion eventually made her first feature-length debut in the mid-nineties with her provocative film *Loaded*, an interesting tale of a group of highly intelligent British teens in the process of making a video horror film. During one strange and confusing weekend in the country, they decide to drop acid and one of the group is accidentally killed. The film is not a typical teen picture and is notable for its sharp evocation of this representative group of young people's confused and desperate search for meaning. They display all the character types typical of many teen films, but with almost none of the stupidity, cliché, cynicism or sentimentality of such films. From a sociological viewpoint, the film is interesting as a commentary on the pressures placed on this generation of young people, including the limits of individual responsibility. It also examines how technology and drugs, so prevalent in today's environment, intrude on our emotional and intellectual life. The questions raised by the film are intriguingly handled and the film is refreshingly free of any kind of moralizing or judgmental tone. It is a visually stylish film, featuring strong performances from its mostly unknown cast of young actors. It confirms that Anna Campion has a real feel for cinema and that she will go on to have a significant career in the film industry.

Campion has also devoted herself recently to co-writing Jane Campion's film *Holy Smoke*, as well as writing the novelization of that film. In part, this was undertaken to pay some of the bills incurred during the making of *Loaded*, which left her virtually broke. The harsh reality of making a feature film is that it is an incredibly expensive, time-consuming business. The struggles of making that all-important first feature, and what one learns about the film industry in the process, became the focus of our conversation. Campion also expounds on being a woman film director in an essentially "misogynist industry" and what ramifications that has on the possibilities of having any kind of "normal" family life, issues of real concern to potential women filmmakers. I spoke with Anna Campion in London.

Can we start with your growing up in New Zealand, and how that helped shape your decision to become an artist and filmmaker?

Well, I grew up in the fifties and sixties, and it was a bit like living in Albania or something, because the whole thing was controlled like a Communist state. It also had a grip on people's psyches, which were far too conventional, apart from the Maori psyche. I really think that if it hadn't been for the indigenous population and their struggle to not be like us, it would've been a totally conventional place. Luckily for me, I was living in a family that was highly theatrical. My parents went to the Old Vic. They trained there and that was unusual. If you grow up in a psychopath's family, the way they bully each other and carry on seems perfectly normal to you, until you live with another family. It's the same with me. I didn't realize that other people didn't read plays and go on in an obsessive way about aesthetics. Passion was my mother's big number, as is reflected in *The Piano*. The bad thing about them was their eccentricities. You always long for what you haven't got, so I wanted people who were around more.

Your parents weren't around a lot?

No. They were touring. My parents started the first professional theater in New Zealand. They were pretty narcissistic and probably Jane [Campion] and I are too. [Laughs] Everyone was driven by their obsessions. The good thing about it is that you set standards. You don't think to yourself that any old painting's good enough because your mother is always showing you that Picasso has done it better.

Were you a film fanatic growing up?

One of the first films I really clicked with when I was young was
Lawrence of Arabia. And then there's school. The best thing they ever
did was take me to *Gone with the Wind*. I thought that was extraordinary; I just loved Vivien Leigh. I still think she's totally mesmeric,
with her level of energy and performance. So, I was introduced to
epics because that's what was around, really. Then another formative film when I was about eighteen was *Cries and Whispers*. That had
a huge impact on me; it was like someone else had gotten into my
mind. Bergman had those strange moments of intimacy and cruelty
with people, which must have been behaviors I either longed for or
recognized.

You decided to go to art school?

No. First I followed my parents into the theater and that was good. I
went to the same place that Mel Gibson and Judy Davis and those
sorts of people went to in Sydney. I was professionally acting on the
stage for six years. I was wired for it.

What do you mean "wired for it"?

To engage properly with a performance you *are* it rather than *perform* it, so you're climbing into it, much the way Daniel Day-Lewis
would approach something. So, I had that ability imaginatively. The
other thing you have to have is great stability on the stage. You have
to be able to remember huge acres of garbage that you have to re-
cite. I stuck it out for a few years. It gave me a feeling for performance,
and also the terrors of it, because you can go on and sometimes an
audience is just rustling newspapers throughout and you have to be
able to rise above that. Unfortunately, I have good hearing and sometimes took these agitations in the audience too personally. So the
imagination functioned, but the stability varied. It made me sympathetic to people who come to the camera. I really do know it's
fantastic for them, but very intrusive for them too. Psychologically,
some days you can handle it better than others. So, your job as director is to feel and see changes in that person and make alterations

for that. Every actor is so different; there's just no prescription that will work with all of them. Sometimes when I was working with the people on *Loaded*, there was the bravery of attack, but the level of invention was quite low because they hadn't really been encouraged to do it.

Why did you leave New Zealand?

I had to leave New Zealand at that point. I just felt too claustrophobic. It's too small. I wanted to do exactly what I wanted to do. I think people should be able to do everything. They should be able to take drugs, do whatever they like because, at the end of the day, it's up to you to make up your mind where your limits are and what you will do. But in a country like New Zealand, it was too repressive. I still think it's repressive for young people. It's fine if you want to go there and retire.

So, this would've been around your mid-twenties or so?

That's exactly right. I came to London, and I lived in a squat, and that was fantastic. What I liked about London was that you could put yourself on the map or you could be completely anonymous. All big cities have that weirdness about them. People could be carving up and eating each other's livers next door to you, virtually, which is weird. It also offers you a chance to retreat and reinvent yourself or reshape yourself.

Did you have a specific plan when you came here?

Yes, I wanted to get into some sort of "psychobabble" stuff. I ended up working with psychopaths, teenage ones, at a unit called the Henderson Hospital. That was a bit like *A Clockwork Orange*. We weren't formulating behavior to that extent, but there was definitely a behavioral element to it, in trying to readjust maladjusted people. I liked doing that and stayed there for three years, but I just couldn't hack it after that. So I decided to go back into the arts. I went to Goldsmith's College, which had a good Arts Department. That was great. Then I went on to the Royal College of Art. At Goldsmith's I started getting frustrated with the Painting Department, even though I think I was okay as a painter. Once I started picking up videos, I became obsessed with watching people and what they do. [Laughs] My full voyeurism came to the fore, as well as what the frame would do. Then I switched completely to film.

Were you exposed to anything other than narrative film at that time?

Yes. I saw some really weird stuff, actually. Jean Genet, Maya Deren, quite a lot of Americans, like Kenneth Anger. I liked that stuff quite a lot.

Was Jane at film school at this time?

No, she had finished, and was doing *Sweetie*. I remember I had to leave the Royal College to look after mum, who has bouts of depression now and again, while Jane was doing *Sweetie*. That was the pact we made. She agreed to do my short film *The Audition*, a film I made with her and mum, and probably one of the most enjoyable experiences I've had.

This is around 1987?

Yes. That worked really well. It was great having a semi-professional crew and all the rest of it. And Jane was a damned good actress, actually. She's provocative, and mum engaged with this.

Did you end up at film school here [London]?

Yes, at the Royal College of Art. That was a misogynist outfit run by Dick Ross and it was a bit of a wake-up and just such a struggle. Some of these film schools are so stupid, playing ridiculous games.

Were they trying to impose their own ideas onto the students?

Yes, and their own anxieties. I think film schools are a bit dodgy because a lot of them are run by failed filmmakers who want to get their aura in on some peculiar level. The best thing they did was invite proper cinematographers and proper writers in. It forced me out of fear to become manipulative, and apply to the New

Zealand Arts Council for money to make *The Audition*, which I finished at the school.

When did you make *Broken Skin*?

I made *Broken Skin* after that for Channel Four around 1990. It was quite cute, although I don't think it entirely works. It's a little too vague.

Miranda Richardson is very intense in that film.

And in life!

I find it an interesting discipline to make a ten-minute film.

I think a short film can either do something poetic or something really funny. They're difficult, and the weird thing is that, in some ways, it's easier to pull off a feature because you can travel into many different areas.

Was the experience of making those two short films a good preparation for the feature? What kinds of things did you learn?

Yes. You learn what you won't put up with. There are so many frustrations. For example, I got on better with the cinematographer on *Loaded* because of my experience on the short films. I concentrated too much on the performance and not enough on some of the lighting in *Broken Skin*. When I look at it again, there's a shot in the kitchen which is just badly lit. I'd be able to call that now.

Did you have any trouble slipping into the role of director?

I remember reading how Kubrick couldn't film a scene unless there was something organic within the scene for him to bother turning the camera on for. It's either working or it isn't. Kubrick's approach was to line everybody up and do a lot of takes. I agree with that fanaticism. I think that it's all too expensive not to have something that's interesting to you to bother with. What bores me is when I know exactly what's going to happen all the time or I feel the level of performance isn't emotional enough for me to get really excited.

Then I would rather write a novel. There are plenty of other things to do with my life.

Was the subject matter of *Broken Skin* particularly meaningful to you?

Well, it was really my mother and me, or me/ Jane. I think I'd attack it differently now. All the time, what you're moving towards is more clarity, synthesizing the alchemy down to where it's just gold and getting rid of all the sculpture and crap around it.

In terms of your own filmmaking, are there particular films or film-makers who have been important to you?

Actually, one person I like that not many people might know about is Donald Cammell. I like *Performance* and *White of the Eye* and a movie he made with Julie Christie, *Demon Seed*.

Yes. I think they're all very interesting.

The vision of that man was a lot higher than people give him credit for. I had previously thought it was all Nic Roeg on *Performance*, but then when you see these other films, you can see that there's a completely different voice there. I also like *Apocalypse Now*. I like Scorsese and Woody Allen. Oh, and Bergman and Polanski and Kubrick. I also liked *Alien* and movies like that, which have been very visionary in taking you on a complete trip. I like some of Tarkovsky's stuff. *Andrei Rublyov*, I thought was just quite extraordinary. I think Cassavetes is fantastic.

What about the idea for *Loaded*? How did that come about?

I read somewhere about a case in America where these young men had borrowed their father's car and had an accident. They freaked out completely, more worried about the car and the father's wrath than the fact that they could've been injured in the accident. So, they robbed a liquor store to get money to fix the car. They were drinking in this car park, and next to them was a policeman with a girlfriend he shouldn't have been with. He saw them waving this gun around, which they borrowed to highjack the liquor store, and he got freaked out and shot them. One of them died, and they just buried him upstate, nothing said, and pretended that nothing had gone on. The idea of people taking the law into their own hands, because of the fear of what it would do, interested me. I couldn't do it with guns in England, because they are not so available. I used the idea of a class-A drug like acid, which would also freak people out if some accident happened. I think it's a big issue the whole business with drugs and the prison terms being handed down to people. I think this is completely wrong and alienating a whole generation. I wanted to address this, which I did, probably clumsily, but those were the things on my mind. The other thing on my mind was the psychopathic behavior of Neil's [Oliver Milburn] character.

I talked to Roger Corman who was quite interested in putting money into it, and he said to me, "Well, try and keep it within a 30-mile radius of London," which we did. It was good to do and a bit challenging because some of the actors hadn't done any film. This was before *Trainspotting*, and there was a lot of hoo-ha about these drugs. We're such a hypocritical society. Human beings are completely peculiar. I got there two years too soon, in a way, because I could have done anything I liked after *Trainspotting*. But before, it was "Gasp! You're using acid."

Also, what I wanted to do with these Thatcher children, who are very concrete in their materialism, was introduce a drug like acid where you actually have another reality. That was quite important for me, to try and get these kids to start seeing that a table was a living, moving atomic experience!

What was the involvement of the British Film Institute? They gave you a bit of development money?

I will say this for the British Film Institute, they did come to the table. You're not paid. In actual fact, I got the writing done quite quickly.

They gave me something like £12,000. In fact, one of the girls at the publishing house at Miramax asked me recently, "Anna, how can people afford to be filmmakers?" I think that's the best bloody question! Part of the reason I went on to do things with Jane was because I was just so strapped for cash after finishing *Loaded*. I did it on deferrals too. Luckily, it sold enough for all that to come back. But, imagine, I could be completely bankrupt. I don't think that's right. What worries me is that you're only going to get people who are middle class, or connected to the industry, making films. You're sustaining yourself, and people say, "Oh, you've got a film festival to go to!" Most filmmakers think, "Oh, no. How much is that going to cost?" [Laughs] It's such an expensive arena to get into.

Did the script give you trouble?

No. The script itself did not give me trouble. What gave me trouble was everybody getting into a doubting mode about drugs. Left up to myself, I could have taken the thing that I'd outlined in six weeks, started improvising, and built it up from there. That's maybe what I would do in the future.

Instead of what? What did you do?

Everybody now feels that they have to completely drive everybody crazy by doing twenty thousand drafts of the script. Bullshit! It's either working or it's not. The problem is you can only say so much in a scene. You then have to move it along. But it's only people like Jane, or other writers, who can tell me these things. If you haven't written, you don't know enough about structure to help a person write.

In terms of character and themes, was this material particularly personal?

Yes, it was, actually. I was pretty dumb in terms of looking at it commercially. There are a few things I'd change now. I would go in tighter with the camera. I might have made the horror film within the film more explicit. The big lesson I learnt was that you can go right over the top, because you can always cut it out later. I felt very close to the character of Neil and also Rose, the girl played by Catherine McCormack. She was a lot like my mother, that sort of creative, sensitive person.

Ultimately, how did the film get financed?

The BBC was interested, but I knew they would freak out because of the drug thing at the time. So I rang up Ben Gibson, and he gave me seed money to develop the script. Then I got introduced to Caroline Hewitt, and she and my husband David Hazlett became the major production team. Then, Bridget Ikin and John Maynard, who were running a company in New Zealand, brought a million dollars of New Zealand money to the table. We made it up of this money, and another company called Strawberry Vale, and Hans Geissendörfer put in £200,000 of his own money. I thought that was particularly bold. But you see what the problem is. You have a lot of voices on the film. Because it was made as a coproduction between England and New Zealand, I had to travel all the way back to New Zealand and do the postproduction and editing there. And that's 12,000 miles.

Did you have a clear idea about how each scene would be filmed before you started shooting, or was there a certain amount of improvisation?

Because many of the actors had not really worked in film, I did about four weeks of improvisational stuff, which was good. Because we did the improvisations, we could call on those memories and get a lot of setups done in a day, probably more than on most films. I went out there on the weekends myself and checked the viewfinder to find the best angles in the rooms. I think I probably did too much of that. When I walked in, I'd say, "The camera is going right here."

I think actors who are very good at improvising are a joy to work with. That's sometimes the difference between here and America; the energy of performance is great in America. We had Holly Hunter doing a read for Jane and me recently for *Holy Smoke*, and the level of energy was amazing. I think that's why people like Eastwood, Cage, DeNiro, and Keitel are so great. There is an energy there, even when they're doing nothing.

So you feel you overprepared because it was your first feature?

I did a bit. I'm convinced now that people like Woody Allen and Kubrick are right. Get the alchemy up there, then worry about it. Because at the end of the day, it's not the angle that's doing it, it's who's wandering around in it.

How important is casting for you?

I tend to cast for type. I think, "This person has these things in them or they do not." I think good directors are pretty manipulative.

Was it a difficult shoot? Was it enjoyable?

It was a bit difficult, but I still enjoyed it. I really like working with the actors. What drove me crazy was the editing. I would do it digitally on an Avid in the future.

The film has a nice rhythm, good transitions. Why was the editing difficult?

Because there was a lot of material and we didn't have an Avid. And people were trying to make unrealistic deadlines. You can't shoot a film in November and then decide to make Cannes in May. It's just not going to happen unless you're a very experienced filmmaker. In the editing process, you're sticking with your best stuff, but you're also trying to make the best of the worst stuff, and sometimes I felt a bit beleaguered. What I would do next time is clear out what was not important to the story line right away, instead of trying to make things work. Forget all that! That's just beginner's crap, really.

What was difficult about the shoot?

It was cold. We had to heat the beds. I had to rub Deep Heat into the actors. [Laughs]

Stylistically, you were going for a long-take style.

Yes. I think what you're looking for really is the great take. I don't know that you need to disrupt it too much. I mean, Jane edits a lot more than I do. However, modern audiences' level of boredom still has to be catered to as well.

Was it difficult deciding on how to block scenes? Was there any aspect of the shoot that was most troublesome?

Yes, table scenes. If you've got a lot of people around a table, it can honestly drive you mental. They are very difficult and quite boring to do because you obviously want something a little different happening. I don't really care if you cross the line of axis, sometimes it can work, but at other times it's just irritating and no one knows what the hell you're doing. Strangely enough, things that appear more difficult like blue screens, CGI [Computer-Generated Imagery], are actually straightforward technical exercises.

Can you describe how you worked with your cinematographer?

Alan Almond shot it, and operated the camera as well, which is very tiring to do. The great things about him were his speed, and his fluidity of movement.

Did you feel fairly prepared in terms of what you expected from your cinematographer? Did you have a good idea of what you wanted?

Yes, I did. Again, I think it's a really good idea to get photographs done, or get three of four films that you like. I quite liked *Drugstore Cowboy* at the time.

Did the fact that you are a woman have any impact on how you worked with the crew?

Ah, yes. It's a misogynist industry, and you're a bit of a curiosity. I don't know that I'd have got on any better being a young guy. It might've been worse, actually. I don't think it featured on the set, but I think it features in the industry in general. I think that the subject matter of this film and the psyche that's presented to the world is male. As a female filmmaker, if you become more masculine and less complex, basically, you'll do better. No compensation is made at all for the fact that you have a child or anything like that.

What does the title of the film *Loaded* mean for you, apart from the most obvious meaning?

Loaded psychologically. You've got a loaded situation. Jane quite liked the title *Babes in the Woods*, which I still like. We went through, I would say, 400 titles. From the beginning, I said, "What about *Loaded*, or what about *Babes in the Wood*?" They'd say "Oh, not *Loaded*." And what did we use in the end? I mean, this is where you waste time. Stupid stuff that goes on in the industry which probably goes on all over the world. I think at the end of the day, it's best to say, "I am not engaging in this subject one more time. This is the title I think will be good."

It sounds like you learned a lot.

I learned more than most people learn in five films. I really did. It was a violent experience in some ways, especially going to Miramax and finding out what they do from the other end of it. There's a sort of violence in filmmaking where people ring you up and say great things, but then devastate you in other ways. The violence to your person is quite heavy. In the end, you have to say, "I'm making dreams. Basically, I'm making up a series of realities that sustain me for whatever reason." You've really got to disengage from taking yourself too seriously. The best way to do that is not to read either good or bad reviews. It can be estranging in both directions. I heard, for example, on Alison Maclean's *Crush* that some members of the crew were heard discussing whether they thought the script was any good. I do think that there should be more protection from that sort of stuff. The producer should come on the set and say, "Have you raised the money? Did you write the script? Is that your job description?" I felt really bad and angry for her, hearing about that sort of violation. It's not really up to the crew to discuss the merits of the script. What it really means is that they're feeling nervous about their contribution. It has nothing to do with Alison. The director really only needs to talk to about five people, apart from the actors. You talk to producers, the musicians, sound, cinematographer, designer, and editor.

The final cut of the film was ten or twelve minutes shorter than what was shown at the Venice Film Festival. The film was also delayed in terms of its release. What was the story behind the delay and the different release prints?

Yes, definitely, mistakes were made. Basically, Miramax played it to people. It was because of the editing thing, and the film-within-a-film not being all-out maniac stuff. Some things in the Venice cut, I liked better. It was spookier. Other things, I thought did go on too long and held up the story. They were just too indulgent, frankly. My problem was going with the BFI in the first place. That's when those decisions really impact on you because they don't have a distribution arm. That means that more than half the films being made here now don't go anywhere near a cinema. At least I wasn't in the dire situation of no one wanting it. Harvey Weinstein was fairly protective of me. When we showed the final cut at the Toronto Film Festival, we got a very good reception. Sundance happened from that. I got quite a lot of interest from people wanting me to do stuff in America. At the time, after *Loaded*, I was really broke.

Why such a long delay, though? It was almost two years before it opened in North America.

To release a movie is so expensive, and Miramax wanted it to be as right as they thought they could get it. Simultaneously, I also agreed to write *Holy Smoke* with Jane, and so I had to finish the first draft of that, and then get back to the film. That was not a very good move. I do think that the BFI probably could have opened it immediately, because there was no *Trainspotting*, nothing on the horizon. I think they'd have done okay for themselves.

What was the most challenging aspect of making *Loaded*?

Sometimes I think it's a stupid thing, like raising the money. The other was getting the right cast. If you miscast dreadfully, it's a nightmare. Strangely enough, the technical things didn't worry me as much as what was going on in front of the camera. I think that has to be your total priority all the time. Maybe the biggest challenge was my own lack of confidence and clarity. You can walk alleyways that are time-consuming, which you don't need to walk. It's very debilitating. The thing you're always coming up against is your own limitations. Everybody is. And that's what drives you crazy.

The film-within-a-film material goes on a bit long, I think. Did you go for them making a really bad movie to have more fun?

Yes. But they could've been more vicious, like tying the girls up. They could've been reading out the psychopathic literature, and saying, "So this is what Ted Bundy, or whoever, would do in this scene. You lie down here." You get into arguments of exploitation. Or what would the girls do if they had a boy and they could do anything they wanted?

Was the death of Lionel [Matthew Eggleton] meant to symbolize the death of innocence?

I think he's the Christ figure, in a way. I don't know that it's the death of innocence. He's someone who is really a sweetheart, and those people often are removed because of our Darwinian trust in the West to trample over sensitive types like that.

Do you have thoughts on story structure after your experience on *Loaded*?

Well, I've learned that you have to keep it moving and get out of scenes fast. I'm more ruthless with myself on the new script. If the scene is long with another major scene to follow, that scene will suffer not because it's not good, but because the scene previous to it has dragged, and it can be cumulative. The problem with film is that it has to be "simple-stupid" in some ways. You can build your complexities in other areas. It was the basic first-time filmmaker's mistake, you know, you want to say everything. Forget it! It's another movie. That discipline's terribly hard.

How much of the structure was determined in advance and how much at the editing stage?

I had to restructure a bit. Setups are difficult for me. The setups were too meandering, and went on too long. We also ended up throwing out eleven or twelve scenes from the script.

But you ended up using most of what you shot?

Yes.

What compelled you to explore some of the issues, like materialism versus spiritualism, with kids in their early twenties as opposed to characters your own age?

I thought the difference between English young people and Americans was that they're articulate. At least the middle-class kids. They're forced to live in their heads more than the Americans or Canadians. There, you have those huge spaces; you can go skiing. This is prohibitive to most people here because it's too expensive. So I wanted to do a movie where people were having to grapple with things verbally. I liked the idea of them being verbally threatening. I also saw the film in somewhat sociological terms, which may have been a bit of a mistake. What you really have to do then is drive it through with character. You don't want them carrying messages that are too weighty. With Neil it makes sense, because you've got this backstory driving through. Also, because I went to film school late in life, I was mixing with people of that age group.

There seems to be a tangent in this film that might have been explored more. I'm thinking of the way Neil uses technology and his relationship to his therapist. Why does he videotape their sessions?

Films really are processes where you're stealing the image of someone and replaying it. That's what he's doing with the shrink, because he can replay the tape anytime he wants. It's like having a lover on tap for you.

So it becomes a bit of a fetish?

Yes. I think there is an element of that with video. This nonstop stuff that we have at the moment is pretty fascinating. Courtroom dramas are better than most films these days. Look at the O.J. Simpson case.

Did you achieve what you wanted to achieve with _Loaded_? Is there any part of it that isn't satisfying to you now?

I look at it with such a critical eye that I can't look at it. [Laughs] I can sometimes play the interviews in the film when I'm feeling strong because they're interesting. I think the film was quite bold. It was trying to mesh the psychoanalytic thing and the psychopathic thing, and I was quite pleased with that, and also the wooliness of our thinking these days, as reflected in Neil and the dangers of that kind of thinking. I think I should've sharpened my sword a bit so that the rapier goes in a bit more cleanly. Hopefully, in the future I will be able to do that. Sometimes I think that it was quite a good start, and I need to build on it. At other times, I think let's give myself a rest and do a comedy, because, for one thing, it's nice to hear right away that people are laughing. You think, that's pretty good, and it would be nice to hear that.

The film received something of a mixed response. Were you upset by any of the negative reactions?

I honestly feel that my main job is to make myself better as a film-maker. So I'm probably a worse critic than any of them could ever be. Sometimes you do feel there's a bit of misogyny amongst the critics. Jane thought that. Rather than thinking that this is someone's first film, it was "this film should be _The Piano_," or something.

Commercially, did the film do much business?

Strangely, where it did quite well was in the Scandinavian countries and Belgium, where they didn't advertise a damned thing. It just stayed and stayed. So that was quite lucky. But at least they gave it a chance. Word of mouth did it. Where I don't think I got a fair deal was with the BFI and people distributing it here, where it was just a mess. Even though it did better than most films in the first week, they were expecting some extraordinary record figures on it. That was unfair to me.

I think Harvey [Weinstein] was quite cunning in the States because he also put it around to the universities a lot, and he would've made his money back with that. But you are up against famous filmmakers and stars. So I think to have any distribution at all is pretty good, really. Especially since so many people don't get any.

How has it affected you in terms of getting your next film made?

I think it hasn't affected me badly because so many first films just go nowhere and we don't even hear about them. It did a lot better than that.

What did you do immediately after finishing the film? Were you offered any scripts?

Yes. There were things that I turned down in the States and Australia. A lot of American scripts start really well, and have a terrible second act, and then kick in with an interesting ending. So they really get you going in the first ten pages and then go nowhere.

So you had this period where you were being courted?

I had a period where I was thrown scripts and things, but immediately Jane got onto the bandwagon and said, "Why don't you come and write with me?" This is *Holy Smoke*, which starts in India and finishes in Australia, and is really a sort of battle about religion and about men and women. I'm doing the novelization too, which is why it's taking me so damn long.

Well, you'll be rich. [Laughs]

I hope so. This is the idea. It was also quite rich working with her. Jane's obsessive and has almost a cruel, or so incisive it feels cruel, helicopter vision, detached in order to really see. I tend to enjoy intense interaction where you get lost. The object is to lose it psychologically and break through to some other aspect of yourself. She provides the searing clarity. Not many people want to do that, there's a wish to brush over the problem because it's just so bloody difficult conquering the material at all, in any shape or form. And we possess comic ability. I love that about Jane.

Is Jane directing the film?

Yes.

There's also another script you're working on.

Yes, *Kirsa, a Mother's Story*. It's a bit like *Picnic at Hanging Rock*, very weird, scary, and interesting. If anything, it's anti-violence, but there's a lot of peripheral violence in terms of what happens to the family. The father's a vicar. It's got a fairly good hammering storyline too. If that works out, good. If that doesn't, I'd quite like to do a comedy, which would be much more Woody Allenish, looking at my family. [Laughs]

Was there ever any competitiveness between you and Jane?

Well, I consider her so far ahead. In fact, I've made up my mind that I'm not going to get involved with this stuff. What I would rather do is make seedier, second-stream movies where the expectation just isn't on you.

But you feel the expectation?

Yes, but I think you can choose. In some ways, it's better to be working than not. So rather than thinking that I want to be one of the twenty big names, I might ironically be able to do that easier if I'm not pressured to do that, if I ring up Roger Corman and say, "What piece of crap have you got that I could turn around for you?" [Laughs] Because that would be more fun, you know?

If you were starting out in the film industry sixty years ago, you'd be making two or three movies a year. You wouldn't be judged so much, and you'd learn your craft.

Yes, I think so. There's too much pressure. I've seen it with my sister. Jane's having anxiety dreams already about this bloody *Holy Smoke*. I appreciate that effort, because it really does make a difference in the movie. But on the other hand, it might be that by being relaxed and a bit of an idiot, you can get to the same place. It's just a different psychological process. You've got to think of your sanity and your family. I don't particularly want to be one of those filmmakers who can point to a shelf and have no life. [Laughs]

Well, what about TV? Have you thought about that?

No, I haven't, but I think why not? It could be good, especially if you go in with secret little expectations. It could be quite fun. The problem with that would be that half the actors would be crap. That would be tricky and it would be boring. Maybe you could steal up on them and say it's rehearsal or something, and try to get something happening. That level of TV is bad. But the speed at which it goes is good. I would fill it completely differently and really throw the camera around in the sense of angles. I wouldn't bother storyboarding it very much.

What I think is really problematic now is the time that it takes to get films made. People wait for three, five years . . . It's so wearing, that when the person actually starts principle photography, they're probably not even interested in it anymore. Their head and psychological processes have moved on.

What's wrong with the film industry?

One of the problems with the industry is that before, people thought, "Oh, well. We've got a studio. Half of this will be crap. Things that we're not thinking will be crap might be great. Or things that we think will be crap might turn out great." They concentrated on big things and hoped that the other things weren't too hopeless. Now, they have huge expectations of every film, even the small ones. Some things should just not get done. I don't even think it's the refining at the script stage, but at the idea stage. If the idea is something that catches the imagination, do it; it may work out for you. If it isn't going to work at that level, forget it! You've got so much competition now with satellite and all the rest.

In terms of content, I wouldn't mind a few more films addressing things like virtual reality and media manipulation, and being a bit more ambitious with their thinking. On that level, things are a bit of a snooze. [Laughs] Generally speaking, that's one thing I learned. Before you spend five years driving yourself crazy with something, it really had better be something that's worth spending that time on.

You also have to be really tenacious. You have to be a nut, really. There's too many people who are not in the firing line barking on. It's like hiring an architect, and then saying that you don't like anything they want to do. Well, hire another one, whose style you like, because then you'll at least agree on something. In other words, the tail is wagging the dog too much. And the tail is the money.

Do you consider yourself a part of any British film tradition or do you see yourself as an international film director?

I consider myself a bit of a weirdo, but I do think the opportunity is there for me now to embrace other weirdoes here if I want to.

But can you also see yourself going somewhere else?

For the sanity of everybody, apart from my big narcissistic self, I think I probably should stay in one place. I do think the industry is in L.A., though. Jane might have made some sacrifices by staying in Sydney, in terms of being the influential player she could be. But then she has to think of her sanity in other things. I mean, Donald Cammell shot himself. I don't think he wanted to be in that arena of madness. At the end of the day, it comes down to whether the script is good enough for you to pour so much of your life into.

Is it important for you to maintain links to Australasia?

I think a lot of ideas that I have spring up from there. *Loaded* didn't happen to be one that I thought should be shot there. But I have lots of ideas for scripts. I really like *Hand-Carved Coffins* by Truman Capote. The problem with some of these damned things is that people just sit on these projects for twenty-five years. They're not going to do them, and they don't want anybody else to do them. This sort of stuff is frustrating. Generally speaking, some of the best stories around at the moment are from the public domain, a really interesting place to start.

Is there a lot of pressure on you to make your next film more commercial?

I would think so. Yes. [Laughs]

Do you want it to be more commercial?

If I went down a silly road with Corman or somebody, and kept it cheap, I could have much more freedom. When you get expensive, the freedom goes. In a sense, I think I'd rather keep my freedom. I don't want to be poor, though, just because I'm in the film industry.

But you also don't want to make anything just for the sake of making it.

No. I could've done it by now. I have refused to partly because I just don't think I could lie to myself that much. I would be half-way through it, and thinking, "God, this is really a turkey, man. You are involved with a turkey. Oh my God! This story is just a shitty story!" My best idea of how to make a film is to make sure these emotional things are hitting the right notations, and the story is a little better than *Loaded* was, a bit more sure of itself. I'd like to feel there's something obsessively interesting for me on the screen, otherwise it's a snooze for me.

If there wasn't a place for you in the film industry, would you write?

Yes. I'm quite enjoying writing this novel. It's great to travel in certain states of mind, and certain sexualities and things that are more difficult to do in a movie.

What does one need to succeed as a filmmaker?

You need to be a nut. You need to be tenacious. You need to sort out your personality a bit. I mean if you're too quiet, you have to work on something inside yourself. I have to do work on clarity and calm-down. For other people, it may be that they will have to modify different facets of themselves. Also, it's a good idea to know yourself enough to know what actually interests you, then you can sustain a lot of grief. You've got to make sure the little wierdnesses you are shooting are enough to sustain all kinds of horrors. If you're an intense person, it's best to make that kind of thing. If you've got funny aspects, you might have to address that in a couple of movies. Basically, you're playing off bits of yourself. You're just tweaking it around. I think if you do that, then you can live with it, with bad critiques, and all the rest of it. It is quite an extroverted industry, and that can be quite hard for people. You have to be a bit of a performer yourself.

What are some things filmmakers should avoid?

Sometimes what you have to do is not take things too seriously, and also, don't let people lead you up alleyways that amount to nothing. For example, "Shall we fire the focus-puller or not?" This conversation can go on for the entire movie. Do it, or don't do it, but don't ring me at two in the morning to talk about it. It's basically making sure that everyone can make decisions, otherwise it just becomes laborious.

I think what a lot of filmmakers who are starting out are not addressing is "Is there really enough of an idea to bother shooting in the first place?" I do think that you have to desensitize in quite a terrible way to make films. The business side of it is boring, really. I wish my sister didn't feel she had to take on every little thing. I do think that drives you a bit potty. In fact, I'll have to pull a reversal here; this is Jane as I previously perceived her. Although still a maniac, her trust's vastly improved. You need to decide that some people are actually capable of doing their jobs. I think the feeling can be that you're alone and that's a myth, but it's weird how you can think, "Oh, God! They're all fools here but me!" And on other days, you can think, "Oh, my God! I'm the one and only fool!" [Laughs] It's getting rid of these extremes. That's the trick.

TERENCE DAVIES

Terence Davies has made some of the most devastatingly emotional films of the contemporary era and some of the most beautiful. He is an uncompromising artist who has charted the pain, loneliness, and terror of growing up poor and gay and brutalized by a tyrannical father in such powerful films as *Distant Voices, Still Lives* and *The Terence Davies Trilogy*.

The Terence Davies Trilogy is a collection of three short films made over the course of a decade. It charts the tragic, painful journey of its male protagonist from brutal childhood to an agonizing death as an old man in a hospital ward. This autobiographical trilogy is among the most fiercely honest films of the contemporary era. As someone once remarked to the filmmaker, these films make "Ingmar Bergman look like Jerry Lewis."*The Trilogy* is a forceful example of how the life and work of an artist can intertwine in curative ways that can literally save the artist's life. I strongly doubt that Terence Davies would be alive today if he had not channeled his painful experiences of growing up into some form of creative outlet.

Davies' best known film, *Distant Voices, Still Lives* starring Pete Postlethwaite, clearly proved that the filmmaker's autobiographical experiences could be shaped into a feature format with great international appeal. A daring aesthetic experiment, the film paints a particularly harsh portrait of Davies' brutal father. Its brilliant formal stylistics, including a marvelous tableau-image strategy, an arresting color scheme, and a rich integration of characters singing songs with no musical accompaniment, combine with emotionally searing material to create a remarkable cinematic experience. The film illustrates Davies' astonishing ability to combine images and sound in creatively ambitious ways that in no sense detract from the emotional power of the film's volatile subject matter.

This is even clearer in *The Long Day Closes*, a film which illuminates the ecstatic experiences of the filmmaker's childhood—the years after the death of his father—and the conflicted feelings and subtle pain of realizing his own homosexuality and inevitable end of this charmed existence. *The Long Day Closes* contains some of the most rapturous images in contemporary cinema. Additionally, the creative use of popular songs and fragments of film soundtracks from such films as *The Magnificent Ambersons, Kind Hearts and Coronets*, and *The Lady Killers* contribute to a complex formal approach that has elevated Davies to the top ranks of world-class personal filmmakers.

Although the specifically autobiographical chapter of the Davies' filmmaking life has now ended, he continues to astonish audiences and take huge aesthetic risks in such films as *The Neon Bible*, his adaptation of the John Kennedy Toole novel starring the luminous Gena Rowlands. This film, set in the American South of the forties, uses a tableau strategy similar to *Distant Voices, Still Lives* but with the added advantage of the wide-screen image and again, a particularly rich attention to sound. But whether he is exploring the working-class Britain of his youth or the American milieu of Edith Wharton's turn of the century novel *The House of Mirth*, his most recent film, Davies has emerged as one of the most original cinematic voices in contemporary Britain. He has created an extraordinary body of work that, hopefully, in the years to come, many more viewers will discover. I spoke to Terence Davies in London.

Davies

Can you talk about your background, growing up in Liverpool, working-class, Roman Catholic, and homosexual. It sounds rough.

I'm the youngest of ten children. Seven of them survived, three died when they were quite young. I went to an ordinary, working-class school. It was okay. Because the way the system works here—or how it used to work when I grew up—from five to eleven you went to primary school, and from eleven to fifteen you went to secondary school. They were always separate schools. The primary school was mixed and really rather nice, and all the teachers were women. I was very happy there. Except one particular teacher who was a martinet, but that was just one brief cloud on what was really a lovely experience. Then at eleven I went on to an all-boys secondary school. That's when my misery really began, because I was bullied and beaten up every day for four years, and I didn't tell anyone. A lot of the teachers were quite brutal, because a lot of them were ex-army [men] who'd gone into teaching. They were just really cruel and sadistic. So that changed my life quite a lot.

At seven, I saw my first film, *Singin' in the Rain*, which was a wonderful introduction. I fell in love with film, particularly musicals because my sisters loved them, and I was very, very close to my sisters. As much as I love my brothers, I was much closer to women, like most gay men. I felt uneasy with most men, because I felt inferior to them. But I went to the cinema all the time. My refuge from this misery of school was my family and the cinema. I was also a Catholic, and very devout. I really did believe, and sometimes prayed until my knees literally bled. I suddenly realized, as I got into puberty, that I was feeling these things towards men that I knew instinctively were wrong. I prayed and prayed to be forgiven and, of course, nothing happened.

I left school at fifteen and went into a shipping office where I was just a clerk. This was a very Dickensian shipping office, around 1961. Like most people from my background, if you were reasonably intelligent you went into an office. I was just told, "You will go into an office," and I did. I was there for a year. Then the shipping office closed down and I got a job as an articled clerk. I was supposed to take articles, which is a fancy way of saying that it was an apprenticeship, and you stayed there for seven years, or whatever, to become an accountant. It was there that I suddenly realized that I wanted to act and write. That's what I did in the evenings. I didn't take articles, because I knew it wasn't what I wanted to do. But really, the writing and acting kept me sane, because I hated the work so much. I was good at it but I hated it. The thought of spending all my life doing only that was horrific.

By this time, all my siblings were married, and my mum and I moved into a little flat where we lived together. I started acting and writing in the evening. I tried for drama school but never got in because I hated London. I used to come down and give terrible auditions because I loathed being here. Anyway, by the time I was twenty-seven, I couldn't really stand office life anymore. I figured, "What am I going to do? I've got to do something. I can't continue like this." So I applied to drama school—not a very good one—in the Midlands and got in, and got an education grant. I went there for two years. It was not a particularly good experience but at least I had got away from Liverpool. Ironically, I did not want to leave home and my mother. I was very attached to her. I'd go home once every three weeks on the train because that's all I could afford. I missed her terribly. It was absolute agony. The fellow students were not very nice, I have to say. If you gave a good performance, you were ostracized for two weeks. I was shocked that people could be so consistently vicious. But I had to stick there, simply because if I'd given up, I would have had to repay my grant to my local authority, and I couldn't afford to.

When did you decide to make films?

I used listen to a program on BBC 1 called *Cinema Now*, and I heard a program about the BFI [British Film Institute] production. I sent off my script, the first part of the *Trilogy* that I had sent everywhere and everyone had turned down. Later they asked me to go down, and they said, "You have eight and a half thousand pounds. Not a penny more. You will direct." And that's how I got into film. [Laughs]

You made your first film, and then you went to film school after?

I still had to complete my drama course. I made the film over the summer. It was absolute agony because the person who gave me the money left the BFI. Everyone on the crew, apart from the cameraman, loathed the script, and they let me know it. They made my life complete misery. It was one of the worst experiences of my life because I didn't know anything.

You're talking about *Children*, the first part of the *Trilogy*?

Yes. The crew's attitude was: "You haven't gone to film school. You haven't made a film. Why should you get all this money from the BFI?" Because in 1972 £8,500 was a lot of money for a short film. They gave me a very hard time, and after it was over, I thought, "I'm never going to do this again." Despite that fact, when I looked down the camera lens for the first time, it was terribly exciting. Anyway, I had all this material and somehow, the sound recordist had wangled the job as editor, and was *not* an editor, and it was a complete disaster. The person who took over at the BFI was Peter Sainsbury, who said, "You know, there's a good film in that." I said, "It may be in there, but I don't know where." He said, "Well, let me try to find you an editor." He got me another editor, Sarah Ellis, who was just divine, and we recut it. It's still too long at forty-six minutes, but it was my first film. The whole thing was my apprenticeship, but Sarah and I got something out of it.

So the structure evolved out of the editing?

Yes, and Sarah was very helpful. Very often I would say, "This just feels right." And she'd say, "Well, if it feels right, you must go with it." But I knew nothing about rhythm and visual dynamic. It's still too long, too languid.

Then I went to do my last year of drama school, which was even worse because now I'd made a film, and there was a great deal of overt jealousy. I was treated like shit, actually. That year was awful. I look at my diary now and I don't know how I survived that year, I was so low. Most of the time, I was suicidal. I ended up having only two friends. But it puts iron in your soul, I have to say. Anyway, I finished. I applied for film school and I didn't get in. I thought again, "What do I do?" I went back to Liverpool and had to take a job as a bookkeeper. One day, I thought, "I've got to get out of here. I can't do this." I applied to film school a second time and, thank God, they took me, and I went down to the National Film School in London.

What are the formative influences on your work as an artist: film-makers, films, novelists, or other artists?

Well, the main one really was the American musical, because that was what I was brought up on. At the same time, the best comedies were made in this country. We still had people like Alistair Sim, Margaret Rutherford, and so many others; real comic talent, and in such depth. If you wanted to see a good comedy, you went to see an English film. You didn't go to the Americans. They were too slight, actually. This was before *Some Like it Hot*, which was one of the greatest comedies ever made. But you must remember we produced films like *Kind Hearts and Coronets*, probably the greatest film comedy ever. It's just incomparable. I don't think *Some Like it Hot* touches it, for sheer stylishness, wit, and elegance.

What about melodrama or other kinds of films?

They didn't have much of an impact until I was older and I started seeing them on television. We didn't have an art cinema. We were lucky if things were recycled. They would be popular things, like the Bowery

Boys, which were constantly brought back. There were obviously popular melodramas at the time which were hugely successful, such as *Love is a Many Splendored Thing.* It's unwatchable now, but then, it was a huge success. It wasn't until I saw films like *Night of the Hunter* and *Letter from an Unknown Woman* and *Rebecca* and all sorts of others on television that I realized there was another culture. Much later, I discovered Bergman and Ozu, an even greater revelation.

What about music? Your love of popular songs and radio, which are so important to your films.

Oh, yes, that's true. Radio was incredibly important. Everybody listened to the radio. It was a radio culture, and that was an enormous influence, particularly comedy. Of course, those were the really rich years for radio comedy in this country. There's nothing to equal them now. *The Goons* was still twenty-five or thirty years ahead of its time and infinitely better than the Pythons, funnier and more anarchic. That was your home entertainment.

You're known for preplanning almost everything. Did you start that way too, when you were working on the *Trilogy*?

I didn't know how you wrote a script, and so I wrote down what I saw. And people said, "Well, you're not supposed to write like this." I'd never seen a film script, so that's what I did. Also, if I write down everything, when I go on the set, I know every shot in the film. That gives you an enormous kind of bedrock on which to base everything.

The *Trilogy* is almost unbearably painful and depressing to watch. Was life as bad as portrayed in those films?

Spiritually, yes. I really was at my lowest because there was no sense of hope. There I was, for a long time believing devoutly that if I was really good, and if I really prayed, whatever it was inside me He would take away. And, of course, it doesn't happen. Because of the way I grew up, and the way Catholicism was taught, any kind of doubt was the work of the devil, and I had to fight it. And I did, a complete waste of time. In the end, when I was twenty-two, I thought,

"This is a lie. It's actually a lie. Why have I believed it for so long?" When you realize that it's no longer true, and that there is no God, there's nothing there, it's very, very hard.

I come from a working-class background where even ordinary sex wasn't talked about. God, if you were light on your feet in those days, it was still a criminal offense until 1967. And so you're automatically a criminal, which is an awful thing to find out when you haven't done anything. So it was infinitely worse than the films. I could never go through that again. Never! I was just miserable all the time, because I had to suppress what I was feeling. I couldn't tell anybody.

I'm curious about your working methods. What is it like to direct nonprofessionals?

Most of the actors in the *Trilogy* were professionals. The only ones who weren't were some of the extras and the kids. What you have to do is try and keep in mind what you felt when you wrote the script and what you're aiming for. With children, it's a much greater strain because you can't say, "You're doing this because it's your psychological motivation." They just don't understand it. You've got to make it seem like play, and say, "No. If you do that, it doesn't look very believable." They say, "Well, can I do this?" You say, "Yeah, try that." You coax it out of them. The only times it wasn't a strain were with Leigh McCormack in *The Long Day Closes*, who was terrific, and Jacob Tierney in *The Neon Bible*, who is actually Canadian. He was terrific. They were really professionals and you did think, "Oh, that's such a relief!"

The *Trilogy* seems to get more complex as it goes along. Parts Two and Three seem more complicated stylistically. Is that to some extent the effect of film school?

Partially, but I also think that the only way to learn is to do. When I'd made *Children*, I actually knew there were lots of things wrong with it. I didn't know what I wanted to do. One shot lasts two minutes and twenty seconds.

[Laughs] That's not long.

Well, I call it my angora sweater shot because by the time it runs through the projector, you can knit one. I didn't realize that there is the rhythm of a piece, and also an internal rhythm. My internal rhythm tends to be meditative and slow.

What were you going for with that long take of the boy on the bus looking out the window? The shot finally cuts to the mother, who is by then in tears. The miserableness of their life?

No, it was something much more modest. Here's the child who looks out of the window at the world, as children do. And then, after he's finished looking, he turns and, to his surprise, his mother's weeping. There's no preparation. I was going for a poetry of the ordinary—because I'm interested in the poetry of the ordinary—not quick cutting, not fast tracks, not lots of things happening at once. I think that's spurious drama, visual fast food. I'm interested in tiny things happening because the majority of people's lives are about tiny things. And when something big does happen—a birth, a wedding, a death—it is huge. Someone goes away, it is huge!

The majority of people do not see people getting shot to pieces or tortured. The majority of people, like Thoreau says, "lead lives of quiet desperation." I also got that from Chekov, because when I first went to the theater, it was to see *The Seagull*. I didn't understand it but I knew emotionally what it was about. And his plays are about tiny things happening in ordinary lives which are stunted and never grow, and that's why they're so moving. So, that's what I was trying to say. Here, the world went by this window, his known world, and then he turns around and she's weeping. When you're a child, the world is mysterious, but adults are just as mysterious because they do things and you don't know why. It's never explained to you because you're only a child.

You have so many introspective characters in your films. There's a little boy who's in a world of his own in just about every film.

Well, I believe children are in a world of their own. And that world can be both wonderful and terrible, as in *The Long Day Closes*. You're terrorized at school, and yet you look out the window and think you see a ship, because that's what I did. I'm sure I'm not unique, all children do it. You hear it and you think you see it. You haven't, of course, but in a way you have. The world of the imagination can be just as powerful, because it's lived with such intensity as a child. And when I was a child, from seven to eleven, I was in a state of complete ecstasy all the time. It was extraordinary.

There's one scene in the *Trilogy* that I thought was unusual. In Part Two, Robert's at the office, and a Kyrie comes on the soundtrack over a slow camera movement. I was reminded of Bresson. I thought you were trying to create a spiritual moment out of this drab existence.

But that wasn't conscious because I'd never seen Bresson and I'd never heard of Bresson until I got to film school. Consciously, I was trying to recreate what it felt like because I actually worked in that office. It had no natural light and I can remember very often, usually over tea in the afternoon, we'd all be working and we'd just look around and say, "God, we could be here forever."It was terrifying. It frightened me so much.

You've been criticized in some circles, and personally by some gay critics, for the negativity and despair of the *Trilogy*. Some of those critics say that you perpetuate negative stereotypes. How do you answer those critics?

Well, as I said to them in San Francisco where they loathed it, "That was my experience, and if it's my experience, then it's true." Sufficient numbers of gay men came up to me and said that that was their lives, too. And one bloke said, "No, this isn't true." And I said, "Have you any idea how arrogant a statement that is. You're very good-looking, you've got a good physique. I expect they're lining up for you in queues. Have you any idea what it's like not to be good-looking, not to be attractive? You don't know, do you?" And he didn't. He'd never had one single doubt about how attractive he was. But lots of us are not like that, unfortunately. And we do despair, and it is negative. I still stand by that negativity because that's how I feel. It has ruined my life and I'm prepared to say that to anyone because that's what it's done.

Do you still feel that about being gay?

Yes, I do. And I'll go to my grave loathing it. I hate it!

You seem comfortable with yourself to me.

Oh, no. I hate me. I wish I could change. I would change me tomorrow. I don't like being me and I never have.

In the third film of the *Trilogy, Death and Transfiguration,* we're very aware of the human body—in the painful screaming hospital scenes especially.

It's an extension of why I moved to London. I didn't want to end up like that. And a lot of people do. Before my mum died, she was in a home. She was okay, though she was ninety. She wasn't senile. But those people sitting there in chairs all day are senile, and that is a horrible thought that you survive that long, and then end up like that. The film is literally charting two things really: his past life and a series of epiphanies. His body is literally disintegrating and painful. He dies of a hemorrhage associated with a brain tumor.

Even in Part One, you have a scene of the boy coming in on his father who is in such pain, on the floor, screaming. It's a very intense scene.

My father took two years to die at home. In those days they were given morphine very strictly throughout the day, and when it wore off, they just waited until the next injection. Very often, he screamed at anything and then attacked us as well. It was awful. That happened when I was between the ages of five and seven. That's an awful time for this to happen to a child, because that's when you are at your most vulnerable. When you see things like that, you never forget. It makes you acutely aware of not just people, physically, but the hostile nature of the world and disease.

What it did do, ironically, was allow me to withdraw into the world of cinema. Here was this world of light and glamour and ecstasy where nothing like that happened. People didn't die, and if they died, it was a couple of coughs, a bit of sweat, and curtains, which was a very nice way to go, I thought. Most of the time, it was a Technicolor world where everything was resolved in the last reel and people lived happily ever after, and you embrace it with a kind of ecstasy. It's only later, when I came to make films myself, that I realized that's not the real world. Much as I would love life to be like *Young at Heart* or *The Pajama Game*, it is *not*. It was a huge trauma to let that go.

The structure of the *Trilogy* is fairly non-linear, but it's quite controlled. The shifts in time are never confusing. Did you struggle with the structure?

Not really, because content dictates form. It will tell you how it wants to be made. Certainly in the *Trilogy*, I was working out my style and looking at things like the nature of time and memory, but I didn't know I was doing that. It was just as you start to cut, you think, "Oh no, this doesn't work," and, "Why doesn't it work?" It was in the *Trilogy* that I decided that once you shoot and put together your first assembly, not to look at the script again, because there's no point. It has to work on its own terms then.

Memory works in ellipses. That's when I worked out the ground rules of the nature of memory and the nature of time. I was also reading a lot poetry, things like *The Four Quartets*, which is about time and memory. I learned a lot that way. I learned a lot listening to symphonic music—particularly Sibelius—about emotional structure, emotional architecture, which is different from a strict linear narrative. When you start to work out the nature of emotional logic behind a memory, it has visually associative things, and that's what you will then cut or dissolve to. It's like dropping a stone in a pond: the ripples are the memory and all the ripples are part of the one stone that initiated it. They have an inner logic, a subtextual logic. I was trying to find my voice in a clumsy way. I think, in *Death and Transfiguration*, I really found my voice. That's the one part of the *Trilogy* that I look at and think, "I got it right then. I found a way to say it." As soon as I knew I could use "It All Depends On You" by Doris Day, I thought, "I know what I'm doing." But for the rest of it, I was in the dark.

What was the reaction to those films?

It was mixed, certainly in the States. I finished them in 1983, after ten years working on them, and it was still very much "glad to be gay" then. Well, that's not what the films are about. They're about the unpleasantness of being gay and the terror of being alive. That's not what gay men, and particularly good-looking gay men in San Francisco, wanted to hear. It was pre-AIDS, so a lot of these people had never come across death or experienced death first hand. It's significant that the reaction of gay men to it is much more positive now. The *Trilogy* was not saying "It's all wonderful," because it's not all wonderful. Nothing is.

They're such powerful films, whether you're gay or not. Those films are devastating, so authentic and urgent. If you hadn't channeled your pain into a creative outlet, you might not have survived.

I think that's true, actually. I think it would have destroyed my soul. I would have just been destroyed inside. Whereas now, it destroys other people. Fabulous! [Laughs]

Let's move on to the film you're probably best known for. You've said that the portrait you painted of your father in *Distant Voices, Still Lives* was actually a softening of real life.

It definitely was. You can't put everything in. Nobody would believe it. It would seem like a parody of what he was. And he was a swine, he was a bastard and a psychotic. So, it had to be refined down to a small number of incidents to get over the impact of just what a bastard he was. It was infinitely worse than that in real life and it lasted much longer.

You don't seem very interested in understanding why he is the way he is. It's more like "He is this way. He's really fucked up, and I don't want to know why."

That's right. I'm not in the least interested, because my attitude is, if you marry and have children, you should want them to have a better life than you. And his attitude was the complete reverse: "I had it tough, so why shouldn't you?" I cannot understand that. I don't care that he had a hard life. I'm not interested. You don't inflict suffering on people simply because you had it hard. That shows a complete lack of humanity, as far as I'm concerned. It is the roots of fascism. I've got no time for that. We didn't deserve it. I'm sorry he died of cancer in that painful way, because nobody should, but that's the only scrap of sympathy I have. I'm not interested in why he was like that at all.

From the very beginning, the film calls attention to its images and sound. Visually, you're very aware of the bleaching process. Why did you take so much trouble with the visuals, when it could have been done in a simpler way?

That's how I saw it in my mind. I didn't know about the bleach bypass method, but that's how I saw it. It had to be within that range of browns, going from pinks, all the way through to very dark browns and blacks. That's the kind of color I wanted. I just knew it was right. We did an awful lot of tests before we got there, I can tell you.

Was there anything that triggered that mood, another film you might have used as a model?

No. That's how I saw it. But, also, going back to what you said about listening to it, people from other countries may not get it, but for me the opening is full of comedy. When I was growing up, there were only three stations on the radio, and the BBC Home Service began at seven o'clock. That was the first one you'd listen to, and it always had the weather forecast, which I didn't quite understand, but it was like a mantra. It was so magical because I didn't understand it. It was fabulous! It gives me immense pleasure just thinking about it, because it's so comic. But, of course, if you don't know that, then you extract some other meaning from it. It's not just what was said but the way it was read. It conjures up Britain in the fifties in an instant. It's like the comedy shows of the period. As soon as you hear them, you know that on a warm Sunday, windows were open all over this country, and people were all listening.

Why was sound so important in that film?

Growing up, I just assumed I was like any other child, and I'm sure I was. I listened and looked all the time. I actually listened to the house because you could hear the wood settling on the stairs. Especially when they'd all gone out to the pub and I was desperate, waiting for them to come home. There were really long vigils. It's always small things that you listen to. Sometimes you don't know where things come from, like the scene of the man falling through the glass roof. I said, "I know we have them going through the splintering glass, and I know 'Love Is a Many Splendored Thing' is on the track, but there's something missing. I want something else." We were in the dubbing theater and there was an open piano. I said, "What would the sound be if we hit the strings with our hand and played it back at double-speed or half-speed?" And that's what we did.

Why did you use a tableau or portraiture strategy in your film?

That wasn't conscious. That was how I saw it. It doesn't seem to me like portraiture or tableau at all. A very boring answer, I'm sorry.

An editing strategy that I noticed in this film, and even more in *Neon Bible*, is what some critics call a retroactive match structure: When you have a shot that you don't fully understand, and either a shot or several shots later, you make sense of it. You have lots of examples of that in your work.

It's so retroactive that no one went to see it! [Laughs]

No, really. It's a terrific narrative device. It makes things much more complex and interesting. In *The Neon Bible*, you have a shot of Sarah [Diana Scarwid] talking to the camera. You see this shot and wonder who she's talking to. You then cut and show that her son is in the room. That's an example of what I mean, where you have a certain understanding of something, but it's not resolved until later.

Very often, isn't that more true to life than doing it the other way around?

I think it is true to life. I just had a conversation with a filmmaker who believes in clarity above everything else. I said, "Don't we go through our lives not understanding things and figuring things out as we go along? Why shouldn't films also have ambiguity?"

If we don't have ambiguity, then we lose a lot of interest, because life is ambiguous. Art is ambiguous. I know there are dangers in ambiguity, of simply not being clear, but when something is genuinely ambiguous, and has several meanings, and may be resolved later or perhaps not at all, that seems more interesting to me. We're no longer passive: We actively try to work out what it means. I've just seen Bergman's *Cries and Whispers* again. I don't know everything it means intellectually, but I know emotionally. Who cares what it means? It's so powerful! If we had no ambiguity, we wouldn't have that film, which, despite its clarity, is all about ambiguity. A corpse that comes alive. What could be more ambiguous?

The time frame of *Distant Voices, Still Lives* is very non-linear, as it was in the *Trilogy*, although it's not in any way confusing. Was the structure completely elaborated in the screenplay?

As I said before, it was written with that idea of ellipses and slippages in time and memory. When you come to cut it, that's when you refine it, and it changes as you refine it. But the blueprint for the film is obviously the screenplay. It's not the finished film. The film has to work on its own terms but the basic structure and ideas were always in the script.

Do you have any thoughts on autobiography as a form, in terms of filmmaking?

What I was trying to do was to make sense of the suffering my family had gone through in *Distant Voices, Still Lives*, and my own direct experiences in *The Long Day Closes*. The *Trilogy* is partially autobiographical, partially a projection of my fears and doubts. What I realized after making them is that it doesn't change anything. Charting the self doesn't change anything and has no point. People are just unlucky in their suffering. That was a hard realization, and it's not cathartic.

What you do is you mine your own life and other people's. But it's only a pale shadow of reality, because you can't put it all in. My mother had twenty-five years of constant abuse. What you do is a sketch, really. You try and distill their experience and make certain scenes stand for whole years of abuse and suffering. But it doesn't really tell you anything about human nature. What it does is tell you about the arbitrariness of suffering. I don't think it has any spiritual value, because people would rather not suffer. And why should they suffer? It's not enough to say that it throws into relief the times when they are not suffering or that it makes them better human beings. On the whole it doesn't.

Even though *Distant Voices, Still Lives* has this brutality, it's more optimistic than the *Trilogy*. Is it, in some ways, an idealized view of the working class?

Oh, I hope not. I hope it's true. Otherwise, I'd feel I failed if it was idealized.

What about in *The Long Day Closes*. There's little sense of pain entering into the home life. Although, when the boy is at school there's obviously pain.

It's a subtle pain in *The Long Day Closes*. There's the pain in realizing that he's gay and in seeing that family disintegrate because they're all going to get married and in the isolation of simply being alone within a family. There's a spiritual pain and loneliness. I think there is a great deal of pain—not obvious, it's implied—but it's there. I would hate to think that it's an idealized view, because that's not what I intended. I wanted it to be as accurate as possible. The story, and the way in which it's told, is poetic. I think there is more hope in *Distant Voices, Still Lives* and in *The Long Day Closes* than in the *Trilogy*, but then someone said the *Trilogy* makes Ingmar Bergman look like Jerry Lewis. [Laughs]

[Laughs] Have you changed the way you direct actors over time?

I think it's basically the same. Obviously, as you direct more, it becomes more refined and you're more supportive of them. Basically, I know what I want and I try to be as supportive as I can to get what I want. You can't always say, "This is wonderful." You've got to say "No" as well.

You come to the set so well prepared. You say you know what you want from actors, you know every camera set-up. Don't you ever get to the set and have your ideas changed by the actors, or find that an idea doesn't work?

Yes. Absolutely. That's the magic, that they'll do something you hadn't thought of and that's tremendously exciting. That's why I watch the actors, even between takes. I also like to have the crew happy, and to have a laugh. I'm very serious about what I do, but I think it's good to have a nice atmosphere. It shouldn't be "Oh it's art, it's got to be miserable." Sod all that! I like a laugh and that helps too.

They can tell if you know what you're doing. You have to be flexible. If someone comes up with a better idea, I'll always say, "Do that!" I'm not rigid. I won't have sentimentality though. As others have said, it's unearned emotion and it's cheap. We can all do it, and I don't like it. Of all the nations in the world, the most sentimental are the English, despite the fact we don't look it. The country which embraces sentimentality wholeheartedly is America, but they are actually quite hard. They're not sentimental at all.

The portrait of the men in *Distant Voices, Still Lives*, except for the brother, is not very complimentary. Were you criticized for it?

Oh yes, and I think one of my weaknesses is the sketchiness of the men. And they're usually not complimentary. I think it's an absolutely valid criticism. It is a weakness and I hope I have addressed that in my new film, where there are lots of men who are quite complex.

The umbrella scene is a great scene. You start the scene and "Love is a Many Splendored Thing" comes on with all those umbrellas.

Who said I wasn't sentimental? [Laughs] It's a wonderful tune.

What ideas do you have on how poetry can function in film?

Well, as in written poetry, it says the obvious but in an unusual way, so that you suddenly say, "God!" and you only realize after it's happened. That's real poetry. And it can be really, really tiny, but you never forget it. The example I'll give is from *The Heiress*, when Ralph Richardson takes Olivia de Havilland to Europe and is trying to make her fall out of love with Montgomery Clift, and they're at that little café table in Paris. They're drinking hot chocolate and he says to her, "Have you changed your mind?" To which she says, "No." He says, "Well, we'll go back to New York." She says, "I thought you wanted to go to England." And he says, "I've *seen* England." That's real poetry. Very tiny, but unforgettable because of the way in which the lines are written, delivered, and shot.

Let's talk about *The Long Day Closes*. Could life possibly have been that happy?

Yes, for that brief moment. For those four years after the death of my father, when I was seven to when I left primary school at eleven, they were. I was literally in a complete state of ecstasy all the time. I mean, the sheer intensity of it couldn't have gone on any longer. I would've been worn out. The tiniest things gave me such huge pleasure, I mean huge! "You're going to be taken to the pictures." God! Or I was allowed to go and buy makeup for my sister and her friends every Friday. Everything was a joy. Getting fresh-made bread and being allowed to have the crust because I was the youngest. Ecstasy! They were tiny things, but they were ecstatic.

Was each piece of music chosen in advance or did the images ever inspire a choice of music?

Sometimes you discover a piece of music and that will be the impetus to write the scene. I had written the whole winter scene in *Distant Voices, Still Lives* and then I discovered the hymn to accompany it. I just knew they worked together. Whereas I knew I wanted to use "Love Is a Many Splendored Thing" and it would determine the shots. It's a mixture of the two, really. Certainly in *The Long Day Closes*, I worked out the shots, and I knew I wanted to have "Tammy," but I didn't know what the shots were until I worked it out by putting pieces of paper on the floor.

That was a particularly complicated scene to shoot, I'm sure.

[Laughs] God, yes. The most complicated, though, was Christ on the cross. That took nine hours.

The technical complexity of some of your work is amazing. Do things need to be that complicated?

When I write it, I think, "This is what the shot has to be." Then when I get on the set, I think, "Oh, Jesus, now we've got to execute it!" You see the shot in your mind and that's the shot you want. I've no idea how they're got. I don't sit down and design them beforehand. The camera was doing nine separate things for the Christ on the cross scene in *The Long Day Closes*, because he was static, and we did all the movement. I thought we'd never get it because it was so complicated, but we got it in the first couple of takes.

The Long Day Closes **is again very stylized, especially in the deliberateness of the camera movements and the shimmering light. I'm sure somebody must have criticized you for that very long, static take on the carpet. [Laughs]**

Oh, yes, they have. A lot of people hate it.

Does anyone ever say you're sinking into a kind of preciousness?

Yes. A lot of people say it's very precious and boring. One critic said, "His films are unbearably tedious." Lots of people don't like what I do, I can assure you. I'm just glad if they stay awake. I do think *The Neon Bible* is too slow, and it's something I've got to watch on my next film. A lot of people didn't like it. It failed, there are no two ways about that. I stand by it though. I'm still proud of it because my commitment to every film is total, good or bad. If it fails, it's my fault. I chose to have it shot and edited like that. But I think there are good things in it.

Do you feel that the film references in *The Long Day Closes* are lost on the younger generation. How does the film work for people who aren't familiar with *The Magnificent Ambersons* or Doris Day, for example.

The ones that liked it [*The Magnificent Ambersons* voice-over] said that they thought it was voices from the street, the people who live in the street. And, of course, it's not. The first voice-over is Margaret Rutherford and the next one is from *The Lady Killers*.

You also have *Kind Hearts and Coronets* in there...

Yes, talking interminable nonsense...

But if one is not film-literate, how does one perceive those things?

I have no idea. It's really impossible for me to say because I know them so well that as soon as I hear them, I know where they're from and the pleasure they have always given me. If someone doesn't recognize "The Carousel Waltz" or Doris Day, then I simply don't know. They have enormous meaning for me and that's why they were in the film. The one for me that is most moving is Miss Haversham from *Great Expectations*. At the end of the film, it's just so sad, so heartbreaking.

George getting his comeuppance from *Magnificent Ambersons* is also moving.

Yes. That's a wonderful voice-over. That's a wonderful piece of writing, and the way it's delivered. Those who were alive at the time remembered it, and those who weren't have forgotten all about Tim Holt. God! When I saw it, with that track in on him leaning by the bed, I just wept and wept. It's so moving.

Was *The Long Day Closes* shot totally on a set?

No, there were some real locations, but we built the street. I was trying to rebuild my street and there aren't many streets like that, not even in Liverpool. So we had to build it.

There are lots of moments in the film that seem infused with added meaning, like the shot of empty space with *The Magnificent Ambersons* soundtrack over it. Maybe it's the poetic quality you're talking about. Your work is related to other filmmakers who also have a belief in the "presentness"of the image. I'm thinking of people like Werner Herzog or Terrence Malick, who have an almost phenomenological belief in the power of the held shot.

I think that's true. But you still have to know when the life in the shot has died, then you have to dissolve or cut. That's always hard, because sometimes what's in the scene just invests that little bit extra, that little extra half a foot of film. You can't say why. And other people will say, "Well, why are we looking at nothing?" They won't get it. But then, if they don't get it, they don't get it. There's nothing you can do about it. One of the strains of editing is you've got to think about it in terms of a shot, in terms of sequence and in terms of the whole film. Where does the life of a shot begin? Where does it die?

Which part of the filmmaking process is most satisfying to you and which is most difficult?

The most difficult is always the most satisfying, and the most difficult is the editing. I'm in a state of permanent worry.

Are you ever defeated by something? Some filmmakers talk about working on something but not ever getting that moment right.

Oh, yes. In *The Neon Bible*, there's a beat missing in the tent sequence. I don't know where it is, but it's not there. Every time I see it I think, we need something extra, and I don't know what it is. There's a beat missing. I got it wrong.

The Long Day Closes finishes the chapter, specifically, on your autobiographical work. Why did you feel you needed to move on at that point?

Because I'd said everything about my family and growing up in Liverpool. There was no point in regurgitating it, although people who didn't like *The Neon Bible* said it was a regurgitation of the same old thing. I've said enough about that. You can't keep repeating the same thing. I felt that I wanted to do something different and that was when my co-producer approached me with the book and said would I want to do it?

Why did you choose this particular novel [*The Neon Bible*] as your first adaptation? Were you attracted to the novel?

No, it chose me, really.

Did you feel a kinship to the tragic life of John Kennedy Toole?

No, not at all, but I did like the book. I thought it was a very mature work for a sixteen-year-old to write. I liked it, and I could see it. I said to my producer Elizabeth [Karlsen], "I'll do it if I can see it, and if I can't see it, then I won't." And the opening two paragraphs tell you exactly where to begin.

The Neon Bible is your first wide-screen movie. Why did you choose that format?

Because it just felt right. It's an emotional thing when you think "It's Cinemascope." What's wonderful about it is when you move the camera in Cinemascope, everything becomes epic. It was thrilling to do that crane shot down into the street with everyone walking towards the tent because it looked epic, and that was one of the few moments where we actually got what I saw, even better.

People have accused you of making "The World of Terence Davies" in the American South.

Perhaps I have. I honestly don't know because I'm so close to it, I can't tell. I think it's different, but I'm going to think that because I'm close to it. At the end of the day, it's for the spectators to say, "Yes, it's good," or "No, it's not." And there's nothing you can do about that.

It's an American South fabricated from the Golden Age of Holly-wood movies, very "aestheticized," very dreamlike. It opens in a very mournful way. The very first tune we hear is so sad.

Well, the tune is an old American hymn: "Oh Lord, How Long," it's called. And the cor anglais [English horn] makes it sound mournful.

Later on, when you use Stephen Foster's "Hard Times," it's just devastating, and coupled with that material, it just shakes you up.

That's a devastating song. Of course, Stephen Foster was the first great American songwriter.

Why did you feel you had to keep the first-person voice-over from the novel?

Well, I had to keep certain bits of it. I kept it down to a minimum because I wanted to use it more as counterpoint and sometimes it's quite savage: "And then the war was over," and we cut to a shot of the soldiers in coffins. A bit of English savagery there.

What's the boy's sexuality? It's sort of uncertain.

At that age, a lot of sexuality is uncertain. He is very innocent, with his fumbling attention to that girl. It's a time in your life when you're clumsy about everything, not just that, because you feel so self-conscious.

Again, you are using a tableau strategy.

That's how I saw it. It doesn't seem like tableau to me. People who don't like the work also say it's very theatrical, and it doesn't seem theatrical to me at all. But I am very close to it. It's like when you hear your own voice, you say, "That's not me. I don't sound like that. I'm much more butch!"[Laughs]

How did you decide on Gena Rowlands?

When I said to Elizabeth Karlsen, "Yes, I'll do it," she said, "Who would you like to play Aunt Mae?" I said, "Gena Rowlands." She said, "So would I." It was quite a coincidence. So we went out to see her. I had not written the script by then. We sent her a copy of *Distant Voices, Still Lives* and the *South Bank* show on me, and she liked it and she liked me. We got on, and she agreed to do it.

Was it always intended that she do her own singing of "My Romance"?

Yes, everyone had to. You can't do it any other way. She said, "I can't!" I said, "Why don't we record something then. Just record it." Then I said, "It's just wonderful!" She said, "But you've chosen the one that's flat." The point is Aunt Mae would not have a good voice. It's not good, but it's sung with feeling and that's why it's moving.

One of the most excruciatingly honest scenes in the film is when Diana Scarwid sings "Turrah Lurrah Lurrah." It's such a naked, risky moment for the actor.

Some people think it's terribly indulgent. I've been accused of real indulgence there. What works for me is the fact that she sings brokenhearted. And you don't know why she's brokenhearted. I said, "You've got a wonderful smile. Play the smile when you come out." And in a minute, she's gone from this wretched creature, to this . . . It electrified the camera crew. We'd done pick-up shots all day, which are really boring, and when we did this, they were electrified!

Yes, it's extremely emotional. Did she have qualms about doing it?

What happened was we'd gone for a drink at the end of shooting one day, and she sang the tune, and I thought, "God, that's so marvelous." I thought at that time, "She really should do it." Because it wasn't in the script, but that's how I am, flexible. So, I came to her and said, "You can say no, and I will not be offended. Will you sing 'Turrah Lurrah?" And she said, "I'd only do it for you." And she did. After it was over, I just put my arms around her, I couldn't speak. I think it's a wonderful performance, I really do. And it hurt me that people said it was indulgent or that I made her look ridiculous. I think that hurt me more than anything else, because I would hate to make anybody look ridiculous. I just thought, "How can they say that?" She goes through such an emotional spectrum.

There seems to be a fairly non-naturalistic, at times melodramatic strategy at work in this film. Do you agree?

No, actually I don't, because I see it as perfectly natural. Perhaps my perception of what's natural and realistic is as perverse as the rest of me! [Laughs]

Things like everybody's clothes, which are so clean. Those little boys are so cleanly dressed and tailored. Little kids in the South wouldn't walk into a store with such tailored clothes.

That's true. Perhaps that's a measure of my clumsiness.

It's a measure of your stylization. You're not making a realistic film.

That might be its weakness.

Were there any photographic or painterly influences on the film?

Oh yes, there were some. Dorothea Lange, Norman Rockwell, Wyeth to a lesser extent.

Your work is constantly walking a fine line between the aesthetically beautiful and tragic content. *The Neon Bible* is a good example of this. There must always be a danger of overwhelming the tragedy with beauty or prettiness.

That's hard to answer because you want the images to be powerful. The drawback with color, no matter what you do, is that it always prettifies. It can't help but prettify. You've got to try and keep that in check, I think.

But in this film, you're after a kind of Technicolor look.

Yes. That has advantages as well as disadvantages. You get the early Technicolor stock, which was usually overseen by an unsung genius, Natalie Kalmus. Any films that she had anything to do with, as technical director for Technicolor, are wonderful to look at. I'm sure that the West never looked half as gorgeous as in *The Harvey Girls*. I'm sure small town St. Louis never looked half as gorgeous as *Meet Me in Saint Louis*. The problem with my approach—and I do think it's a problem—is if you have all this knowledge of what's gone before, that may be the very thing that kills it stone dead. That's the risk.

I get the sense that you're trying to be more experimental here than in your earlier work. There are more sound overlaps, for example. It's also very non-linear. You seem to be challenging audiences even more than in the other films.

With each film, you try and do things, not for the sake of it, but because content dictates form. That circumscribes you to a certain extent, but what you're trying to do is say, "Well, if I did this, what does it mean? Can I get across these two ideas?" The white sheet sequence, with the music from *Gone With the Wind* over it, when you go into it, it feels like wiping the character's life-slate clean. But it also informs the scene with this romantic idea or myth of what the South was. It never was that in reality. It was a slave-owning society. People owned other people; there's nothing romantic about that. But it's the juxtaposition of wiping his slate clean, thinking about all the things that have happened to him up to this point, and hearing this huge, romantic sound. I was trying to do that, but that might have been "too clever by half," as we say. I honestly don't know.

You've worked with a lot of the same people in your films. How important is that for you?

It's crucial, because my costume designer, Monica Howe, is a designer of real genius. I wouldn't use anybody else. I have only used the production designer, Christopher Hobbs, twice, and I will use him again, obviously. The cameraman will change this time because he's not available for the next one. You work out a rapport with your collaborators; they know what you want. It's a huge help when you come to do it because they understand and they're on your wavelength. They know what you mean when you say that you want this part of a room decorated, and that's all you want. You're not going to turn around and say, "Sorry. I'm going to do shots from here now," when they haven't decorated it. They know I wouldn't do that. It's a kind of shorthand. They know what I want. And I know that I can say to Monica, "This is the sort of thing I want," and that she'll go away and do it. She'll give each character not only clothes which are right for that character, but she'll give them eight or ten choices.

I always work with Olivia Stewart because, not only is she a good producer, but she's got a wonderful sense of color and she knows a great deal more about painting than I do. And she can analyze a script. So it's things like that that you can't do without. I'm very lucky in that respect. I've got an agent who is a wonderful analyzer of a script, and I wouldn't send it out without him reading it. And any notes he gives me I take seriously and I incorporate, and the same with Olivia. Those things really are important. Obviously, you tend to want to be with the same people.

Have you found the way you work is changing to some extent?

No, not my method. My method is very much the same. I only ever write two drafts of the script. The first draft takes usually a year, and that is over a long period of accretion. Sometimes I'll write whole sequences, sometimes bits of dialogue. By ten months, I've sort of got the film in the back of my mind, and then I sit down and write it. I write out a first draft: every track, pan, dissolve, everything is in. Then I wait four to six weeks and write a second draft, usually quite quickly, and refine it. That method has not changed.

What do you find changing?

What's changing is the fact that my next film, *The House of Mirth*, is a more linear narrative. It can't be as elliptical as the other work.

Is what you do on the set different now than ten years ago?

Yes, I think it's more confident. Although I'm always nervous. Since I only make a film every three years, I'm always nervous that the people I'm working with will complain and get angry with me. I'm terribly neurotic. The first few days of working with Gena, of course, I was intimidated. She's a big star. She's done more films than I've had hot dinners. I thought, "This is absurd!" She's agreed to do it.

What you're requiring of yourself in each film is something different. This new one will be much more formal because the dialogue in the novel is extremely formal. That will be a completely new thing. And they speak a lot; that will be different. But the way you get the performances has remained the same, with some refinement. You try to be as supportive as you can whilst being as critical as possible. That's the whole point of doing separate takes. I hope it's become less neurotic. The thing I can't hide—and Gena said this in many interviews at Cannes—if something goes well, you can tell I'm ecstatic. If it goes badly, I'm very dejected. I can't hide it. I get very down.

Have your ideas about cinema changed over the years? Can you relate to a lot of the films being made now?

I can't. In that sense, I feel like a dinosaur. I'm not interested in violence. My father was violent, I do not want to see it. I'm not interested in people taking drugs. I don't want to see them shoot up, thank you very much. That's not my idea of entertainment. And when they swear all the time, I think it's monotonous. Someone says forty-six fucks in the first two minutes. Great! That's really something. It really takes talent to write that! So there are very few films that I can actually enjoy. There are few films now where I can suspend my disbelief for more than ten minutes. I go less and less because I think the cinema's changed. The younger generation doesn't want what I do. I'm not interested in those subjects, and if that's the new cinema, or urban cinema, then it's definitely not for me.

Could you see yourself working in Hollywood?

Oh, God, no! Been there once, and once was quite enough.

Do you ever get sent scripts?

No, not from Hollywood. To them I'm just an obscure director who makes films that few people see. No, I can't imagine anything more awful. I loathed it. Loathed it!

Do you like being an artist?

Not especially. I don't think it achieves anything.

You can't really believe that! What would the world be without art? It would be horrible. What if we took away all of those movies that you love? Wouldn't the world be a lesser place?

Yes, but I don't know what it actually achieves. It doesn't change anything. If you're in Rwanda, you couldn't care less about the latest Michelle Pfeiffer movie, because you're worried about getting hacked to death by some rival.

Yes, but when you're watching a film, and it has a profound effect on you, it *is* changing you. It does affect you. That experience is important to you at that time. And experience is necessary for us.

I agree with you. I agree that I couldn't do without all the films that I love. But I don't know what it achieves in the long run. It's not a cure for cancer or AIDS. There's something rather trivial about it.

But it makes us more complete as people.

I did believe that for a long time, but that's taken a battering these past few years.

Is it because of the junk out there or because the film industry has changed?

Well, that is part of it. I mean, the majority of people certainly don't want what I do. Because too few people go and see what I do.

The majority of people don't want poetry, but that doesn't mean we shouldn't have poets.

No, but in a way, it is easier to say that when you're not involved in it. When you are, it's very disheartening. It's even worse for poets. I don't know how they do it. There must be people who are writing wonderful poetry that nobody has ever read. Now that strikes me as being very disheartening. And the stuff that does get published, a lot of it is not very good. It's just disheartening when people are telling you—without naming any of the films in Britain—"This is wonderful." No, it's not wonderful. A lot of people have gone to see it, but that doesn't make it wonderful. For many people if it earns a lot of money, it's, ipso facto, a good movie. It's exactly the television mentality, where twenty million people watch this particular soap, but no one ever says that it might be because twenty million people actually have no taste. No one dares say that. That's like peeing on the chips. You're not allowed to say it.

But there must be a tremendous satisfaction in making something good which will be around for a long time, even if it's appreciated by smaller numbers of people.

Yes. Well, you see, that feeling doesn't last. Any film that I make, I will make to the best of my ability, because my name is on it, and I've got enough ego to want it to be good. But I'm relentlessly attacked and your confidence dwindles away. You think, perhaps it is crap, perhaps they're right. I've convinced myself that it's better than that. That's what happens with friends who kill you with faint praise. "I liked the photography" is the equivalent of going to a stage play and saying: "Well, the scenery was good." You might as well not say anything. People do it quite consciously. They know that they're undermining you and they still do it. It's very hard because I come from an ordinary background, and my brothers and sisters and my mum—although my mum and two of my brothers have died—were not sophisticated. They're proud of me because I'm their brother and I've made something. But they don't really understand. I'm disappointed because I want them to. But they don't, and I can't do anything about it.

But they must still have a sense of pride. You don't make films for the working class, do you?

No, I don't, and ironically that's precisely what I want. A lot of ordinary people loved *Distant Voices, Still Lives*. The nicest compliment I ever had was when I was showing it to my family in a cinema on a Sunday morning in Liverpool. These two cleaners were also in the theater and they said, "It's really a good film." That was one of the nicest compliments because they were just ordinary people, and it has quite a complex structure. A lot of working-class people in Liverpool did respond to it and I was very pleased about that. But with your family, it's something extra. But they didn't really get it. Of course, that is disheartening, because you want the people you love to say, "Oh, yes. That was really smashing!" They were proud of it, as you said, but they didn't understand it. They would rather watch *Coronation Street* or *Brookside* because that's what they understand.

Do you think your films are difficult?

Well, clearly they are, otherwise more people would go. When the films are seen, the audience is expected to work quite hard. The majority of people don't want to work hard. The only way I can enjoy a film is if I am completely participating and interpreting what I see, and not just passive. If everything in the film is made explicit, then what is the point of my being there? But that's not what the general public want. They want to be told everything in films because they've grown up with television where everything is told to them. I don't want to do that. It's much more interesting if there's a reasonable amount of visual, and emotional, and narrative ambiguity.

If you weren't making films, what would you be doing?

I don't know. Begging? It might come to that! [Laughs]

[Laughs] Not in that accountant's office in Liverpool, though.

No, I couldn't go back to that. I mean, death is preferable to that.

Would you be a writer?

I honestly don't know. I do want to make films. That's what I feel is my raison d'être. But whether anybody is prepared to keep giving me money to support me is another matter.

Presumably, after each film, your stature gets higher?

Well, I don't think it works like that anymore. What gives you stature and clout is if your film makes money.

Do you feel pressure that your next film be commercially successful?

No, because that's never been a consideration, but it should be. If I had any sense, I'd think, "How can I make this film so that it'd have the maximum audience." Whereas I write and make the film because I want it to be the best I can make. In a way, that's ostrich-like; it's not taking into account that it's going to cost a lot of money and that producers need to have a return on their money. In a way, you could say it's arrogant. But I don't perceive cinema like a mass audience does.

We are in an era of niche or specialized audiences, aren't we? The whole American independent film scene seems to be based on the idea that you can make a small film and still make it commercially viable, that it doesn't have to be released in two thousand theaters to make money.

To be truthful, I don't think it works like that. I think the overriding aesthetic now is money. Everyone wants to make lots and lots of money. And when an English film does well in America, everybody wants to make that. Well, that's one way of making film, but it's not the only way, and it doesn't allow—or allows less and less—people like myself who make different kinds of films. It goes back to what we said at the beginning of the conversation. If it makes $100 million, people say it's good, and you think, "Well, it's not." All it means is that it made one hundred million dollars. If you look at the great films of the last fifty years, many of them failed when they first came out. *Citizen Kane* failed, *The Magnificent Ambersons* failed, *Letter from an Unknown Woman* failed, *Night of the Hunter* failed, and they're four of the greatest films ever made. That's not to say that if something fails, it's therefore great. Just as I'm not saying that if something makes $100 million it's bad. No. I thought *Tootsie* was terrific. I don't think it's a great film. It's very funny, very enjoyable. It does what it sets out to do perfectly. It deserves to do well. But a lot of the time, you just feel that everything ends up at the lowest common denominator. I'm not interested in dull actors shooting a lot of people and blowing things up. I just—physically, emotionally, and intellectually—can't see the point in making a movie like that. But, obviously, millions of people go. They want to see someone shooting someone else. I don't.

Are you optimistic about your ability to continue to make films?

I don't think I'm an optimist. I always think, "This film will be the last film, because it's so costly." Each time I make a film, I'm trying to do something slightly different because the story dictates it and that costs money. Unfortunately, it's expensive, and I don't know how long I can expect them to put money in if they're not getting a return. You can't expect that subsidy forever. I am fairly pessimistic because I see a kind of homogenization of things. The films most successful here are pale imitations of what they do in Hollywood, and it has been ever thus.

Are you optimistic about the current state of the British film industry?

Oh, I never have been. We're going through a boom at the moment, and it will be followed by a slump. It's the same old thing. It's gone on for the past fifty years, and it will never be different because we unfortunately share a common language with America, and they are the dominant power, whether we like it or not. It's now all over Europe as well. They dominate everything. Last century, it was the British; now it's the Americans. I can't see how you can build up an indigenous film culture when you're trying to imitate someone else's. That's what we've always done, and we always do it badly without exception. The times we have not done it are the films we remember. Nowhere else could *Kind Hearts and Coronets* have been made; nowhere else could *The Lady Killers* have been made. They're just unique because we looked to ourselves and said, "This is what we want to make," and that's what was made.

And nowhere else could *Distant Voices, Still Lives* and *The Long Day Closes* have been made!

[Laughs] Yes.

TOM DICILLO

Tom DiCillo began his film career as a cinematographer on several independent films of the 1980s, most notably Jim Jarmusch's first film, *Permanent Vacation*, and his seminal *Stranger than Paradise*. This early experience seems to have happened almost by accident, since DiCillo claims he knew nothing about cinematography at the time, not even how to take a light reading. DiCillo did not make his own first film until 1990, when he directed a young Brad Pitt in *Johnny Suede*. The intervening years were partly spent studying acting, which may account for the high level of performance in DiCillo's films. Even after he made his first film, the frustrations of financing his own projects continued. It was another five years before he made his next, and most well-known film, *Living in Oblivion*, perhaps the funniest film yet made about the trials and tribulations of filmmaking.

DiCillo's work is characterized by an almost classical devotion to story structure and written dialogue and a great respect for actors, although never at the expense of cinematic invention. DiCillo's films are quirky, laced with humor, and often quite stylized, but his characters always project a strong sense of realism and humanity. His films are witty, intelligent, and highly imaginative, which makes their lack of popularity baffling. This lack of commercial appeal can sometimes be attributed to inept handling by the film's distributor, as happened with *Johnny Suede*. At other times, the public simply has not connected with DiCillo's vision, as was the case with *Box of Moonlight* or *The Real Blonde*, a witty and imaginative satire whose commercial failure is confounding. It may be that the films' frequent shifts in tone, and mix of comedic and tragic elements, are difficult for mass audiences accustomed to the easy payoff of genre films with their more conventional characters, structures, and formulas.

DiCillo's work in the 1990s is a testament to his imagination, tenacity, and sheer doggedness in the current filmmaking climate. He is a filmmaker who cares deeply about his art. Through his characters, he is a chronicler of American life and male-female relationships who has few equals. I spoke to Tom DiCillo in New York City.

Can you talk about where you grew up and your background?

My father was a colonel in the Marine Corps, which meant we moved to a different state every two years, and lived mostly in small cities and towns that were around the Marine bases. Most significant about that period was the fact that my father refused to let us have a television until I was about seventeen. So I never watched television. Consequently, whenever I did go to the movies, it was almost like an addiction to moving images, because I had never seen them before.

I got my undergraduate degree in Creative Writing at Old Dominion University, in Virginia. I was heavily influenced by Joyce, Kafka, Thomas Mann. I thought I was going to write, until a friend of mine said, "We have this film-appreciation class starting. It's a film series. Why don't you come tonight?" I said, "What the fuck," and I went. I was about eighteen or nineteen, and the first film they showed was Fellini's *La Strada*. I literally can remember the physical sensation of having my mind blown by this movie—the acting, the quality of the story, and the fact that someone would choose to make a film depicting life this way.

You weren't going to films a lot before this?

Oh, I would go to films, but not art films. I wasn't aware of them yet. I never lived in places where that stuff was shown. You go out of the big cities and the awareness of film as art is practically nonexistent. The film that affected me the most, when I was around eleven years old, was *Rebel Without a Cause*, because it was so familiar, yet disturbing.

So, it's mostly writers who influenced you?

Painters and photographers too. I was greatly influenced by Walker Evans and Robert Frank. There was just something about those images of America, and the use of black and white that really moved me. But, yes, I would say, principally, writers.

Why did you decide to become a filmmaker?

My visual sense was developing. I applied to New York University Graduate Film School, got accepted, and moved to New York.

Did you make films as a graduate student?

Yes, I did. My first film was an absolute disaster, but it contains many things that I've continued to put in my other films. It deals with people on a street and the contrasts of life in New York that most people take for granted. For example, in *The Real Blonde*, when the guy harasses Mary [Catherine Keener] on the street, I've never seen that in a movie, but you see it every day here. I learned an enormous amount from the first film. A rule I still try to apply to cinema is to take three seconds of time and make a twenty-minute movie about it. My second film really turned out quite beautifully. I wrote and directed six short films at NYU.

Was your experience at film school good or bad?

It was both. My final experience there was pretty bad. My thesis film didn't turn out well, and I knew exactly why. However, the faculty felt compelled to keep telling me why it was no good. It did a number on me. That's why an overly negative criticism at school is not very helpful. My last experience at the school literally kicked me into an area where I felt, "You know what? I need to learn more." So that's what I did. I began to study acting and shot a few films for other people, which wasn't anything I particularly wanted to do but just ended up doing. So, I took an eight-year detour before I finally came around to directing.

Why did you go into acting?

On the set of my last student film, it became absolutely clear I had no idea what to say to these people. If you look at my films, they deal with very specific, human emotions. It's the kind of acting that requires the actor to understand, and feel free to really go there. I had no concept of how to talk about that. So, I began studying, and did it for eight years.

You studied acting with Frank Corsaro, didn't you?

Yes, he's a good teacher. The motivation for my character sketches for a guy called Johnny Suede evolved out of the acting classes.

Did you have ambitions to be an actor as well?

Only after acting in front of Frank. The first scene I ever acted in was at his insistence. I did a scene from Mamet's *Sexual Perversity in Chicago*. Frank looked at me afterward and said, "You never acted?" I said, "No." He said, "I don't believe you." I said, "I've never acted." He said, "Well, you should continue." And based on that, I said, "Wow, maybe I could be an actor." I had enough success to keep me hopeful. A lot of that experience went into those humiliating fucking auditions you see in *The Real Blonde*.

How did your experience as a cinematographer enter into your aesthetic?

To be quite honest with you, I see my cinematography period as a passive period. I don't say that in a negative way. I got into it by accident. My degree at NYU is in writing and directing.

Jim [Jarmusch] and I were in the same class at NYU and became friends. We had a little project and the teacher said, "Okay, Jim, you write something. Tom, you shoot it. Someone else edit it." That's how it happened. I knew nothing about cinematography. I didn't know how to take a light reading. But we worked together and something clicked. There was something about the melding of our minds that was very exciting. I shot *Permanent Vacation* for him, and *Stranger than Paradise* is the last thing I did for him. What I love about that film and my work in it is that it is not technical, it's emotional and dramatic. To me, that's the eye of a director.

Do you think you both influenced each other in terms of directing?

I don't think so. I have a tremendous respect for Jim. The fact that he made a very personal film with the potential of going into regular theaters was very important. Before *Stranger than Paradise*, that possibility did not really exist. I like the way Jim's mind works, and I think he has a very interesting sense of humor. I have a sense of humor, too, but mine is different than Jim's. The influence for me was simply opening the door, and I give Jim credit for doing that. If you look at his films and my films, they're very different. My films are very specifically human, and the actors are encouraged to be as real as possible, almost over-real. Jim's characters are always in the realm of ideas—and that's what's interesting about them.

After I shot *Stranger than Paradise*, I started to get some attention. Everywhere I went, people would talk to me about the fact that I was Jim Jarmusch's cameraman, and I got calls to shoot films. Nothing for any money, mostly for first-time directors who wanted me to do the same things for them that I did for Jim. For a while, it was okay, but then I realized that I was basically directing films for these people, and it seemed like a waste of my time. Artistically, it was actually destructive, so I quit doing it. I started painting apartments and working as a waiter—stuff that was not artistic, but emotionally it wasn't as destructive as shooting films.

I was in Barcelona doing press for *Living in Oblivion* and someone asked me, "Will you ever shoot a film for Jim Jarmusch again?" This was in 1995. I shot *Stranger than Paradise* in 1984. Ten years had gone by. I said, simply, "No." The next day they had a big headline in the paper, "DiCillo says he will never shoot for Jarmusch again!" Even now I still read "ex-cameraman for Jim Jarmusch." Listen, I'm not embarrassed about my work at all. My experience as a cinematographer did enable me to watch people make mistakes, especially in the way directors dealt with actors. It was very helpful on that level.

Johnny Suede **began as a play?**

Right, a one-man show.

How did the play come about? Where did it come from?

One basic place it came from was Corsaro's class. I started writing short monologues for myself, simply as acting exercises. Eventually, I saw a central theme and collected all the monologues into a one-man show. I created this guy who, on the surface, looked like he had everything together. It was something that really interested me, and still does: How people's desire to be one thing is so different from what they are within. Here's a guy who thinks he's someone who understands women, but actually doesn't have a clue. So all that stuff began to come out of me, the things I was going through in my life, the things I was learning about myself. I also saw Johnny in a lot of other men, and I tried to illustrate that. I'm also interested in somebody heroic, who has this questionable side to them. Woody Allen's heroes are mostly jerks—they're funny, but it's a little pathetic. I said, "Why couldn't you have someone heroic with the same sort of weaknesses as the Woody Allen hero?"

Was it well received as a play?

It was. It ran for six performances. The most positive and interesting responses came from women. They said, "Man! I've never seen this aspect of the male psyche presented this way." That's what encouraged me to turn it into a screenplay.

Was the character different in the play than he is in the film?

No, it was pretty much the same. But Brad [Pitt] unfortunately took the direction I gave him and misunderstood it, and I didn't find out about it until well after we shot. I said to him that, in some ways, Johnny is like a child. What I meant by that was that he had a child's attention span. A lot of attention here, then a lot of attention there. He took that and reduced the character's intelligence.

There is something child-like about the character. You didn't want that?

I didn't want that dull quality. Anybody who's a poseur works very hard at the pose, so there's a tremendous energy in keeping that pose up. Whenever someone threatens that pose, you've got to quickly cover it up. Brad really didn't give the character that agility.

How prepared were you as a film director when you went into production on *Johnny Suede*? Were you clear about how the scenes would be filmed?

Yes, I was. My style has not really changed since then. I went to every location; designed almost every costume; chose the color for every apartment; designed Johnny's hairstyle; chose the elements in his apartment. I'd been on enough sets to see that accidents happen all the time. Chaos intrudes at any moment. The only thing you can do is prepare as much as possible, so that if an accident happens, you can deal with it. I rehearsed the actors a lot, and we had storyboards.

What kind of things did you do in rehearsal with Brad Pitt and Catherine Keener?

Basically just getting them to understand scenes. I learned that you can't really fine-tune a performance in rehearsal. The most important thing is to make sure they understand what's going on and what they're about and why their character does something. So when they are in front of the camera, they're ready to act. My work with the actors was basically getting them to feel comfortable with each other. You'd be surprised how most actors are extremely untrusting. I put a lot of effort in slyly defusing that.

Was Pitt's conception of the character much different than yours, apart from the misunderstanding you mentioned earlier?

Johnny was a tough role to cast. Most people didn't quite get it. Brad came closest. I still don't think he completely got it. I wasn't the most articulate person in telling him exactly what I was thinking. I'm constantly discovering how specific you need to be.

How many films had Pitt done by then?

He had finished shooting *Thelma and Louise*, but it hadn't been released yet.

Can you talk a bit about the shooting of the film? Was it difficult?

It was extremely difficult. *Living in Oblivion* is a testament to what it was like on the set of *Johnny Suede*. Everything that could go wrong went wrong. The building that we shot Johnny's apartment in began to collapse after we shot there for two days, and the fire department wouldn't let us finish shooting. We had to find another apartment, paint it, dress it, and hope it matched—all in about eight hours. I will say that I did not enjoy myself on the set of that movie. I was just working as hard as I could to get the thing shot.

Were there things that didn't get into the final cut?

There was a lot. The first cut of the film was two and a half hours. I was the one who was solely responsible for cutting an hour out of the film, stuff that tied things together, and a bit more about his character. I think it ultimately affected the film.

Can you tell me about working with other creative people: the cinematographer, the editor, the production designer? You say that you did a lot of the editing yourself.

Yes. I'm very intimately involved in every aspect of the film. Even now, in *The Real Blonde*, I chose every one of those bathing suits that the guys were wearing, the squash rackets on the wall in their apartment, everything. It's not in a controlling way at all.

Working with a DP, I haven't really developed a working relationship, except with Frank Prinzi, who has now shot two films for me. I find a lot of DPs are technically oriented. They do not understand how to help you with the drama of a scene, and that annoys the hell out of me. I have no patience with that.

I'll give you an example from *Johnny Suede*. One of Brad's greatest emotional moments was at the end of the film, when he goes into this donut shop in the middle of the night. He's lost his shoe, and he's sitting there utterly lost, and Catherine appears and starts talking to him. Then he notices she has blood running down her leg. I wanted Brad to just break down and cry. I saw he was there emotionally, and I said to the DP, Joe DeSalvo, "Okay, let's go." He said, "No, I'm not quite ready." I didn't push him. We waited ten minutes, and I said, "Are you ready?" He said, "No, I'm not ready." Forty-five minutes go by, and I said, "What the fuck are you doing?" The shot was of Brad with a window behind him. Four blocks away, down the street, this guy was putting a light on a building's facade. This is what we were waiting for. I went insane. It's inexcusable. That's why I have to be so involved.

I see *Johnny Suede* as something of an absurdist piece, almost East European in tone.

The main thing I tried to do was let people know it was not reality. I'm not interested in naturalism. I wanted everything about the film to be somewhat heightened, almost in the form of a Tex Avery cartoon. I tried for a little twist there, a little bend here, a little exaggeration.

The physical locale has an important place in the film, the use of empty landscape, for example.

Right. That was based on my sense of the East Village at that time. By the time we shot the film, the East Village had completely changed. It became more gentrified, and I had to go out to Brooklyn to find that same sort of feeling, the empty streets. We recreated a fictitious image of the East Village as it was when I knew it twenty years ago.

But in a way, that works better, because it's not really the East Village or Brooklyn. It's not a landscape you can quite recognize.

I'm glad you said that, because some people were telling me at the time, "That's not the East Village, man. What did you do?" But that was precisely the idea.

Your music and sound are pretty effective in the film. Can you talk a bit about that? You wrote some songs, didn't you?

I wrote all the songs that Johnny sings.

"Midtown" and "Mama's Boy."

I loved those songs because they were so stupid. Johnny was not a musician—he just looked like one.

Did you have a background in music?

No. But I started playing different instruments. I enjoy music a lot, and I have a sort of simplistic ability to hear things musically. To me, it's so critical where every piece of music starts and stops. It's so critical what the instrumentation is, the pace of the music, the tempo, everything. I lucked into working with a composer, Jim Farmer, who is absolutely ego-less. Our relationship is one of the most trusting, in terms of composition, that I have experienced. He allows and encourages me to be very intimately involved. On *Johnny Suede*, he did everything on his synthesizer, even though I said I wanted all natural-sounding instruments. He would take the videotape, play a little piece, and we'd talk about it. We were literally trying things, and manipulating them before we even got to the mix.

Most composers don't work that way. What you do is talk in general terms to the composer. They are so prideful of their ability to compose music that they want to be left totally alone. Most of the time you end up not having the music with the film until the final mix, which can be disastrous. They may sketch out something for you on the piano. But you don't even hear the music next to the movie until the recording session, in which you're paying thousands of dollars an hour and it's too late to question it. If you read my diary for *Box of Moonlight*, that's exactly what happened. With Jim, he gets my sensibility. I encourage him to get as loopy as he wants. He did some incredibly beautiful stuff in that movie. The trickiest thing I try to do with each film is come up with a tone for the music that has not been heard before. I would never want music in my film that sounded like twenty other movies.

Did you find that it was difficult to strike the right tone for *Johnny Suede*?

Yes, but I find that with all my films. Look at *Living in Oblivion*. That film could very easily have become a horror film.

Johnny Suede gets quite dark in the last part.

Yes, it does. *Box of Moonlight* has that same shift in tone, and even *The Real Blonde* has it. I'm not sure what that means.

Do you do it because you consciously want to add some emotional depth?

I don't know. It just feels right to me. When I look at one of the most influential movies of my life, *Midnight Cowboy*, there are moments of absolute hilarity in that film, and other moments where you're just devastated. It goes together for me. I don't see why they have to be separate. It's a tricky balance. At times, Johnny Suede is a fool, just a buffoon. At other times, I needed to see him disintegrate. I really needed to see that facade just blown away.

I think Johnny's naivete is very charming, but that dark undercurrent is there. Was the character always conceived that way?

He was even darker. One of the scenes that was cut was a woman walking down a street with this truck driver harassing her, swearing at her. Johnny goes into a quick fantasy where he just walks over and beats the shit out of this guy. There was that whole aspect of his character, which I had written to make him more dimensional. Due to pacing, most of it got cut.

The decision to cut it down wasn't really about the way Brad was playing the role then?

Brad's pacing put a kind of a structure on the film that I was forced to deal with. His slow delivery meant I couldn't cut within scenes to speed them up. So, if I was going to take out scenes, I had to take them in their entirety.

Are you talking about his delivery of lines?

Yes, his delivery of lines was very slow.

And you didn't want that?

No. But I take responsibility for that because I was there by the camera, and I could have stopped it. It's something that I'm continually experiencing, even with *The Real Blonde*. I look at scenes now, and I just say, "Come on, let's move!" It's a very strange thing. One of the things, as a director, I never wanted to do was simply say, "Faster!"

The actors get very insulted when you say that to them. But sometimes, you have to.

There are a lot of long takes, and long shots, full-figure shots in the film. Did you have an aesthetic reason for that?

One of the reasons was my respect for acting. I just wanted to let the actors do their work. In some ways that was good; in other ways, it didn't help me in the editing room. I have since come to learn that if an actor is really good, they can do the take again, and you can shoot the whole scene in a master, and then go in for a closeup and get something different. Most of that style was just to get a sense of the spontaneity of a continuous take, as opposed to breaking it up into short pieces.

So you would shoot it differently now?

Definitely, because I have experienced what it's like to be in the editing room with nothing to help you put together a score.

You didn't have enough coverage on that film?

I didn't have the right kind of coverage. One of most interesting things I heard John Sayles say is that editing is where you do your final rewrite of the film, and it's absolutely true. The movie actually changes form in the editing room. Every time you say this is the way the scene is going to go, you get in the editing room and something happens to change that. "We don't need that line there. How do we get that line out?" And you can't cut it out. If you need to make a change, and you don't have the right material, you're fucked. It's a very critical lesson to learn.

It's always refreshing when people don't cut needlessly. I like to think that filmmakers should have a reason to cut.

Look at *The Real Blonde*: I did a lot of the stuff with Matthew Modine and Catherine Keener in wide shot because I just love to see the two of them together. There are scenes in that where I just locked that frame! I love that. Godard does that. If anything, *The Real Blonde* was directly influenced by films like *Vivre sa vie*, those sort of relationship movies that he does so well. I even took Catherine's glasses from Anna Karina.

Where do you think Johnny and Yvonne are at the end of *Johnny Suede*?

I think they're at a good point. Emotionally, at least, he is more real. And she is very real, so at least they have a place to come together now. He's done something horrific to her, but he understands it. To me, this guy realizes that his life, up to this point, has been an exercise in futility. There's the potential of hope for the two of them. Again, some people criticize me for not making his realization bigger. After *Box of Moonlight*, somebody said, "Well, when Turturro goes home, why doesn't he squeeze his wife's ass, and be loose and free?"

Well, he's not going to suddenly change his personality.

Exactly. Johnny could not change his personality, but he could come back and say, "I'm sorry." To me, that's real and believable.

What happened with the film's release?

It's a simple story. We went to Locarno, the first film festival I had ever been to. Beyond anyone's expectations, we won the Best Picture. This was 1990. *Thelma and Louise* was released. Brad Pitt became a star. Miramax bought the movie. Harvey Weinstein bought the film without even seeing it, and I am convinced he never knew what he bought. He thought he was buying a teen comedy, and he never knew how to sell it. Consequently, he waited a year and a half, hoping that Brad's star would become so huge that he could release this film effortlessly and it would just take off. It never happened. We played two weeks in New York, and they dropped the movie. That's the story right there. I could go into detail, but the film never really found an audience.

In your own mind, did you achieve what you wanted to achieve with the film?

No, to be honest. If I had, I think more people would have gotten it.

But are you proud of it?

I'm very proud of it. I think there's stuff in it that has never been put on film, and when I look at the film, that's what I respond to. Just in terms of the acting, the scene with Catherine Keener and Brad in bed, when they make love, is a beautiful scene. I love the way that scene is shot. I said to myself, "You know what, Tom? I think you really got it." Essentially, I think what's missing from the film is a sense of urgency. Originally I had thought it would come from the complexity of the character, but the character ended up not quite as complex as I had wanted, and the film just seems to meander. That was never my intent.

The pacing is off?

More the focus. I look at some of my favorite films, and there is a sense of tension, something just driving them. I don't mean tension in the way of *Cliffhanger* or *Demolition Man*. But something that's really making the next thing happen. Look at *La Strada*. You watch the film, you see what's going to happen between this slightly retarded woman and this brute of a man. There's always that feeling of what's going to happen.

Were you disillusioned after the release of *Johnny Suede*?

Enormously. It was either suicide or kill someone else. It was rough. *Johnny Suede* was finished and completed in 1990. I did not make *Living in Oblivion* until 1995.

What did you do during those years?

Every day, on the phone. The deal for *Box of Moonlight* would come close to happening once every three months, and then it would crumble. And each time I had to start over from scratch. The amount of effort and energy used toward getting a deal to almost happen is enormous: phone calls, letters, meetings. I did that blindly, relentlessly, until finally I realized that five years had gone by. Something had to give. I couldn't take it anymore.

That's when you decided to write the short film, which became the first part of *Living in Oblivion*, just to do something? Were you interested in making a film about filmmaking?

No, not really. I was at a wedding, and the deal for *Box of Moonlight* had fallen through for, I guess, the fifth time. I'd had a couple of martinis, and this guy who had been in one of my acting classes, and who I hadn't seen for six years, comes up to me and says, "Tom, it's so great you made *Johnny Suede*. You're so lucky to be working in film. Lights, camera, action! How exciting!" I literally said, "Hold on a second. Let me tell you what it's fucking like. Especially for an actor, making a film is the most tedious, frustrating experience. You can be in the middle of the most incredible, emotional moment, and it's fucked because a guy just didn't get the focus right, or a light explodes." And that was it. I was in the middle of a sentence with this guy, and I said, "That's interesting. What would happen if I just took that idea and put an actor in a situation and just kept bombarding them with things fucking up?"

It's interesting that you took the point of view of the actor rather than the director when you thought of the idea.

Right. I didn't in any way want to say, "Oh, look how hard it is for me." It wasn't the point. There are many ways in which you can blame specific people. For example, I had to fire the guy who shot *Johnny Suede* because he was intentionally screwing up the film. I suspected that, but I couldn't quite believe it. I actually called him from the editing room because I was looking at some material that was so unusable I couldn't believe it. I called him and said, "I have to tell you, if you want your name in the credits, you have to allow me to ask you, 'Why did you do this?'" And he starts crying over the phone, "I was so jealous of you, directing your first film. I was intentionally sabotaging the film." Now, that is evil. I couldn't put that in *Living in Oblivion*. There was a part of me that said, "I'm going to try and trust these people." The cameraman's problems in *Living in Oblivion* have more to do with the fact that he's not getting it from Wanda, the assistant director, than wanting to just blatantly fuck somebody over.

That's an interesting point that you made, that the film takes the point of view of the actor. Honestly, my experience working as an actor and studying acting with Frank Corsaro and Freddy Kareman showed me the absolute beauty of a single living moment, and how rare it is. Freddy said to me, "You may get that once in twenty years." That's how rare it is—when you see something happening in front of you, and you just can't believe how incredible it is. I witnessed that in his class. You're half asleep, and then suddenly something starts to happen, and it's the most compelling thing you've ever seen. I will always respect that. Many times I've sacrificed the shot, the style, something, just to get the acting. One thing that has been consistent in criticism of my work is that the acting has been impeccable, and I'm proud of that.

Can you talk about your decision to shoot various sequences in black and white and others in color in *Living in Oblivion*?

Just to play with it. The film was originally conceived as a short film, in black and white, with the shots the crew is shooting in color, in a way to show my belief in the magic of filmmaking. When I conceived of it as a feature, I didn't want to do the entire film that way. It just didn't make sense artistically. So I messed with it a bit. In the second part, we have them shoot what appears to be almost a 1930s love scene, with a very different kind of black and white than the first part. It's luscious and creamy—compared to the ragged graininess in part one. And I had the reality be in color. Then, in part three, it's all color. It was just a way of trying to keep it visually interesting.

Your work always has an emotional aspect, even when it's meant to be funny. Is that because you don't want to create caricatures or cardboard characters?

That's it, but it's odd because even the emotional moments do something to embellish the humor. In *Living in Oblivion*, I had the most emotional moment of the film when Catherine Keener and Rica Martens, the older woman, do their mother/daughter scene. These two people are absolutely caught up in an emotional moment. Yet, it's a very complicated moment in the film. Steve Buscemi [the director] is alternately horrified that he's not getting it, but he can't help but be awed by what he sees. Meanwhile, the crew is in tears!

It's a great moment.

It's emotional. I consider that a different moment than, for example, in *Box of Moonlight*, when the guys get beaten up and Sam [Rockwell] breaks down in John's [Turturro] arms. To me, this is what Kid [Rockwell's character] is about. He is absolutely terrified. I wanted it to look on the surface like it was an idyllic, goofy thing: "Hey, yeah, man. Spend some time with me!" But in that scene we see in an instant what Kid is about—something darker and more complicated.

Why didn't you pursue that more? There is a sense that we'd like to know more about Kid's emotional life.

I agree, but the intent was to keep Turturro off balance. A part of me is as interested in that as much as in the humor, and I think it somehow makes the humor more valid.

Do you do much improvisation in your work?

There's a lot of improvisation. Sam Rockwell made up a lot of stuff in *Box of Moonlight*. I'm very much into it when it becomes critical to the film. But there's also something utterly fascinating about a beautifully written scene that the actors do word-for-word and it just seems improvised.

Was anything improvised in *Living in Oblivion*?

Yes, although most of it was scripted. We were under the most incredible time restraints. We had five days to shoot the first half-hour of that movie. And fifteen days to shoot the rest, so we didn't have time to stop and talk. One thing that was improvised was Buscemi's rant to the crew at the end of part one. I had designed that simply as a shot of the crew, and I said, "Steve, stand right by me while we shoot this. Say whatever you want to them." And he just went crazy off-camera, "You fucking AC, you dumb shit..." And those reaction shots were real because that was exactly their shock in watching Steve. I just said, "Okay. Turn the camera around." We didn't even re-light. I said, "Steve, go ahead." He just made that whole thing up and we filmed him doing it.

What's your working relationship like with Buscemi?

Well, it's one of the most rewarding, because he is one of the most willing actors that I have ever worked with. It's a joy simply to go up to him and whisper something in his ear. That's how I work with him. Just before the camera's rolling, I say, "Steve, try this." And he just does it. Afterward, you see a little twinkle in his eye: "How was that?" He's one of the most gifted actors we have. I love working with him. I never know what he's going to do next, and he always makes it interesting. I particularly like it when he gets angry. To me, he's hilarious when he's angry, genuinely angry!

All of your films are very concerned with story structure, and creating strong central characters. Where does that come from?

Probably from my writing background. I'm fascinated by things that appear to have a solid structure, that aren't just thrown together.

I think you're a very American filmmaker. You take the virtues of classicism, in construction and character, and work with them.

When I talk about some of the films that inspired me the most, there are not too many in the last twenty years, so maybe that's what you're talking about. Fellini's early films were incredibly well-structured, and character-driven. And Buñuel's films are rock-solid. Kurosawa, John Huston, George Stevens, everything in their work needs to be there.

Do you think your strengths as a screenwriter are in structure or your ear for dialogue?

I put a lot of effort into both. The dialogue comes easier for me. I have an ability to put words into people's mouths and have them sound believable. In terms of structure, I like writing scenes, and I think my sense of scenes is very clear, but structure in a feature film is incredibly complicated. Just contemplating the idea of having a film for an hour and thirty minutes. And then there's got to be a scene at the end, which ends the movie. It's a very difficult thing to do.

What was it like having a successful film, *Living in Oblivion*, after the failure of *Johnny Suede*?

Well, I'd have to qualify the word "successful." *Living in Oblivion* was definitely more successful that *Johnny Suede*, but it was not a "hit."

Was it also mishandled?

Completely mishandled, and it also got very mixed reviews. Again, it's so bizarre, even with *Box of Moonlight*, and currently with *The Real Blonde*, people say these films are not as good as *Living in Oblivion*. These are the same critics that trashed *Living in Oblivion*, that said it was a one-joke film only for filmmakers. That tenor of review killed us in this country. Killed us! We made more money in France than we did in all of the United States. The release was incredibly small, very timid. It never did anything in terms of getting the film out there. But *Living in Oblivion* was a more vital film than *Johnny Suede*. I like its artifice, I like the way it just keeps the ball in the air. People are aware of the movie. So, at least in an artistic sense, the success was very beneficial.

Before you made *Box of Moonlight*, had you already decided that John Turturro and Sam Rockwell would be in it?

Sam Rockwell, I knew. I almost cast Sam as Johnny Suede, but I found he was too young. I vowed to put him in my next film. The part of Al was a tough one to cast. I went to Alec Baldwin, Michael Keaton, Kevin Kline, John Malkovich. You could see the kind of actor I was going for, strong but also comedic. All these actors either never read the script or scoffed at me for even considering them. It wasn't until I saw Turturro do Herb Stemple in *Quiz Show* that I realized he had such an emotional range. I knew Al Fountain [the lead character in *Box of Moonlight*] needed to effect people from an emotional point of view. Many people would see him as an unsympathetic character for a while. Whenever you play a guy who's a little uptight, and you really commit to it, there's a danger people won't like you. I said, "They may not like him, but I want them to understand him." That's why I cast Turturro. He's an incredibly strong actor. And I wanted Al not to be a wimp. Why can't a strong, good-looking guy have an identity crisis that makes him utterly helpless?

Was that film a difficult shoot?

Yes. It was so intense on location, dealing with all the elements. We had thirty days to shoot that movie. We had to rush the filming. To rush and get something good, you work eighteen-hour days, and that's what we did. It was grueling.

Do you see *Box of Moonlight* as a development in terms of your work as a director?

I think so. I feel like I moved out into a different direction. I don't know if it's always going in a straight line. I think *Box of Moonlight* is a complex film that, strangely enough, most people see as utterly simple. The most common response was, "Oh, it's a hippie film." I cannot comprehend why people would classify the film this way when it is so absolutely the opposite. It's strange to me how, with a subtle idea, you lose people by the millions. To make a statement about spirituality is definitely a step into uncharted waters for me.

Once again, you had to strike a delicate balance between comedy and drama. Did you feel that you hit that balance?

I think I did. I'm very proud of that movie. Of all the films I'd done, I really thought that film was the best. It would just come out, and people would go see it. I think it was artistically successful. It's funny, though, because a lot of people criticized the film because Turturro does not become a great guy by the end of the film. They want more. They want that *Good Will Hunting*, kind of resolution. But I'm very proud of what Sam Rockwell does. I'm very proud of the intimacy these two strangers achieve.

Can you talk a bit about working with John Turturro on that character? What kinds of discussions did you have?

My main discussion with John was making him a little bigger than life, and trying to make the character's rigidity humorous and exciting to John as an actor. He couldn't quite get that at first. He admitted to me that he didn't know why I cast him. I said, "Mainly, John, I want you to have fun with this part." He said, "What do you mean? How can I have fun?" I said, "Okay, this scene when you're in the restaurant, and the waitress comes up to you. I think you can have some fun with that." He said, "How?" I said, "What if Al Fountain is the kind of guy who never really talks to people, but in this scene, he's going to try to show that he's a regular guy." And he goes, "Oh! I've got it." And if you watch that whole scene, John is going, "Really? Really? Oh, yeah! Okay!" To me, that's one of his funniest scenes. Or when John gets up and dances around the fire, he can be absolutely hilarious. John is an amazingly disciplined actor. He prepares himself for every take, and you never know what he's going to do next. A lot of my work with John was just saying something and then stepping back, because he took a lot of pride in wanting to find it himself. What I wanted him to do was just be as much of John Turturro as he could be, and a lot of our battles were trying to get him to take off some of the veneer of character. When John is just being himself, he is an incredibly warm and hilarious person. I said to him, "Just because this guy is mean or rigid with his son doesn't mean he can't have things about him that are enjoyable. I don't want so much of a character that we can't see into this man."

I don't know if Turturro often communicates that warm side in his work.

I agree. That's what I like about what I also achieved with Steve Buscemi. Steve is often cast as "that funny-looking guy," as a character in *Fargo* describes him. In *Living in Oblivion*, he comes closest to being as real as he can, which many people found to be warm, sexy, and even attractive.

I've spoken to some people who find Kid from *Box of Moonlight* irritating. What do you think about that?

Well, I've spoken to as many people who felt that John Turturro's character was irritating.

I think Kid's touching, but I could see why he could rub people the wrong way.

I wanted him to be the antithesis of Al. He would be a guy that Al Fountain would not want to grab too tightly because he might get some bird shit on his hand, who might say to him, "Listen, man, You've got to get your life together." And we should believe it when he says that, because he's not this Peter Pan spirit that changes Al's life. That's not what's going on in this film. The film is about two strangers who meet, and somehow, there is an exchange. That's part of the reason why I had him be annoying in a certain way. He's the exact opposite of Al—he steals, he's loud. I wanted him to be able to affect Al, and then have Al affect him.

So you think that Kid has more of a sense of responsibility about life because of Al?

I think so. Listen, he's gone through a very heavy thing, and he's trusted another human being. Al came through for him.

And you think that Sam's spirit gets into Al?

Yes, I think so. That was the idea.

How else is it a spiritual film?

One of the things that I believe, and find to be true for myself, is that the most powerful belief you can have is one which you arrive at through some personal experience. Most of the time, it's painful, but you arrive there. I wanted to show Al turn his back on organized religion, which he does by rejecting the minister's appeal for his soul. He flouts the laws of fidelity and marriage by sleeping with another woman. He violates the trust of employment by blowing up his workplace. Then he comes to an understanding about himself and how he feels about his job and his wife. The fact that he sleeps with Floatie [Catherine Keener] doesn't mean he doesn't love his wife. Maybe he now thinks of his wife in a different way, a more inclusive, vital way. People have been burned at the stake for expressing those kinds of thoughts.

Structurally, the film seems quite focused on the relationship between Al and Kid. It's a long time before you introduce the two women characters.

If they were introduced earlier, the audience would expect them to reappear. I wanted a feeling that we don't know what's going to happen. Because that's the way it is in life.

Do you favor a particular way of structuring your work?

I believe there should always be something that is moving the film forward. Some people look at my films and think it's just like watching paint dry, but when I look at *Box of Moonlight*, everything that happens to Al leads to something else. I think it's very plot-driven. What's plot other than what happens next? Some plots are more intricate than others.

Do you have a sense of where you want your characters to go?

Absolutely! At all times. To me, *Box of Moonlight* was broken down into a series of days, which is why I had Al Fountain constantly saying what day it was out loud, like "July 2nd." So we had the sense of each day, and what was happening to Al during those days. Each scene with the wife and son was calculated to illustrate a bit more clearly how he treats his son, the effect on his son, how they enjoy him being gone. I don't write frivolously. It may not appear to have meaning, but every single thing I put there is what I feel should happen next.

You basically achieved what you wanted to achieve?

Yes. But there are things that I would want to change in every one of my films. Filmmaking is one of the few art forms where you don't have the freedom to go back and change things, because there's so much money, and people's schedules, involved. When you're there, you've got to get it. If you don't get it, then you don't get it.

Can you imagine an ideal way of working?

Yes, I approached it on *The Real Blonde*. The little more money gave me time to stop in the middle of a scene and just say to people, "You know what? We all know that this isn't working. Let's just stop and get it together." There's a scene with Catherine Keener and Matthew Modine in the apartment that wasn't working. I cleared the entire set. The actors and I worked on the scene for three hours. People were totally freaking out. I said, "Don't bug me." We rewrote the scene, and it's in the film as we rewrote it. To me, it's exquisite. *Living in Oblivion* came the closest to being exactly what I wanted. Interestingly enough, it was the one film in which I only cut out one scene. Everything we shot is in the film, except for that one scene.

How did *The Real Blonde* come about, and what motivated you to write the script?

For *Box of Moonlight*, I felt limited by the idea of "hipness." That road is so narrow. Having done that, I said, "I want to get back into the city." I wanted to get right back and deal with stuff that I felt was very immediate—what's going on in terms of men and women today. That was my primary concern. I think the film illustrates that there is no simple answer. I wanted to show a relationship the way I experienced it, in terms of intensities between two people. I wanted to investigate what it's like to be in a relationship in which both people are right in an argument. It's very easy to have one person right and one person wrong. But what if both people are right? What if Modine's desire to somehow maintain his integrity is as valuable as Keener's "How will we pay the rent? You're thirty-five. You're unemployed. What are we going to do?" That was it. I wanted to use that as a framework to then hang these ornaments of the soap opera onto the Madonna video, the fashion world. Just to illustrate my sense that our entire world seems to be unable to tell the difference between what has value and what doesn't.

So, the character study, or that aspect of the film, was more important than the satire?

No, both were equal. One of the things I learned from *Living in Oblivion* was that I really enjoy satire. I came up with the idea when I saw all these fashion spreads with women beaten up. I thought,

"Christ! What's next? They'll probably have a perfume called Depression." And I did a sketch of a perfume ad showing a depressed woman with a bottle of perfume called *Dépression*. I had the idea for this two years before I made the movie, and I put it in.

What about the casting for the film?

Pretty easy. The only person I was specific about was Catherine. I wrote the part for her. Modine was on a very short list of actors who I thought could play this part. Again, like Turturro and Buscemi, the part is very dual in what it requires. I wanted somebody who could have a certain nobility, yet be really goofy. I wanted someone who could be strong, but have a childlike inability to deal with the world. I met Modine, talked to him, and thought, "He's got it!" The rest of the actors came to me on their own. Daryl Hannah approached me. I was amazed at how much interest actors like Kathleen Turner and Christopher Lloyd showed in the script.

Was it difficult finding the balance in this film between the satire and the character study?

Not really. As I was watching the actors work, if I laughed, even during the quieter scenes, I knew it was working. I felt no matter what was going on, if something created a giggle of recognition, then it was right. So, that's what I went for. Again, the film is not naturalistic, but it has a reality that's definitely locked into the film. You believe it, but it's very exaggerated. That was the trickiest, like how far would Marlo Thomas go before her character became too foolish.

Talk a bit about Modine's character. When he finally gives that speech from *Death of a Salesman*, he does it so well. How does he get to this point as a character?

The same way Buscemi gets to the point he does in *Living in Oblivion*; Turturro gets to the point he does in *Box of Moonlight*; and Johnny Suede does—he gets to the point where he completely lets go of everything. Joe [Modine] reached a point where every single thing supporting his image of himself has disappeared. The only thing left is the reality of himself. When he gives that speech, he is finally speaking the words that he feels. That's what makes him do it. He realizes that he's having very specific problems with Mary, the woman that he's in this relationship with. Madonna did not call him. He is working as a waiter. He's thirty-five years old. He has finally accepted the reality of where he is in that film. When we first see him, he's a very different person.

You have a lot of fun with the advertising world, the fashion world, the soap opera world. Is there a danger in satire that the thrust will get lost because it's so much fun to watch?

There's a danger in anything. I could show you the range of reaction to this film, and it's pretty much every note on the musical scale. Some people say it's too bitter, other people say it's about nothing. I did it the way I felt it would excite me, and that's all I can do. I wanted to do the fashion world that way. I didn't want to show them as inept, because they're not inept. They're very good at what they do. I did not want to show them in a cynical or bitter way. Even if you look at the Marlo Thomas character, she definitely wants to do a good job. The model wants to be a good model. They care about something.

The Real Blonde **is an ambitious film.**

Yes, I wanted to try things visually. I wanted to create a different world of New York. It's a very complicated city. I wanted to venture into these different parts of the city: the catering world, the world of wealth, the soap opera world, the fashion world. Each one is a very specific world. The visuals are extremely playful in this film.

Do you see a danger that you will be corrupted by the studios, or run the risk of watering down what was quirky and original in your work?

No, I don't. I don't see it in *The Real Blonde*. I see scenes in *The Real Blonde* that I have never seen on film. I don't even want to hear that it's been watered down. All you have to do is look at the film and see what's in it. Just because it makes you laugh doesn't mean that it's just a joke movie. There's a lot of very complicated stuff going on in the film. I'm disappointed that more people don't see that. I think what happens with Joe and Mary is just exquisite, the way that Modine and Keener pull that off. I'm tired of seeing people in films in relationships where it's this gooey shit. I don't believe it. I would rather see two people the way they really are in relationships. That was the intent.

So, you don't see yourself working in Hollywood?

I'll put it to you this way. If they give me twenty million dollars, final cut, and whatever cast and script I want, then of course I would work in Hollywood. But that will never happen. Hollywood functions utterly by committee, and when you get thirty people making decisions, they always make the weakest ones, and I'm not about that.

It's tricky making any kind of distinction between being an independent and working for a studio these days. I'm not sure I know the difference anymore.

Well, there is a difference. It's that the independent people are completely affected by the possibility of making money. There was always that possibility, but when the budget for a film was $500,000, you had more freedom. They were a bit more willing to take a risk. Now, you can't even make a film for $500,000 without hearing, "We'll give you the money if you put Harvey Keitel in it." The kinds of films that are being released or financed by independent people are the kinds of films that they think are going to make money. Maybe it's always been that way. I know that when *Stranger than Paradise* came out, no one would have conceived of financing that movie. If Jim had given that script to Miramax, they would have laughed him out of the room. Independent films have proven that they can make money. Therefore, they now face the exact same box-office requirements that Hollywood films do.

What's the most difficult part of being a director? Is it the business part?

Yes, it's the business part. It's also dealing with disappointment on the artistic level. It's a creative process that is endless, twenty-four hours a day. And you're dealing with a tremendously large group of people who are all looking at you, all the time. And if something happens that you are affected by, say disappointed or angered, it's difficult to find a way to express that. Now, if something doesn't go right, either with the producers or on the set, it really affects me tremendously. I have a hard time hiding it, especially when I know that the film would be better if that accident hadn't happened. The casting of Catherine Keener is an example. I almost didn't make *The Real Blonde* because I had somebody telling me, "You can't cast her." That was the most excruciating thing I've ever been through. When I saw the list coming from these people, "Here, why don't you put Tea Leoni in that part? Why don't you have Nicole Kidman?" I said, "No. Why do I have to go through this shit? I want Catherine Keener. I wrote the part for her. I know she is the right actor for the role."

Honestly, you want to know what it is? Mainly, it's the disappointments, but those disappointments take many forms. It's incredibly frustrating when you make a film like mine, to have people dismiss it critically. It's not as if I, or filmmakers like me, have 30,000 people rushing to give us money. I can count on one hand the films that I have seen in the last five years that seem to me personal films, that were trying to be about something. Why doesn't someone take a film like *Eraser*, trash it, and go, "That director should never work again. What the fuck was this movie about?" They don't do that, but with more personal films they do. It's very strange to see how the director or the writer is attacked and cut down with reviews that say, "He shouldn't be doing this." Especially with a film like *The Real Blonde*, it's very clear where negative reviews have influenced our audience, and there have been some pretty bad ones.

Really? In Los Angeles?

Yes. It did best in New York. But, literally, we go from people like Janet Maslin saying, "It's great," to Kenneth Turan from the *L.A. Times*, who would not review it.

As a film director, is there one stage of the process that you enjoy most?

I enjoy the creative process. And that is one of the shortest times in the entire process. I greatly enjoy writing scripts. When I just sit there alone and know that I have three of four months by myself writing a script, it's exhilarating. I love it. I love being alone, and I love the writing. At a certain time, I reach the point where I want to get around people again, and so the whole filming becomes very exciting. I love working with actors on the set. I love working with the shot, going to the dailies, all of this stuff is tremendously exciting. And the editing to me is equally exciting. To have that material there, and you can change it, speed it up—create this thing right there in the editing room. That is the most exhilarating thing. The other thing, peripherally, and this happened most with *Living in Oblivion*, is taking the film into a theater and sitting with an audience, seeing people react to what you've done. When their laughter is the laughter of recognition, that's a very pleasurable and satisfying thing.

What's the most crucial thing you've learned about directing in the last few years?

As Buscemi says in *Living in Oblivion*, "I've just got to roll with it." In other words, the problems are built-in. You can't expect it to be any different. The only thing you can do is somehow take the accidents and try to make them work for you. That's one thing that I have learned. And I find that if I am excited on the set, usually what I end up with is exciting. It's not a matter of forcing each square into each peg, right? It's the thrill of finding it. That's where the joy is.

ATOM EGOYAN

Atom Egoyan's Armenian immigrant roots are undoubtedly a key to his aesthetic development and identity as a filmmaker. Egoyan's family moved from Cairo when he was three years old and settled in Canada's West Coast province of British Columbia in the early 1960s. This background as the outsider who never quite fits in has been crucial to the formation of Egoyan's cinematic world. The focus on family and identity characterizes many of his early films such as *Next of Kin*, *Family Viewing*, and *Speaking Parts*. As Egoyan states, "When you are aware of absorbing a culture at an early point in life, that colors you somehow. You become aware of the idea that we are constructed, that there are things we drape ourselves in to become functioning members of a community." Another important thematic investigation of these early works is the nature of sexual desire and how it is stifled and distorted in the modern individual. Egoyan's early work is also a meditation on the very nature of art itself, in particular, film, video, and photography—art forms that not only invade our lives and help shape our sense of identity, but mediate our very understanding of reality.

On a stylistic level, these early films have a carefully determined feel, perhaps lacking some spontaneity, in part necessitated by their sometimes minuscule budgets. As Egoyan says, "because I've always wanted the films to have a certain visual look, and to get that look on a very limited budget, everything has to be carefully planned." Always popular with festival audiences and those attuned to the art cinema, Atom Egoyan's early films were sometimes criticized for being mere formal exercises, or not creating believable characters. But believability of characters hardly seems the point in these films, which do, in fact, have emotional characters and use music in deeply felt ways. It is undeniable, however, that a certain detached quality prohibits easy audience identification.

Egoyan's more recent work, especially *Exotica* and *The Sweet Hereafter*, has taken on new emotional depth and accessibility. This may have something to do with the birth of his son, Arshile, around the time that he made the very personal, semi-documentary *Calendar*, which seems to have been some kind of watershed for the director. Egoyan's new-found depth also coincided with wider critical and audience acclaim. He received two Oscar nominations in 1998 for his film of the Russell Banks novel *The Sweet Hereafter*, including one for best director. His most recent film, *Felicia's Journey*, is based on William Trevor's novel, and was produced for Mel Gibson's Icon Productions. It may be that in adapting the work of other writers, as he has done in his last two films, Egoyan has found a voice missing in the hermetic world of his earlier films. I spoke to Atom Egoyan in Toronto.

Egoyan

Could you talk about your early history, coming to Canada from Cairo and growing up in British Columbia?

The family came when I was really young, and they settled in Victoria, which was an odd choice, since most of the other Armenians were settling in Montreal, Toronto, and Vancouver. We were the only Armenian family in Victoria, which came to mean a lot in my early childhood. I was very aware of trying to fit into a community which was quite different from the atmosphere and feelings I had at home. It wasn't a traditional Armenian family, since my parents were both painters, but I was always impressed by how happy they were when they were painting. So, the idea of creating and celebrating art was very much a part of my childhood. I was also trying to become like all the other kids around me. So life was full of contradictions, and I can see how those contradictions have informed aspects of my work now.

Such as not speaking English until later in life?

Yes. The idea of language, when you let a language go, when you let a culture go, has important implications later in your life. The feeling of what a culture means and what defines a set of communal values, familial values and personal values, and the intricate play between those three. When you are aware of absorbing a culture at an early point in life, that colors you somehow. You become aware of the idea that we are constructed, that there are things we drape ourselves in to become functioning members of a community. When

I started writing drama, it was so liberating for me to be able to create a system of behavior for other people.

This was at college?

I started writing plays when I was really young. I remember my first play was an idea I gave to a drama teacher at my school when I was in grade five. It was called *No Hope for Canaries*, about a bunch of boys who are trapped in a mining shaft somewhere and have a canary, and know that once the canary stops singing, their lives are over. As I became older, I veered towards a style of drama influenced by Theater of the Absurd, writers like Ionesco, Beckett, and Pinter. Those were really strong influences on me. I think I've always been attracted to the more extreme sides of human behavior—the ways people can bend themselves out of shape.

Particularly non-naturalistic manifestations of behavior?

Yes. I've never really had a lot of patience with naturalism. I always found drama in the more extreme situations people find themselves in. I think that idea of an absurdist world finds its clearest expression in *The Adjuster*. It's a film I have some difficulty looking at now, because it's so extreme. But that's certainly the film in which I could see the most direct lineage between my earliest dramas and influences.

You studied international relations at university. Why didn't you do something artistic?

I was attracted to international relations because there was a group of people in Victoria who were retired diplomats. I always found it such a romantic world. There is a writer, a very well-known Canadian poet called P.K. Page, who is a close friend of my mother. She was married to a high-level diplomat, Arthur Irwin. I just loved their stories of travel and her ability to write and have contact with other cultures. There was a huge sense of romance and adventure around that, and I was attracted to it.

Were you also attracted to non-Armenian culture?

Yes. By the time I was in my teens, the Armenian side of my background was virtually extinguished.

Had you forgotten the language?

Yes. I didn't have any need to use it, and I was just a regular Canadian kid. I played hockey and was totally involved in popular culture. It wasn't until I was eighteen and I moved to Toronto to go to university that I became acquainted with the Armenian community here. That was a shock to me.

What do you count as some of your formative artistic influences besides the theater. Were you film-literate?

I wasn't so much film-literate as I was theater-literate, and certainly, I read a ton, and the writers who left a strong impression on me were people like Jonathan Swift and George Orwell. I just ate up Orwell. I'll never forget stuff like *The Road to Wigan Pier*, the chapter where he discusses socialism. For someone to feel passionately about something, and yet be critical of it, was very exciting to me. As he says, "The greatest enemy socialism has are socialists." I remember this biting account he wrote of the typical English socialist of that time. He had humor and an ability to self-criticize that I found really interesting. I guess the other person that influenced me was Sidney Peterson, those psychodrama movies from the late forties. And certainly Maya Deren's *Meshes of the Afternoon*. Those were all really strong influences.

Music was also a part of your life.

Music was a huge part of my life. Like any kid, I had aspirations to be a rock musician. But someone told me quite early on that the way to become a really great rock guitarist was to study classical. And of course, one of my other idols at the time was Jimmy Page. I remember listening to his acoustic guitar and thinking that I wanted to play like that. So I started studying classical guitar very seriously, and became so involved with it that I put aside the idea of the electric guitar. I really devoted myself to that, to the point where by the age of seventeen I'd won the British Columbia music competition. One of the other reasons I came out to Toronto was to study with Ellie Kastner, the legendary guitar teacher. Those first few years in Toronto were very exciting because I was doing so many different things: studying international relations at the University of Toronto, Trinity College; weekly music sessions with Ellie Kastner, which were really intense and took a lot of time; and writing film reviews for the U of T newspaper.

So, you were interested in film?

Oh, I was very interested in film from the moment I saw some of Bergman's movies in Victoria—they just blew me away—and Fellini and Antonioni. There was a film club in Victoria called Cinecenta, which is still there, and that was an important source for me. I also had a romance around the idea of experimental film. By the time I'd graduated, I remember organizing an evening of experimental films at the Art Gallery of Victoria. That was a huge success. This was before I graduated from high school, the summer before I left for Toronto. I remember I brought in Kenneth Anger's *Scorpio Rising*, some early shorts by Polanski, *Un Chien Andalou* by Dalí and Buñuel, and I put in a short film I had made as well. I couldn't believe the audience we drew that night. We had to turn away 200 people. And I thought, well, this is interesting.

So this would've been around 1977, 1978?

Yes, exactly. I had started making short films on Super8. I remember being excited about experimental films before I actually saw any. My only source really was The National Film Board of Canada, which had a branch in Victoria. There was no video at the time. Everything was on 16mm, and I remember bringing a borrowed projector home and setting it up in our basement and looking at these early Norman McLaren movies, where he was drawing on film. Those were really mind-blowing for me. I remember seeing *Nobody Waved Goodbye* [dir. Don Owen]. It was the first Canadian feature I ever saw. That's something the younger generation probably finds weird because everyone's so used to popping cassettes into a VCR, but somehow when you rent a 16mm film, you're much more aware of how that movie was made. You're quite close to the actual mechanism which captured those images, and there's something quite touching about that. I have a distinct memory of watching *Nobody Waved Goodbye* in my basement and feeling very close to it.

Did you make any more shorts while you were at U of T?

I did. What happened my first year was that I had written a play that I submitted to the Trinity College Dramatic Society, and they turned it down. I remember being so upset, and thinking, okay, I'll make it into a film! It was almost out of spite. There was a film club at Hart House, which was a sort of cultural center. I became really involved with this film club and got a small grant. Then I shot that first film, *Howard in Particular*, in my first year at U of T. I made it in 16mm, black and white reversal for $300. It was strange, having never been to film school, that I submitted it to this festival called the CNE Student Film Festival, and it won first prize in the dramatic section.

Can you talk a bit about your working methods?

I was basically interested in finding a language to address the subconscious. Anything that immediately immersed the viewer into this other world, where they had to leave their rational expectations behind. Like the first part of Bergman's *Persona*, that really fragmented section where you're trying to resolve the elements and it ends with this boy touching the screen.

Did you understand the complexity of a film like *Persona*, the fact that it contained very complex editing? Or was it more an emotional reaction?

I think it was just an emotional thing. I look at my early short films and it's very interesting to see how I attempted to deal with the complexities. I didn't understand the notion of film rhythm. But I certainly understood what it was about the imagery that was attractive. But not having been to film school, it took a long time to understand how to work with rhythm.

This notion of film and its relation to the unconscious or dreams seems to be an important part of your work. Were you attracted to Stan Brakhage's work?

I was, but later on, because I didn't see it until I got to Toronto.

It takes an enormous commitment to deal with that kind of work.

Yes, but I remember there was an important screening of *Dog Star Man* at The Funnel, an experimental film theater in Toronto. I remember that was a really important piece of work. *Mothlight* and films like that presumed the viewer was open and ready to go on this journey. To me, one of the most influential films of that period was Michael Snow's *Wavelength*. What was exciting was that the film had this relentless structure, this strong formalist exploration, but within it were these narrative strands just thrown in. Like this person who just comes across the screen and drops dead. You don't even know if they died. You think about all the things that might have brought the person to that point, as the camera continues doing what it's doing. That was also a part of *Dog Star Man* as well. I'm sure that wasn't Brakhage's intention, but I always loved this idea of having to impose a narrative on something that resists it. There is a natural desire to find narrative, and the more you resist that, the more tension you create.

You were also growing up during a pretty interesting period of the American cinema. Were you also interested in Scorsese or Coppola?

Yes, Coppola especially. *The Conversation* had a huge influence and can be seen in a lot of my stuff. This idea of someone losing oneself to a process of recording or investigating others. Gene Hackman's character is so incapable of communicating and he's so involved with that process. That was a film that left a huge impression.

How much preplanning do you do for your work? Do you storyboard?

Yes, I storyboard. I had to on the early films, because I've always wanted the films to have a certain visual look and to get that look on a very limited budget everything has to be carefully planned. I had to know exactly what I needed to see, to focus whatever resources we had on that frame. A film like *Speaking Parts*, which is a very rich-looking movie, was made for nothing. There was no surprise about where the camera was going to be. I think where you start wasting a lot of money is when you make those decisions during the shoot. It also makes sense from a business point of view. If you shoot a film like *Family Viewing* in fifteen days, you have to be extraordinarily well organized. You have to have things planned.

In a film like *Speaking Parts*, is there a danger of not letting some spontaneity in, or some element of chance? There can be an almost antiseptic quality to the work.

Yes, and that's one of the things those early films were quite weighed down by. It wasn't until a film like *Calendar*, which is really important to me, where I found a comfortable balance between structure and improvisation. That was quite liberating.

Let's talk about *Next of Kin*, your first feature film. How did this film get made? Where did the idea for it come from?

The idea was something that just evolved. I had a friend who worked as a videographer at a therapy place downtown, and I was intrigued by his stories. In particular, this story about meeting, outside of the session, somebody whose family he was taping. He wanted to approach them on the street, but realized that it would break some code, and the people wouldn't know who he was and would be quite alarmed by it. This is somebody like me, in their early twenties, who happened to have this job where they had extraordinary access to these people's lives. That idea of access began to percolate and emerged with this story *Next of Kin*. It was quite a long process, because I had submitted some skeleton of a script to the Arts Council in 1982, and I remember they liked my previous short films. But they weren't sure if I was ready to shoot, so they asked me to reapply in six months. So I reapplied six months later and, at that point, the new jury didn't like my previous films or the idea and I was told to reapply in a year. It was very frustrating, but that period was helpful because I kept trying to develop this idea, and finally the script for *Next of Kin* emerged.

That was a very important experience because, first of all, the film was made for so little. It was really a labor of love on the part of a number of people. Also, a big influence at the time was a film by Peter Mettler, a friend of mine, called *Scissere*, which was the first real feature to come out of what some have called the Toronto New Wave. That was made for $12,000 to $15,000 through Ryerson Polytechnic Institute. It proved that a feature could be made for no budget.

Next of Kin was at once a very sweet but frustrating experience. A lot of people really embraced it, but the central concept, or what I wanted the film to do, never really worked. I had this idea that the use of a handheld camera would somehow give the viewer a sense of the spirit of the real missing boy watching the family drama unfold. But it never came off that way. In fact, what the handheld camera did was give it a feeling of documentary. I was horrified that a film could go so wrong and that an effect could be so miscalculated.

Did you feel that when you were making it?

Yes, because people were enchanted by Peter's [Patrick Tierney] journey as opposed to finding it disturbing. I resolved that in the next film, there would be no doubt as to what the intentions were. That's where I think the formal distance of *Family Viewing* comes from. Even in that, there was confusion about the whole idea of shooting all these scenes in the condominium on video, a soap opera with live television switching. A lot of people didn't really get that. But it didn't matter because I knew that there was something about the intentions of that film which were really clear. That was a much more confident piece of filmmaking. I'm much more forgiving of *Next of Kin* now than I was at the time. It's an interesting first feature, very warm, and a lot of the ideas that came into the other films were introduced there, but there was a central failure of technique. In a way, there's a casualness to it, which I reject.

Do you see it as an apprentice work?

Yes. Another problem with the film was that my ideas were way beyond my filmmaking ability at that time. I didn't understand coverage, I didn't understand building up a scene or rhythm through cutting. That was all mysterious to me and that's why I used these long masters, because it was something I could understand. I remember having this purist sense that the moment you cut a scene, you're admitting failure. You're admitting that you haven't been able to resolve a choice.

Rather than having every cut serve a purpose or finding the right moment to make the cut?

That's right.

There's a nice attention to slow zooms and internal rhythms in *Next of Kin*.

The first part of it is very strong that way. I love the first part, I love the dreaminess in the airport, when this person arrives. I also love the stuff with the therapy session, which was my introduction to live television switching. Once he finds the family, the film goes slack in terms of its construction, not because of the performances or the spirit of that family, which I think is well created, but it suddenly becomes quite linear. Maybe that's just something I have a problem with in terms of my own cinematic language.

Are issues explored to your satisfaction in that film?

One of the ideas I'd take further, if I were to do it now, is the notion of an incestuous relationship between Arsinée's [Khanjian] character and the boy she obviously knows is not her brother. There's an attraction between the two of them, but I made a decision not to develop that. More could have been made of it, but it was something murky at that time. I think it was a real opportunity lost. It could've been very interesting.

There is a leap technically, and in ambition, between *Next of Kin* and *Family Viewing*. You did some television work in between. Is that what accounts for your development?

Well, the television work had a huge part in it. After *Next of Kin* I made a TV one-hour film called *In This Corner*, which was a traditional boxing story, and I was the last person you'd think would've gotten that. But, politically, it was a good thing for the CBC [Canadian Broadcasting Corporation] to do at that point. And I quickly learned what it meant to use coverage. It was a crash course. There was no way I could have shot that film just with masters. Suddenly it became very exciting, this idea of, when you're shooting two-shot coverage, *not* seeing someone's face, withholding that, and playing with the scene. *In This Corner* actually holds up pretty well. *Family Viewing* was purposely overcut through the live switching. In fact, the cutting is quite brutal. I was basically learning the craft and language of editing.

Wasn't *In This Corner* part of the *For the Record* CBC series?

Yes, it was one of the last in the series. I learned some real filmmaking skills, especially since it was an action film. There were car chases, boxing sequences, a terrorist attack at the airport. I remember storyboarding that so carefully. I looked at *Raging Bull* over and over again, trying to see how those fight sequences were designed. It was my education. Going to the CBC archives, and going through all the old *For the Records*. Seeing the early Claude Jutra, all the Don Shebib films, the Peter Pearson movies. There's a really great story of Canadian filmmaking told through that series, which has sort of been lost now. But there are some real little masterpieces there. I had complete access to those vaults, so I was able to watch the films in 16mm prints. A lot of them critiqued psychiatric institutions. It was a very compelling series. It was a great introduction and education, and where I really learned the more conventional side of filmmaking. Then I directed some episodes of *Alfred Hitchcock Presents* and *The New Twilight Zone*, which were also great learning experiences. A couple of those are actually very good little films in their own right. That allowed me to make a living, and learn through the actual process of filmmaking.

Family Viewing **is probably where your exploration of ambiguous narrative really begins. For example, we are presented with narrative** information that we don't quite understand when we receive it, and only later make sense of it.

Yes, and to me it's also about seduction. I've always found it a very seductive way of entering a story. Not mystery in the sense of information clearly being withheld, as in a spy thriller, where you know that's one of the conventions. It's more a sense of whether or not, on a fundamental level, a story connects. It's a really exciting place to situate the viewer, as long as there's a certain degree of seduction. It doesn't work if there isn't seduction. Marcel Duchamp was the first person who made that clear. He wanted to invest objects or ideas with degrees of exploration, or layers of meaning, but he understood that as the first step, there had to be a seduction. If there wasn't, there was no reason for the viewer to begin the journey. How do you create that? I love the idea of music giving you a strong emotional impulse, and then including elements that work against that. The images, like in *Speaking Parts*, are very fragmented, but the music gives you a sense of an emotional cohesion. I found the tension between the two, at an emotional level, intoxicating.

Explain this idea of tension.

The music makes you want to feel something, but the images don't let you know what you should be feeling. So there is a frustrated sense of desire. The music is very lush and you want to lose yourself in what you think the music is saying you should feel. But the images withhold that for the longest time.

At times, the dialogue of *Family Viewing* is very explicit. There's also a lot of humor, but it's very black.

To be sure, a lot of the film is extraordinarily blunt. There are people who don't get the humor at all, but when I see it with the right audience, I find it quite artificial how the father and son relate to each other. It's all so formalized and brutal. There's something about this young man being raised in that environment which is obviously going to affect him. Like that scene in the nursing home, where he has the argument with Aline, and he's talking about her relationship to her mother and he doesn't seem to be aware of how insensitive he's being. He's been brutalized into this lack of feeling. He's on the cusp of a life where he can either become like his father or make a last-moment reprieve where he can access that part of his background that gave him some humanity. I find sometimes that my feeling about that film is so much the result of who I'm watching it with. I remember watching it at a festival in London and I was just delirious because I thought, oh my God, all the humor somehow came through and people understand the absurdity of it. But when I watch it with a really dry audience, it's very awkward because all the stuff that's meant to be harsh and extreme just comes off being crude.

In terms of technique, it's more sophisticated than *Next of Kin*. Your understanding of screen characters, and how to work with actors, seems to have developed. How aware were you of the acting process itself?

I was really involved in theater, but just working with professional actors in *Family Viewing* like David Hemblen and Gabrielle Rose helped. You can never ask an actor to be inexpressive without some discussion about why. What is it in their life that has led them to the point where they cannot express their feelings? There's a process of trying to articulate what it is that these people are holding back and where that comes from. That's a really important part of the rehearsal process.

That's interesting, because there seems to be an almost anti-psychological process in your work, at least up until *The Adjuster*, a feeling that you don't want to psychoanalyze these characters. Yet the actor probably needs some sort of conventional motivation.

Except if you look at something like Gabrielle Rose in *Family Viewing*, where he asks her very bluntly, "Are you a kept woman?" And there's this discussion. You can see from her conversation that she's made a choice. She says, "Lovers can't be kept." Someone who formulates a statement like that has something else going on in their brain. This idea of what someone has to hide or suppress in order to maintain a certain life is fascinating to me. Again, the Gabrielle Rose character in *Speaking Parts* is a woman who feels this tremendous sense of guilt over her brother having donated his organs and dying in the process, and she tries to create some testament to him. It's a fascinating situation. I think what's provocative in that movie is that she's written a really bad screenplay. I'd make that clearer now. It puts the viewer in a strange quandary because you want to support what she's doing, but on some level you can't because her writing is mediocre. I was always disappointed when I showed *Speaking Parts* and some people didn't get it or would be frustrated by it.

Speaking Parts was not that well received, right?

Well, it wasn't well received in light of *Family Viewing*, which was incredibly well received. What happened with *Speaking Parts* was that a lot of people saw it as being the same movie, which I've never understood. People just went, "Oh well, that's the video thing." And they discounted it, but it's a very different movie. I have also learned that the idea of coming up with one film right after the other is not necessarily the smartest thing, because you spend so much of your life talking about the film that you are releasing. All the discussions around *Family Viewing* were very much in the air when *Speaking Parts* came out, so people couldn't help but join the two films together. I think *Speaking Parts* is the best script I've written.

Something about the film must make people fail to connect with the characters though, or not see them as real somehow.

Because they're all neurotically inspired. At no point are you prepared to feel for Lisa's [Arsinée Khanjian] love for Lance [Michael McManus]. There's no point of identification. And certainly he's not sympathetic. He's just like an automaton. It resists the exploration of romantic love. There's nothing that you're invited into. There's no point at which you go, "Oh, I can imagine doing that." Which is what makes it different from *Calendar*, where, for whatever reason, people could imagine getting to that point.

Some have criticized your characters for being cold, especially in *Speaking Parts*, and you've also been taken to task for a certain slickness in your work. How do you answer those critics?

It's the one thing that I've never quite got, because the films are almost operatic in terms of the emotions they are dealing with. I think when people say "cold," all they are saying is, "I don't want anything to do with projecting myself into these characters." They're cold because those characters are cold to them. They don't ask why these people are holding back emotion. It goes back to what we were saying about Duchamp. None of this makes any sense unless there's a process of seduction or intrigue. I could talk to you about how fascinating and complex, how driven and intriguing these people's situations are, but I cannot force you to follow this story.

But if you, as a filmmaker, keep the viewer at a distance in something like *Speaking Parts*, then you are setting up the framework for whether people are going to find the characters cold.

It also comes down to the casting and performances in *Speaking Parts*. With all these characters we find ourselves in the middle of a ritual that they've already established to protect themselves.

That's how *Calendar* is quite different. With *Calendar*, we are seeing what made this person, the photographer, into the emotional wreck he is. He watches his relationship fall apart in front of his eyes and he does nothing about it. We see that develop, and so, by the end, we understand his ritual. But in *Speaking Parts*, we never really understand why Lisa goes to the video shop. We understand it in terms of information, but we're not given access to the degree of anguish she feels. We only see the result of her already having found this ritual which deals with her pain, but we're not given entry into how she got there. If you want to create identification, you have to show how the person arrived at that, then there's some sense of pathos, or a sense of feeling about wanting to see these people get out of that situation. A lot of that has to do with performance. Look at *The Conversation*. We don't quite know, with Hackman's character, why he is there, but I will never forget this scene where you suddenly see him at some conference or trade show for surveillance gear. He starts talking with one of his colleagues about how exciting this new microphone is, and suddenly his face bursts into excitement, and he's like a little boy. Your heart goes out at that point because you see the human being there. But with films like *The Adjuster* and *Speaking Parts*, the human being is behind a fortified wall, a wall of their own making, and you're not allowed to see how they got there. Although *The Adjuster* is the first film where, at the end, suddenly you have this glimpse of Noah Render [Elias Koteas] having met this family, and you get a sense of why that all began, but it's too late for there to be any kind of catharsis.

Do you see *Speaking Parts* as a more complex work in terms of style? The montage sequence toward the end is pretty amazing.

Again, it's exciting because if you actually break it down and look at what you're seeing, it's quite remarkable. It's an incredible study of delusion and people needing to project images of others in order to help them to extend themselves. And this whole process of people extending themselves to others becomes this circus of images.

There seems to be a new level of character empathy in *The Adjuster* that we haven't seen in your other films. How did you get to that point of wanting to create more sympathetic characters?

Well, because it was something that was happening to me at that point. My parents' place went up in flames on New Year's Eve 1989, and we had to deal with this adjuster. He was a very kind man, but I found it an extraordinary thing that he would come into our lives. I don't know if you've ever experienced a fire. You just don't want to do anything. Depression sets in where you think about what you want to recreate and why it's important to have things the way they were. Things have to be done quite soon after a fire, but there's also a desire not to do anything. And the adjuster in the film is in the middle of that process and extends himself to these people, and tries to understand their pain. He's a severely depressed character himself, obviously an insomniac, and the only brief moments of self-worth he has are when he's able to help other people reconstruct their lives, while his own life is a complete disaster zone.

The idea of using an abandoned housing development is a great idea. How did that come about?

Yes, it's a great idea, and it almost drove us crazy realizing that. It was just one of those ideas that I loved.

Did you build that?

No, we were just able to make it look like that. We ended up finding a situation similar to it in a development site, but it was crazy. It was one of those situations where I really understood what it means to be limited by budget, where you have a strong concept and an idea and you just don't have the means to create it. We almost had to make a serious compromise with that film, until the last moment when we found a location close to what I had in mind. It was difficult to actually locate it with the budget we had. If you have a huge budget, it's no problem. You either find the site or build the house. I think that house in flames at the end of the film is one of the absolute miracles of low-budget filmmaking. How we actually got it to look like that without digital effect is quite stunning.

Was *The Adjuster* also a commercial failure?

No, it was fine, especially in some territories. It would've done a lot better in the States if Orion Classics, who picked it up, hadn't gone bankrupt. It was a very difficult time. It was the first film of mine to actually get a wider distribution in the States, and it's still available on video. I think those three features, *The Adjuster*, *Exotica*, and now *The Sweet Hereafter*, are the three which are most available. Strangely enough, I was just in L.A. recently, and *Calendar* made its way back into video as well.

Do you find yourself taking criticism to heart? Did you find yourself reacting to what people have been saying about your work?

At the beginning, I really didn't. I would get frustrated sometimes. I would see other filmmakers develop a following based on a kind of hipness in their work, people like Hal Hartley or Jim Jarmusch. Yet I really benefitted from not having that. I wasn't weighed down by a hard-core group of fans who want you to be one type of thing. I never felt that I was responding to an image people had of me, and that's been liberating. There was a flipness to the way I was making those films because I didn't have the financial expectations. Each film was made with a slightly larger budget and was able to somehow respond to that budget. But I never felt I was suddenly in a zone where I had made such a huge step forward that I had to accordingly find a new audience. It was never about that. I took what I'd earned to make the next film a bit more elaborate, and make a different type of film, or a different-looking film, but I never tried to placate people. To me, it was all about trying to find expression which was honest, which conveyed what I was feeling and to preserve the freedom to do it without interference.

Why are you so interested in creating slow rhythms in your films?

I find a languid pace in a film really seductive. That's just a personal predilection. That comes from the movies I've watched, like Antonioni and Resnais. I find that very mysterious; it's like looking at things under water. It also comes from watching glorious, beautiful images projected on a big screen, where your sense of pace is different. To see *The Adjuster* on a huge screen in a proper scope format is fundamentally different to watching a pan-and-scan video. It always tears me apart that people have to watch these movies on pan-and-scan. I'm not quite sure what they're getting, or what they are seeing. I don't think it's the mere fact of projection, because you can show a 16mm pan-and-scan, and it's not much better than video. As a matter of fact, it's probably not as good, because the sound is better on video. But to see it on a really big screen in the proper format is phenomenal. To see *The Adjuster* on a huge screen, and to see this blank landscape and tiny little house, and a jeep arriving at it, with this wonderful music welling up all around you, really is a phenomenal experience. It's one of those few times you get to show it that way where it's really gratifying.

You speak in interviews about wanting to critique the technological world we live in. But you also create these images that are quite wonderful technologically, and that obviously depend on technology for their effectiveness.

Yes, but they take consideration and time. A lot of the seductions of our time depend on our ability to have media access to things. There's the pure seduction of being overwhelmed, as in the last part of *Speaking Parts*, which is essentially an MTV-like barrage of images. The whole last reel depends on that type of fast cutting. By that point, that type of imagery becomes a shock, because of everything that preceded it, and you realize that most of these characters' lives are spent watching images on television which resemble that section.

You obviously felt that you'd run as far as you could go with that idea by the time you finished *The Adjuster*. Yet people expected you to always deal with these issues of technology?

Yes, and that's something I find frustrating now, too. I still love that stuff, and I could be in that world forever if I wanted. And maybe this adaptation I'm doing now will include that. I don't know how it's going to work, the William Trevor book *Felicia's Journey*. In a way, I see that as a modern retelling of *Peeping Tom*, which is one of my favorite movies. I find it fascinating, the ease with which we make these archives and document our experiences.

So you've abandoned that critique?

No, I haven't abandoned it, but I'm also aware that the very thing I like about it—that it makes people self-conscious and uneasy—is also what people came to expect. So any attempt to use it in a critical way was somehow diffused because it was what people wanted to see. It was quite liberating in *Exotica* to leave that behind, to show that you could have more theatrical forms of image-making and use them as persuasively.

It's so dangerous when the audience expects things of artists.

And in a way, it chronicles why an artist has to sometimes work on other people's material. It happens at a certain point. It happened with Scorsese and it happened with a lot of filmmakers I respect, where at a certain point they come to inhabit another person's world. Maybe I'm going through that now with these adaptations. You think you know your own world and what you're drawing from, but it's also great to surprise yourself and inhabit someone else's world.

Some people say *Calendar* is a departure in your trajectory. Do you feel that way?

I have very strong feelings about that film.

Was *Calendar* completely unscripted?

I knew there were twelve scenes. The structure was clear, but what happened within those scenes was largely improvised.

Calendar is an unusual film in the sense that it doesn't seem like a natural progression from _The Adjuster_.

Yes, but *The Adjuster* was as far as I could go in that vein. I continue to believe that. It's funny, there are people who really admire that film. One of the interesting things about this is that there are people who fixate on different films as being their favorite for whatever reason. For me, I know where I was at any particular point in my life when I made a film. *The Adjuster* so violently rejects any form of identification and that's very much where I was at that point. My attitude towards the idea of portraying characters sympathetically on screen was really quite caustic and violent.

I quite enjoyed the inscrutability of the characters in *The Adjuster*. I also enjoyed its surrealism and the emotional intensity you try to reach, but ultimately withhold. A friend of mine uses *Calendar* to illustrate screen time.

It's interesting because there is a division of time, and there's an attempt to heal time. There's also an attempt to understand, because during those twelve months he gets further away from the source of the pain that created this ritual where he invites these call-girls over, and wants them to speak a foreign language so he can lapse into a memory of how he lost his previous relationship. You get a sense, by the end of it, that time itself is removing him enough so he won't need that ritual anymore. Yet there's something very regimented, and at the end, we're suddenly given an explanation of this very immediate moment with these sheep and what that actually meant. These scenes in Armenia are excruciating to him, but they set the blueprint for the next year of his life.

It's hard to know that they're excruciating for him when we see him in the twelve scenes with these women.

Yes, because he's in such denial. It's shocking to me with *Calendar* that some people don't get that these women are prostitutes. Some people think it's actually me auditioning actors for a movie.

That's because it doesn't seem like a world of fiction. It seems like Atom Egoyan shooting scenes over and over again with different people.

Maybe that's part of it. Maybe if it wasn't me playing the character, the film wouldn't be as strong. I was intending to have a better actor and the reason we shot these scenes in Armenia with me behind the camera was so that I could have someone come in and dub over my voice, and then shoot scenes with those actors and the women. But, technically, it didn't work out that way, because there's so much overlapping. So it necessitated me playing the part.

It wasn't really a budgetary consideration?

Well, it was a budget thing in as much as I could not afford to re-dub everything. But that film was made for nothing. Including getting the crew to Armenia and back, it was made for $100,000.

Were you surprised at the responses to the film?

Definitely. It was really just made for German television, an experimental program on German TV, and I was very surprised at the response. I was really surprised to see stacks of it at the Virgin Superstore in L.A. Yet I also understand the pleasures of the movie. It's true about this medium that there's a magical way in which a camera can convey what is going on behind that instrument, what is not shown. My problem with much commercial, studio-driven film is that behind the lens, there's just a committee, there's no governing force. There is no one person feeling something. And what you're really experiencing behind the lens is groups of people who want to delay decision-making and film as many choices as possible and mold that according to test audiences. You can end up with a very sleek product and something that people will watch effortlessly, but you don't really get the magic or mystery of what a person was thinking if they made a decision to shoot those scenes in a particular way. To me, that is the most attractive quality of a film camera.

Have you found that the audience for your films has changed?

It started to change around *Calendar*. Up until *The Adjuster*, the people who appreciated my films were, essentially, an extension of people who would go to a festival or expect to be challenged and would have some preparation. With *Calendar*, a strange thing happened. When I showed a rough-cut of that film to Alliance, they almost didn't want to release it, because they felt it was so marginal. They decided instead to give it a short run at the Cinematheque, around a retrospective of my stuff. Not only were there really great reviews, but there was a different feeling in the audience. They were responding to it. People felt something about this relationship. People felt that it was documenting the actual break-up of my relationship with Arsinée, which was so weird! I remember showing the film in Berlin, and Arsinée was pregnant at the time and she couldn't come, and people found it strange that I was there alone, because we'd always traveled together. They thought we'd actually broken up. That taught me something as well. I was amazed that people who know what goes into the making of a feature, could believe that one could actually be breaking up and still have the wherewithal to plan and document that process in such a formal way. That people would be so lost in the world of the movie, that they could actually surrender their common sense, was a real eye-opener. People really wanted to believe that what they were seeing was real. That was a shock. I never really experienced that desire to identify before. Also, what the character I'm playing is doing is so torturous and extreme, yet viewers found that touching, especially male viewers. They understood what he must have been feeling. I found that quite liberating.

Do you think *Calendar* was a watershed for you? It clearly marks a change in your use of identification as a narrative device.

It certainly marked a desire to use identification and the idea that you can go further by creating characters that are identifiable, and then perhaps the viewer will be prepared to go on a more exhaustive journey. That's certainly been the case with *The Sweet Hereafter*, where the film moves back and forth through something like thirty-five different time zones and people are not aware of it. People just accept it, because the characters and the situations are identifiable, and they know what they are relating to. So they're prepared to invest more. That was true of *Exotica* as well.

It's frustrating that people were not getting the emotions I'd projected into these movies like *Speaking Parts* and *The Adjuster*. With *Calendar*, it was very gratifying that they were, and I suppose I tried to investigate what it was about the film that allowed that. It was just a degree of emotional vulnerability. To me it's like those scenes in *Exotica* where Elias Koteas' character says, "What is it about a schoolgirl that gives her a special innocence?" And those scenes were painful to write because they're actually very revealing. At a certain point, I remember one of the investors—the Ontario Film Development Corporation—called and said they were uncomfortable with the extremity of some of those passages. They asked if there was any way to tone them down. Because I was in the middle of wanting to shoot it, I said, "Sure!" I got this great call from Elias who said, "What have you done? That was what I liked about the character." It kind of shook me, and I realized how easy it is to be swayed by the needs of other people. I was able to bend it back to what I wanted. The reason those scenes are excruciating, but also quite compelling, is because I am actually making myself vulnerable in a way that I didn't in those earlier films.

I found that of all your work, including *The Sweet Hereafter*, *Exotica* has the most intricate structure.

Yes, it does. Because *The Sweet Hereafter,* at a certain point after the accident, becomes quite linear.

When you wrote *Exotica*, was that structure originally there?

Yes.

It's interesting to me whether a film changes shape in post-production and when scenes get moved around.

The only things that shifted were the scenes in the field where they're walking. They were originally extended scenes and not as fragmented as they are. What I found was that rhythmically, it was more useful to use those scenes in a fragmented way. A scene that did take shape during the editing—and one of my favorite sections—is when Elias is in the room playing with the light bulb, flicking it on and off. The film goes into a reverie of him remembering that day in the field and culminates with him meeting Christina [Mia Kirshner] in the hallway. In the screenplay, it was just a scene of him in a room and then meeting her in the hallway.

At that point you have the voice-over of him from the past, talking about his ambitions, and we see him in this frustrated state. That irony is very strong.

Yes and that was found in the editing. I remember that happening one night when I was just so frustrated and working on this flat-bed, which seems like such a dinosaur now that I've worked with a computer.

You have a lot of characters in your films who are obviously very self-absorbed. It's a running theme in your work. You have characters looking in mirrors all the time. Why do you think you're so interested in this investigation of the self or in characters who are trying to figure out who they are?

It's because it's what I do, too. I spend much of my time in situations like this, or situations where I'm writing and I'm wondering. It's a very personal thing to me. Any artist allows himself a tremendous degree of self-indulgence. It's almost one of the job requirements. I don't think you can keep doing that without wondering what the effects are. It's very much like when I show characters in the process of making images. I'm naturally attracted to people who are involved in a process close to what I do.

We are constantly with your characters in this process of self-absorption. They're looking inward, instead of trying to figure out who they are through a process of social action in the world, as they might be in a Cassavetes film.

It's also because there are so many images thrust at them as to who they could be, or how they should be acting, which creates a sort of paralysis. I've noticed that in starting a family. There are so many images thrown at you of what a family life should be. And, of course, you're constantly weighing yourself against those images. That can be paralyzing and produce a degree of passivity. I find that passivity fascinating, and how you work out of it, how to empower yourself with the ability to create your own images. I think a lot of my characters are really depressed. The Maury Chaykin character in *The Adjuster*, or Elias' character in *Exotica*, are very depressed individuals who are trying to find some way to ignite some feeling of meaning into their life, but it's really quite desperate. In the case of Maury's character, it culminates with a double-suicide, in that scene where he says to Noah [Elias Koteas] "Are you in, or are you out?" What is it that finally pulls Elias out of that house? It's just some glimmer of knowing how this started, and maybe in that, there's some hope.

It's very moving, that speech about how he has everything that he wants, but he doesn't know what he needs.

It's moving but he can't really articulate it.

But he's articulating it very well, in a way. He's actually pinpointed the problem to some extent.

Yes, but he's telling it to a complete stranger, so there's absolutely nothing. There can't be anything coming back. It's not enough to be able to understand the source of your alienation. It's also being able to reconnect. A lot of these people in the film are just doing it the wrong way and creating rituals which they think are answering questions, but are just opening up other ones, creating patterns of behavior which they think are dealing with their pain but ultimately are just elaborating it and twisting it more out of shape.

That seems to be part of *Exotica*.

Yes, of course! My God, what a terrible situation Francis [Bruce Greenwood] has got himself into. What is he expecting from this? "Faulty mourning" is a term I've found only recently, a compelling psychoanalytic term to describe people who have found a way of mourning their loss or their sense of grief, but in a way that exaggerates it, as opposed to really dealing with it. A lot of these films are dealing with people who've found a faulty mourning.

Certainly that's in *The Sweet Hereafter*.

Of course, but in our culture, we're seduced into thinking that there are ways of dealing with our pain that are socially sanctioned. At some level, they are comforting, but they don't really deal with more fundamental issues.

Another interesting thing in *Exotica* is that you don't make moral judgments about the characters. You resist the temptation to judge them.

I liked the Miramax trailer.

Which was?

Well, they were just trying to sell it as a sexual crime thriller, and it's all about guns going off.

***Exotica* was a very successful film in terms of Canadian cinema. I would think it had a great effect, in terms of what you could and could not do and how people perceived you. You got great reviews.**

How do you think it effected you artistically?

Well, it confused me because it started this terrible dalliance with a studio project at Warner Bros. which didn't come to pass. In some ways, I can look back and think of it as a lost year. A lot of the year was spent in L.A., meeting actors and various people on what would never have been more than a mediocre thriller, but which I convinced myself I had to do because it was my moment. *Exotica* was the hip film I'd always dreamed I would make one day. It was the independent film that lived up to the hype of what independent film is about, and it was marketed that way. I thought that this was my moment, and if I didn't grab it, I'd always regret it. And it ended up being a really terrible year because I almost gave up what was clearly a better project, *The Sweet Hereafter.* The best thing that happened to me during that year was being invited on the jury at Cannes, and seeing these great movies, and realizing that this was the tradition that I really was part of, and not some Hollywood dream. Seeing *Breaking the Waves, Secrets and Lies, Crash,* and *Fargo* shook me into understanding what I was doing.

Do you think it's impossible for you to get into that system and create a personal work? Some people seem to do it.

Yes, but I need to have final cut. I'm having that problem right now with the William Trevor project. It's quite interesting since I could do really well with this project, but the final cut issue is very murky. *The Sweet Hereafter* now has been on over 200 top-ten lists in the States, *The New York Times, Los Angeles Times, The New York Post. Newsday* called it the best film of the year. You can't dream of getting a more unanimous critical response, but the bottom line is that it has yet to make as much money as *Exotica,* and it probably won't. For that reason, an American producer will go, "Well, should we give him final cut?" I realize this now, and I'm taking a really hard position on this. It's ridiculous. That's how I make my films. I understand that they feel uncomfortable giving me that, based on how this film has done. So fine. Let me just leave this project now. There's nothing more to be said. If this is the way you work, then I understand that.

If they really want you, it doesn't make sense not to give you final cut.

Anyway, that's the issue that will break the project if it doesn't work.

Is this the one with Mel Gibson's company?

Yes.

The Sweet Hereafter **is the first film you adapted instead of writing the original screenplay. What was your reason for doing that and what were some of the challenges you faced in adapting that novel for film?**

The biggest challenge was the technical one of how the book was written.

You mean in the first person?

Yes, four first-person narratives, and wanting to preserve the idea that this literary device gives you a sense of storytelling, and why people need to tell a story, and what they expect to get from the stories they create in their lives. So I had to find a way of mirroring that idea, and also dealing with the notion of how to portray the psyche of this community. How to show all these people's lives, how they were, as they are right now, and how they become. I wanted the notion of "before and after" to really play an important part in the way the story was formatted. So I spent more time writing this adaptation than I've ever done writing any of my own screenplays because I wanted it to be absolutely right. I knew what I was serving, and I had to honor the spirit of that book and do justice to it. I didn't want to fuck up, you know?

How did your point of view differ from that of Russell Banks in the novel?

The main difference between Russell Banks and myself is that Russell has a moral position, and that's the result of being a novelist. A great novelist, it seems to me from the writers I've met, feels more comfortable defining that sense of morality. That's a role a novelist is expected to fill.

You don't think you did that in *The Sweet Hereafter*?

I think I had to. I think there's a huge issue about Nicole [Sarah Polley] and I think that her lie is substantiated, in that it makes sense for her to tell a lie to express a greater truth.

Was the elaborate time structure a way to replace the multiple perspectives of the novel?

No, I don't think it was that. When I was thinking about replacing the multiple stories, it was a matter of seeing who these people could tell their stories to. In the case of Mitchell [Ian Holm], there's no one. If I wanted to preserve his story at all, I had to find someone he could tell his story to, and that person certainly wasn't in the community, so I had to invent the character of Allison on the plane. That became interesting because it was dealing with a period two years after this event. In the case of Nicole, it was a matter of replacing her story with another narrative, and that's where the Pied Piper came in. The time issue seemed the most organic way of telling a story. You're dealing with people who are drifting in time and the structure has to mirror that.

What narrative problem did the Pied Piper device solve?

I wanted it to have the quality of a fairy tale. I also wanted it to show how she needed a narrative, and that narrative came from an external source, and at a certain point she uses that to define her own narrative within this community. That's the narrative which is imposed on her by her father, and which she's then able to reappropriate. To me, the most convincing and emotional aspect of the story was this young girl who goes through a passage.

In terms of the film's complicated temporal structure, it still feels very seamless, which is a great accomplishment. On a directing level, it's your most complex work. Yet it's also a more classical film than *Exotica*. I think that's partly because of the emotional empathy with the characters.

Yes, it's more conventional. The part where I get dissatisfied is after the accident and from the time Nicole comes home. At that point, the story becomes quite linear, and has to, in a way, because we have to find the most expedient way of getting to the deposition hearing. But up until that point, I'm just so proud of that movie. It's just floating and finds this really well-achieved sense of dispensing with the notion of time, and yet allows the viewers to locate themselves quite easily. In a way, that's something I've been working on for a long time.

Some people have trouble with the way you handle the incest question.

That stemmed from a desire to present it from the point of view of what a young woman would actually have to believe was happening in order to justify it to herself. The whole film is an attempt to construct people's experience of things. So you see an accident from the point of view of what a father would have seen, and it gets into the helplessness he would've felt. In the same way, with this young woman you get a sense of what she would have to believe was happening to justify these horrible events to herself.

But why does a powerless person need to construct a justification of a situation she obviously can't control?

Because any child has to rationalize why a parent is engaging in this incestuous behavior with them. What is interesting is what people get offended by. I think what happens is that people go, "Oh, are you suggesting that it's consensual?" Well, yes, incest is consensual until the point at which the truth is revealed. The question is, how is this consensus arrived at? It's arrived through some means of coercion, whether it be through physical or psychological violence. But there is a degree of consent. That's how it continues. How is consent manufactured? In this case, it's by her believing, and her father leading her to believe, that there is a creepy romance about it all, that it's okay and that he really loves her. She's only able to understand how untrue that is when she sees his fear and weakness after the fact. He doesn't even address it. At that point she knows that it's terribly wrong. She might be able to get to a point where she feels hate towards her father, but it's very misleading to say that she's capable of that as it's happening. I think it's presumptuous for someone to say, "This is what incest is really about," because it's different in every situation. From what I've observed, it's about people trying to rationalize and understand the unthinkable, which is that a parent is destroying you.

Did you struggle with that at the script stage?

Oh yeah, because in the book it's quite different. I could not portray it as it was in the book. It did not seem true to my experience and to what I'd observed. It was a major departure, but I also feel vindicated by it, because what happens in the film is that when she brings it up at the end, you have to dredge up and deal with these images that you've almost sublimated as a viewer. The film implicates the viewer, and it's a more exciting world, I think.

Your work with actors has gone through an interesting trajectory over the years, and it culminates in Ian Holm's monumental performance. It must affect you in terms of your own expectations of working with actors and what you can get out of them.

I don't know if I could ever get anybody this good again. I mean, he's one of my favorite actors, and it was an amazing opportunity to show him off.

But do you think your ideas about screen characters have been affected by this experience?

Sure, they have. Just to see someone create that amount of detail. You realize what an incredible talent he has, to be able to have that control over his face, and to know it. To be so conscious of that and yet to be natural, is a tremendous gift.

Do you think his character is redeemed?

Not enough. He's redeemed himself in our eyes, but not enough to himself. He can't understand why Nicole said what she said at the hearing.

What about by the time he's on the plane, which is two years later?

Hopefully, but I'm not sure.

He's terribly moving. He's in tears. The character has obviously been changed by the experience.

It's interesting because some people say that his daughter has died.

You did a Bach film with Yo-Yo Ma this year.

That's an interesting project. It was like going back to something from my own world. There are people who haven't liked *The Sweet Hereafter,* and who prefer the other films, and I find that a bit odd, because I really feel it's a huge step forward. But then they look at this Bach film and say, "Oh, yeah. He's going back to what he does." I find it very dissatisfying in a way, because I know the way my mind works. There's no surprise to me when I have quirky characters doing unexpected things. I know that's going to be delightful, but it seems indulgent to me right now. I feel I have certain talents and my responsibility is to find material which could be served and elevated by those particular talents. Something like *The Sweet Hereafter,* which a lot of people would have read and thought, "Well, this is impossible to film. It's so sentimental..." Somehow, through the combination of our talents, we were able to create something quite unexpected.

Tell me about this project with Antonioni?

You know, *Red Desert* was a great influence on me. I spent a lot of my first year at U of T just watching his films. Michelangelo really wanted to make this new film in L.A. and it's his great final wish to make a Hollywood film, which is bizarre. Not a Hollywood film in terms of genre, but to actually make it *in* Hollywood. He's been there for seven months and he's so frustrated. I just talked to his producer and I think they're now going to relocate to England. It's such a mess because there are all these agents and other people who are not being straight with him. I don't think he understands just how duplicitous people are. They're huge fans, they want to support him, but they also want to please their clients. And their clients, when they read the script, and when they meet Michelangelo, don't know what to make of him. It's such a youth-obsessed culture. He is quite paralyzed and a senior statesman who doesn't articulate his ideas in a way that they can quite understand.

Surely some of the actors who are interested can get over that?

They can, but it hasn't worked out. People string him along and at the last moment say, "No." It's been really frustrating.

That's terrible. So you think he'll go to England?

Yes, but because I've got other obligations coming up, these opera projects and the new film, *Felicia's Journey*, I don't think I'll be attached to it. But it's been a great mentoring process. One of the most amazing notes I got in Cannes, the evening of *The Sweet Hereafter* screening, was a handwritten note from Antonioni saying, "Augure" [Congratulations]. I was so moved.

KEITH GORDON

Known to many as an actor from his early work with Brian DePalma (*Dressed to Kill*) and John Carpenter (*Christine*), Keith Gordon is now primarily a writer-director, although he still does the occasional acting job. He has been involved in making films since the mid-1980s, when he co-wrote, co-produced, and starred in the cult film *Static*. His first directorial effort was an adaptation of Robert Cormier's *The Chocolate War*. Because of his acting and theater background, Gordon's films are notable for their strong performances. From the ensemble playing of the group of remarkable up-and-coming actors in *A Midnight Clear* or the relatively inexperienced young actors in *The Chocolate War* to the superb performance of Nick Nolte in *Mother Night* (his adaptation of Kurt Vonnegut's contemporary classic) the acting in Keith Gordon's films is always impeccable.

Gordon's films are also stylish cinematic works that play with space and time in inventive ways. They always feature interesting structures, imaginative visuals, and emotionally involving music. From the first-person point-of-view shots of *A Midnight Clear* to the use of Arvo Pärt's music and the audacious mixing of tones in *Mother Night*, each aesthetic decision is carefully thought out and is always at the service of the film's narrative and its characters. His films are classical in the best sense of the word, in that they are interested in creating intensely believable characters and an involving cinematic experience. They have a certain solidity. They are never trendy or flashy. Gordon is not interested in reworking the grammar of film as much as he is in finding the right cinematic shape and creating the right cinematic universe for his characters to inhabit. Gordon's characters are often in the throws of tackling difficult moral questions, none more so than Howard Campbell (Nick Nolte), the doomed hero of Vonnegut's *Mother Night*.

All of Gordon's films to date have been adaptations from literature. This desire to work with established properties bespeaks a respect for the written word as well as an interest in tackling significant subject matter. It is reassuring to know that there are filmmakers who still believe in the power of literature to illuminate our moral landscape. And even more reassuring to know that they still believe in the power of cinema to translate those moral issues into significant cinematic experiences for audiences that seem less and less interested in the act of reading. I spoke to Keith Gordon in Montreal while he was shooting *Waking the Dead*, his adaptation of Scott Spencer's novel.

Gordon

Where did you grow up?

I grew up in New York City, but I've lived in L.A. for fifteen years. When I was small, I lived in the South Bronx, which was a multi-racial, lower-middle-class neighborhood. As it started to get tougher, we moved to the Upper West side of Manhattan, where I spent my formative years.

You got into acting fairly early.

Yes, I started acting professionally when I was fifteen or sixteen. My father is in the theater. He's a teacher, director, and actor, so I was always around it. But I was much more interested in making movies. Even as a kid, I made Super8 films and videos. The turning point for me was when I saw *2001: A Space Odyssey* at the age of six. I didn't even know what it was, but I knew I wanted to do that because it was so cool. I had no idea how people got to make movies. The acting thing was something I also liked and locked into. I was in a school play, and somebody saw me and said, "Why don't you come audition for this professional play?" I did, and got the part. From that play, I got a part in *Jaws 2*, which was my first movie. So, I started to work. I liked not being in school, so I just started working all the time and supporting myself.

Were you thinking about directing movies at this time?

I was, but I didn't know how people got to do it, and I thought there was no reason that I would ever get to make a film. When I started working as an actor, I felt maybe I could use this as a way to get into directing. I kind of apprenticed with the film directors, asking them endless questions. I was lucky enough to work with some very kind people who gave me big chunks of time and let me hang out in editing rooms and look through the camera. Even when I was doing theater, those directors talked to me about how they directed actors and why they did what they did. So, I went to the most wonderful university of all, with Brian DePalma, John Carpenter, Michael Bennet, Joan Macklin Silver, and others.

What other cultural influences did you have?

Obviously, I was very affected by television. And I was an obsessive moviegoer. I worked at the Museum of Modern Art as an intern in the film archives, filing old films. In turn, they'd show me weird old movies. I'd also go to the film series there and revival cinemas in Manhattan.

Are there any filmmakers or films that were particularly important to you?

Well, Kubrick was my hero from very early on. From *2001* on, he's always stayed the key director for me. I see his influence all over my work. Certainly there are a lot of other people like Scorsese, Truffaut, Fellini. It's very eclectic, it wasn't one style of film. But definitely Kubrick was the one. When I was a kid I read all the books about him. Painting was also important for me. I loved MOMA [the Museum of Modern Art], not just working in the film archive. Literature has always been a little harder for me because I'm mildly dyslexic, and I don't read all that well, which is why I was drawn more to visual arts than to literature. I enjoy reading, but I'm a slow reader.

DePalma's *Dressed to Kill* and Carpenter's *Christine* are the two film acting roles you're best known for. What do you think you learned from those directors?

Actually, I did two films with DePalma. Before *Dressed to Kill*, I did *Home Movies*. That was an even bigger educational experience, even though it's a movie almost no one has seen.

That was the film he made with students at Sarah Lawrence College?

Yes. They had some professional actors, like Kirk Douglas and Vincent Gardenia, but the crew was made up of students. Brian was willing to treat me as one of the students, even though I was hired as an actor. I said, "I want to be a director, so can I use this as a classroom?" He was very kind about letting me do that and answering my questions. That film was set up to give young people a chance to be part of making an independent movie. It was a huge education on how to make a movie for no money. I studied what he chose to shoot and not shoot, how he covered scenes, all the basics. Then being in the editing room, seeing how it went together. I went to all the dailies on both that and *Dressed to Kill*. I liked watching dailies, because you saw all the raw material, and what worked and what didn't. Brian had a way of working with actors that I liked. He'd get one printed take that was what he wanted, then we'd always do a couple more. He would say, "Okay, we've got that, now try one this way or that way." There was a great freedom in that because actors have those little ideas in their heads like, "What if I did it this way?" But you're scared to do it, because what if it's stupid, and that's the one that ends up in the movie? More than anything, with Brian, I learned about visual style—watching his use of a crane and the Steadicam, and lenses, filters, and lights.

The moment I started acting, I was already trying to get into film production. I was writing scripts at sixteen. I didn't have a rich family that was going to pay for my first film, or send me to film school. I didn't have a plan, but I knew that's where I wanted to end up. I didn't want just to act because it was such a horrible life. I mean, I loved acting, but I hated being an actor. They're two very different things: the work of getting a job as an actor, and acting. I still love to act, but the job of being an actor is terrible.

With John Carpenter, I loved the way he ran his sets. John worked with the same crews over and over again. *Christine* was a lot of fun to make, even though it was a hard schedule. It was an $8 million film with a lot of special effects, but John just laughed all the time and played practical jokes. He kept the air light. When you've got a lot of people working long hours, it's important that they feel appreciated and part of the process. There wasn't this big division between cast and crew, it was very egalitarian.

How did *Static* come about?

One of the kids who worked on *Home Movies* was Mark Romanek. He wasn't going to Sarah Lawrence, but he became a hanger-on of Brian's. He became the Second Assistant Director. Mark and I struck up a friendship, and talked about eventually doing a project together. Mark had some family money. He had an idea for a character, which I thought sounded like fun. So, over the course of about a year, we hammered out the script. I would write sections, he'd write sections, then we'd trade and edit each other's stuff.

Was it clear that you'd be playing the leading role?

That was the whole idea. The role was written for me, and he would direct.

Where did the idea come from?

Mark started out with the idea of a guy, an inventor, living in the desert, working in a crucifix factory. Everything else came out of our imaginations. It took forever to do. We were able to cobble together some money, and we put together a cast at the same time. It was helpful that I was doing enough in New York theater that I could get people like Amanda Plummer to work in it. It was made for under a million dollars. That was my biggest education, being co-producer on that film.

Were you satisfied with the way that film turned out?

At the time, I was frustrated by some things, since I wanted to be a director, and had my own vision of the film that was somewhat different than Mark's. I'm sure I drove Mark crazy. I would have made a different movie, but when I look at the movie now, I think it's pretty neat. It's pretentious, but I accept it as a first film with flaws. It also shows a lot of talent on his part, and it's visually strong. There are scenes in it that I love, and a couple of things where I cringe.

This is 1985. Were you getting frustrated with acting?

Yes, I was already moving away from it. Acting was less and less thrilling to me. After *Static*, when the opportunity to do *The Chocolate War* came up, it was, "Okay. So much for acting." I kept acting a little after that. I kept an agent for a while, but I just didn't have the energy. The reality of independent films is that you spend so much time putting together the financing, there isn't any time left. You can't have a life as an actor, auditioning, and a life as an independent filmmaker begging for money. I'll still do little acting jobs here and there, because I like it.

Why did you choose *The Chocolate War* as your first film to direct?

It was a book I loved. I was familiar with all of Robert Cormier's work. *I Am The Cheese* was given to me on the set of *Jaws 2* by somebody who wanted to make a movie out of it, and thought I'd be good for the role. That never happened, but I wrote a script for *The Chocolate War*. I thought it could be made independently on a small budget.

I met this guy, Jonathan Krane, who was one of the few people in America who actually saw and liked *Static*. He asked if there was anything I wanted to make. I told him about *The Chocolate War*, and that I thought it could be made pretty cheaply. He basically said if I could make the film for half a million dollars, I could do it. It was an incredible piece of luck and good timing. This was when the video market was flush, and Jonathan was running a company that was fed by the video market. He knew if he made a film for half a million dollars from a book that was even vaguely known, even if it was a bad movie, he could cover his costs.

How personal is the material in *The Chocolate War*?

Everything I've ever done is personal to me. I don't know how you can direct something and not make it personal. It's an actor's thing, to make something personal, to find the connection, even if it's not like your life. *The Chocolate War* spoke to me on a lot of levels. I felt very much like an outsider as a teenager. I've always felt like life is a strange thing, where you keep trying to do good, and things blow up in your face. The moral ambiguities of life have always fascinated me, and that runs through everything I've done. The world seems like this complicated, messy, screwed-up place where good things turn bad, and bad things turn good. What I liked about *The Chocolate War* was the sense that there is value in the effort to do good, and a knowledge that it's very difficult to do. I couldn't identify with a nihilistic view, yet I also didn't identify with the hyper-optimistic, American view of things. So, there was something in that story that spoke to my own adolescence, my own sense of the world.

How prepared were you when you began shooting that film?

I go into all my films well prepared. I created a shot list of the entire movie, my version of a storyboard. Since I don't draw, I write everything out. What lenses I think I want to use, the color of the lights, where the light's going to come from. I imagine everything. Then, as the film becomes more concrete, it gets modified. Things change when I see the locations and when I start to rehearse. Things evolve, and you start giving up some of your earlier ideas. So, the shot list is like this guidebook that keeps evolving throughout the making of the film.

Was the structure of that film worked out completely in advance?

Yes. Very little of my films change, structurally, in the editing. They get shorter and tighter. But I have a decent idea of what I want the structure to be. There are exceptions, but it's usually a scene here or there. The idea of flashforwards and flashbacks is something that I had going into *The Chocolate War*. I love Nicolas Roeg's movies, and that was something I wanted to play with. I'm often attracted to novels with odd structures, and I like keeping those structures. Interesting novelists will not do things in a linear way, and I don't think linear films are very interesting.

The script didn't change that much. Things would come out of rehearsal where actors would find a new line. But there wasn't a great deal of improvisational stuff. Of all my films, that one is the closest to the original script because the money was so limited.

Were you insecure making your first film?

Much less than I thought I would be. I remember walking on the set the first day, and saying, "I'm home! I know how to do this." Before shooting started, I was terrified. I thought "Oh my God. Everybody on the crew is older than me. Who's going to listen to me?" I walked in the first day, and they were all really nice people, and they wanted to hear what I had to say. They seemed to like my ideas, and we all started having a really good time. That was one of the happiest days of my life, the first day of shooting on that movie. The night before, I was completely ill.

How many shooting days did you have on *The Chocolate War*?

It was about twenty days. It was only difficult in that we had so little time. It was a great deal of fun. I was very supported by the money people. They left me alone.

Let's talk about how you work with actors. You say there is a rehearsal period. How long would that last?

Well, it depends on the film. On *The Chocolate War*, it was one very intense week. It was like doing a play: we'd rehearse ten hours a day, no one else around, no producers, nobody else in the room. We locked ourselves away and really worked on the scenes. I tried not to worry too much about the blocking. I concentrated on the core emotions.

Did you encourage them to create a backstory or just work with the text?

On that one, we worked more on text. I made the assumption that anybody who wanted to create a backstory would create one. Actors work very differently. The best education in directing actors I ever got was from Michael Bennett, the late theater director. I was in a three-character play he directed, one of the few things he ever did that wasn't a musical. We were three young actors, and we couldn't have been more different in personality and training. I was very intellectual and approached things that way. There was one guy who was very "Brando," you know, "in the moment," and there was another guy who was doing his first play and was terrified.

Michael was the most deferential director in the world. I talked to him about what he was doing because I was interested in directing. He said, "My job is to figure out how you work. It's not my job to teach you how to act. My job is to figure out what is going to help you do your work the best way, and then help integrate each of you guys into the same play." That was the best lesson you could possibly give on directing. A director should not try to act for the actors. Part of what I try to do is ferret out, Who likes to talk a lot? Who doesn't like to talk? Who likes to do backstory? Who's screwed up if you get into too much backstory? Who likes to improvise? Who wants to stick to the words? And then, How do I piece those people together so that everyone gets what they need?

How did you work with John Glover on his characterization?

John was endlessly inventive, as most good actors are. He came in with so many good ideas, which made my job fairly easy. With most of the really good actors I've worked with, the truly fine actors, your job is to be a filter as much as anything else. You don't have to tell them what to do. They've done their homework. They know more about the character than you do by the time they start. My job is to say, "Yes, John, this is a little too big. Maybe go over that way a bit, a little more subtle."

Did you ever have an experience where the actor's understanding of a character was different than yours, or different than what you wanted?

Never in a major role, because I'm really careful with casting. I've had this in minor roles, and it's a big pain. If you begin with a really good actor, there's always something valid about what they're doing, even if it's not what you had in mind, and you just find a way to work the compromise. Casting is the single most important decision you make.

Did you ever consider acting in *The Chocolate War*?

No, I knew I didn't want to act in the film. It was hard enough to direct the movie. To me, acting and directing are very separate things, like left brain/right brain. When I'm acting, the whole idea is to be as stupid as possible, and be lost in what's going on. As a director, you've got to be aware of everything. In the episodes of *Wild Palms* that I directed, I had three lines and I hated it. I had no idea what was going on in the scene. I couldn't watch objectively. I think too many other young directors think they can do that. I think it takes a very specific genius to do that. I think Spike Lee's a terrific director, but I think his films are weaker when he's in them. And the scenes he's in are weaker than the scenes he's not in.

I find the music well chosen for that film. Had you preselected all the songs?

Some of them. There were some things in the script we couldn't get. I couldn't afford David Bowie's *Heroes*. It boiled down to who was willing to be kind to us. Peter Gabriel was incredibly kind, and worked with us, as was Kate Bush, and some of the other people. And some people just weren't interested. They were like, "My song will cost you $100,000; call me when you've got it."

The style of the film is somewhat non-naturalistic, almost absurdist. There are lots of subjective images and dream sequences.

I've always been drawn to people like Kubrick, Roeg, Truffaut, and Sidney Lumet. I seem to be drawn to this weird mix of stylization, but with humanity. And that was what I was trying to achieve, a somewhat absurdist, somewhat distanced movie that you still got emotionally involved in. And that runs through all my films.

You use a lot of long takes in the film. Do you think that comes from your understanding and respect for the acting process?

A little. I think it also came from the fact that I like long takes in films, and find them more interesting. It's not just understanding the acting process, it's more interesting in a certain kind of movie to watch a scene unfold. Style is often dictated by economic realities.

And when you've got to shoot seven or eight pages a day, you don't have time to do all sorts of coverage. Most of what I do, I do out of instinct.

There's a lot of moving camera in the film.

I love subjectivity in film and that's one way to communicate it. I love point-of-view shots, and I love shots that make you feel what the character's feeling. Again, it's that weird "Kubrickian" thing, like when Alex is beating people up in *A Clockwork Orange*—you get involved with the thrill of that. As much as you're being repelled by it, your heart's also beating, and there's something very sexy and very involving about it. Something about the circling camera makes you feel uncomfortable.

Where do you think Renault [Ian Mitchell-Smith] is at the end of the film? How much of a rebellion has he really made?

Ultimately, his rebellion failed, which is what's tragic about it. The guy has gone through all of this, and I believe he's right when he says, " I didn't change anything." But even that realization is a growth. I don't think it was pointless. I don't agree that he should have just sold the chocolates. Ultimately, it was a failed attempt to do something wonderful, and he ended up serving the system he wanted to bring down. It was a cautionary tale.

It seems a very accurate portrait of Catholic school.

I didn't go to Catholic school. I went to a comparatively liberal school, but I still knew that sense of not fitting in, so I think it's more about adolescence. That film was also about power, and the problem with power anywhere.

How was that film received?

Critically, we did very well. I was real happy, and somewhat surprised. It never made a lot of money, but it did make money in relation to its cost. That was probably my most successful film so far, in terms of cost-to-return. It did well on video because of the book—schools bought a lot of copies. Theatrically, it also did well, in terms of playing in a lot of cities for a number of weeks, and getting good reviews. It worked its way around the country.

What was the genesis of *A Midnight Clear*?

That was brought to me by Dale Pollock, who was one of the producers. He had seen *The Chocolate War* and said, "Look, I liked your movie. Let's talk about this. Why don't you read the book?" I read the book, and I said, "The way to make this is to keep it inexpensive. Make this film for a few million dollars. Don't make it for $25 million. If you do, you won't be able to make your money back." So, I wrote a script, which they were happy with.

Was it difficult to adapt William Wharton's novel?

More than the script for *The Chocolate War*, which is a short book written very cinematically. *A Midnight Clear* was the first one where I had to take a 400-page book and edit like crazy. There were things in the book I didn't like, that I thought were too heavy-handed, but I liked the overall feel of it. So, there was more work to do, but the book and movie are still very similar.

Why does the film use a first-person, voice-over point of view?

I wanted it to be a very subjective experience of war. There's never a point-of-view shot that's not his, and there are a lot in that movie. There's never a scene that he's not in. It's always his experience, so in that sense, it's very subjective. I thought it would be more powerful to see a specific point of view. I thought it was such a surreal story that if it wasn't specific, it would look like I was just making some kind of surrealistic comment instead of the way it was experienced by this particular young guy.

Did you ever think about playing more with the voice-over? It's fairly straightforward narration.

If anything, we cut it down at points, because it started to get too obtrusive, and it was telling you too much that you were already seeing. I had terrible fights with the money people and the producing staff on that film. Ultimately, there are many things in the final edit of the film that are not my choices. It's still my movie, but it's the only experience I've had where not everything is mine, including where there's voice-over and when there isn't. That was not a happy experience, and that experience almost made me stop making movies. I went through a real depression, and just thought, "I don't want to do that anymore. It's horrible."

The actual shoot itself was not unhappy?

Oh, it was terrible. The actors were wonderful, and the creative process was wonderful, but I was having my ass kicked every day by the money people. I was told every day I could be fired, my cinematographer could be fired, that I was a hired hand, and they didn't care if I had written the script. And the producers also didn't like each other, so basically I became a child of a bad divorce. It would be one in the morning, and I'd be trying to sleep when the phone would ring: One producer would say, "We don't like the green of that wall. What are you going to do about it? We can fire you!" And then I'd hang up, and the phone would ring again. It would be another producer crying, "Did that son-of-a-bitch just call you? He's not your boss, I'm your boss. If you listen to him, you're fired!" Every day on the set, people financing the movie would come over and say, "We have to talk about the dailies from last night!" I have actors and crew there, and I'm going, "Guys, we're on the clock now. Do we have to talk about it right now?"

One time, one of the producers flew up when we were shooting on this mountain. We had to snowmobile up and back to do the scenes. He said, "We have to talk!" And, I said, "God, can't we wait 'til lunch?" "All right, all right. I'll wait." He stood there to irritate me, for the whole day. Everyone else went to lunch but he stayed on this mountain alone with me and said:

"We saw the last scene of the film."
"Yes?"

"It's really sad."
"Well, yes."

"No, I mean, it's *really* sad."
"Well, that's how it is in the script."

"Yeah, but it's like *sad*."
"Well, we talked about it. This is a movie about the death of a soul."

"Can't we just make a movie about the *wounding* of a soul?"

The whole experience was like that. At a certain point, I just dug in my heels and said, "This is the script, fire me if you want to." Everybody on that film thought they were a writer. It made it much harder to stay open to even good ideas, because there was just too much coming in. That was my education in what Hollywood could be like, although it was in fact all independent money. It was tough in that way, and I think it affects the final film.

There are things that I would have done differently. I'm fine with almost everything in the film but there are a lot of minor things I'm unhappy with. There were pieces of music I wanted that I wasn't allowed to have. There are pieces of music that I didn't want to have that are in the film. There are shots I wanted in the movie that aren't in the movie.

You got a very good group of actors for that film.

Yes, we spent a long time on the casting process and fought a lot because they didn't want my choices. I was being pushed to use that week's teen star. I kept trying to point out, "By the time this movie comes out, this person won't be hot anymore, and you'll be sorry you've got them in your movie." Again, I ultimately won those battles, but it wasted a lot of time and energy.

How did you work with some of the actors on their characterizations?

On that film, we had two weeks of rehearsal, and it was really fun. You could have had a bunch of young actors together and their egos could have been all over the place, but they weren't. They were just cool people. We rehearsed every day for two weeks. We did a little more improvisation, because they were more experienced actors. We also put them through a minor military training with some local militia guys. They learned how to be soldiers, and they bonded. We didn't have girlfriends around. They ate together. They played ball together. They did everything together all day for the two weeks before shooting, so by the time we started, they had histories with each other.

Dramatically, the sequence where the boys and Germans try to stage that fake skirmish, which goes horribly wrong, is one of the high points of the film.

I wanted the death of Father [Frank Whaley] to be hard to look at. I wanted it to be like a real death, not a movie death. I wanted it to be bloody and ugly. I wanted blood dripping from his mouth. We've seen so many war movies where death is glorious and heroic, and I wanted his death to be painful and tough to take. That's why I get very close on his face, and on the wound. I wanted some tension, and to make you think it was going all right. When it went wrong, I wanted you to experience their shock. So we made the same dolly tracking move past the German soldiers over and over again. You get very lulled by it. It's only by the third or fourth time you see that somebody suddenly is shot in the middle of it. I tried to frame it so when he got shot, he wasn't perfectly center-framed. The camera just keeps going, and doesn't stop on the guy who's been shot. You sense that something could go wrong, but when it does go wrong, it's not where you're looking. It's a little sleight-of-hand thing.

The religious symbolism in the film, the washing of the body, the transporting the body on a cross, the Christmas setting: How much of that is from the novel?

Certainly the feel of it is from the novel. The incidents are from the novel. If anything, I pushed it further because I like people trying to find meaning in the most meaningless thing. Being in a war is the most anti-religious act there is, and here are people trying to find some grace in it. I'm an atheist Jew, but to me it doesn't matter what the religion is, it's about finding a sense of ceremony, and meaning, and grace. They found it in something that is vaguely Catholic. But the incidents are in the book, and the idea of washing Father's body was in the book. It wasn't something that I created, although I tried to get more of a *pietà* feeling to it.

It's clear you believe in the concept of a just war. Do you think it's possible to remain a humanist in the midst of war?

Well, that's the question. I think it's possible to try. At a certain point, as a participant, you can't. And that's the problem. To me, that is the dilemma of World War II, because, yes, you had to stop Hitler. You had to go to war. But the second you do, you are condemning souls to death, not just the people who were literally killed, but the Will Knotts [Ethan Hawke], the people who come back forever scarred. My conversation with the producer was about that, the death of the soul. I mean, Will can never be the same. He may grow up, he may have children, he may have a life. But he has lost a very deep part of himself because he's been involved in the killing of other human beings who are innocent. I don't know how you can send a bunch of innocent young people to kill a bunch of other innocent young people, and not do permanent damage. And yet, there are certain times when you can't avoid it. I think it's one of those horrible dilemmas of human existence. And certainly, for every just war, there have been fifty unjust wars. I think you can probably count the number of just wars on one hand.

The pace of *A Midnight Clear* is nice. It's steady, but it never feels rushed. Was it tricky to maintain that?

Yes, particularly in light of the producers all having different scenes they thought should be cut out, put back in. Pacing was one of the hardest things because everybody had their two cents about the structure of the film. Some people argue that the film is too slow, but I like that pace. I like the idea of a war film that is deliberate, and all about mood. This film is as much about mood as it is about incident.

There are incidents, but the mood that the action creates is just as important. None of the producers liked it. So, I had to fight for it. It was amazing when the reviews came out on that film: All the producers who hated me suddenly called me up and said, "Oh, congratulations, we always knew it was a wonderful film; we were always in your corner."

It strikes me that you're interested in creating somewhat classical films. They're character-driven, with strong structures, and character empathy is important, although they are also stylistically interesting.

I am interested in time and space, but only in how they inform character. My films reflect what I am interested in seeing. I make movies that I want to see. I was raised on seventies movies, on Kubrick, Pakula, Lumet. Films like *Klute* or *The Parallax View* or *Three Days of the Condor* are all stylish, but not about style. I grew up on movies that combine style and content in wonderful ways, like *The Conversation* or *The Godfather*, as opposed to a lot of what I see now, which is style for style's sake. Really neat shots that don't tell me anything new about these people. So, yes, for me, that's a goal, because those are the movies I like. You can't make a more stylized movie than *The Conversation*, but it's all telling you about Harry Caul [Gene Hackman], and why he is the way he is. There's not a shot or cut, or sound in that movie that isn't informing you about that man and his paranoia, and his sense of loss. To me, that is what a good film is.

What's your relationship like with your editor? Do you work very closely together?

Yes, I'm not somebody who goes away and lets somebody else cut the movie. On *The Chocolate War*, the editor sent me his first couple of days of cut footage. I said, "Just stop right now. Do not cut anything more. I will be there soon." And we cut the film from scratch, together. Since then, I've let the editors do assembly, but then I'm in the editing room all day, every day. I don't give notes and then go away. This new film [*Waking The Dead*] is my first film cut on the

Avid system. It's an experiment since I'm shooting and don't have time to go to the editing room. The editor sends me cuts of scenes, and I send notes back on what he's done. But once we get in there for my ten-week cut, I'll be there all day and every day, and I'll be very specific about what I want to try and what I want to do.

When did your television work start?

About a year or so after *A Midnight Clear.*

You took acting jobs during that time?

No, I was just trying to put projects together. Most of my life since *The Chocolate War* has been having meetings and chasing down money. *Mother Night* took six years of ridiculous, silly money-chasing. We had Anthony Hopkins, we lost Anthony Hopkins. We had European money, we lost European money. It's just this roller-coaster, which was going on before, during, and after *A Midnight Clear.* It's so hard to get somebody to give you money to make a movie that has any artistic pretensions. If you don't have a car blowing up and naked women, you're already on an uphill battle.

Did you take the television work just to be doing something?

Yes, but they were still interesting jobs. I have never taken jobs I didn't like. I haven't done something just for money.

Wild Palms was really interesting. I liked the people involved. I went in and said, "I don't know how to do this. I've never done this before." And they said, "Look, we're getting feature directors, and we want you to bring your style. We don't want to tell you what to do. Oliver Stone's attitude was "Let's get good directors and let them make these little movies." It wasn't as dear to my heart as certain things, but it was fun. And, because it wasn't mine, if it didn't work, who cares? It's a TV show, and Oliver will take the blame. It was the perfect antidote at that moment. It also paid the bills, which was great, but more than that, it was a chance to have a good time. And I liked working with the other directors, especially Kathryn Bigelow. Because we were working at the same time, we could go to each other's editing rooms.

What about *Homicide*?

Homicide was less fun. It was a series I really liked, and still like. The problem for me was, unlike *Wild Palms*, I didn't feel they were very interested in what I had to bring to it. They were enmeshed in their style, almost to an absurd point. I knew I was in trouble when, on the second day, we shot the end of the episode. It was supposed to end on the Andre Braugher character sitting on the steps of a church. It was a very sad, lost ending because they found the murderer, but he'd lost his faith. I shot that scene on a tripod, and I did not move the camera. The whole idea of the story was he had come to a point where he's stuck, the story's stuck, there's nowhere to go. I thought, "Okay, we were moving the camera during the whole show; in this scene we're not moving the camera." Well, the next day, the executive calls: "We move the camera in this show. Every scene!" I said, "Well, yes, but I'm making a point." "No, no, no. We can't!" So, they made me reshoot the scene with a moving camera, at which point I thought, "Okay, you don't want me. You guys know what you want. Why am I here?"

Then you're given two days to edit, and I edited it in the way that I wanted. It was completely re-edited into something that bore no relation to what I did. There were scenes that I hate that were put back in. There were scenes that I love that were taken out. I also don't like the convention of arbitrary jump-cuts. I like them when they mean something. So, when I cut my version of it, the only jump-cuts I had were informing you of something. And it was, "No, no, no. We put jump-cuts in every five minutes. There has to be a jump-cut." It was that kind of thing. Whenever I look at it, it's just not mine. It's fine, but it has nothing to do with me.

The main reason I took the job was that there was a twelve-minute interrogation sequence all in one room. To me, that was the most interesting thing about the episode—they were stuck in this room. Of course, they intercut it with five other things, which blew the whole structure of the story, and blew the way I shot it. If I'd known they were going to do that, I wouldn't have shot it the way I did. The shot was designed to keep you in this very tight place.

Will you talk about how *Mother Night* came about?

Bob Weide, who wrote the script and produced it with me, is one of my oldest buddies. He's very close to Vonnegut, and a very good documentary filmmaker in his own right, and has been doing a documentary on Kurt for years. We started talking about doing a project together, and Bob brought up *Mother Night* as a book of Kurt's that was comparatively linear, and could be done on a relatively small budget. So, Bob wrote a script while I was doing *Midnight Clear*. He'd never written a feature script before, but he wrote this really good script. I didn't have to do anything to it except edit it down. And Kurt loved it. Everybody loved the script, but no one would make it, because it was too dark. In Hollywood, they have these little one-sentence sum-ups, like "Young boy falls in love and beats up villain." Ours was "Nice Nazi hangs self." It wasn't exactly something to get people to hand over the cash.

We almost had it come together several times. It was a long, long road. Nick Nolte was actually the first person I ever tried to send the script to, and his agent said, "No, he's not interested." This was years earlier. Then five or six years later, Fine Line said "We'll make this movie, but there are three actors we'll make the movie with: Nick Nolte, Robert DeNiro, or Daniel Day-Lewis." So, we went back to Nick Nolte, and again his agent said, "He's not interested in doing this." I know how often agents say that, and it means the actor never saw it. So, as luck would have it, the casting director on *I Love Trouble* called me and said, "I know you're not really acting anymore, but I'm doing this movie, *I Love Trouble*, and we're getting all these New York actors to do little cameos. Do you want to be in it?" I said, "If you can put me in a scene with Nick Nolte, I'll do it." I didn't want to tell her what my real motives were. I have two lines in *I Love Trouble* as Andy the photographer.

The first night I was there, I started chatting with Nick and said, "I'm only here for one reason, and that's to give you a script." Luckily, Nick is the nicest, most gracious man in the world. He said, "No, I like Kurt Vonnegut, and my assistant tells me your films are good. Give me the script, and I'll read it." And I gave him the script. Weeks went by and I didn't hear anything, and then I got a call from the assistant, who said, "Um, Nick lost your script. Can you send another copy?" I sent the script and weeks went by again, and I didn't hear anything. Meanwhile, we were chasing Robert DeNiro, and he wasn't interested, and we couldn't even find Daniel Day-Lewis. Then I get this call on my answering machine, going, "Hi. It's Nick Nolte. It's great! I want to do it. Come up to the house." I went up to his house in Malibu, and we spent four hours talking about how I like to work, how he likes to work, how I saw the film, how he saw the character. When I left, he said, "I'm in. I don't care about the money, I don't care about anything, I want to do this movie." We just caught him at a good moment. He'd done all these big Hollywood movies, and he wasn't having fun. He wanted to be an actor again.

Did Vonnegut have any input into the film?

Bob sent him the script. But he never really gave notes or anything. He said he was really pleased with the script, and he was always very articulate about saying, "A movie is a movie and a book is a book, and if you guys want to make this movie, I trust you." He loved *A Midnight Clear*, because it was his experience of the war. He had been an intelligence and reconnaissance guy in one of those platoons where it was only really intelligent guys. It spoke to him. So, he felt confident in me as a filmmaker, and he'd known Bob for years. If anything, he felt flattered and pleased by our passion. I think he also felt a little burned on things like *Slapstick*, where they had taken his book and thrown it out the window.

What was important to you in terms of remaining faithful to the integrity of his work?

Well, not being afraid, first of all. We were dealing with the Holocaust, and making jokes. We felt it was important not to be afraid of mixing humor and drama. It was important to let each scene have its integrity, because what Kurt does so wonderfully is make you laugh and then punch you in the stomach, and then make you laugh again. You never quite gain your equilibrium. We really wanted to do that with the film. Part of the challenge was also creating different eras, and shifting between black and white and color.

Did you do much research for the film?

I didn't have to do much, because Nick Nolte does more research than any human being in the history of the planet. I've never seen an actor work the way Nick works. Nick is the most tireless, relentless guy you've ever seen. He read every book written about the Holocaust, about writers during the Holocaust, about spies during the Holocaust. He wrote his own biography of the character. He wrote biographies of every character that he would have known in the film. There's a huge book I have at home of what Nick created for this character. So, Nick became our researcher. It was fabulous because he loves to share what he's found.

He had tapes of German propaganda and American propaganda. He was looking for a sympathetic, friendly voice, so he started listening to Arthur Godfrey tapes. Nick was an amazing resource. I did some reading, but I didn't want to do too much, because it is an artificial world. We weren't even pretending to recreate the Third Reich. We were creating a Kurt Vonnegut Third Reich.

Nolte is great in it. He's very moving.

He is so wonderful to work with. I think he is the best actor I've worked with to date because he combines the best of everything. He understands film, he knows what cameras do, he knows what lenses do. He was making suggestions like, "If I move here, the shadow's going to hit me this weird way." But at the same time, he's very much an actor who is in the moment, who can improvise. He just brings those two disciplines together in a completely seamless way. Just easy, and funny, and doesn't take the whole thing too seriously, even playing such a heavy character.

Was the structure pretty much as it was in the script?

In general, yes. The film was very long. Our first assembly was three hours and fifteen minutes, and the final film is an hour and fifty. So, a lot of material disappeared. There was this fabulous eight minute scene with David Strathairn, who played O'Hare. A scene between Nick and him at the end that was amazing. I was really heartbroken to let it go.

The movie has some nice stylistic qualities. What were some of your ideas for the film's style?

I liked the idea of slow zooms. We'd start on a detail in a room, then slowly reveal where you are. You always start not knowing what's going on, and then slowly find out, just as Howard is finding out himself. Certain shots, I just knew I wanted, like the shot of Nolte up through the typewriter keys. It was something I knew I wanted for months before we shot. I didn't know how we'd do it, but I thought, "Oh, the typewriter keys on an old typewriter can look like the bars of a cell. Let's do something with that!"

Some of the material with Dr. Jones [Bernard Behrens] is played for black humor, almost burlesque. Was it hard striking the right tone for that material, and marrying it with the other scenes?

Marrying it was the hard part, getting it to blend was hard. *Mother Night* is an atypical Vonnegut book. Some people, who didn't like the movie, said it wasn't funny enough, and that we lost Kurt's humor. But this book is not as funny as Kurt's other books. This book has a lot of serious stretches, leavened by the odd sudden blitz of comedy, as opposed to the more overall comedy of, say, *Breakfast of Champions*. We tried to stay true to that.

What are your views about Howard Campbell, Nolte's character? Is his notion of trying to separate private and public morality a doomed idea?

Doomed and wildly selfish. Nick always said that, ultimately, it's not a film about an evil man, but a selfish man. It's a film about a man who wants to have his own reality, and doesn't see the real world. He doesn't really do evil, and he'd like to do good.

Nick's performance is very sympathetic.

I don't take the Hollywood view that a flawed character is a character you can't sympathize with. We're all selfish to some extent. It doesn't mean you can't feel for someone who is selfish. It doesn't mean that Howard Campbell is a bad person. Nick and I felt that the flaws of the character made him lovable and interesting.

The character presents some complex moral questions because of his role as a propagandist for the Nazis, which is as damaging as whatever good he might have done as an American spy. Also, since the government created him, they have to bear some responsibility for the situation.

Our goal was always to have people walk out of the theater and argue. For me, the interesting thing in art or filmmaking is to raise questions. I mean, I'm thirty-seven years old. I don't have a lot of answers. I don't know what the meaning of life is. I don't know what's good, what's bad. But I know there are good questions to ask, so I feel I'm doing my job if I can make people think about that stuff.

It takes a certain kind of arrogance to tell people what to think.

My own life feels full of compromise, morally. Life is nothing but moral choices, and I flounder around as much as anybody, but I like to get people to think about it. What I love about Kubrick's films, or Roeg's films, is walking out and saying, "I have to think about this. I don't know what's right or wrong." In *A Clockwork Orange*, is Alex ultimately a victim or a hero? I don't know if Harry Caul is ultimately a victim or a hero. I love the puzzle. It's what a good book does, and I think that runs through all my films. I'd love, at the end of my movies, for people not quite to know how they feel. To be moved, yes, but not quite know. Then I've done something.

How do you think Howard saw his actions? Did he really believe he helped the Allied cause?

I honestly believe that he could care less about helping the Allied cause. I believe he was apolitical. I think he was a ham, a guy who was really self-centered, an actor in a writer's body, who didn't want to hurt anybody. He relished the role, and it was a chance to leave some of the pain of his life behind. He had this horrible childhood, this horrible life, and here was his chance to be his greatest creation. It's an act of tremendous ego. At the same time, he gets Brownie points for doing a good thing. I'm sure he didn't love the Nazis, but as Nick would always say, he didn't hate them, either. They paid his salary. If you were a playwright working in Berlin at that point, it meant the Nazis liked you.

But if he was really apolitical, would he be in that position? It's already a political act.

It's the difference between a political act and a moral act, which is what Kurt Vonnegut more than anyone writes about. He doesn't say, "Do you hate the Nazis?" He says, "Do you believe in good?" It's different. Believing in good is a trap, because it reduces things to simplistics. That's where Howard gets into trouble. He thinks it can be reduced to good and bad, and suddenly it doesn't work that way.

Does Howard achieve redemption for his actions?

I think he does. I always loved the idea that the only real thing Howard does is kill himself. It's the only time he takes control of his life. A lot of the movie is ultimately about passivity. To me, there's a great parallel between him and some members of the Nazi party. Most people in Germany who joined the Nazi party probably didn't support the Nazis, but they did what was easy. It was how you moved up socially, and there were perks that went with it. So, you went along with the tide. Howard went with the tide wherever it took him. Until he is in that jail cell, and looks at that last page of his life, and decides, "I'm going to kill myself. They're not going to judge me. They're not going to set me free. I'm judging me, okay? I'm making this decision. I don't care if anybody thinks I'm not guilty. I am guilty." And to me, that's an heroic moment. That's a moment of grace.

One of the great things about the movie is your choice of Arvo Pärt's music. It's a brilliant stroke because it adds great emotional weight.

That was the one thing I had to fight with Fine Line about. They wanted a more traditional score. As it was, they got Michael Convertino to write in the style of Avro Pärt, and mixed it with Pärt's music. I didn't go in knowing that was the music I wanted, but I went in suspecting that I wanted some kind of modernist classical music. Howard is emotionally stuck. I knew that most classical scores or a John Williams kind of score, would have too much emotion in it. What I love about Arvo Pärt is that the music doesn't change, but it breaks your heart anyway. That to me was Howard. He's stuck on the street. He's not going anywhere, but he still gets to you.

How do you feel about it as a film?

I like the film a lot. I'm very proud of it, but there are places where the transitions from comedy to drama or back again don't work as well as I wish they did. I think they're too jarring. I think they alienated people.

Do you feel that *Mother Night* is a directorial leap for you from *A Midnight Clear*?

In some ways, it feels like a leap, and in some ways it just feels evolutionary. It's a leap in that it is the most ambitious film I've done. *The Chocolate War* was very small scale, and in its own way *A Midnight Clear* is very contained. *Mother Night* jumps around in time and place a lot more. It's a much bigger movie. It's a leap in terms of working with actors of Nick's stature. It's a leap in terms of stylistically going from black and white to color. In some ways, I feel *A Midnight Clear* is a more finely realized film, or a more complete film, but I think *Mother Night* is a more ambitious film.

You've had bad luck with distribution for your films?

Yes, it's not my strong point. But I'd rather have a great experience making a movie and a bad experience with distribution than the other way around. Having had the nightmare of *A Midnight Clear* took a lot out of me. *Mother Night* was sad, but I still made the movie I wanted to make. I'm still proud of the movie. Ultimately, whether

10,000 people or ten million people see the movie, it's still the movie I wanted it to be.

Waking the Dead **is also an adaptation. All four of your films are adaptations. How faithful to the material do you have to be as a filmmaker?**

I feel I have to be faithful to why I liked it in the first place. There's a tendency in Hollywood movies to take wonderful books and then throw out the character, the structure, the dialogue, the settings, and then wonder why the film doesn't work. Good books are largely cinematic. They have a lot of the same elements. I'm very happy to re-write scenes or add scenes or subtract scenes. I think part of the advantage of being a director-writer, instead of a writer-for-hire, is that I don't have to prove anything. I'm the first to say I'll steal what is good from William Wharton. I'll use all his dialogue wherever I can. Scott Spencer's a better writer than I am. So, if there's stuff from *Waking The Dead* that I can use right out of that book, I'm going to use it. I'm only going to write what I need to write, as a filmmaker, to make it work as my cinematic vision. But I don't go in feeling I have to put my stamp on it. My stamp is going to be put on as a director.

Do you still consider yourself an actor?

Well, I don't consider myself a non-actor. Put it this way, it isn't on my tax returns anymore.

So you consider yourself a director.

Yes, a filmmaker, a director-writer, a director-writer-producer. I found that on small films, the only way to do it is to be a producer. It makes a big difference. *A Midnight Clear* is the last film I will ever make that I do not produce.

Are there big distinctions between being an independent director and working within the Hollywood system?

Waking The Dead is an independent film, but it's certainly not an independent film the way *The Chocolate War* was. *Waking The Dead* is an $8.5 million film, made by Polygram Films, with Jodie Foster's company, Egg Pictures. You could make a really good argument that this is not an independent movie. On the other hand, compared to a world where the average film is $40 million, and this material would probably not get made, it is very independent. It's all relative. I know I want to continue to make films that are mine. I don't care if they cost $40 million or $400,000.

I don't have an anti-studio attitude. To me, it's in the material. And as somebody who reads ten scripts a week, the reality is that the studios are doing a lot of garbage. When I get a studio script that's wonderful, I know one of two things is going to happen: It will never get made, or if it does, I ain't gonna be the one who'll get to make it. Because somebody bigger, and hotter, and more famous than I am will get first crack at it. I've come close a couple of times, but it's always ended up that I've lost out to people who were just bigger names, which is okay.

What is the most difficult part of being a director? Is it dealing with the business side of it?

Certainly it's the least pleasant. That's the part that I wish I didn't have to do. I wish I had that producer relationship that Quentin Tarantino probably had with Lawrence Bender, where somebody else does the dirty work and sets up the deal. Somebody else structures it and does the initial budgeting. Somebody else fights those fights. I hate meetings. I hate selling people on how much money my movie's going to make for them. I don't know how much money my movie's going to make, even if it's a really good movie. I mean, I'm going around with *Waking The Dead*, saying, "It's *The English Patient* meets *Ghost.*" But I don't know how much money it will make. I know it's a good movie, and I'm really proud about how it's turning out. But I don't know if people are going to go see it. Sometimes I feel like Howard Campbell. I feel like I'm selling my soul.

What is the best part of being a director?

Getting to create your own reality. There are so many things, it's hard to highlight one thing. Working with actors is wonderful. Right now I'm working with Billy Crudup, a young actor who is very talented and still forming, and helping him get a performance. There's emotionally wrenching stuff in this movie, and I'm helping him get to places that he didn't know he could reach—some very dark, raw places in his soul.

Last night, we were creating this artificial snowstorm in the middle of the warmest day of the winter in Montreal. On some pure level, you're creating magic. It's amazing. I was like a little kid. I said, "Look at what we're doing, we're creating our own reality. We're making a world to tell a story." To me, that's exciting, and doing it with people you like is very exciting. I enjoy everything about it. There's something about being on that set, when it goes right. And it doesn't go right every day. But when that thing happens, when the actor, and the light, and the moment come together, you go "Wow. This is bigger than me." I love shooting. But I'm terrified when we're shooting. The producer in me is always a nervous wreck when I'm shooting. I'm terrified of the budget. All my films are made on limited budgets. You make this pact with the devil: "If I come in on budget, you leave me alone." On a movie like this, for example, we have no contingency. I wanted everything on the screen, so that means if anything goes wrong, I'm dead.

On the set, I just break down and weep sometimes. There was a scene in this film we were doing a couple of weeks ago, where this love of Billy's life, who is dead, calls him on the phone. And we improvised the scene. I'd written it out very floridly, and we did a couple of takes. Then I said, "Okay, now just tell your story." And he started doing it and started crying, and I started crying.

You know what it is about shooting? There's no way you know what is going to happen when you're shooting. If you're going to make a good movie, there's a certain amount of complete uncontrollability. I can have all the shot lists in the world, but there's something that's going to happen that day that we could not have prepared for. Editing is much more predictable. You know which scenes you're going to work on, what ideas you want to try, but on the shoot, anything can happen. Some days are good, some days are bad. Some days the actors aren't cooking, or the light doesn't quite work, but it's full of adventure.

Editing is a really intriguing puzzle, but it's a more cerebral process. There's nothing about filmmaking I don't enjoy, but editing's more removed, it's much more cooly solving a puzzle.

What's the most crucial thing about film directing you've learned in the last few years?

To keep the joy of it alive. And not only for my sanity, but for the quality of the movie. The more I can find the joy in that magic, the better the movie's going to be. The more I resist things, the worse it is. I have to let it be what it's going to be. My job, more than anything else, is to bring the best out of everybody around me.

NICHOLAS HYTNER

Before Nicholas Hytner embarked on a film directing career, he was a highly regarded theater director in Britain and New York, a parallel career which he maintains along with his increasingly frequent film assignments. Hytner's films are characterized by an awareness of earlier film traditions and a conviction that popular work can still be intelligent, stylish, and imaginative. Hytner's first film, *The Madness of King George*, confirmed he was as well suited to the film medium as he was to the theatrical world of The Royal National Theatre and Broadway. Exuberantly and unabashedly theatrical, *King George* featured superb performances from a brilliant cast headed by Nigel Hawthorne and Helen Mirren. The film takes a scathing look at the eighteenth-century monarchy while offering an intimate view of marriage and a virtual treatise on medicine of the time. Describing *The Madness of King George* as theatrical might give the inaccurate impression that it is a stage-bound film. In fact, *King George* dynamically embraces the film medium. It is a stylistically audacious film that dazzlingly evokes the era.

King George was followed by Hytner's screen version of Arthur Miller's *The Crucible*, a play about the Salem witch trials written in the early fifties. The play itself notoriously drew strong parallels between the seventeenth-century witch hunts and the anticommunist McCarthy hearings at the time. But transposing the work to the nineties proved a daunting task for Hytner. The film was not a commercial success, despite strong performances from Daniel Day-Lewis, Winona Ryder, Paul Scofield, and Joan Allen and, once again, bold stylistic choices on the part of the director and his collaborators. What may have been a miscalculation was the notion that contemporary audiences, and in particular young audiences, would be interested in such a strong morality tale in an era that seems to have lost its moral compass.

Hytner followed the tragic high drama of *The Crucible* with the stylish romantic comedy *The Object of My Affection*, co-written with American playwright Wendy Wasserstein, a film which not only takes an intelligent, mature view of gay relationships but also evokes the best of Hollywood in its allusions to screwball comedy and the musical. He recently completed *Center Stage*, a film set in the ballet world, and is preparing the film version of *Chicago*, Bob Fosse's stylized musical set in the twenties. In only four films, Hytner has covered a remarkable range of cinematic genres including historical drama, the musical, and romantic comedy. His film work is proving as varied and astonishing as his stage work. Although Hytner has deep roots in the theater, his films never sacrifice the integrity or uniqueness of the film medium. I spoke with Nicholas Hytner in New York City.

Let's start with your background. Where did you grow up?

I was born and brought up in Manchester [England]. I went to school there.

Did you see a lot of films growing up? What kind of films were you attracted to?

I did see a lot, and my taste was very eclectic. Like everybody in my generation, the French and Italian cinemas seemed to be the most interesting, the most alive in the sixties. When I started to go to the movies, Truffaut was still working, Fellini was still working, Bergman was still working. The European art cinema was alive and kicking. But the stuff that was easiest to see was the American cinema. My influences are incredibly catholic.

Did this notion of commercial and art cinema inflect your theater aesthetic, and how you directed theater and opera?

The interesting thing about English theater—and this applies to English moviemaking as well, although perhaps not to someone whose vision is as severe and single-minded as Terence Davies—is that it exists absolutely straddling the art theater of continental Europe and the commercial theater of the U.S. Each nation's theater springs from the flowering of its classic period. From the social circumstances of each nation's classic theater you can derive the way theater in that country operates now. The American theater was a commercial theater, the Broadway theater, so the great American playwrights sprang from Broadway. In France, they sprang from the court of Louis XIV; it was a court theater. It was a kind of intellectual court theater in Germany, invented self-consciously, in that very German way, by Goethe and Schiller, and it still has that severe, self-inventing experimentation. It's very definitely an art theater. The English theater, as everything else in England, is an uneasy mix of commercialism and state subsidy. Elizabethan theater had to earn its keep at the box office, but wouldn't have survived without patronage from the Monarch or the Lord Chamberlain or whoever patronized the company. That still operates. We still are brought up in a kind of quasi-academic tradition. As I said, my training is classical theater. There is no real director training available in Britain as there is in France and Germany, although there is a little more now than there was when I was growing up.

Did you go to theater school?

No. Like so many of us, I had an academic training. I went to Cambridge, read English, and studied and directed a lot of theater. My background and training is in classical theater. As soon as I was old enough, I was regularly going to the theater in Manchester, which was very lively. I was going to London and Stratford as often as I could. When I left Cambridge, I briefly tried to be an actor, but I realized I was no good. In the absence of a talent either to act or to write, I wanted to learn how to direct. The English theater is geared to a system of informal apprenticeships. You're expected either to act or to stage-manage, which I did. I was stage-manager, then an assistant, and eventually I was directing stuff of my own in the regional repertory theaters. During this time, it remained a fantasy that one day I might direct a movie but it wasn't what I was learning.

You had it in the back of your mind to direct a film?

Always. The British culture is a theatrical culture and you have to be very determined to flourish as a filmmaker. When I was a kid, it never occurred to me that it was possible to make movies in England. It all seemed dead. In any event, I was very much a creature of the theater. Although we saw as much film as we did theater, it all seemed to come from continental Europe or the U.S., and very little seemed to be going on in England in the sixties, apart from the obvious stuff.

I qualify the statement that essentially the English culture is a theatrical culture. It's changed now. Nowadays, any theatrical culture exists in the context of what is essentially an international cinematic culture. It's not altogether unhealthy for the theater. It encourages you in the theater to focus on what is quintessentially theatrical. By the time I got a chance to do lavish shows on a grand scale—and I did two or three, such as *Miss Saigon*, before I recoiled in horror— the shows were imitative of the movies.

One thing I got to do relatively early on was direct musicals and opera, which broadens your horizons in terms of scale. Technically, as a director, it was enormously helpful. When I eventually came to direct a movie, the one thing I wasn't daunted by was the scale of it. There's nothing more daunting than putting on a Broadway musical. Technically, it's as difficult as directing in any medium. There's just so much to do.

How did directing theater and opera in the late seventies through the eighties affect your work as a film director?

Well, it's easier to say how my experience as a moviegoer impacted the theater work, because in a sense there's only one proper way of being a theater director in today's international cinematic culture, and that is to be monastic about it in the way Peter Brook is. The job in the movies is to write the script. As far as filmmakers are concerned, the difference is between the ones who write and the ones who don't. I specifically don't. I've always worked with writers for whom I not only have respect, but affection, even awe. Arthur Miller, for example.

Obviously, directing for the theater gives you a different sense of how to work with actors. Working in opera gives you a different sense of how to use mise-en-scène.

Opera is a tricky one. That's another conversation. [Laughs] Yes, you come to the movies with the experience of six-week rehearsal periods and three weeks of previews. Quite often, the process in a theater rehearsal is to recreate the spontaneity you get the first time you read through it. Sometimes, if you cast it right, the first time you read through a play is dazzling. It takes you six weeks to recapture that because the process of performing a play involves being spontaneous eight times a week. You have to examine all options and reject those that stand in the way of an apparent reproduction of spontaneity each night. I didn't realize until I'd made *The Madness of King George* that you have to stop rehearsing a movie at the point where your theatrical experience tells you it's about to dissolve.

It was interesting with *The Madness of King George*, because half of us had done it for two years in the theater. Half of us could have rehearsed six weeks and it wouldn't have harmed us, because we already knew it. But for those who came to it new, I realized very quickly I couldn't push it much further right away. I do obviously rehearse in detail. One of the things that coming from the theater enables you to do is to speak with precision and economy to actors. I realized then that working with actors in movies requires a different technique, obviously a precision that enables and encourages an actor to strike out in a new and unexpected direction, but essentially less of that kind of vaguely democratic atmosphere of discovery that you encourage in rehearsal in the theater. Only the film director knows how one scene is going to cut with the previous one or the next one: That's the job. In the sense that an actor is totally dependent on the director to know that, the director's function is clearer with an actor in the movies than it is in the theater. In the theater, an actor, within a six-week rehearsal period, can gain as great a feel for the totality of the event as the director can, but not in a movie. Funnily enough, the best training I had for directing actors in movies was directing opera in French, which I've done a couple of times. My French is not so terrific, so I only spoke when I had something really worthwhile to say. When it's an effort to say something, you realize how much crap you speak when it's no effort to speak at all. So much just pours out for the sake of hearing the sound of your own voice. That's really dangerous on a movie set. It's almost as if you have to trick yourself into thinking it's an effort to speak.

You hadn't tried to make a film before *The Madness of King George?*

No, because I'd never written one. That seems to be the way most first-time filmmakers get to make a film, unless they've come from commercials or music videos. The things that were sent to me—and a lot was sent to me—was very much the kind of stuff you wouldn't be interested in. The kind of slightly upmarket studio fare, which was plainly never going to get made. Why else would they send it to a theater director who hadn't made a movie?

The reason I got to make *The Madness of King George* is very straightforward. Alan Bennett would not release it unless Nigel Hawthorne and I went with it. Goldwyn was the only one who would pick it up under those circumstances. They were less worried about me than Nigel. That says a lot about the studios' priorities. Me, they kind of thought, "Yes, why not? He's a theater director. He's done a couple of successful shows." Nigel was a big thing for some of those idiot studios to swallow.

You had already done *The Madness of George III* **at The Royal National Theater in London. What kind of specific preparation did you do to direct the film? Did you rethink the material?**

Yes, it was totally rethought. I was very fortunate in that Alan Bennett had written, with huge success, many screenplays.

Describe the relationship you had with Bennett working on the screenplay.

When we did the play, that material arrived from Alan in a slightly chaotic form because that's how Alan often works. We workshopped it as a play and knocked it around quite a lot. It goes back to when he once adapted a children's book which I did as a kind of Christmas show at the National [*The Wind in the Willows*]. All the time I was sitting with him, he'd say, "I don't know how to do this." And I'd say, "Don't worry about that. I'll do that." He said, "A train comes on stage. How does a train come on stage?" I would say, "Leave that to me." It was a new thing for him, because he was a writer of well-made plays.

The *George III* play was written with a much freer, looser, you might say, cinematic structure, precisely because we had worked together before, and he just thought, "I'll just let them sort that out." Therefore, when we came to do the screenplay, the play seemed to me to be a screenplay in disguise, a play written for an empty stage, with cross-fades, and dissolves and cuts as the mechanics of its forward motion.

Did the focus change from play to film?

We were able to have more fun with more stuff. The heart of the play and the heart of the film remained the same. And I think, quite genuinely, the whole event would not have connected so much with people if it hadn't been for one of those rare occurrences where the part and the actor create a kind of alchemy. Being able to move in close to Nigel, I saw things which I'd never seen. The play opened with a tremendous flourish, but it was totally theatrical. The set was a plain wooden platform with a wide flight of stairs at the back. That's all you saw, with a big blast of Handel. Up over the top of the steps, the king and the entire royal court came thundering down the steps. It was like a Gainsborough painting materializing over the top of this flight of stairs. And he always moved quickly. It was just one of those theatrical lifts. That's quintessentially theatrical. You can't get that in film, the manipulation of real people in a real space. The assassination attempt happened ten seconds after this initial opening.

I remember saying, "Well, let's start with the State opening of Parliament. That's easy!" It's not hard. The stuff that seemed startling to me was getting in close. In an historical movie like *King George*, we deliberately were not going for the dusty, pompous feel, not going for the French historical movie style, not going for the slow unfolding of detail. I mean, there is no better historical movie than *The Rise to Power of Louis XIV* by Rossellini. It's fantastic, but it is so cool, and allows detail to unfold so much at its own pace, you feel you're there. Well, we went for a more "Rowlandson" feel. The way it's written, the way it's shot, the way it's acted, the whole feel of the film was like a Thomas Rowlandson caricature. Those were always the visual references.

Did Alan Bennett make any important changes from the play to the film?

I think we were essentially telling the same story. The politics in the film come across stronger because we were able to give it a context, because we went into the House of Commons. I think the Prince of Wales in the film comes over stronger because we are able to see with greater vividness how he operates.

You've mentioned that when it was first written, it was more a satire on medicine and politics, but it changed when you saw it as a play about a man with an illness.

Nigel was the first to change because Nigel just grabbed that part. I remember a final scene, which I was never keen on, that we performed once and then threw out. Alan tried to bring the whole thing together and seemed to be saying that "This is about medicine. This is a Molière play about medicine." But Nigel had already highjacked the play by then and quite rightly so. The movie is about a marriage. The movie seems so strongly to me to be about the marriage and it has a lot to do with Helen Mirren's performance as well. It's not so much in the writing, you see. Their scenes are not so different. What I was discovering as I was going along has to do with getting in close and going behind the eyes, as much as, or more than, the creation of a world.

So, for you, it was less the idea of opening up the play, and going outdoors, as one might normally do when going from stage to film. It was about getting more intimate with the characters?

Opening up is the fun bit. You do it anyway. But yes, getting more intimate. It was also fascinating and challenging to take a basically ironic look at a period of English history and the English court with a definitely anti-heroic, historical movie very definitely not in the American or Hollywood tradition of historical movies, and still be able to pull out of that a genuine emotional center.

When you started shooting, did you have a clear idea of how you'd stage each scene?

Yes, I did, although I didn't necessarily have a clear idea about how to shoot each scene. When I'm staging a scene, I still find myself in the scene looking at the camera, rather than behind the camera looking at the scene. That's just how I work. I'm in the scene, I'm in the space, and suddenly I realize that I've drifted from behind the camera, and the camera's looking at me. Weirdly, the DPs love that.

I have been very fortunate with the two DPs I've worked with, Andrew Dunn on *The Crucible* and *The Madness of King George* and Oliver Stapleton on *The Object of My Affection*. Andrew was an educator as much as a cinematographer on *Madness*. I tried to storyboard and he persuaded me to stop. Because I had a firm idea of each scene in its space, I would grow less fearful of not starting each day with the scene cut together in my head. Three films on, that happens with greater ease, and I'm less fearful of it. If there's a set or a space and three actors, it's actively a mistake to know how you're going to shoot it. To know exactly where the camera is going to be at every moment of the day is a creative mistake.

So, you were prepared, but not overprepared?

I was prepared in every respect, except in knowing where the camera was going to be put. In every other respect, I was heavily prepared.

Does that explain why the camera is so liberated in the film? It's swooping around and following actors everywhere.

Yes, and everybody's moving all the time. Partly the scheme behind it is let the camera reflect his state of mind, the state of his body. When he starts going haywire in the palace, it seemed the obvious thing to do. The first couple of days, I looked at it and thought this is a bit careful. I remember realizing early on a difference between directing for the theater, where everything the director says is challenged immediately, and directing a movie, where you only have to offer a tentative suggestion and they're already doing it. That's the training, because time is so precious in moviemaking. You only have to say "What if we . . . ?" and they're doing it before you've finished your sentence.

It was also about the disruption. It's about an image of order, an image of decorum. There's already bustle at the beginning, it's hyperactive. I love all that stuff at the beginning. I haven't seen it for ages, but I loved doing all that stuff of dressing him, and the pages dashing back and forth. It is very self-conscious in that it's playing with the façade of royalty, the façade of power and authority. It starts at a high pitch because that's what he is, that's what he's like, and then it goes completely nuts.

At times, the camera doesn't move much at all, but there is still a sense of movement.

The scene of the bell ringing is a good example of that. It's just two shots and a couple of closeups of the bell-ringers and the royal party watching. I don't think the camera ever moves we just cut from one to the other. We have two shots of the king enjoying himself, and two shots of the princes, exhausted. Then back to the bell-ringers, back to the king, the camera never moves. The king leaves the room, and the camera doesn't move there, but the court goes "Whoosh!" It's just a matter of personal taste. Often, in movies, the camera moves because the director is not in there directing the action. It's easier to get some spurious energy from a camera move than it is to get in there and direct the actors. I can remember thinking, "Is this completely ridiculous? I'm getting them to do what they did on the stage here!" I was getting them to exaggerate that big collapse because they're all so tired, and taking off their shoes, and so on. But it's a cartoon. And the camera stayed still there.

In terms of visual style, did you look at specific films for inspiration?

Yes, several. Kubrick's *Barry Lyndon,* of course, had the same designer, and that's why I asked him. I thought, the worst that can happen is he'll say no.

Did you do painterly research like they did for *Barry Lyndon*, looking at a lot of paintings?

Very much so, but that's part of my training. That's the way I come to

everything. Yes, there's a huge number of French and Italian historical films which you could point to. As I say, it's not so much
Gainsborough, not so much Reynolds or Zoffany. Although they are
the naturalists of the period, the spirit of the film is Thomas
Rowlandson.

Was it a difficult shoot? Did you shoot any extra material?

Yes, I was inexperienced in that respect. The first cut was an hour
longer than the final cut. *The Crucible* was only about ten or fifteen
minutes off, so I think it was my inexperience. There was a lot of
hugely entertaining material cut, but it was just saying the same thing.
You can do that in the theater; people are more forgiving of that.
But it wasn't a difficult shoot; it was very fast. We did it in forty-two
or forty-three days, and there was something very invigorating about
going all over England doing the film.

**Did you find the authority of a film director different from that of
a theater director?**

Oh, totally different. I realized that I had to bring Andrew very firmly
into that pool of authority. We pushed each other. Any time I was
being too careful, he'd push me. A huge number of those set-ups are
his creations. These guys, like Andrew Dunn and Oliver Stapleton,
have shot so many films. They've spent every day of their professional
lives moving the camera. It's obvious that if you are going in a certain direction, they're going to know how to do that, and often a lot
better, so you must listen to them. Also, the whole point of the film
is that this man, partly through temperament and partly through illness, totally disrupts the formal frame of the Gainsborough painting of the English Court. So there is a concept there.

**Can you say a few things about working with Nigel Hawthorne on
his characterization? Since he had played the role on stage, did he
rethink it as well for the film?**

One thing I discovered from watching which actor friends of mine
succeeded on film, and which failed, was seeing them make the

mistake of scaling down, doing nothing for the film camera. It's a huge mistake to be less demonstrative, to allow the camera to discover rather than demonstrate. That's by and large the note I'm constantly giving in the theater anyway. A big mistake many theater actors make is that in scaling down and doing nothing for movies, they shut down their imaginations. In a sense, you have to be even more imaginatively engaged with a camera close to you. You get away with much less than if you're standing in the middle of a stage, spouting it to a thousand people. Nigel and I discussed this. It's why he's also a master of television acting. There's not that much difference.

His performance in the film is very fearless. You see that he's taking risks and going through a range of emotion.

Yes, he did that on stage too.

Did he surprise you on the set?

Oh, constantly, and particularly looking at it blown up the next day. You would say, "Wow." It's emotionally much rawer because when you're doing it once you can afford to go places that you can't if you're doing it night after night. It's just too exhausting.

Was his performance as physical on the stage? It's quite an energetic performance.

Yes, it was, but within the confines of the single space we had to perform it in. I was able to do a lot with space in the film.

I read an interview with Hawthorne in which he said the only reason he did *Demolition Man* was so he could get to do the film version of *The Madness of King George*.

It's true. In any event, it didn't matter because Sam Goldwyn would no more go see *Demolition Man* than he'd put his hand in a fire. That's not where he comes from. Goldwyn's great. He's the best. He's completely on his own. So interesting, and so complicated because he carries his father's legacy, but he's totally committed to filmmaking.

One of the most interesting things about the film is that you see a world behind this façade, the marriage and the king's treatment of his son.

Although we pretend not to be, that's what we are mesmerized by in England. It's very English. We prefer toilet humor. From the age of two and a half, the image of the queen going to the toilet is the funniest thing anybody can imagine! It's like one of those ironic secret images. What is it like when the queen takes a pee? It's the image of authority, the image of decorum undermined by a kind of rampant chaos.

Was there ever a feeling that, since it was your first film and you were coming from the theater, you had to overcompensate by emphasizing the visuals, to avoid making a stage-bound film?

No, not really. The whole experience infected me, though. It had nothing to do with worrying about being accused of anything. I didn't know when I set out that the camera would move quite so much.

Many people look at this portrait of the monarchy as a comment on the present-day monarchy. Did you see it as a political film, contributing to the debate about the monarchy?

It's more mischievous than that, actually. I hope it's unpretentious in its portrayal of the monarchy. I think it is a humane portrait. At its heart, it is interested in the man and his wife, and his sanity and his image of himself. It's interested in the tension between the man and the role. That's what all the Shakespeare kings are about. We were deliberately mischievous, and we added that final caption to nudge everybody into being mischievous with us. We were not "po-faced" about it, and I think it caused irritation in some quarters.

To me, the institution of the monarchy is so absurd. The best thing we could do is to get rid of it. Not because I have anything against them. They're in a terrible situation—and they don't seem to be anything other than decent folk—but because it would be a tremendously invigorating thing for us, the English, to do. I'm not sure how we can get rid of the whole stranglehold of class. Maybe it's all dissolving anyway, but how can it totally dissolve whilst we defer to these people who are there purely because of an accident of birth? Alan Bennett is, in a gentle way, a monarchist. We slightly disagree about this, and yet we never disagreed about the movie.

How did *The Crucible* become your next project?

I had no idea when I made *King George* whether I'd be any good at it, and whether I'd enjoy it. It was released just a few days after it was finished, and suddenly there was nothing to do. *The Object of My Affection* was still not a script that could go.

When you say you had nothing to do, you don't mean that you weren't being offered work, because you're working all the time.

I was being offered a lot of work, but there was nothing that I particularly wanted to do, and I had no theater projects in the offing. I remember *The Crucible* arrived from Fox, and the idea of working with Arthur Miller and creating that world seemed to me so enormously alive. The interesting thing is that it plainly wasn't. I think *The Crucible* is a good film and I'm very proud of it, but there's absolutely no denying that it failed to catch the public imagination. People thought the story was dead. The analogy between the Salem witch trials and the McCarthy witch hunt was so specific that the idea that *The Crucible* had something to say that transcended the specific circumstances of the events portrayed, or the events that gave rise to its initial composition, was not entertained. In the end, all you can do is make the film you're interested in. But it was completely unpredictable why *The Madness of King George* caught the public imagination and *The Crucible* did not.

Did you work closely with Arthur Miller?

Enormously closely. And that was a tremendously exciting thing to do.

What were some of the challenges in adapting that screenplay?

It was a more tightly constructed play than *The Madness of King George*. *The Crucible* is a very well-made play, particularly the first act.

Unpicking it was quite a job. The first act of the play is an unbeliev-
ably skillful example of how you can do forty-five minutes of
exposition without it seeming like that. The first draft, which had
been knocking around for five or six years, hadn't really restructured
the play cinematically. So that's what we did.

**Did you feel restricted in terms of your input, or overly reverential
to the material because of Miller?**

Not at all. Miller put a stop to that immediately.

**Was there discussion about changing the dialogue to make it a more
contemporary vernacular?**

No, on the contrary, I never mentioned that in my first two or three
meetings with Miller, because it genuinely never occurred to me to.
By the third meeting, he said, "You know, I've spoken to a lot of directors about this, and every single one except you said I had to mod-
ernize the dialogue." If we modernized the dialogue it would have
made absolutely no difference to the people who came to see the film,
and it would have been horrible! I believe that. These Puritans, their
thought processes were finer than ours. They were more articulate,
better educated than us. Language was drummed into them, beaten
into them, whipped into them from infancy. Language of muscular-
ity and expressiveness, which we find now impossible to comprehend.
These Puritans were brought up on the King James Bible, and on the
sermons of hugely articulate, creative divines who had preceded the
ones who were doing the preaching at them. They just simply spoke
better. It would be a grotesque betrayal of the people you are trying to
portray, the world you're trying to create, if you dumb them down.

How did Daniel Day-Lewis get involved in the film?

I asked him, and he said yes. It was that simple. He's now a friend,
but that's how he works. He says yes or no, almost always no. When
he says yes, he does it. He never ever backs away.

**The visual style of the film is very vivid. Did you have clear ideas
about the style of the film before you started?**

Yes. We talked about the devil getting into the camera. From a camera point of view, it was a virus of fear and paranoia that starts the film. It's a similar process to *King George,* that rather than starting with the image of decorum, you present the virus first. That's why we had to go to Massachusetts, where the landscape is not wild, but austere, demanding, beautiful, rough but not wild. They were trying to shove us up into Nova Scotia, which is beautiful but wrong.

Can you talk about some of the stylistic choices like the use of blue light, the moving camera, the wide-angle lenses?

But that's to do with the devil, or fear, paranoia, whatever. The devil is the way we described it because we were being Puritans. I can re-member the yellow bird's point-of-view shot, which was a tremendous shot to do, and very satisfying because it felt right. When the girls were outside the meeting house and they're pointing up, and the camera swoops down on them like it's the bird. That was fun to do.

The first half of the film strikes me as being more melodramatic than the later trial scenes, the excessive hysteria of the girls, the sweeping camera movements and the music.

I think it was, probably. But I'm not sure that I would use melodrama as a judgmental term.

I don't mean it in a negative way. It's a wonderful genre. I love it.

I'm unashamed of that. That's how it's written. The play is a thriller. Late in the day, Daniel turns into a tragic hero. In that sense, it's Abigail's [Winona Ryder] film until halfway through. I always used to say to Daniel, "This man is trying so hard not to be in this film. He is trying so hard to stay out of it." It's when he steps forward that there is a change of tone. Up until that time he says: "The little children are jangling the keys of the kingdom, and common vengeance writes the law." It's such a great line. I'm so proud of the writers I've worked with: Alan Bennett, Arthur Miller, Wendy Wasserstein, and now Larry Gelbart, who is writ-ing the screenplay for *Chicago.* These are writers, and for me, if you're not a writer yourself, why piss around with some Hollywood hack?

Larry Gelbart said to me "You know, I was an investor in *The Crucible* when it was first played on Broadway in '52, and I know that play off by heart. I keep thinking about that line 'The little children are jangling the keys of the kingdom, and common vengeance writes the law,' it's what's happening in Washington." And I think to myself, "He can see that, I can see that, and yet, there are no witches, so nobody else can see it." One of the things I kept saying while we were making *The Crucible* is that the witch hunters now, the McCarthyites, are the press. They have such an abysmal sense of constitutional self-importance here. At least the English press can look in the mirror and see pigs, I mean they know they're pigs. They know they're disreputable. It's the American press now who are fulfilling the function of the witch hunters, the judges, and the McCarthy tribunals. They are judge, jury, and executioner, looking at it from the outside position of an Englishman who spends a lot of time here. It's the Abigails who are in charge. But you're right, when Proctor steps forward and takes control of the drama, there is a change of tone.

Anybody can tell any lie now, and people run with it. We talked about child abuse, witch hunts, the hysterias, the whole business of political correctness on college campuses. The mistake maybe was trying to find specific analogies. Any Abigail Williams can tell any lie or exaggerate the truth or put herself into the spotlight, and people are like lemmings, they'll run with it. We have the lemming shot, when they all thunder down the hillside into the sea. We did that deliberately. It's way over the top. People don't see themselves doing that as they buy *The National Enquirer*.

I can see all those analogies, but maybe it's the moral question that's difficult to deal with in the 1990s. The idea of creating someone who is so moral that he is willing to sacrifice everything. Proctor's love for his wife is solid at the end of the film, yet he's willing to throw that away for a principle. It's an impressive thing, but how many of us would make that decision?

No, and there is a spokesman for the position that you've just touched on—Reverend Hale—who says, "No truth is worth dying for. God forgives a lie, if the lie brings life."

He is your liberal voice.

Yes, but he's also, if you like, my voice. I kept faith with Arthur all the way through. I wasn't prepared to say, "Change this play. This is now the voice that should be heard." Certainly I couldn't change the ending, because that would not be true. When the play was written the issues were clear cut, emerging from the war with Hitler and these Cold War years. It was possible to go to the scaffold and, as it were, take the public with you. But now you can't.

I'm not sure that many of us would have the moral strength to make Proctor's decision. I'm not even sure that Miller made the right one. One would have to believe that John's death served a purpose apart from rhetoric.

If there is a reason why the film didn't find a wider audience, I think this may be it. We live in morally pampered times. We have not been required, those of us who live in Western Europe and North America, to make serious choices based on principle. With the collapse of religious and philosophical certainties, the only certainty that remains for most of us, the only circumstances under which we would be prepared to sacrifice everything, fall loosely under the heading of love and family. I think that's why it's hard to take.

I've spent time in Northern Ireland, and the principles to which most members of both communities attach themselves are fairly unattractive to most of us. There are many there who in defense of their so-called principles would be prepared to sacrifice their wives and families. It plainly happens the whole time. The thing I found hard was to underline, to highlight, the one person in the last twenty minutes of the movie who does posit the proposition that there is nothing, there is no principle worth sacrificing your life for. That's Hale. By that stage in the movie, he is so compromised a figure, and in dramatic terms a relatively weak figure compared to the Proctors. It was hard, cinematically, to say this may be the correct position. Also, movies, much more than the theater, are not conducive to that kind of ambiguity. They're not conducive to the idea that Reverend Hale might be delivering the emotional and philosophical climax.

It may be also that we live in a more pragmatic age. How many of us believe that an individual sacrifice would really change the system or combat evil?

By saying it in that way, Mario, you're making my point. Proctor didn't think he was changing the system. He did not make that sacrifice to have an impact on the community. He did it for his own soul. And that's what we've lost. I don't believe that those individuals—the millions of individuals who sacrificed themselves in Germany in the thirties and forties—did it because they thought they would defeat Hitler. They did it because they couldn't live with themselves otherwise. All is compromised now, because we don't have those choices to make. There seem to be no religious, political, or philosophical causes that are precious enough or threatening enough to die for.

Perhaps it was inevitable that *The Crucible* would not get a large audience?

It's very hard to get a wide audience, because we also live in a selfish, self-involved, solipsistic age. It's very hard to get audiences to believe that under different circumstances, in different times, people thought differently about these issues. There are at least two reasons to tell a story set in the past, to make a period film, or to stage a Shakespeare play. And they are opposite and complementary reasons. One is that things never change, and the other is that things always change. Both apply. The only interest the mass audience has in something like *The Crucible* is that things never change. There's an arthouse audience for the idea that things are always changing, in constant flux, but not a mass audience.

The performances are often at such a high pitch, was it difficult striking the right tone with the actors?

They came from very different places, all of them.

What about the issue of British versus American actors?

The most interesting thing was actually that Daniel Day-Lewis and Paul Scofield came from diametrically opposite places, and they both had enormous respect for each other. They both have mysterious processes, but Paul's is from the outside-in, and Daniel's is from the inside-out. I never think it's a problem if people are using different ways to get to the same place.

What about the American actors; would their training have been different?

Joan Allen is a stage actor. She spent years with Steppenwolf Theater Group in Chicago. I think her scenes with Daniel are the best thing in the movie.

Winona Ryder is also very strong in the film.

She's unafraid of the language and totally in command of it. She was anxious to be part of it all. She rehearsed as much as everybody else.

How did you work with Daniel Day-Lewis?

Daniel does not like to reveal his hand until the day you shoot. It was clear early on that that was his process. We spent a hell of a lot of time together before we started the shoot, and, indeed, during the shoot. We talked in considerable detail about the character and the movie as a whole. He's an actor who likes to know about each scene in some detail, in fact, the whole movie. There are many actors to whom that's a genuine distraction. I always knew that there was a huge emotional climax in his big scene with Scofield and the tribunal, but with Daniel you don't even know during the camera rehearsals. You don't know until the camera's rolling exactly what he's going to do because I'm not sure that he knows quite what he's going to do.

The interesting thing about *The Crucible* was that there were so many different approaches to acting amongst that cast. One of the differences between directing actors in theater and directing actors in film is that in the course of a theater rehearsal period, you have some chance of getting everybody acting in the same way. The theater ideal is a permanent repertory company where everybody approaches the business of acting in the same way and evolves through months, years together. I'm not sure it exists anywhere anymore outside of the Peter Brook Company in Paris.

In directing actors for film, what you have to do is create some kind of territory in which they can all peacefully coexist. In many ways, it's like brokering a deal. As long as what happens in front of the camera looks like it's happening in the same world, it doesn't really matter how we get there. I rehearsed *The Crucible* for about three weeks, with various agendas. The girls needed more time together, although I didn't do very much on the text with them. I did a lot of improvisational work with the girls because they obviously had to behave as one, as if they lived in the same tiny place all their lives, and were infected by the same virus. That came through the kind of theater exercises that kids do in drama school.

When you talk about Daniel Day-Lewis' process being so personal and private, did he interact differently with the other actors on the set?

There are myths about Daniel Day-Lewis that just aren't true. He's very genial and hardworking and personally approachable, very giving. But Daniel won't let on in rehearsal what it is he's going to do because he is constantly at war with the whole business of acting. Daniel has to trick himself at every take into believing that what he's doing is utterly spontaneous. Some would say that's what acting technique is about. There is no chance of total spontaneity. Daniel won't learn a scene until the moment before he starts to do it. In rehearsal he will do what he can within the limits of his own requirements to help the others. There are some actors who are putting together a performance in rehearsal. That's not his way. His performance is delivered from hidden psychic depths at the last moment.

Scofield puts it together bit by bit, syllable by syllable, vowel sound by vowel sound. The result is just as deeply felt as the Daniel Day-Lewis performance, which comes fully formed at the last moment. At the beginning, Scofield wants a broad outline of what's required, and then he wants precise, succinct technical advice as in "too fast," "too slow," "too loud," "too soft." Whereas an actor like Bruce Davison, who played Paris, wants the whole thing, a constant barrage of suggestions and a hundred ideas that he can play around with to choose from. Winona Ryder wanted to be coached and pushed as if from a completely blank sheet, as if she were a total beginner. Nobody objects, nobody finds Daniel's approach difficult because once you are on the set in front of the cameras, you get everything you want and more from him. When you are actually doing it, he is an utterly selfless actor. He's selfless to the extent that sometimes he will give his best performance off-camera. Even if it's the other guy's closeup, he'll still do it, and if that happens to be the best one, then that's the best one.

How did *The Object of My Affection* come about and what attracted you to it?

Five years ago, Wendy Wasserstein, who is a friend of mine, sent me the novel. She had a draft of the screenplay that she wrote five years previous to that and it had gone nowhere, nothing was happening to it. That script bore only a slender resemblance to what we eventually shot. This was before I made *The Madness of King George*. I was tremendously attracted to the novel, to the material, to the central relationship, and to the idea of doing something with Wendy. I said at the time I'd better do *The Madness of King George* first to see whether I like doing this, whether I'm any good at it. That's how it came about. So on and off for five years we worked on it and tried to get someone to make it.

What kind of working relationship did you have with her on the script?

In the end, we did it in the same room together, although she wielded the pen. It was the closest relationship I had of the three movies.

What was the challenge in working in a lighter, romantic-comedy vein?

In the theater, I've never just stuck to one genre. I've done period work, contemporary work. I've done funny and serious. I think the romantic-comedy genre is a wonderful, often debased genre. If you stretch it back to include Shakespeare, and in cinematic terms, to include the great movies of the thirties and forties, it's a staggeringly rich genre. The rules of romantic comedy are that the hero and the heroine overcome a variety of obstacles and then they marry. They must marry. Now obviously, as in all genres, the obstacles evolve as society evolves, but the rules tend not to. But the rules of romantic comedy have been undermined over the last twenty years in the same way that social institutions have been undermined. Marriage no longer seems to be the only possible end for a romantic comedy, as it is no longer the only road to a fulfilled life. It's just a fact that fifty percent of marriages collapse. So many people now are looking outside of marriage for the kind of stability and fulfillment and emotional satisfaction that was only imaginable within marriage these last few centuries. As I started to think about it in terms of romantic comedy, it interested me very much to try and reconcile the genre with the lives that are led by most people I know.

The film pays homage to the classical Hollywood cinema, both the musical and the screwball comedies of the thirties and forties. What kind of cinematic research did you do as preparation?

I watched all the films again. I was also very careful about the casting. It was cast with smart, literate, articulate actors. Most dramatic comedies now are made with cute dummies.

The film clearly respects the genre, and what was good about Hollywood movies. What other key issues were there for you? The gay issues are obviously there, but I imagine you don't want this film to be ghettoized as a gay film.

Certainly not, but the gay issues were important to me. It seems that Hollywood has found two ways of dealing with gay characters, either as victims or in comedic terms. Somebody else—not me, but it's a good line—once said that it's either "slit wrists or limp wrists." None of the gay characters in this film have an issue with being gay, and none of them are screaming queens. It's a film where half the characters are gay men but no big deal is made of it. Whether they like the movie or not, I suspect the majority of gay men who see it will breathe a sigh of relief.

It's the victim movies that get up the nose of gay men more than the screaming queen movies because there are screaming queens, and they're very funny, and a lot of gay men *are* fairly "faggy." For instance, the Greg Kinnear character in *As Good as It Gets*. That movie had a lot that was good in it, but that character, though well acted, made me furious. In reel one he is gay bashed, and then spends the rest of the movie with no friends, lonely and sad. He's always going to be desperate. So he goes off on a long car journey to be abused by Jack Nicholson's character.

Everybody is abused by Jack Nicholson in that movie. But I see your point. So, for you, if there's a political aspect, a political edge to your film, it's primarily in creating a positive image of gays?

I don't think art or entertainment is about creating role models. If it has the effect of creating positive images in middle America, I'm delighted. But it's not a movie that's meant to preach.

Do you see the film working differently for gay audiences than for straight audiences?

I don't know. What is the gay audience? The fact is there may be theaters in New York and in San Francisco where there'll be an unusually high proportion of gay men, but I don't know where the gay community is.

Do you think it's as disparate as the heterosexual community?

Exactly. And in a sense what the movie is saying is that there is no such thing as one gay community. We all have boyfriends, ex-boyfriends, friends, jobs. We're in the world.

Did you consciously try to make a more commercial film after the weak performance of *The Crucible* at the box office?

Not consciously after *The Crucible*. But there was no point in doing this movie unless it was a popular movie, and when the decision had to be made whether Jennifer Aniston's character would be alone or not, there seemed no point in her being alone. Either would feel true to me. In fact, it feels truer to me that she's with someone because she's not someone who would be without a boyfriend. We did try an epilogue in which everybody was more miserable, in which George [Paul Rudd] and Paul's relationship was on the verge of collapse, Rodney [Nigel Hawthorne] was very miserable, and the only two that were fine were the characters played by Alan Alda and Allison Janney. That would also have been true. But this version is as true. And to be frank, since it's romantic comedy, there seemed no point in providing five minutes at the end that would probably decimate its appeal. I wanted it to be popular. There have been plenty of specialist films in which the kind of issues that arrive out of the different sexualities of characters are explored. The challenge here was to make a mainstream film in which sexuality was the obstacle, and see whether there's a wide audience that's cool about that. What we're hoping is that there is a wide audience.

Do you think that stylistically there's a pulling back? Do you see it as a more conventional film after the first two?

I see it as a less theatrical film.

And more classical?

Yes, certainly. Although there is a certain theatrical sensibility to it not least because the writer and the director come from the theater and were just fine with song and dance.

The one part of the film that left me a little unsatisfied was the relationship between Paul and George. I couldn't see what was so great about Paul.

I'm not sure that there is much that's so great about Paul. I'm afraid I think that's life. I think he's the right boy in the right place at the right time. And he's a man.

He doesn't seem good enough for George.

No, I'm sure he's not. But then how many of your friends are with people that are good enough for them?

There was something undeveloped about the character and that relationship.

Yeah, I think you're probably right. When you're trying to keep seven or eight characters going, it's tough. Rodney has relatively little screen time, yet you don't feel he's underdeveloped. But that's partly because it's beautifully written and brilliantly acted by Nigel.

Was it tricky striking a balance between comedy and drama?

It's something I love to do. If I look back on all the stuff that I've done over the past fifteen years, *The Crucible* is more single-mindedly earnest than I'm usually comfortable with.

So you don't see this as a departure?

I don't. No, not really.

I'm interested in hearing your thoughts about the notion of theatricality and how it relates to cinema. Do you think either of your first two films were too "theatrical?"

I think the style is very theatrical. I wasn't after low-key naturalism in either of them. I guess you mean by theatrical, a fixed point of view. The camera emulating the audience in the theater.

I mean more than that. Obviously it's a tricky discussion because the cinema owes so much to theater to begin with.

Yeah and I don't know why everybody is so ashamed of it.

How do you view the relationship of theater to film?

The Crucible is plainly from the theater. *The Object of My Affection* isn't from the theater. It was made for different reasons, although it's very much writer-related. Wendy Wasserstein is maybe my closest friend here in New York, and the film is very personal for both of us. It would have been inappropriate to shoot it either like *King George* or *The Crucible*. It's shot in a calmer style. And now I'm going to make *Chicago*. I'm not a writer. I don't come from a background of low-budget, guerrilla, independent filmmaking. I come from the theater. I have four or five things which I'm trying to develop. *The Object of My Affection* is more personal than *The Crucible*. Of course, I was in on *The Madness of King George* from the beginning. *Chicago* was actually first brought to me two years ago, and I couldn't do it, and didn't think I knew how to do a film musical, and now I think I do. And I hope after *Chicago*, I'll do one of these things that I'm currently in the process of developing. They all have something theatrical. Even in *The Object of My Affection*, we couldn't keep away from the theater. It's who we are, it's where we're from.

You don't think film as an art form has to keep some distance from the other arts?

No, I absolutely don't. I very specifically don't, and this may be because I'm not someone who was born and grew up with a camera in my hands. I have to admit it, and to be honest, it is the action towards which I gravitate. I start behind the camera and I end up in front of it because it's the action I start with, not the image. It's the scene in a space that I start with, rather than the sequence of shots. I'm aware that there are many kinds of films that I couldn't make, and there are films that I recognize as purely cinematic, which I couldn't make and aren't me.

In terms of your next project, *Chicago*, does the prospect of working on a lavish musical worry you?

Of course, the prospect of shooting a musical worries me. It's complete lunacy!

It's seems like the right moment for such a project.

I hope so.

Are you worried that Madonna will automatically make some people expect a "Madonna" movie?

You can't worry about that kind of thing. And I don't know what a Madonna movie is.

Just that she brings her persona.

The great thing about *Chicago* is that her persona would be just fine for that material. I think she's capable of a lot. When Madonna hits the target she's really good. And there's always a gap between the public persona and the actor.

Do you think that the project needs a star?

I think musicals do. The stage show, particularly in its current Broadway form, is such an odd hybrid. It offers no blueprint at all for a movie, which is a huge advantage for me. It's so presentational, it's vaudeville. There is no real cinematic equivalent to vaudeville.

Will the choreography play as big a role?

Well it won't be Bob Fosse. You can't start doing all that. The single most daunting prospect is that this musical was created on stage by Bob Fosse who was the last director who cracked the musical form, who actually succeeded substantially with the musical form in movies like *Cabaret* and *All That Jazz*. The interesting thing is that they aren't musicals in the pure sense. With the exception of the "Tomorrow Belongs to Me" scene, all the music happens on stage in *Cabaret*. I can't imagine I will shoot dance as well as Bob Fosse did. How could I? Fosse was a dancer and a choreographer and a camera maestro. One of the astonishing things about all Fosse's films is how inventively and authoritatively they're shot, just as films. But I can have a go at it. It's going to be choreographed by Graciela Daniele, one of the great Broadway choreographers at the moment.

Do you see yourself as part of any British film tradition? Do you see your film work as basically an extension of your theater work?

Oh God, those are such hard questions to answer.

Do you see yourself outside the British tradition?

What would you call the British tradition?

Well there's probably more than one.

Yeah, cause I'm definitely not within the . . .

. . . kitchen-sink school?

Exactly. I'm not *Taste of Honey* or *Billy Liar* or anything like that. I've never done theater work like that either.

There's a very stylized British tradition, you know, Nic Roeg, Ken Russell.

No, I'm not there either.

But you do put a lot of emphasis on the visuals.

Yeah, I do. I suspect I'm a kind of throwback to the days of the English studios, the days of Ealing and Alexander Korda and Powell/Pressburger. The English film has always had a give-and-take with the theater. Even Michael Powell directed plays and had a tremendous respect for the theater. Many English actors and directors went back and forth between the two.

In a sense, you're probably considered an international director as opposed to a British director.

Well, you know, I'm New York and London.

It's hard talking about the international film industry, whether you can ever escape the studios or the Hollywood industry, which has so much of the money and distribution.

Not in the English-speaking world you almost can't. There are those that do, like Mike Leigh and Terence Davies. They're different and very admirable.

In terms of the actual process of making films—preproduction, shooting, postproduction—is there any particular phase that you enjoy more?

I enjoy the shoot most. I genuinely do, I love that.

That's a bit atypical from other people I've spoken to.

Yes, I know. Of course, everybody loves postproduction. But I've had three very good experiences. I don't work from conflict and tension, in fact, I hate that. I know there are directors for whom it works and who consciously set out to create conflict and tension during the shoot and then have calm postproductions. I love the congeniality, the energy and sense of constant creativity that goes on during the shoot; I'm very hands-on with the actors and with the script during the shoot. That's where I find the transformation from page to movie the biggest leap, and most exciting and revelatory. The most surprising leap happens on the set. And particularly in *Object,* of the three movies I've made, I shot much more selectively. On *King George* I shot more film than I did on *The Crucible* or *Object* because I was less experienced. A lot more happened in post on *The Madness of King George* than in the other two because I'd shot far more and had to give it shape.

Do you feel more comfortable on the set now?

Oh, much more, much more.

What is the most difficult part of being a film director? Is it dealing with the business side of things, or can you navigate that pretty well?

It's very frustrating. Not the business side so much as the constant uncertainty. That can be very wearing and painful. Since you are being written a check for large sums of money—$12 million in the case of *Object,* $22 million in the case of *The Crucible,* and probably $30 million in the case of *Chicago*—it is understandable that they will really put you through the wringer first. Literally, the single most difficult thing at the beginning of every day is telling the first assistant director what we're going to do. That's still hard, coming from the theater where, at the beginning of every day, you can just launch into the day and let it unfold itself, and nudge it here and nudge it there. You can come with a very fixed agenda in the theater, but you have to hide it. On a film, you have to have answers all the time, and that's really hard. It's getting easier, though!

NEIL JORDAN

Writer-director Neil Jordan is Ireland's most acclaimed filmmaker and a key international film artist. Before beginning his directing career, Jordan had earned a substantial reputation in Ireland and Britain for his superb poetic fiction in such novels and short story collections as *A Night In Tunisia* and *The Past*. Jordan burst onto the international film scene in the early 1980s with his first film, *Angel*, starring Stephen Rea, who has become something of an alter-ego for the filmmaker, and who has appeared in many of the director's films such as *The Crying Game, Interview With the Vampire* and *The Butcher Boy*. *Angel* recounts the journey of one individual (Rea) through the Northern Ireland landscape during some of the worst sectarian killings of the late seventies. The film is notable for its poetic, stylized evocation of character and landscape, and recalls the unsentimental, art-film sensibility of such European filmmakers as Werner Fassbinder and Wim Wenders.

Jordan's work, whether in literature or film, is thematically consistent and often revolves around such issues as desire, death, and violence, and the often doomed search for love. These themes are clearly in evidence in such films as *Mona Lisa*, starring Bob Hoskins, or the hugely successful *The Crying Game*, which takes the character of Fergus (Stephen Rea), an IRA gunman, into the transvestite world of the London club scene to explore the notion of whether an individual with such a clearly defined political identity can, as Jordan says, live a truly engaged life as a human being. Can he actually embrace humanity? At times, his films also highlight the very act of storytelling, as in his fascinating excursion into the Gothic world, *The Company of Wolves*, Jordan's highly imaginative collaboration with the late Angela Carter.

Neil Jordan's films run the gamut from such small, low-budget, personal films as *The Miracle* to such expensive studio-backed efforts as *Interview With the Vampire*, starring Tom Cruise and Brad Pitt, and the historical epic *Michael Collins*. This latter film recounts the birth of the Irish Republic, a story that Jordan believes many in Ireland have never come to terms with or adequately debated. As he says, "To pretend that we had a bloodless transition to a Republic is ludicrous. It was actually very bloody."

Jordan's career seems to flow effortlessly between such intimate efforts as his brilliant adaptation of Patrick McCabe's novel *The Butcher Boy*—a film that explores the violent, imaginative world of its troubled young protagonist, Francie Brady—and such large-scale endeavors as his adaptation of Anne Rice's vampire tale. But whether large-scale or small, Jordan's films are always intensely personal, visually audacious, inventive, and compelling works of cinema. He is the epitome of the serious filmmaker, absolutely committed to the complexity of his medium while still creating characters of depth and humanity. Because of his stature as a filmmaker, and the commercial success of his films, Jordan has also achieved what many regard as that most precious of all commodities: complete artistic control. I spoke to Neil Jordan in Dublin.

Can you talk about your background, and growing up in the fifties and sixties?

I was born near Sligo [Ireland], in a little town called Rosses Point. My father was a teacher. When I was about six, we moved to Dublin. So, I'm really a Dubliner, though I was born in the country.

You went to University College in Dublin, right?

I went to university because I wanted to study literature, and I quite enjoyed that.

Is that when you started writing?

No, I started writing when I was about fifteen. I don't know why. I suppose I always felt a bit isolated. My mother was a painter. She taught us how to paint and she brought each one of her kids up to want to do that stuff. So I grew up in a large, bohemian household, in a very pedestrian environment. I began to write short stories and poetry when I was about sixteen or seventeen, and I just kept on writing.

Were you involved in theater at university?

I did a lot of theater with the drama society in the university. When I came out, I got a job teaching

Who were some of the cultural and aesthetic influences on you?

Well, I come from Ireland, so William Butler Yeats, James Joyce, and Samuel Beckett, basically. It was a writer's culture; it always has been.

Were you interested in film at that time?

Yeah, very much. I always was. When I grew up, I used to love movies, but they didn't seem to belong to the culture I lived in. Nobody Irish had ever made a film. I absolutely loved films, but I didn't think they were made by human beings and certainly not by people like me. When I left university, I tried to go to film school. I got into a place called Beckinsfield, a major film school in England, but I couldn't afford to go there, so I began to write. I published novels and a collection of short stories. I began to write for television and film scripts, some of which were made as independent movies. Then I began directing, really. That's my story.

What were some of the films that had an impact on you growing up? Was there anybody particularly important to you?

I was interested in European art cinema and American films of the forties and fifties. I was into everything I saw. Nicholas Ray, Fellini, Buñuel, Kurosawa. I grew up in Dublin and there was an art-house cinema here. I used to go and see every movie that went into that cinema. It's a thing that's gone now, that kind of repertory movie theater. When you say to me, "What are you influenced by?" I don't know anybody who's not influenced by everything they see. There's no one specific thing.

   You must have seen *The Twilight Zone*, for example, which could influence you as much as anything, couldn't it? It could be as profound as anything else. When you're that age and you're looking at movies and reading books and you listen to music or whatever, you realize that any human being could sit down and write or play an instrument, but for any human being to master the art of cinema, it seems a huge stretch of the imagination.

How did you make the leap from writing to direction?

I only began to direct because I wrote a script, *Traveller*, which was made into a film, and some other pieces for television. I was so depressed by the experience of seeing them realized that I had to do it myself. That's the only reason I began to direct. If I had been able to write out exactly what I wanted to see on the screen, and get some-one to realize it, I would never have directed.

Did you become disillusioned with writing?

No. *A Night in Tunisia* was the first book I wrote when I was twenty-four. It was a collection of short stories, and then I published a novel called *The Past*. And if you grew up in this country, writing was the main culture. When I began to make movies, I felt a huge internal conflict because I was dealing with a medium that had basically nothing to do with words, which I loved. A lot of people who ad-mired my work as a writer were outraged.

They felt you were betraying the art of writing?

I did myself, too, in a way, because writing is a totally internal voice and procedure, and movies are a big public fact.

Music plays a big part in your life; you're also a musician, aren't you?

Well, I wouldn't say I was a musician. I had to make a living by play-ing music because I got married very young, and we had two young children, and I was overwhelmed, basically. So I played in a bunch of bands trying to make some money. That was it. But I used to play the classical guitar and stuff like that.

You've written poetry and your fiction is also considered poetic. Do you think the idea of poetry works differently in cinema?

I think cinema's probably the most poetic medium ever invented, in a strange way. Even in the most vulgar, noisy movies, it can lead to a kind of poetry you don't find in any other medium. It's an odd thing; it's what keeps people obsessed with movies. On the one hand there are these crass vulgar facts of the world we live in, but on the other hand we've got this potential to express this extraordinary poetry you don't find in any other realm of expression.

Is there something more immediate about creating poetry with film?

It's very simple. I grew up in Dublin, but was born in Sligo. And William Butler Yeats was born in Sligo, and wrote about Sligo. James Joyce was born in Dublin. So every facet of the landscape that you grew up in has been explored endlessly. There's probably more words per square meter of turf here than there are anywhere in the world, so a writer has this huge weight of stuff, of precedent in front of them. But when I began making movies, I felt this tremendous burst of feeling, because nobody had ever done this before. Not to my knowledge anyway.

Was there any Irish film industry at that time?

No, there wasn't. I'd never seen a film that depicted the landscapes that I knew when I grew up. So I just got a tremendous burst of freedom. I suppose I'd been longing to do it for many years without knowing it.

How did your first film, *Angel*, come about?

I was working with John Boorman. I had written a script for him and he asked me to go through the last draft of *Excalibur* with him. So I did a rewrite job of that. I had written this screenplay and Channel Four had just started up, so I sent it to them, and they said "We're very interested in it." There was a guy called Walter Donohue there, who was the commissioning editor of projects for Channel Four, and a lovely man called David Rose, who was head of Film on Four. It was a new venture in England, to use television to stimulate independent moviemaking. They liked the script and they said they wanted to make it, and I told them I wanted to direct it. They were very nervous, but were interested in an author's cinema. They were worried about me never having directed before. I asked John to produce it for me, which gave them some security, and so they let me make this movie.

Where did the idea come from?

I'd been playing in a band. We'd been traveling up and down around the country, driving up to Belfast and playing gigs. It was the worst time of the sectarian killings in the North of Ireland. It was very scary, around 1979-80. You always thought, as a musician, you were safe. We'd always be driving back at three or four in the morning, and sometimes you came to a roadblock, and you'd be stopped by guys in balaclavas and all this *shite*. Then a band called The Miami Show Band was stopped and they were all machine-gunned. Seven of them were shot dead. It was such a horrible fact. The idea of music, and the kind of tawdry pleasure it gives people, and that kind of violence, was shocking. It led to the idea of Stephen Rea's character, the saxophone player in *Angel*. It was the instrument I used to play. He hides the gun in his saxophone case.

What was it like directing your first film? How prepared were you?

I wasn't prepared at all because I'd never gone to film school or studied any aspect of filmmaking. I had no knowledge of the rules. But I had a great cameraman, Chris Menges, one of the best cameramen in the world, probably. I just kind of shot that movie out of naivety.

Did you storyboard?

No, no. I was very conscious of the things I wanted to see on the screen, though. Very clear images, but I didn't know how to realize them. That's the problem with a lot of first-time directors. You get a very clear image in your head, but you don't realize that to actually get it on the screen, you've got to do all this basic preparation.

Did the film change much from the written text as you were shooting it?

No, it didn't change at all. I just shot exactly what I'd written, probably to a fault. But it's a great thing to make a movie out of that kind of naivety. You've got a freshness that you'll never have again in your life.

Did you feel confident?

I felt terrified! I was getting death threats because I was making a film about sectarian killing, and some people thought it was about the IRA. People visited my house, and there was all this stuff in the newspaper, because this is such a small country. You can imagine a young guy making a feature film; it's a big deal. It was all over the papers back then. There was an independent cinema movement in Ireland, and other directors who had only had the opportunity to make short films saw me, a writer, making this movie. They really got pissed off. It was hard. I had to go the Special Branch, because we had some threats to my house. I asked them, "Should I be worried?" They said, "Yes, you should be worried," which made me even more worried.

Did you feel comfortable working with actors?

I think so. I just loved actors. I really loved watching them.

Did you know how to talk to actors?

They would talk to me. When you make a film for the first time, you're surrounded by the crew, grips and electricians, all these people who've done all this stuff, probably really crap work, and they keep saying, "Who's this little fucker telling us what to do?" Yet you're employing them. The actors are your only mates in a way, so you conspire to make this thing work.

So your inexperience was a disadvantage in working with the crew?

Yes, in terms of organization. But it was a blessing too. If I tried to imagine the rules of this medium, I probably would have got it totally wrong. You're better off trying to realize exactly what you see in your mind when you wrote the script, when the project was conceived. So that's all I shot, really.

Had you known Stephen Rea before?

Yeah. I didn't know him that well, but I kind of wrote it with him in mind. There was a saxophonist at the time called Keith Donald, who was a very good musician, who I knew well, and he did the saxophone riffs for the score. He also taught Stephen to play. They were both from Belfast. The film was about the life that was affecting youth

in the North of Ireland. So we all hit it off. But Stephen's a remarkable actor. I'd seen him on stage once or twice. I always thought he
was a film actor. He reminded me of Humphrey Bogart or somebody
like that. He's one of the best, genuinely one of the most intelligent
actors in the world.

**Although this was your first film, so many of your obsessions are
already in place.**

Well, nothing changes. They're all there, aren't they? They're all
there in the first collection of stories I wrote. I've used the same
locations in about seven movies, certain places I knew as a child.
We do a movie like *The Crying Game* or *Michael Collins*, and people
say, "Where will we put the scene?" and I'll say, "Oh, I know where
we can do it."

Did you and Stephen agree on the interpretation of the character?

We agreed totally. He wore my clothes, basically, because we hadn't
enough money to really work out the costume. If any piece of the costume seemed wrong, I'd take off my coat and say, "Well, maybe this
will fit," and of course it did. I don't improvise. I've never done that.

Do you rehearse with actors?

Not a lot. What's important to me is the central meaning of what
people are doing, and either that's there or it's not. I didn't know
how to rehearse then. I didn't know what it meant. We would just
discuss the implications of the scene. The whole thing of photography, to me, was just such a beautiful thing. I'd never done it before,
the kind of reality and accidents you're able to capture.

What was central for you about *Angel*?

The story, to me, was musical. It was a contrast between the world
of music and the world of the downbeat, concrete-and-clay kind of
thriller. So there were these contrasts in my mind, all this glitter and
colors like gold, purple and pink, and the greys and khaki green, stuff
like that. The thing to me was all about contrasts. In the end, it was

about having this guy in this pink suit wandering through a rural landscape, being exposed like a peacock, being out of his place.

The film has a very elliptical structure; it seems barely finished.

It's not finished at all. It makes gestures towards telling the story and the genre, and then it just goes on.

It certainly makes references to European art films.

Yeah, it does. I suppose it's most like the early films of Fassbinder and Wim Wenders. It's kind of an anti-narrative, in a way, and it's there for the purpose of getting certain themes and emotions onto the screen. The major problem in that movie is that I didn't pretend to tell the story persuasively, to do the thriller bit of the story and the B-movie bit of it. I used a slight shorthand to get there.

There's something very subtle about the film.

Maybe. I think it's a very beautiful thing. I haven't seen it for years. I was down in Italy years ago with Karel Reisz at some festival, and they were showing *Angel*. I had to watch it and I hadn't since I made it, because I find it very difficult to watch the films I've made. I was glad that it was such a naive thing.

Basically it chronicles the main character's descent into violence.

It was about negativity, about a guy being eaten up by a black hole. There was a word I used in the movie, "nobodaddy." I think it came from William Blake, I'm not sure. It was the force of just this emptiness that takes people. It's about the attraction of violence, killing, and nihilism. It was about this man, Stephen Rea's character, who, through a series of coincidences, loses his soul, and the awful glamour and persuasiveness of it.

You call the film an "anti-narrative," so was the most important thing to create poetic images with emotional impact?

I was more interested in trying to use this medium to do stuff that it doesn't normally do. Stanley Kubrick was asked if the important thing was having something to say, and he said, "No, no, the important thing is actually disguising it." That's oddly true in movies, because the world wants these things to perform a certain function, but you want this thing actually to perform a very strange kind of poetic function. You have to disguise it, because if you admitted what you wanted it to do, nobody would go see what you're doing. I wanted it to be like painting or like art.

Were you upset at the controversy when the film was released in Ireland?

Oh, that was all bullshit. That was because I got money. It was because I became too well-known, too young. That's a specifically Irish thing. It's still going on. Some people hated me here. There were directors who wanted the union to stop me making that movie, because I was too young, and a writer. Anybody who did anything back then, they just literally tried to chop your head off, rip your guts out. It was a bitchy little controversy, quite unpleasant.

What were the other responses to the film?

The British press were hugely generous towards it, and it was shown at festivals throughout the world. It was shown in Cannes and different places. It became a *succès d'estime*, you could call it. People in Dublin went to see it, and either they were gob-smacked by it, or they said, "What the hell is that?" It didn't get a huge release here. I finished this movie and the making of it was terribly traumatic. It was surrounded in this country by all sorts of controversy. The manager of The Miami Show Band, whose members had been killed, came to me and said, "I believe you're making a film about my band," and I said, "It's not true." There was all this stuff in the paper about me expropriating money and bullshit like this. People in the literary community were saying, "This man should not be making movies. He's betraying our language and our culture." So it was terribly traumatic.

When you finished it and looked at it, did you feel you had achieved what you'd set out to achieve?

Yeah, I achieved more than I'd set out to achieve. I thought that photography was such a beautiful thing.

Let's go on to *The Company of Wolves*.

The Company of Wolves was very simple. The guy who released *Angel* in England was Stephen Woolley. He saw it in Cannes and really liked it. He bought it because he was setting up distribution in Britain, so he released it. He wanted to be in production. I really liked this guy. He was a very passionate cineaste, and still is.

For the centenary of James Joyce's birth, there was a festival in Dublin where they invited these writers from all over the world. They had Borges, Anthony Burgess, and among them was Angela Carter. Somebody had shown me a short story she'd written, or a short radio play based on a short story, "The Company of Wolves." And they asked me to read it to see whether it could be made into a film. It would have been an amazing movie, but it was too short to make into a proper film, so I began talking to Angela, and I proposed this structure of a story within a story within a story, where this old granny is telling the central story to this young girl: "Don't go into the woods; don't stray from the path," and to illustrate this basic premise, she tells her other stories, and the people within the stories tell their own stories. Angela had written this book of stories that basically went through Grimm's fairy tales, with this kind of strange Freudian, modernist take on things. So we began to write the script, and it became this strange, rather wonderful script for *The Company of Wolves*.

Did you have any cinematic models in mind?

Yeah, I had. There's a movie called *The Sargasso Manuscript*, a Polish film. And Pasolini's version of *A Thousand and One Nights*.

Was there anything in the horror genre that specifically inspired you?

I love horror movies, but not formally. There was nothing in the horror genre that I was thinking of, but it was definitely meant to be a horror movie.

When you were writing the script with Angela Carter, how much research did you do into fairy tales and Gothic literature?

None at all. I mean, there was a popular book by Bruno Bettelheim called *Uses of Enchantment*, which everybody referred to after they saw the movie. I never read it. I still haven't read it. Angela wrote the story as a feminist metaphor, really. I was following her imagination. She knew the power of the fable. She was an absolutely unique writer; there's been nobody like her since. She died very tragically. Like Gabriel Garcia Marquez, she knew the power of story to have many meanings. I was really just trying to do justice to her imagination. I saw it as a wonderful opportunity.

I think Angela Carter called it a kind of "menstrual" movie.

Oh, yeah. It was a movie about little girls and wolves. There's all this blood, this symbolism, and hidden sexuality and sensuality. Even the forest itself. I worked with Anton Furst, a magnificent guy who had just designed one movie. I was trying to eroticize this forest, and he knew exactly what I was talking about. We built this set at Shepperton with these trees that had these vaginal propensities to them [Laughs]. We looked at a painter called Samuel Palmer. If you want to see how to eroticize landscape, look at his paintings; they're beautiful. It was all about sensuality and beauty, really, but one was very aware that at the heart of it is a cautionary tale and bloody dark stuff going on.

This was a studio-based movie. It was like going back to those strange realities of movies you saw in the forties, where artificiality was so prominent. A bit like *Black Narcissus*, or something like that. We used painted sets. We did these archly naive effects shots. I just thought it was a blast. We were actually just painting everything we saw, and finding these ludicrous means to achieve it.

What was the budget on the film?

Two million pounds. To me, it was huge.

You never felt limited by the budget?

No, not at all. I felt limited by the imagination of the crews that I was working with. Every day we'd go out to Shepperton Studios and they'd just laugh at me and say, "Okay, it's your funeral." These guys had worked on *Star Wars* and these big American epics, and to get me and Anton Furst saying, "Okay, now the set is going to change from winter to summer in the same shot." They said, "Well, is it winter over here, or is it summer here?"

You created this very tough, pre-adolescent, very strong girl, who chooses to join this "other" society, to join the company of wolves.

Absolutely. Well, it was about her embracing this beast. The only thing I wasn't happy with in that movie was the ending. That's where the limitations of budget came. The theme of the movie is a young girl's discovery of her own power, so to end it with her screaming was not enough. What we had written was her waking from this strange dream in her bedroom, standing up on the bed and diving into the floor. The floor is like a pool of water. She vanishes and this floor kind of ripples and goes back to wood again. I just didn't know how to realize it.

I think the ending now blunts the film as a whole, because she'd actually mastered these wolves. She'd made them do her bidding and she ends up embracing this wolf. I had to have that little girl, Sarah Patterson, sit down there with a timber wolf and put her arms around this thing. It could have ripped her neck off, so even the actress had to kind of master this monster.

The ending can be seen as a kind of fall from innocence into experience.

It was a tragic fall. That's the only way it can be seen. It can only be seen in generic terms.

After *Angel*, everybody said, "Why are you doing this strange thing?" because they got it into their brains that what I was good at was "poetic realism." You want to do these things because you actually haven't seen it on the screen: that's often the reason why you want to do difficult stuff. We opened it in the biggest cinema in England, the Odeon Leicester Square with this huge party, and everyone was saying, "You're insane to open it at this cinema," because, at the time, they only opened the biggest American movies there. I remember, we had to sit in the premiere and watch it, and the audience was going, "What the fuck is this?" I walked out with Steve Woolley, and there were lines of people everywhere, and I was saying, "What are all these people doing?" and he said, "Well, they're queuing up for the late-night show." [Laughs] It was so funny, and we made a hit with this strange film, which was weird.

Did it do well in North America?

No, it didn't. It was bought by Cannon and they released it as a horror movie. I don't think they actually saw the movie. I think they just saw the trailer for it or something and they paid a lot of money for it. So the financiers made all their money back out of this one sale. I went to America to publicize it, and it was appalling what they'd done. They basically pushed it like *An American Werewolf in London*, and all these slasher, gore movies. They released it this way and the audience felt cheated. I read an article about some woman describing her experience of seeing *The Company of Wolves* in Times Square on the opening night. All these people in the theater just wanted blood, and instead, they saw this strange fairy tale, so they went back and ripped up the theater and everything. So it wasn't released correctly there, but it's become this cult thing. It seems to be the favorite movie for all these heavy metal bands. Every time I meet anybody who plays in a heavy metal band, like Metallica, these guys have seen that movie thirty times. I don't know why.

How did *Mona Lisa* come about? What interested you in particular about this genre?

What is the genre? It's a love story, really. It was a story about the journey of one guy's soul, really, a guy with a beautiful soul, a bit like *The Butcher Boy*, like Francie Brady. He had this wonderful comprehension and openness to experience, but his experience never matched what he hoped for. It was about a naive heart, I thought.

Also, I wanted to do a kind of London movie. It was the first big city I ever encountered. I went over there when I was seventeen or eighteen.

You didn't consider Dublin big?

No, no. Back then, Dublin was provincial, totally narrow-minded. London was my first experience of a metropolis. To me, it was full of darkness and mystery around every corner. I had this image of the city in my mind which I'd never seen in movies, because it's very difficult to photograph London. It's not like New York, with these angular facets to it. London's a collection of suburbs. I had this feeling, this thing in my mind, of a great metropolis with all these lovely shadows and secrets behind the public surface. That was the attraction for me to make *Mona Lisa*. Also, I wanted to make a love story about a man and a woman who didn't understand each other, a love story where somebody was just saying to their loved one, "Just tell me what the story is, dear, please." I had to model the city to make it part of Bob Hoskins' brain when he's looking for this girl. I created a version of London that people hadn't seen, because it probably isn't there.

The music is very important of course.

The music is basically Nat King Cole. It's Nelson Riddle, really. A very good composer called Michael Kamen did the rest of the score. There was too much music in it. That was an argument I had with the production company, Handmade Films. I wanted to take a lot of it off, but they thought that the subject matter was kind of repellent and it needed all this music. The musical motifs in the movie, the Nat King Cole songs, "Mona Lisa," "When I Fall in Love," and all those songs of the fifties, are songs of male isolation and romantic confusion. They're very beautiful.

I find *Mona Lisa* different from your first two films. It's a successful film artistically and commercially, but narratively it seems more conventional to me.

Oh yes, it was much more conventional. I wanted to make a movie about direct human emotions. I wanted to make a movie about the characters, not about artifice. I just wanted to put real emotion on the screen.

You called it a film about yearning.

Yes, that's what it was about. It was about the way men misunderstand women, and have this fixation on this love object that is in their own brain, and rarely in the person they choose. Bob Hoskins wanting this woman to be something that he imagined, and she turned out to be something quite different. That's what I thought the film was about.

Do you want to talk about *High Spirits*?

Yeah, we can talk about that. You should have seen the director's cut.

Is there such a thing?

Well, there should be but there won't be. A comedy is like a mathematical form, and it's got a great appeal to me, though I can't actually do it. There are some absolutely magic comedies like *It Happened One Night*, or *Bringing Up Baby*.

I read this story in the paper about this guy who was running these ghost tours in Ireland. I thought it would be an opportunity to make an elegant Restoration comedy. A bit like an Irish *Whiskey Galore* or *The Man in the White Suit* or something like that. I wrote this little story out. *Mona Lisa* had been quite a success and I wanted to do this tiny little thing in Ireland on a low budget. Then all these Hollywood people got interested in it and it became bigger and bigger and, in the end, it became something different. That's all I can say about that.

Did you lose control of the film?

Yeah, I totally lost control.

Were you unhappy with the actors in the movie?

Nobody engaged in the reality of that movie except Donal McCann, and some of the other Irish actors, who did some thrilling stuff, but none of it ended up on the screen. It was the first time a film had been taken out of my hands. We shot some really wonderful stuff, with Irish characters, caricaturing what they imagined were the caricatures people imposed on them, and a lot of lovely, gentle stuff, and none of it was in the final movie, which ended up being very loud and noisy. If you see the film you can understand what I wanted it to be because it was about this eruption of these dead people. I thought it was a necrophiliac comedy—that's what it should have been—all these dead people falling in love with living people, and at the end, embracing in the grave, embracing corpses.

I found the reaction of critics pretty brutal to that film.

But that's what happens with films. If you get a reputation, they're pitiless when you fail. They come down with hobnailed boots on top of your head. Pauline Kael saw it and liked it. She rang me up and said, "I can see this thing has been cut to ribbons. Can I see the director's cut?" There was no director's cut because I never got to the stage of even compiling my cut. Even before we finished it, they previewed it and started chipping away at it. George Fenton, the composer, who did a beautiful score, said to me, "We've never even seen the movie that we shot." We never had time to consider it, to look at it on screen, you know.

It's lost forever?

I tried to go back to the vaults in Shepperton, and I hired an editor—the editor who cut *Angel*, Pat Duffner—and I said to him, "Pat, just go back and get all the footage out, and look at it," to reassemble what we actually shot. Shepperton wouldn't release it because they hadn't been paid. I got involved with the bad end of Hollywood there. I found the experience horrible. Anton Furst started building these beautiful sets in Shepperton. I was over in Los Angeles and I could see this thing was going really bad, because I was involved with these producers from hell. I rang up my collaborators back in

London, and I said, "Look, I'm going to have to call off the movie." And they all said, "We're doing this amazing stuff, you can't. You've got to keep going and make it work." And I was saying, "Well, it doesn't look good from over here." But when you should say "stop," you don't, and then you end up in manure up to your neck. You imagine you can make it right, and the more you try to make it right, the worse it gets.

I quite liked *We're No Angels*.

Yeah, that I liked. That was a beautiful script by David Mamet. David was being affectionate about a cultural world to which he was an outsider. It was this little Catholic fable, a bit like *Il Miracolo*, or something like that, about these convicts who were redeemed by goodness. I was a director-for-hire on that, really.

You had no input into the casting?

It was written for Robert De Niro and Sean Penn, basically. Mamet actually wrote a play about it called *Speed-the-Plough*. It was a merciless portrait of the Hollywood system. The characters in the play are trying to write this script about two escaped prisoners on the run. I think David wrote the play about the experience of the movie.

Did you have input into the script?

I changed bits and pieces, and there's a visual structure to the thing that is mine, but as to the basic subject matter, it was not my property. It was the first time I'd ever been, I suppose, what you call a "director," and I didn't enjoy the position very much. It was a bit odd.

So it was an unhappy experience?

No, not entirely. I sat with Sean quite a lot. He was splitting up from Madonna at the time, so we had this kind of love-hate relationship going on. I think Sean's performance is marvelous. Because of the kind of relationship that we had, it was slightly fractious but mutually engaged. I think I ignored Robert and should have concentrated more on what he was doing.

There are sweet moments with Sean.

Oh, he's fucking great. They're both great actors, but I think Sean took a lot of my energies. The truth is, working with actors you're always trying to get them to take it down. De Niro is such an actor that if you want him to go into a mad gesture of his own, he can do two million variations of it, and that was fascinating to me. I probably did him a bit of a disservice in not reining him back enough.

The film doesn't have much relationship to the film made in the fifties.

It didn't. The fifties film is terrible.

So you came back and made *The Miracle*, a small film. I find it charming.

I think so. It was me just trying to get out of Hollywood, that's the truth. I wrote the script based on these Irish short stories, and weaved it around these two adolescent kids who were telling stories of the world they were about to experience.

It's interesting that you frequently use people who've never acted before, like Eamonn Owens in *The Butcher Boy* and Jaye Davidson in *The Crying Game*. Why do you do that?

Just because I write these parts. In *The Miracle*, I wrote these parts for kids who were about sixteen or seventeen, and if you want to cast people like that, they're often people who haven't acted before. When I cast Jaye, I couldn't have cast Wesley Snipes or Prince because everyone would know they're men. I had to find some unknown to play that role.

Is there anything about *The Miracle* that you're unhappy with?

I have no idea. Well, it is this Oedipal drama, you know, there's no revelation in the story. You know the story a third of the way through and the characters don't know the story.

The narrative is very subtle.

Yeah. You've got to accept it on a different level. I haven't seen it since I made it. If there is a problem with the movie, it's with the central character, the boy. You're saying, "Come on, you know the story, man. Cut to the chase." To me, the film wasn't about the story. The story was like a mechanism just to explore these themes.

I wonder if the characters are a bit too vague?

Maybe. It was me at that age, really. It's a very personal film. I shot it in my house, and wrote it for the actress [Beverly D'Angelo] who I was having a relationship with at the time. There's one beautiful shot in the film, where she sings "Stardust," and the boy comes up behind her. It lasts for about three or four minutes. The film is about emotion unfulfilled or satisfaction deferred, and it's got all these characters who discover these things too late.

You have good feelings about it?

Yeah, absolutely.

***The Crying Game* obviously struck some kind of incredible nerve. Do you think it was just the taboo subject matter, or great marketing by Miramax?**

I don't know. People liked it a lot. I think it was because it was about the exploration of identity. I don't know why it hadn't been done before, a love affair where somebody is persuasive as a woman and then turns out to be a man.

The story of *The Crying Game* was written after I wrote *Angel*. The film was a kind of inquiry. This guy Fergus [Stephen Rea] is a Catholic and a nationalist, and he identifies himself with certain parameters. He thinks this is what he is, a political animal. He's wedded to violence. He feels that he's a soldier, and is justified in killing people he doesn't know for this cause. I was interested in setting this person up with his polar opposite, someone who is so far away from his experience: a black soldier who is gay, although Fergus didn't know it. If you throw this character on this journey, will he survive and will he change? To me, that was what it was about, really.

He certainly changed.

He changed and survived. To me, it had a lot to do with the IRA at the time, to see if they could change. Could people's narrow identifications of themselves change? This country has been blighted with a sense of exclusive identification of people who see themselves as Catholic, Protestant, Unionist, or Nationalist. It was an exploration of self. That's what I wanted to do with it. If you strip away all these masks human beings wear, is anything left underneath? Is anything left of Fergus when all this stuff is stripped away from him? In fact, there is, and he turns out to be a human being.

Did people criticize your portrayal of the IRA?

Oh yeah, of course they did. There were two criticisms: on the one hand, I made Fergus too sympathetic, and on the other, I made them caricatures. An example is the part that Miranda Richardson played. She was a snarly, psychopathic killer, and I was criticized for that. I was also criticized for daring to make a character, Fergus, a member of the IRA, a cogent, intelligent, rational human being. Did people criticize my portrayal of the IRA? Yes, they did, with great vituperation. At the time, there was this huge argument going on in this country about the issue of the North of Ireland and terrorism. That was such an emotional issue. The minute you even broached it, you were accused of being in sympathy.

Does the criticism bother you?

No, it doesn't bother me. Basically people were saying, "How dare you? Representing these people as anything other than psychopaths does a disservice to the body politic at large." They need to be seen like this to be dealt with and got rid of. The problem, actually, with those kinds of organizations is precisely that they're not psychopaths. If they were, they'd be easy to deal with. The problem is that they are people who've got a decided political agenda and have made rational decisions to blow other people from the face of the earth. The problem is not the psycho-pathology, the problem is the rationality. The film was not an exploration of terrorism or of the IRA or anything like that. It was looking at a character who's a familiar one in the Irish landscape.

I'm curious how you hit upon the twist of unveiling Jaye Davidson's sexuality mid-way through the film?

I'd written the first third of the story, and every time I took the character to London, it didn't seem to work. I'd written the story of Fergus, who kidnaps Jody [Forest Whitaker], who was black, so you've got all these cultural facts that are turned on their head. Fergus regards himself as a member of a repressed minority, yet he kidnaps a black British soldier who took the only job he could get. So you've got this strange thing of the victimized minority victimizing another minority. He inadvertently causes the death of Jody and goes to London, and he does what he was asked to do—basically, tracks down the guy's wife—but Fergus can't reveal his own identity. Every time I came to the London section where he tracks down the wife, it became a bit like a Ken Loach movie, a documentary-realist thing. I didn't know where to go with it. I wasn't really exploring what I wanted to explore.

Then I thought if I'd make the character a man, a transvestite, and Fergus gets absolutely fascinated with her, falls in love with her, has sex with her, and then finds out she's a man, he'll be confronting the person he really killed. Then the story began to make sense to me and that's when I wrote the script. The first part of it is like a one-act play. People say, "There are too many issues going on here," but I think that's bullshit. I think there's such a reductive perception of cinema going on at the moment, in the last ten years. It makes me sick. I think movies should be about something. They should be explorations of ideas, and you should be able to explore anything you want.

Some critics say that the parts don't cohere that well.

Oh, they do. The first part seems to be about politics, and the second part seems to be about something else, but, if anybody thinks politics is not about something else, they're insane. The second part is a mirror of the first part, and everything that happens in the first part happens again in the second part, but in a different way. I'm sure there are things wrong with the movie, of course. There are things wrong with every movie I make.

Do you think the film is essentially about the redemption of Fergus?

It's about whether this man can truly live. Can he live a truly engaged life, as a human being? Can he actually embrace humanity, even though it had a different face to what he always thought it would have? I think it's also a kind of cosmic joke. He's made a promise to look after Jody's "wife," and that's what the act of love is, making a promise, so he's bound by that promise. Will he live up to that promise? I think he will, and that's what I think is heroic about the movie. And if you're in jail for twenty-five years, and you have this pretty thing coming to you, wouldn't you say, "Yeah, I do love you."

We don't know what's going to happen to them.

Well, in twenty-five years, we don't know what's going to happen to anybody, do we? That's all the fun. It's not a movie about a guy discovering that he's homosexual. If it was about that, it would be something quite different. It's about a guy loving another human being. That's all.

After your previous experiences in Hollywood, did you have any trepidation about doing a big Hollywood movie when you agreed to make *Interview With the Vampire*?

David Geffen [the producer] is a very persuasive man. A great guy, actually, a lovely man, very powerful. I didn't know him and he sent me the script. I'd heard about the book, but I hadn't read it. So I read the script which Anne Rice had written, and it was very theatrical but kind of fascinating. It was a vampire movie that took the issue of vampires seriously. After we finished *The Crying Game*, one of the things I was going to do—because Angela Carter had wanted to write a vampire movie—was to do a similar thing to the vampire nexus of things that she did to the werewolf in *The Company of Wolves*. She had written a script called *Vampirella*, which, again, was too short and not quite there. I would love to have worked with her on it, but I didn't get the chance because she died. I really wanted to get back into that Gothic stuff again; I love it. It's like going into a dark, mysterious wood.

I read the Anne Rice book and thought it was a wonderful book. I thought it was one of the best pieces of Gothic fiction since *Dracula*, and really interesting. Not entirely literature, but that only makes it more fascinating in a way. So I said to Geffen that if I could get the script right, I would try and make a movie out of it. I went back to the book and adapted Anne Rice's script, and eventually came up with something I was happy with and sent it to David. He got very excited about it and said he wanted to make it. I was very nervous about making a Hollywood movie, as you can understand. He said, "Look, I'll enable you to make it as an independent film, so you can do exactly what you want," and David is powerful enough to get the studio to do this big movie that cost about seventy million dollars and let me make it the way I made *The Company of Wolves*. To me, it was a blast.

Did you cast Tom Cruise?

Yeah. David had always wanted Brad Pitt to be in it, and at the time, he wanted Daniel Day-Lewis for Lestat. I met Daniel, but he hemmed and hawed for about three or four months and eventually said he didn't want to play a vampire. We were looking around for someone we could cast, thinking of different people, and Tom Cruise's name came up. I went to meet Tom once and then twice, and you know, I thought I'd love to do it with this guy because he's really a fine actor. He's got a kind of pitiless logic to him that would be good for the role. It was obviously casting against type. I'd do another movie with Tom in a minute; he's really a force of nature. Then everybody began objecting, Anne Rice and all that. But, in a way, what happened with Tom and Brad gave us another kind of power, because the world was all against us. We had to run this closed set, and it was as if we were making a tiny movie like *The Company of Wolves*, except with big resources.

Was it a difficult film to make?

No, it wasn't, no.

And the controversy never really affected you very much?

I thought it was all rubbish. I mean, what are you going to say? It was on every talk show, it seems, every week in the United States. You know: "They are doing this. They are taking out the gay subtext. They are doing that," and Anne Rice is on the radio and TV saying all this stuff. But, to me, it was a film about guilt and longing, and if there is a fault in the movie, the fault is also in the book, because once Louis becomes a vampire, they kind of bitch through the ages, don't they? All that changes are the centuries. But I loved that in a strange way. I was aware that it was a picaresque narrative; it wasn't driven by narrative concerns. I was very happy with it because I had the freedom to make it the way I wanted.

There's a kind of airless quality about it.

Of course, it's an unreality. You make a movie about people who are dead, spend two hours with people who are dead, you'll feel a need for fresh air. The problem with it was that, in a way, you couldn't scare people, and I kept saying this to David. When all your protagonists are monsters, you cannot get the scares that you get in normal horror films, because you know they can't die. So it became something different, something about the fascination of repellent things, about decay, and stuff like that.

They became quite a dysfunctional little family. [Laughs]

[Laughs] In a way, yeah, to some extent.

The erotic elements are interesting.

I think so. They're as interesting as they are in the book. Lestat loves Louis, and Louis loves to be punished. And he's punished through eternity, although he doesn't know he loves to be punished.

I'm curious about the kind of discussions you might have had with Cruise and Pitt about the erotic elements of their roles.

What erotic elements? They never had sex, but they never had sex in the book. Their transformation into vampires is always done in a sexual way. They loved to punish each other!

Did you have a rehearsal period? And did you have a lot of discussions with them about their characters?

Yes, I did. We rehearsed for about a week, but I'm not a great rehearser, really. With Tom, it was about the beauty of cruelty in a way. We had a lot of discussions about this. We watched a lot of animal footage, leopards killing rabbits and stuff like this. And with Brad it was about suffering, this beautiful soul that suffers and suffers. That book you could discuss endlessly, so we just got down and made it. To me, it was about visually trying to make this beautifully rotten fruit, in a way. It was a bit like Gustav Klimt or Aubrey Beardsley, that slightly decorative or decadent art at the turn of the century. I just read Flaubert's *Sentimental Education* and realized where Anne Rice got a lot of her stuff for the novel.

So, stylistically, you were going for a painterly look?

I was just trying to create something that was dead, like a funeral home. The whole thing is a series of funereal interiors. I worked with a great designer, Dante Ferretti. I mean, they always lived at night. There was daylight in the first ten minutes of the movie, and after that you're in night until the very end. It was about making their entire world like a coffin: Los Angeles, Paris, San Francisco.

The Paris scenes were quite intriguing. Stephen Rea's character brings a nice humor to the film.

He does, yeah. Stephen based his stuff on the *Comédie Française*. He took these *Comédie Française* videotapes and looked at them all.

Did you feel restricted in any way? You didn't even take credit on the screenplay.

No, I didn't. Nobody restricted me in any way whatsoever.

We come to *Michael Collins*, which is obviously a project very dear to your heart. What was the biggest challenge in writing the script?

Just reducing the whole historical information to under two hours. I had to make the story cogent. But the historical epic form is dead. It's vanished.

Did you feel an obligation to the facts of history?

Yeah, absolutely. You feel leadened, you feel weighed by the facts. You want the narrative to take flight, but the facts make you do this and that. *Michael Collins* was a film really specific to Ireland. It was an odd situation of using the resources of major companies to make a movie that was directed towards an Irish and British audience. When I showed it in America, people were kind of puzzled by it, because it didn't follow the rules of epic movies like *Braveheart*. They want to see the reasons for the character's need for justice. They probably wanted to see Michael Collins [Liam Neeson], as a young man, being kicked about by British soldiers, or something. But I just wanted it to be about very simple logic. People say, "Okay, to resolve this situation, we shall use violence," and they engage in a series of acts that actually do have a result. But out of that result, a punishment comes. The very fact that they're using violence to achieve this aim extracts an inevitable price to be paid and the price is terrible. I suppose that's the story of the Irish War of Independence. I just wanted to present it as barely as possible, so the first part of it is these guys, and you see the horrible nature of the killings they involve themselves in, and in the second part, they've unleashed a kind of a beast which will consume them. I thought it was quite simple.

You portray Michael Collins very heroically.

I thought he was heroic in a strange way. I thought he was a realist.

You were criticized for your portrayal of deValera, the character played by Alan Rickman.

Yeah, I was. I was harsh on deValera, very harsh.

You focused on his worst period.

I did, but I was probably a bit too harsh because he behaved very badly then, he really did.

What was his career after that?

After that he became a great statesman, a very admirable figure, really. And I feel bad, not that I gave a bad portrait of him, but that I just gave a portrait of that period of his life. In many ways, he's quite an admirable man; he was a very good mathematician, a very brainy man. I think what was admirable about the guy in the end was that he was a democrat. What was amazing about all those characters was that they came out of this period of 1910-20, where, all across Europe, others were led to fascism. In the case of these poor Irish geezers, they actually were kind of stumbling democrats in the end. That's what I thought was remarkable about Collins. In the end, having forged this military machine to achieve a certain purpose, he tried to decommission it and learn the rules of democracy. He failed, in a way, but in the end, a certain kind of democratic state did emerge.

But compromise is also a part of democracy.

Oh, sure. But people in Ireland have been so afraid of that period of history, afraid of any examination of it because of the activities of the provisional IRA in North of Ireland. It's been interpreted and misinterpreted and revised, and making *Michael Collins* was like throwing a little grenade into the whole proceedings.

To start a debate?

No, I just wanted to show it as barely as I could, and as pitilessly as I could, because I thought it would be very healthy for people in Ireland to look at this aspect of their own past. It's very recent and most of their parents were involved in it. And to pretend that we had a bloodless transition to a republic is ludicrous. It was actually very bloody and perhaps unjustified. Blood is always unjustified, isn't it? To pretend that didn't happen is a kind of schizophrenia.

Was there a big debate here about the film?

Oh yeah, there was. A furious debate, absolutely furious. While we were making it, when I announced I was going to make it, after I'd made it, and probably still, bits of it are going on. I always thought they would say, "Great, people are taking an interest in our subject!" But, I was accused of being a Nationalist, a Republican, I was accused of being a lover of violence, and I was accused of the opposite.

Do you think the characterizations in the film are fully developed?

The relationship with Kitty [Julia Roberts] is underdeveloped. I couldn't afford to take them to London. If I had taken them to London, I could have got involved in Lady Lavery and all sorts of stuff. It would have been very boring cinema, but we would have fleshed out our historical perspective. I read the letters from Kitty to Harry Boland [Aidan Quinn], and they were every innocent, almost Victorian. I just based it on the letters, really. Maybe they should have had sex, I don't know. You've got to look at what you know, rather than what you surmise. And what you do know is that Collins and Boland were in love with this woman, and they both proposed to her. In the end, she fell for Collins and agreed to marry him, and towards the end of his life they were planning their wedding. That's what I do know. But the movie was not about sex; it was about the moral questions that acts of violence give rise to. I cast Julia Roberts. I think she's very beautiful and she's very good in the film. If you cast stars, people can't accept them as ordinary human beings, that I understand. People had a bit of a problem with seeing Julia Roberts in a movie about Ireland.

The film is pretty linear in its narrative construction.

Yeah, I tried to keep myself out of it as far as possible. I wanted to be as objective as I could, and when it was released in America people said, "Well, this isn't a Neil Jordan movie." It was very odd. What do they imagine a Neil Jordan film is? They said, "It's not what we expected of this guy," and then when I came out with *The Butcher Boy*, they all went, "Ah, here's a Neil Jordan film. Where has he been?" It's very strange.

The look of the film is quite beautiful.

We tried to reproduce the effect of gaslight. It was a khaki and white movie, rather than black and white, and a bit of blue; not bluish, it's kind of pale greens.

It must have been an extremely difficult film to make.

No! It was lovely to make. It was delightful to make. Logistically it was huge, but that's great fun. No, seriously, there's nothing more pleasurable than that. It was very well planned, a bit like military manoeuvers. We hadn't very much money, and we had to achieve a huge amount in the twelve weeks that we shot it in, but it was quite inspiring. All the actors who got involved researched their characters like crazy. We were reenacting quite large historical events, and trying to recreate things through whatever we'd seen, out of photographs and documentary footage. It was very thrilling to make.

Is it inevitable in a film of that scope that you have to compromise with the facts? You've got so much material to deal with, so you eliminate characters or create others?

Yeah, of course. But you've got to concentrate your mind. You've got two hours to tell a certain story, so you say, "Well, what is this story about?" Because there could be many movies made about Michael Collins. You could make a ten-hour movie about the guy's life. There could be many movies made about the Irish War of Independence. To my mind, it was about the use of violence and the consequences of the use of violence. I centered everything around that theme.

Did Liam Neeson do a lot of research for the role?

Oh, he did, yeah. We looked at the photographs and documentary footage. Liam was huge about research. We went and looked up Michael Collins' family. Liam was great. He gave this rural energy to the guy, a feeling that you can almost smell the straw off his boots.

He's fierce in the role.

Oh, yeah, pitiless in a way, the way Collins probably was.

So, in your own mind, you're satisfied with *Michael Collins*?

By the time you finish a film, you've done the best you can with the resources at your disposal, and you've exhausted your brain through the effort of making this work. I generally try to do the best I can, and it's hard to say that you regret something. If you have a child, do you regret that it has blonde hair rather than brown hair, that kind of thing? I'm sure I could have done a better job if I were a better director and a better human being, but this was the best I could do.

Let's talk about *The Butcher Boy*. It's a great movie.

Well, it's Pat McCabe's novel. I read the book when I was doing *Interview With the Vampire*, and I bought the rights to it. Pat's an amazing writer. I commissioned him to write a screenplay. He did a draft and then another draft, and I did the final draft. Coming off two big movies like *Interview with the Vampire* and *Michael Collins*, the main thing about *The Butcher Boy* was a weird feeling, kind of naked. That was a difficult film to make, really hard, because it was like stripping down what we do. I wasn't making a big movie anymore, but this tiny little film, entirely about the character, and about emotions and nuances of emotion and the rawness of emotion. It's much more difficult to do than use 2,000 pounds of explosives to blow up buildings.

What was the most crucial element for you to retain from the book? Was it the tone or the voice-over?

It was to reinvent the novel for the screen, really. If you were faithful to the way the book proceeds, it would make a very bad movie. It was to recreate the emotional feeling I had when I finished the book; that's what I wanted to get on to the screen. There was something very cinematic in the middle of the novel, in Francie's obsession, in the way he sees himself as a cartoon character, and his obsession with cartoons. Yet the book was written in this beautifully dense language, and through the voice of the kid. It seems to happen inside the boy's head, so it seems unfilmable. But on the other hand, it absolutely is filmable. I worked with Pat McCabe the way I'd worked with Angela Carter on *The Company of Wolves*, trying to find the cinematic equivalent for his unique book.

Where did you find Eamonn Owens, the boy who plays Francie Brady?

I found him up in Killeshandra. I saw thousands of kids.

How did you work with him on his performance? He must be a very rambunctious little guy.

Well, he's a very sweet, lovely, but tough guy. I videotaped a lot of the kids that came in. He came in, and I got him to play the part and followed him around with the video camera, just to read through the scene. I looked at that stuff and it was really good. I called him back and we did more stuff with the video camera, and explored it some more, almost like play. Then we went out to Ardmore studios, and I photographed him again in the real environment, in the open fields and stuff like that, and so his engagement with the part got a bit deeper. That's the way it happened, really. Through that series of tests I saw that he was quite a remarkable actor, and then we started doing the film and his performance grew deeper and deeper. I realized I'd found a remarkable talent here.

It was also the way that Pat McCabe had imagined this world of childhood, had recreated it. It was so true that all those boys just stepped into it like stepping into their own suits or something. It's very difficult to be accurate about childhood, but I think McCabe wrote one of the best books about childhood ever written. So I didn't have to do anything to get those kids to act, because the parts just fitted them rather beautifully.

In some ways the voice-over narration is the key to the work.

Oh yeah, of course it is.

What's interesting is that Stephen Rea is supposed to be narrating from the perspective of an adult, but he's actually narrating from the perspective of a grown-up who is still a twelve-year-old.

And you feel that.

Absolutely. It seems like he's actually imitating Eamonn's voice patterns.

Yeah, of course. The whole film was structured around the voice-over. There's a very interesting relationship between the narration in that film and what actually happens on screen: very funny, deeply ironic. So, the first two drafts Pat had written had no voice-over, and I said, "We've got to have the voice in here, because the voice of Francie Brady is obviously central to the book," and I wanted it to have a specific relation to the action in the film, because the voice is saying one thing and the film's doing another. Sometimes the voice would intrude in the narrative and talk to the boy. I just thought it could be used in a unique way for this film.

When Stephen came to do the voice-over, obviously he was finished with the movie, so he'd acted with Eamonn and seen his performance. He'd heard his voice and vocal speech patterns. By the time he came to actually put the voice-over onto film, he knew all that stuff, so he could link his own mental words right to Eamonn's.

You suddenly shift tone in the middle of scenes. It's like pulling the rug out from under the viewer. You're laughing and suddenly it's shocking.

The difficulty with the tone was that you could never put caricature in. It had to be kind to its characters, because the book and the movie is longing for a villain, and if you gave the story a villain you would have messed up the whole film. Even Mrs. Nugent [Fiona Shaw] is not a villain. You see her from her own perspective. The difficult thing about directing the movie was actually getting that tone right. If any of the actors veered into a kind of caricature, it was like a red flag; you could just see it instantly.

It's a film with a simple logic, because Francie always laughs, he always makes you laugh, and he always laughs at himself. The book actually is far more sardonic. In the book he rips out Mrs. Nugent's intestines, and all this stuff, and he walks around with her chopped up parts. What I'm saying is the book is a comic book, but about these horrific things. You couldn't actually read the book if it wasn't comic, because laughter is a great way of looking at the unmentionable. It a very simple logic: the more Francie made you laugh as an audience, the more you liked him. The more you liked him, the more you felt for him, and the more you felt for him the more you laughed with him, so it was laughter and horror. A rhythm was established in the telling of the story, and the balance between laughter and horror gets faster and faster towards the end of the movie, so by the end you're horrified one second and you're laughing the next, whereas at the start, the tone shifts, but at a slower pace.

You implicate the period, in a way, because this society isn't equipped to deal with Francie: not the church, not the psychiatrists.

Even now, perhaps. Some things never change. And, in a way, I thought the guy had a soul too beautiful for the world, you know, a heart too big. And the world is inevitably going to disappoint him. I mean, it's about 1950s Ireland, but it's not an indictment of Ireland in the fifties. There obviously were no social services. Actually, the kid led a great bucolic life. He was left to run free. I'd love to have had a childhood like that. You couldn't have nowadays.

But in some ways Francie also represents something we fear, this kind of irrational aspect of our psyche, or the uncontrollable aspect of the self.

Yeah, he's a human being of that culture. He's the unaccommodated man. He's somebody who refuses to learn the rules of disappointment. He refuses to civilize his feelings because that would do his feelings an injustice. Pat McCabe struck gold with that character. I suppose it's a bit like Holden Caulfield. You can explain who he was, or what he was, but you don't know why or how.

Stylistically, you deliberately went the way of surrealism, or at least non-naturalism.

Well, the book is like that. It happens in the boy's imagination, and real events and unreal events have the same weight to him. The Virgin Mary [Sinead O'Connor] appearing in a field is as real to him as a bogman wolfing down his potatoes. He hadn't learned to separate these things into different categories.

I saw that movie *Heavenly Creatures*, which I didn't like. They had these claymation figures going on, and they didn't seem to have any emotional resonance or connection with the world of the characters, and it seemed wrong to me in some way. I wouldn't have done all that imaginary stuff in *The Butcher Boy* if it didn't come directly out of the character. It had to come directly out of his voice and his mental world and his soul. I don't like movies where they strain for significance. It seemed to come out of the perspective of a child's world, and particularly Francie Brady's world. You've got to lead the audience through this film, and they follow the journey with this boy, so halfway through the movie they realize they're watching somebody go mad in front of their eyes. All the connective tissue is broken and separated, but it's the same things you were looking at in the beginning of the movie, except they're in a different place now.

What is your perspective on Francie at the end of the film, when he comes out of the hospital?

Has he changed? Yeah, he's changed. He knows he's done a bad thing. He does! [Laughs] He says, "No more chopping up." He hasn't changed his language, and he doesn't regret, but he's changed. He's a sinner who's finding redemption in the only way he knows. The sinners never regret their sins, do they, really? Regret is not the same thing as repentance.

What's been the response to the film in Ireland?

They absolutely loved it.

And your portrayal of Irish life?

It wasn't an unkind portrayal. It was deeply sympathetic to all, even to the priests, the old priest that Milo O'Shea played. It wasn't un-sympathetic, and it wasn't untrue. I think they saw that it wasn't untrue. There's a lot of caricatures you could make of those figures, like the town drunk or the parish priest or the pedophile priest or the suicidal mother. I think they were portrayed accurately and with sympathy, and I think people saw that. They also saw an aspect of

Irish experience that they never thought was worthy of fiction, and how fascinating it is, that small town thing. You think, "Oh, if you make movies, they should be about more obviously dramatic aspects of our experience," whereas when they saw this, and they saw how true it was, they liked it.

What is your relationship to Hollywood exactly? Do you consider yourself an independent filmmaker?

Yes, I do.

You've somehow worked it out that you can work for the studios and retain your independence.

Well, I think it's more simple than that. I've got a very visual imagination, and sometimes some of the projects I want to do involve creating stuff that you can only do on large budgets. So unlike Mike Leigh or Ken Loach, I'm condemned to have to encounter the system to explore the things I want to do. Mike Leigh can quite happily work in London because his artistry expresses itself through the fabric of real people's lives, whereas I do movies like *Interview With the Vampire* or *The Company of Wolves*. I suppose I've got large tastes every now and then, as well as small tastes, so I'm condemned to be there or not be there. But it's not a bad place to be. I don't make commercial movies, really. I'm only a marginally successful director, commercially, but, for some reason, they continue to allow me to make films. It's silly to pretend that you've no relationship with Hollywood. Every director does, anywhere in the world, even independent directors, because in the end their films have to be distributed by that system. But I won't make a movie where I haven't got the freedom to do what I want to do. I won't do that ever again.

Are things wrong with the film industry?

Oh, dreadful. But things are wrong with the culture, not just the film industry. The film industry reflects the broader culture we live in, very sad times. If there was a way of measuring the state of the soul through the cultural artifacts any culture produces, I'd say we're in a pretty bad way. You've got to realize I'm also a novelist. People bemoan the state of the film industry, but they haven't ever encountered the publishing industry; that is appalling. What's happened over the last twenty years, since I began writing fiction, is shocking. It's a justification for major violence if I was that way inclined. The publishing industry is dominated by numbers. It's in as appalling a state as the film industry. It's the culture that's fucked, I think.

As an Irish artist, do you ever feel the weight of your cultural past?

No, I don't think so. But you only know what you know, don't you? That's what I know. I grew up in a Catholic country, with a strange pagan kind of Catholicism that you get in Ireland; it's different from elsewhere. It was very superstitious, but a lot of that's gone now, thank goodness. It's a world that teaches you the value of fables. I suppose it teaches the rules of imaginative behavior, in a strange way. The only thing Irish people are good at is imagination. They're not good at football; they were never good at painting; they haven't got great architecture; they didn't build great empires. All they're really good at is their wit and their brains, redeeming the world through the way they imagine and perceive it.

What gives you the greatest pleasure in being a filmmaker?

The whole thing is a great pleasure and I should do it more. I could probably do it better, because it's a great gift to be allowed to make a movie. I like the whole thing. Most of all I like the activity of doing it, being engaged in some fiction which, in many ways, is more rewarding than life. You can aim at a certain kind of perfection in fiction that you can never achieve in life.

RICHARD LINKLATER

Richard Linklater's first theatrically released film was the seminal *Slacker*, a film that became a kind of touchstone for a certain segment of the twenty-something generation at the end of the eighties and into the early nineties. With its fragmented narrative structure and huge cast of characters that only briefly pass through the cinematic terrain of Austin, Texas, *Slacker* remains a key film in the director's oeuvre and a significant cinematic experiment. Along with such key works as Douglas Coupland's *Generation X* and the music of Seattle grunge band Nirvana, it seems to have tapped into a certain generational zeitgeist in remarkably prescient ways. Linklater claims that the portrait is an essentially positive view of this generation, although he also says that it's pretty dark... "there's a certain pissed-off, on-the-verge-of-anarchy quality."

Linklater followed *Slacker* with *Dazed and Confused*, easily one of the best rock n' roll films of the contemporary era that perfectly captured the teen angst in small town America of the mid-seventies. *Dazed and Confused* confirmed that Linklater was a filmmaker of genuine substance and that *Slacker* was no fluke. The director skillfully orchestrated a large ensemble of actors into a coherent narrative, creating recognizable characters and truthful situations familiar to millions of Americans. He also incorporated a great soundtrack into its narrative, using the music not simply as background to the action, but as an ironic commentary on the actors and situations. The film introduced several notable actors, including Matthew McConaughey and Ben Affleck, to a wider audience, something the director has continued to do in all his films, most recently in *SubUrbia* with the attention-grabbing performances of Giovanni Ribisi and Steve Zahn.

SubUrbia was an honorable attempt at translating to the screen Eric Bogosian's acerbic play about another kind of lost generation of disaffected youth. It was not a commercial success, although it has built a strong afterlife on video as almost all of Linklater's films continue to do. Both *SubUrbia* and *Dazed and Confused* also illustrate one of the problem that has plagued Linklater's career: the relatively poor handling and distribution of his films. Because his work tends to play with genre convention, or combine several genres, it is not easily pigeon-holed, and presents a definite marketing challenge that has often not been met by the films' distributors.

Linklater's riskiest venture—in many ways—was the two-character romance *Before Sunrise*, starring Ethan Hawke and Julie Delpy. The film basically has two lovers meet, talk, and stroll around the streets of Vienna in the course of an evening, and eventually fall in love. The film illustrates many of Linklater's strengths as a director: a sincere commitment to his material, superb work with actors, strong character-centered filmmaking, a solid structure, yet a willingness to experiment with form (the actors contributed much of the dialogue as the film was being made), and a keen awareness of film history and previous cinematic models.

This awareness of earlier cinematic form is most evident in *The Newton Boys*, a large scale western/gangster film that echoes the classical work of such great directors as Howard Hawks, John Ford, and Nicholas Ray. *The Newton Boys* has all the ingredients of a successful film: strong acting and colorful characterizations, a compelling story and well-structured screenplay, and exciting action sequences. The film ultimately proved a commercial disappointment and one wonders if part of Linklater's problem is that he is simply too tasteful a filmmaker for the contemporary film market. In the span of just one decade, Linklater has created an extraordinary body of work, and he must be ranked as one of the best directors to emerge in the 1990s. I spoke to Richard Linklater in New York City.

You grew up in the sixties and seventies in Texas. What was life like?

My parents got divorced when I was a kid, and I lived with my mom. She had a teaching job in a small town in East Texas. So, my real crucial years, ten to seventeen, were in this East Texas town called Huntsville, which only hits the map when they execute people. The state prison is there, so I grew up in this world where the state prison dominates the landscape.

Was it culturally disadvantaged?

Yes, but I did have one advantage. When I visited my dad in Houston on the weekends, he would take me and my sisters to museums, movies, and things like that, so I wasn't that deprived. There wasn't any money, so I never travelled or anything, but my mom and dad were educated, literate, and pretty culturally aware.

Was it a particularly difficult childhood?

Looking back, it was something of a struggle, especially living with a single mom with three kids in the inflationary seventies. I remember working all the time. From the sixth grade on, I always had summer jobs because I had to. So, there was no privilege, certainly, but at the time it just feels like your life.

What was your interest in film at that time?

Oh, nothing special other than I liked every movie I saw, like most kids. It was always fun. Though I do remember *2001: A Space Odyssey* having a really profound effect on me. I was in first grade or something and I remember it was really stunning, and I somehow felt I understood it completely. That's a tribute to Kubrick's genius, I guess, that it could communicate so clearly on so many levels. In the fifth to the eighth grade, movies were the cornerstone of our social lives. There would be a new one every Friday on the one screen in town, and we'd all meet there.

When did films become more serious for you as a moviegoer?

It was very gradual. I always thought I'd be a writer. Making films wasn't really in the realm of possibility. It's just something no one in Texas did.

Did you go to college?

I ended up going two years to the school in Huntsville, Sam Houston State.

Were there any other special films growing up?

I remember when I was a senior in high school, I saw *Eraserhead* at a midnight show. Four of us went, and the three people I went with left. I refused to go with them, completely mesmerized by the look and the tone. I'd never seen anything even remotely like it. When I was in college, and writing plays, I saw *Raging Bull*, which became another touchstone for me. I loved the depiction of the characters so much, their psychology, and the film was so beautiful, so poetic, the period detail so perfect. It was like "Oh my God! Film can be that?" I remember telling everyone they had to go see it. I hadn't seen that many great films, but that one really opened up something. From then on I considered myself serious about cinema and started actively seeking out other films. I still lived in the backwater, but when I eventually moved to Houston I discovered the many venues that were going to be my education.

How did you start making films?

It was a couple of years later. I had dropped out of school and was working on off-shore oil rigs in the Gulf of Mexico. At that point my future was truly a blank slate. I wasn't in school. I didn't have a term paper due or any kind of social life. I spent all my time reading, all the classics, with a particular emphasis on nineteenth century Russian literature. Some days off shore, I'd get ten hours of reading in. Everybody out there thought I was crazy. When I was back on land, I found myself at movies more and more. I also saw films on the university campuses and local museums. I'd go home from racing around to two or three movies and read up whatever I could about the director or the studio or the actor, whatever impressed me about the movie. I did that very systematically. I'd write down details about every film I saw. I'd check out books from the library on the French New Wave or whatever, and I studied books on the history of cinema. I hadn't even thought about touching a camera. I was buying books on film, not technical books, strictly history and aesthetics. Eventually I did buy a book called *The Technical Aspects of Filmmaking*, but I didn't open it for a while. I didn't think I was quite ready. I kept watching tons of movies and reading. I'd seen some low-budget features and student-type films, both in 16mm and Super 8, so I had in mind what I was going to be doing when the time was right. That point came when I got laid off the oil-rig job and decided to move to Austin [Texas]. I'd saved up a lot of money—about $18,000—so I bought a camera, some editing equipment, a projector, and a ton of film stock.

You were going to make Super8 or 16mm?

Super8 because it seemed the most cost-effective way to learn. It's sort of comical looking back, I had no experience whatsoever and no indication I had any talent for it at all. I was just going on pure passion. I sort of planted my flag and said "Okay, I'm a filmmaker. This is what I'm going to do." I started shooting films. I'd spent a lot of money on this equipment and I knew I couldn't just blow it off easily. I was really systematic with my days. I wasn't in school, I wasn't working. I just created this cinema world for myself where I could watch two or three movies a day, read and write what I wanted, shoot a lot of film and edit all night. It was all purely technical exercises initially. They had no ambition to them other than learning. I wasn't expressing anything. I would do a film on editing or lighting or camera movement. I did that for about two solid years. At that point, I was still thinking maybe I would get into film school.

Why did you decide not to go to film school?

I actually applied to University of Texas and a couple of other schools, but I didn't get accepted, which was fine because by that time I'd sat in on a few production classes and decided it wasn't for me. I was already kind of getting ahead of it all just on my own and I didn't like the idea of others judging what I was doing. I felt I was on my own path and wanted it to continue as long as possible. I knew I'd be in for plenty of feedback and criticism eventually.

Were there any screenings around of experimental film groups.

Yes, there was one, which I submitted a couple of my shorts to, but they got rejected. [Laughs] This is just in Austin. I went to a couple of meetings and I met a guy, Lee Daniel, who was actually finishing up film school. We were both shooting Super8 and became friends. There weren't many around like us. I remember he came over to the room I was living in and I showed him all the shorts I'd been working on. Hardly anyone had ever seen them.

Had you lost your interest in theater by this point?

Yes. It practically went away over night. I'd completely lost interest. No one ever describes the specific skills you need to be a film director. There's no written description but I would say one of the absolutely necessary talents is a visual memory. I can edit a whole sequence in my head. I remember all the shots in a movie. You have to be able to edit in your head while you're shooting. I remember everything, really, every conversation I've ever had, however many years ago. That is until more recent years, when I meet so many more people than I used to, and often under fairly fleeting conditions. The short-term memory tends to be more strained these days.

When did you start the Austin Film Society?

During my second year in Austin, the fall of 1985, mainly out of a frustration with what was showing. As many films as they were screening, there was a certain academic redundancy to their scheduling and some huge gaps. Lee and I wanted to see other kinds of films. So, we started renting films from distributors and trying to get an audience to see them. I enjoyed that because my own films were private undertakings and it was a good thing to learn how to hustle in a more public way. It's a very outgoing endeavor to get a theater, run ads, put up flyers, and create an event out of it all. It's also a lot of fun. I always say that by running the Austin Film Society, I learned everything I needed to produce a movie like *Slacker*; how to cut corners, how to make something happen out of nothing. That's what you do with a film. I always suggest to people that, while you're making or trying to make films, you should have some parallel film activity like running a film society or a theater or helping to distribute a film. I got a lot of joy out of showing movies and I still do. Last year at the film society, we showed 139 movies, and it's very satisfying to me.

At the same time the Film Society was getting going, I'd started to work on my Super-8 feature, *You Can't Learn to Plow by Reading Books*, which ended up taking two years. It was about a year of shooting and a year of editing. I was really honing my instincts to work a bigger canvas. That was the first time I was actually attempting to say something, however oblique.

Is it more like a diary film?

Kind of a visual diary, with hardly any dialogue. But it's definitely a narrative. It's about communication, or lack of communication. It's the most alienated film I've ever made. People thought *Slacker* was an upper in comparison. It's a lot about the mechanics of everyday life, getting from one point to another and keeping moving. There's a kind of modern alienation thing going on that's pretty Bressonian. I'm also in the film. I had a tripod, my camera and some sound gear, and it was just me making this film, completely alone. I had no help on any level. This little Super8 feature was actually a big step in my development.

There were also other films I wanted to do. I had the idea for *Slacker* even earlier, or at least the structure of it. I'd had a lot of years to think about how it would work and that never went away from me, so I did that next. I'd written a script for something else I was trying to get made, a slightly more conventional picture, but I could never get it off the ground. I never raised even a penny. *Slacker* was a reaction to the failure to get this "real film" made. I thought I could make this other experimental film [*Slacker*] in my own neighborhood and get people to work for free. It was designed around its economic limitations.

How did *Slacker* come about?

I was living in a warehouse in Galveston during the week, where I was trying to get this other film going and failing miserably. I'd go back to Austin on the weekends usually to project for whatever film series we had going. When it became fully apparent that I wasn't going to make this other movie I said, "Okay. I'm going to go back and make that experimental narrative that I've been thinking about forever." For five or six years, I'd been keeping notebooks of ideas, weird little things, dialogue or whatever. In one twenty-four-hour period, in spring 1989, I sat down and wrote the entire script: where it starts, where it ends, what every scene is about. I had the structure. What was important was the through-line. If I had dialogue already written, or scenes, I would jot that down, but it was really the interconnectedness that was important.

But where did the idea come from?

The idea came when I was driving to Houston from Austin. It was about two in the morning and it hit me. It's such a youthful idea, "Oh, why couldn't you make a film like this?" It was an idealistic thing where you're getting into cinema for the first time and are so excited about the possibilities, wondering what it can do and feeling no restriction. I think it's good to attack a medium that way, looking for new territory.

In the films I made earlier, several with Lee, we would do things like put the camera on the end of a fishing line—a little Super-8 camera found at a garage sale—and cast it off a building and reel it back up, just to see what the footage looked like. Or wrap it up and throw it off a building. That's where the last scene from *Slacker* came from, where these people make a movie and throw the camera off. So anyway, this idea just hit me like a thunderbolt. It was like a whole world opened up and I realized film would be the perfect medium to utilize this story structure. There are lots of literary precedents. I'm a Joyce fan, and there's even a scene in the movie where a guy is reading from *Ulysses*. I thought it could be in seemingly real time, and you would experience the day and night through all these different characters. It's really the film that holds it all together, but the characters are interchangeable.

Did the structure change much from what you had written?

Not much. I played with it a little. The idea originally was to be talking, and in mid-sentence, the camera would whip around and go somewhere else. That seemed too random and drew too much attention to itself. I wanted the viewer pulled in the way you get pulled into a conversation when you're at a party, talking, and someone else comes up, and you start talking to them, and then you realize you've kind of drifted off to another conversation. It all makes perfect sense where you start your day, and where you end your day. You can look back on it and go, "Yes, well, I talked to her and I ran into him, and I went to a movie." There's an interlinked chain. All our lives are one continuous link that you couldn't get out of even if you wanted to. I wanted the film to seem like that, too, that you went through a day, and ran into these people, and experienced different things and different opinions. Austin had that kind of atmosphere, and that's why a lot of it is on foot.

Stylistically, does it relate at all to your earlier shorts?

No, not really. The style of *Slacker* was to move the camera a lot. I didn't move it at all in my first film. In this one, I wanted to do the opposite. There's a lot of movement. Even when the camera is stagnant, like in the cab ride, we're moving. So, I wanted much more movement, and it was all about talking, like one continuous monologue. And one-sided, too. It was about obsessions. I'd been in acting classes for a few years at this point, and I realized that in most acting classes you get up and do a monologue. You do a scene, maybe with someone else, but usually by yourself, just talking.

How personal is the material in *Slacker*?

That's an interesting question because on one level it's really personal and on another level it's just things out of the blue, little episodes I'd seen in the world. I guess they become personal when you choose to put them into your film.

***Slacker* seems like the kind of film you'd only want to do once in your life.**

I don't know. My mind really does work that way, so I wouldn't rule out that I might do something similar at some point. But *Slacker* was so much of its time and place and mind set. I haven't seen it in several years but the last time I saw it, I thought, "Oh, I was kind of crazy." Nothing's happening in the film, but it's pretty dark, what the characters are talking about. There's a certain pissed-off, on the verge of anarchy quality.

Did you do much rehearsal with your actors?

Yes, extensive rehearsals, depending on the scene, but often it was the night before. We rehearsed and the next day we'd shoot the scene.

You used a lot of non-actors.

Yes, casting was crucial. I would cast the most interesting people I could find, nonprofessionals. We handed out cards, me and my little group, particularly Ann Walker who is now my producer. I was just rounding up anyone who I thought would want to work on the film and not get paid. [Laughs] They would come in for a video interview, and I would say, "Hey, how's it going? What do you do, what's going on, what are you thinking?" And then as they're talking, I would cast them in my mind, like, "Okay, she could be the paranoid lady. He can be the guy in the bar." I had all these parts. I did write some episodes with people in mind. I have a friend who's a JFK assassination buff, John Slate. I think he's pretty funny, so we worked up a lot of that in rehearsals.

Did you stick pretty much to what you had written.

Yes, I would often write the dialogue right before the first rehearsal, and I'd rewrite it as we did it. Or the actors would make their own joke, and I'd say, "Hey, you know, that's perfect!" So, you're picking and choosing and manipulating. It's a real balancing act. But by the time we were shooting the scene, it was one hundred percent scripted.

Did you have any professional actors?

Almost everyone had some acting experience and a few had been in acting classes with me, like Charles Gunning, who plays Slim in *The Newton Boys*. I always remembered him and I custom-wrote his scene, at least the first part where he's talking about his stepfather. That was based on an improv he did in class three years before. I remembered it verbatim. Then, as he was reading the scene, he goes, "Well, shit, I can relate to this. I had a stepfather I really hated." He barely remembered me from the class three years earlier.

In a film like this, I'm curious just how much the characters were encouraged to create a backstory?

No one had a backstory. They had no names, they had no desires outside what was going on in their head. It was kind of like a Godard film; there's no history to these people. They're just mouthpieces for the film. I was really strict about that. There's no depth to the characters. You don't get to know them, you don't want to know them, it's impossible. Why confuse the issues? None of them knew what the film was about, because they only knew the episode they were in.

They didn't know what other people were doing?

No, and there wasn't a full script available to anyone. It was kind of a D.W. Griffith film in that respect. It was only when they saw the final film that they said, "Oh, it's a series. Everybody's kind of like me." No one put it all together. Even the people I was working with, as we were making it, would say, "It seems like everyone's giving a long monologue, someone's doing all the talking and someone's doing all the listening, they're not really communicating."

What was the shoot like? Was it difficult?

Now that's the film I would only want to do once. I had a camera and a Nagra, and about five to seven of us would usually show up. It was like, "Okay, we're shooting tomorrow. We can do that scene in the morning." So, we'd all show up at 6:30, and I rehearsed all night with the actors. But we had days off. If Lee, my cameraman, was off doing a commercial or working as an AC, then we would shut down for two days. Because there went our camera and our cameraman. But that was okay, because I needed that time to plan, to rehearse and to keep casting. The process was continuous. It's amazing how quick it all happened though. We had our first production meeting in May 1989, and we were shooting on the fourth of July weekend. We shot it in thirty-five days over a two-month period and a lot of those were half-days. That's pretty fast, especially for a no-budget film.

Did you shoot any extra material that didn't get into the film?

Yes. I had no concept of how long the film would be, I liked the idea that it might be three hours long, and when it was finished, it was long, but not in the good way. I went back and cut out some sections, re-shot a few links to tighten it and shot a couple of scenes which could make new links. Like most movies, I cut out some really good stuff that just didn't quite fit.

But it didn't give you any problems in terms of restructuring?

No. It was an easy film to edit. It was like one long take, and you have an in and out point. And I used the same lens, the same look for the whole movie. I didn't want anything to distract. I wanted it to seem like documentary. There's a lot of very choreographed movement with a dolly. We borrowed a dolly all summer from the TV show *Austin City Limits*. They had a particular dolly they weren't using, and we just went up there one night late and, how do you say, borrowed it. We returned it a couple of months later. It was that kind of production [laughs].

Did you feel like your inexperience as a director was a disadvantage, either with the actors or with the crew?

No. In those acting classes all those years, my teacher would let me direct a lot of scenes in class. She'd go, "Rick, go work with them and make that scene work." I think I had a natural thing with working with actors. I liked all the people and even though they were non-actors, it was fun to work with them. It was interesting for the first time to work with a crew. I had to learn to articulate my personal ideas to others, and not be shy or defensive.

I found out how egoless a director really has to be. On one level, it's the most egotistical thing you can imagine. On the other, during the actual production, you really have to put that away and deal with the reality in front of you. To work with a group, you have to become the master manipulator of everyone's time and energies. You bring everybody aboard, and it's only when the film's done that they realize you've brought them in to help make your film [laughs]. But we were all friends back then, and we're still all friends.

You used a lot of long takes in the film's style.

It's just the way it felt natural to me to tell that story. Consciously it was anti-MTV and quick-cutting. I wanted it to seem real and have a kind of documentary feel.

Following the characters around?

Yes, I wanted that. I wanted it to seem unmanipulated and real, and the more cuts you make, the more the audience, on some level, is aware of being manipulated. Of course, sometimes I had to cut, and it felt like some kind of a moral violation. When I started cutting, I didn't like doing it at all. Every cut was a big deal.

Did the narrative experiment dictate that this movie had to keep moving, that it had to have this momentum?

Yes. The narrative was all about movement, whether it's the camera moving or the characters. They're all on their feet; they hardly ever sit down. I never questioned it, I felt that was the right way to tell that story. Also, on an economic level, that was the best way. I didn't need a continuity person.

The film seems to be crammed with so many details and stories?

Definitely. *Slacker* is like fifty movies and you're jumping from one to the next. It's almost like channel surfing. You're getting a glimpse of this person here, and then you're over there. Sometimes they talk about things, like the girl who runs up excited, and tries to sell the Madonna pap smear. She's recalling a story that she heard on the news. A fantastic scene, but the camera wasn't there for that, you just hear about it. It's about secondary information. There's not that much happening in the movie, but what they're talking about suggests a pretty rich, wild world, and they're all obsessed with violence.

Some of the style obviously comes out of its economy of means, and shooting very quickly. Do you think the film would've been any different if you'd had more money or more shooting days? Is this the film you wanted to make?

I look back on it and I think that's the film I wanted to make. Of course, it's frustrating while you're making it. You think, if I'd just had a few more thousand dollars, I could have done things differently. But you look at it, and you just say "Well, that was the right way to make that film." It might not have been as good, if I'd had more money. It wouldn't have been as good to even shoot in 35mm. That would have been a disaster. It's much better in 16mm, that's the documentary format.

Did it bother you that some people took the film as a kind of portrait of an entire generation? It must have put some kind of burden on you to be the spokesman of a generation.

[Laughs] Yes, that's the downside, but the upside meant that my little film, which I thought I'd be carting around to art museums and festivals and selling in underground videos, was actually getting seen and people were excited about it. I was surprised that so many people were able to find their way into it. But yeah, a lot of the people in the movie were in their twenties, the entire crew was in their twenties, so it was taken as a portrait of this twenty-something generation. A few things happened along the way to create an official media trend. There was a *Time* magazine cover called "The Twenty-Somethings: What do they want?" right at the time the film was first being seen. An older generation were looking at what youth wanted. And then Douglas Coupland's book, *Generation X*, came out, and Nirvana hit. Suddenly, it's like, "Oh, there's something going on!" They just tied a lot of these things together and suddenly *Slacker* was the film that filled the cultural niche, it became part of the overall dialogue. But, you know, *Generation X* is an experimental novel, and *Slacker* is an experimental film, and that to me is what is interesting about them, their narratives. But when people in the larger media picked up on it, they—for the most part—hadn't read the book, hadn't seen the movie. They were going for the sociological broad strokes they could package for the public. So, it's was only truly interesting for about a month, and ever since it's been a misrepresented symbol that me and the movie have nothing to do with. [Laughs]

When you made *Slacker*, how aware were you of, let's say, the more conventional rules of filmmaking?

I knew all the rules, but they simply didn't apply much here, although I didn't make the movie just to break the rules. I had some people on the crew who had worked on other movies saying out of frustration, "Just do a cut. Shot, reverse shot. What's wrong with you? Why are you tying all this in?" And my answer was "No, I just want it to be one take." I could barely articulate my reasoning, but left in other hands, it would've been more standard TV-movie kind of coverage, which I couldn't stand. I wanted to do something different. At the same time, I don't know that I could have made a more conventional film. It just wasn't part of my thinking.

Why is it such a verbal film?

To me this movie is about people trying to articulate what's in their mind, and it's a reaction to my first film, which was almost one hundred percent nonverbal. I also love conversation. I like people that express themselves just in the way they talk. Also, an element that was paramount in my mind was secondary sources. Like the JFK assassination guy, people are describing things they've read. It's further away from personal experience. He's not even obsessed with the assassination any more, he's obsessed with books about the assassination. He's like a generation removed.

A lot of the characters are very bright and have a lot of energy and a good facility with language. Isn't there a danger in creating this kind of character that what they say won't seem organic to their characters. It will just seem like line-readings?

Well, they don't have characters. They don't have pasts or futures. They're just these moments in time. They're just people talking, mouthpieces for the film.

Why does the film end self-referentially with the kids photographing each other.

It contrasts with the rest of the movie. It was a physical break from the town. It refers back to the scene where she's says, "Oh, we never leave this one square mile area. We never go to the lake, there's all this pretty stuff." There's a certain release and this group isn't talking. The film becomes nonverbal at that point and the music takes over. The music has had no importance in the film whatsoever, and suddenly you've got all this music, and it's playful, and it's Super-8 film blown up to 16mm, and then to 35mm. There's as many cuts in that sequence as there are in the rest of the movie.

It's like the experimental film I would have made with Lee, throwing the camera off. It was just a good formal release, and a celebration, too, of these people's lives. They were filming each other. Their lives were worthy of cinema. I was depicting people who usually don't show up on the narrative map. My attitude was that everything's worth making a film about. When you're living cinema, personally as a filmmaker, everything is cinema. Oh, my trip, my love story, whatever I'm doing you could make a film about. Every thought in my head, every thing I'm seeing or hearing or interested in could be cinema. So, I like the image of them filming each other. Just making a film about their trip out of town in an old Cadillac, and running up a mountain and throwing their camera off.

Do you think it's a positive or negative portrait of those people at that time?

I think it's positive, with some dark corners. I can't say I don't have mixed feelings about quite a bit of the milieu it captures. I'm not a guy who sits in a coffee shop all day. I think it has affection for its people, but everyone can judge it however they want. My intentions were, these are my friends, these are my selves, and I can be self-critical and critical of anything. I think it was positive in the fact that people were trying to communicate, trying to express themselves. People have this endless potential, and that's a good thing. I thought it was positive that you show people being active. They have their art projects and they're lives are more important than their jobs, and that's all positive for the individual.

But if they're all monologues, how are they really communicating with each other?

They're trying, like we all try. The communication really takes place later. The communication is the cumulative effect of all these inputs you've had and it makes sense in retrospect, or when you tie it all together. Film is a safe place to eavesdrop, in the safety of a darkened theater, a good place to overhear conversations and see obsessions at work.

I always kept the listeners in each scene as neutral as possible. I'd tell them not to judge. Like, "Okay, here's this crazy guy who's ranting on about how we've been on Mars since the fifties," and I was say-ing, "Just look at him. Don't give him a funny look, don't laugh." If you look at those people, they're very neutral. I didn't want to steer the audience. Even the camera angles were all the same. I was going for a truly neutral experience, and let the audience decide.

You're obviously satisfied with what you accomplished.

As a filmmaker I learn to accept my limitations. Here's what I had. Here's what I did. I wouldn't change a thing. I did the best I could at that time. I knew I had pushed myself to the limit of my abilities and energies at that time, which were pretty immense. It was full-on. I would dream the film. It was just my whole life for those months we were shooting and I liked that feeling. I like being completely obsessed with a project when everything I do is feeding into it. So, I accept it and wouldn't change a thing. It was a good working method for me for the future. I look at all my films now, and I wouldn't change a thing, not because they're perfect, but because, given all the circumstances, that's what it was; and that's the best I could do at the time.

How did *Dazed and Confused* come about?

Well, that was a huge jump. People make a link between that and *Slacker* as if they are similar, and in some ways they are: big ensemble cast, time structure, etc. But for me, they couldn't be more different. Suddenly I'm making a period piece. It's the seventies. *Dazed* was about being fourteen to seventeen years old. Before *Slacker* came out, I'd been thinking about *Dazed* for a few years, like I said, "Someday, I want to do my teenage, rock 'n' roll movie." I knew what it would be so I started writing it. I knew it would require a larger budget, but I thought maybe I could raise a few million or so. I knew just the music rights alone would be a big deal. So I started with the music, and started writing the script. Then this guy from Universal, Jim Jacks, called me. *Slacker* had been out for a little while and Jim had read an interview with me where I was talking about doing a rock 'n' roll movie next. I told him I was working on the script and was really excited about it. He said, "Why don't we meet?" So I went out and talked to him and Sean Daniel, who's his producing partner. I had to do the "pitch," which was just me talking about the film. I made it sound fun. It's kind of hard to describe the actual story, and I'm still amazed that I got the thing made, because it is so much more a character piece than a great story.

How formed was it when you were talking about it?

Oh, pretty much. I had a good outline and characters and knew where it was going. So, pretty soon I had a finished script, and everybody really loved it. It never had to go into development. There were about thirty projects in development at Universal, and they liked the *Dazed* script so much that it leapfrogged over these other projects right into a production slot.

How much did it cost to make?

About six million dollars.

You suddenly had a big crew and people you were responsible to.

Yes, I had department heads and a big crew, not just my close friends. We were building sets like the pool hall and the moon tower. That was when I learned to make a real film. It was a big challenge: to take on the huge undertaking of a professional production with all of its mind-numbing realities, and still stay inspired and centered with what you had in mind in the first place. And then there's another layer of bullshit going on all the way up to the film's release. *Slacker* had got some recognition, so you feel the scrutiny a little more intensely. They're really judging you on that next film. It's almost like everyone but your closest friends wants you to fail. They ask, "Are you just someone who got lucky, or are you a real filmmaker? Do you have more than one movie in you?" Then rumors started that the film wasn't working. The word was that the dailies were terrible, which started at the studio. It's the kind of film that makes little sense out of context. The studio would watch the dailies, with things out of order, and they just didn't get it.

Was there any improvisation in that film?

In the same way there was in *Slacker*, in rehearsals. I'd rewrite characters. A lot of those actors would have lines that we'd come up with in rehearsals. The structure and characters are from the script, but we came up with a lot of fun stuff. They were a great group of actors. It was the first movie for a lot of them, so we were all learning at the same time. I had that rehearsal time, and I treated them as collaborators. I think for a lot of young actors it's mostly "Hit your mark. Say your line. Here's who you are," whereas this was real flowing, very natural.

Did you choose most of the music in advance?

Yes, I had the music before I'd even finished the script.

And you knew which music would accompany each sequence?

Yes, anything you see in the movie that's a largely musical sequence, like when Mitch gets paddled to Alice Copper's "No More Mr. Nice Guy" or they walk into the pool hall during "Hurricane" or the ZZ Top they're listening to when they're riding around busting mailboxes and stuff or even the opening credits to Aerosmith: a lot of that was in the script. You don't find that stuff in postproduction, you have it in mind before shooting. The music is ultimately the single most expressive element in the movie, and that was how I felt as a teenager. Teenagers often can't express things. You don't even know what you're feeling, but the music's there for you. I wanted to use the music sequences in a narrative way, pre-MTV, more like *Scorpio Rising, Mean Streets, Easy Rider, American Graffiti*. If you play a song and you do a series of shots, your narrative information is there, not just imagery for imagery's sake. The lyrics of the music are often tied in to what is going on, sometimes ironically.

In what way do you see *Dazed and Confused* and *Slacker* as autobiographical? Just that they come out of your experience?

Yes, one hundred percent. *Dazed* is probably beat by beat the most autobiographical thing I've done. Almost everything in that film, I did, saw, heard or was a part of. I was Mitch. I was initiated.

Everything that happens to Mitch [Wiley Wiggins] happened to me. When I was older, I'm more like the guys on the newspaper, Tony [Anthony Rapp], Mike [Adam Goldberg], and Pink [Jason London].

Right, the Poker Club.

Yes, we thought of ourselves as the intelligentsia of our high school.

Yes, I like them. [Laughs]

They're wonderful. I'd tell the actors, "You guys are really the cool ones, but it won't be recognized until college. There's no appreciation of your mind here. You've got all these jerks who run the school on pure testosterone." And that's why the female characters kind of take a back seat.

So, we see you in all the characters?

Yes, I'm all over. Even Ben Affleck was giving me hell as O'Bannion. He's the bad guy. He goes "Rick! I think you were O'Bannion in high school. You seem to be having so much fun with this, we're all wondering who you are in here." But I wasn't. Officially, I was in the first class that took the beating as freshmen, but didn't dish it out when it was our turn as seniors.

Is the structure of the film pretty much the way we see it, or did that undergo a change?

No, that's definitely the structure of it, but there were also a lot of things cut out or reduced.

The film doesn't seem to have much of a dark side, outside of O'Bannion. Teenage years can be pretty horrible.

I think it's pretty dark. I mean, it is a comedy, but I find it a little horrific.

Not like *River's Edge* or *Over the Edge* kind of horrific.

Over the Edge, If and those kind of movies are taking it into teenage fantasy, where they can enact a revenge, fire-bomb the school, gun down the administration. That's the optimal ending to a teenage movie, but that just wasn't my experience. *Dazed* is more about initiation and trying to be cool. By the end, Mitch is sort of a jerk. He's been initiated from a somewhat wide-open kid to a teenage male jerk. He responds to the line about the girl he's hooked up with, "You gonna be fucking her later?" with "How do you know I haven't already?" It's funny and people laugh, but it's kind of sad. You have to talk bad about women to get a laugh. To male bond you have to be a jerk, break things, bust mailboxes. He's a hero when he throws the bowling ball out of the car and breaks a windshield. His big triumph is to create some high-dollar damage. [Laughs]

Was the experience with a studio a happy experience?

Happy to get the film made, and happy with the final film, unhappy with the way the film was ignored within the studio that made it. You spend all that time and energy, and it's your life up on the screen, and you think it's good and entertaining, and then the studio ignores it.

They didn't get behind it?

Not really. It got a modest release, like 183 theaters. Universal was never very excited about it and it got passed off to a smaller distributor they had recently partnered with, Gramercy. The downside to working with the studios are the previews, and all the draining things you have to put up with, the notes from all the execs, the pressure on album deals. I could go on about the nastiness of the music industry and album deals, and all the sabotage. So, I had all the crap of working with a studio, and a smaller, independent-type release, which is too bad, because I really loved the idea of the film showing in all these little shitty towns across the country, like the one it's set in. But ultimately, I was happy with the film. That's my film completely, but I paid the transgressor's price. The studio's attitude was, "Okay, you can have your film, but fuck you." I'm having a very similar experience with *The Newton Boys*.

How did *Before Sunrise* come about?

In the fall of 1989 I was visiting my sister and brother-in-law in Philadelphia. I was out one night and met this woman, and we ended up
walking all night, talking. I was still finishing up *Slacker*, but typical
filmmaker, I'm always thinking in film terms. We were having this
great evening. I though, "God, I don't really know this woman," but
we were talking and it was very intimate. I said "That could be a
movie. That should be a movie." Just this relationship. Just this
moment. Could it be done? Make it one night in a life where two
people meet. I'd been to Germany and thought, "Maybe I'll set it in
Germany, and make it cross-cultural." Can you make a movie that's
just about two people talking? I made one with 100 people talking,
but can you do it with two people in one night in their life, and with
the romantic aspects of that. It had a long gestation period. I thought
about that for years, and then worked on a structure for it.

Then I asked this friend of mine, Kim [Krizan] who is also in *Slacker*
and *Dazed*. She's very serious, hyper-intellectual. She was writing her
thesis at that time on women's diaries and women's literature. I really liked the way her mind worked. She's not frivolous, she just
jumps into real subjects. So, I asked her to help me write this script.
We wrote it in eleven days.

Did you work with her specifically to work on the female part?

I just knew a man and a woman working on the script together was
more likely to have authentic results.

You just wanted someone to bounce off of?

I wanted a male and a female in the same room, because on *Dazed*,
I feel like I failed a bit with the female characters. I had wanted to
achieve more of a feminine point of view but the testosterone of the
male characters just took over everything. That's not unrealistic to
that environment, but I was hoping to impose more femaleness on
it. I felt it was my shortcoming, both in the script, and in my approach to the movie. After *Dazed*, with its huge cast and studio production, I was craving a smaller film. Long before *Dazed* came out,
I'd committed to *Before Sunrise* being the next film.

Did any films inspire *Before Sunrise*?

I don't know specifically, but a model would probably be European art cinema in general.

Like Eric Rohmer?

Yes, like a Rohmer, although it's more pointedly romantic than Rohmer.

The process of making this film, and the input from the actors, was unusual.

The script that Kim and I wrote in eleven days was definitely the beginning, the end, and some points in between. It had these themes, but the working method was that that's not enough. Casting the right two people became crucial. For a while I thought it would be an American woman and a European guy. It could've gone in any direction. I was meeting young actors of both sexes, all nationalities. If I was in Germany, I would meet some actors there. I was fishing around.

Did you know when you tested Ethan Hawke and Julie Delpy that they were the ones?

I met Julie early in my L.A. casting. The film wasn't even financed or anything. The day *Dazed* opened, I was casting *Before Sunrise* in New York and meeting a lot of young actors. I saw Ethan in a John Mark Sherman play that Anthony Rapp, one of my *Dazed* actors, was in. I went backstage, just talking to Anthony, and met Ethan briefly. He'd seen *Dazed and Confused* and really liked it. I liked Ethan's energy. He seemed like a man now; he wasn't like the kid I'd seen in *Dead Poet's Society*. He was twenty-three or twenty-four. So we got together a few days later and just talked for an hour. I liked the way his mind worked, plus I think he's a really good actor, technically and otherwise.

Did you have specific ideas about who the characters had to be?

Yes. Really intelligent, sensitive, romantic, all those things. You just know when you meet them. They couldn't fake it. I wanted someone with an active imagination and the verbal quality that Ethan's definitely got. With Julie, I had met a ton of other actresses. I had a final call-back with two women and two men. Julie was one. I had a hunch that she had a fascinating mind and I wanted to see her again. During the call-back, Julie and Ethan did a scene and kind of improvised some things. When I saw them together, I knew they were the right two. Ethan wasn't fully sure he wanted to do the movie, but we reworked a scene a little and it got better, and he got a sense of what I was like as a director. At the end of the day he looked at me and said, "Hey, that was fun." To make the film, he took a big cut in pay, and the film was risky. The script's not that great, nothing happens. He had a hunch that it was going to be hard to pull off, but was worth the try.

Why did you finally settle on Vienna?

Initially I thought it would be Berlin. I also thought of American cities like San Antonio and Philadelphia, towns I'd spent walking the downtown areas. In Germany, you meet with the government agency in charge of the film office, and you could tell that they didn't really want me there. I was treated like a film student trying to make my first film. But I'd gone to Vienna for the film festival and they showed *Dazed and Confused* and it was like a big deal. I met with their film board and they really wanted me. I said, "Well, I'm trying to do this film, just looking around." And they said, "Why don't you do it in Vienna?" They all speak English. I wanted it to be realistic that the two lead characters would start off in German and then speak English. In Vienna people have taken eight years of English, and they can speak it. I really liked the people in Vienna. They had a great, laid-back spirit, and the city has that slightly morbid, rich cultural history.

What do you think it contributed as a physical location to the meaning of the film?

I think the tone of the movie was set, and would have been the same in other cities. But Vienna was special in a lot of ways. It had a richer history. We'd be walking down streets that were built in 1320, and then you go, "Oh my God. The United States was just a field then." Your day there is really fleeting in an historical context. Neither of our characters lived there; they were like ghosts. They were there for one night, and they were both gone. The next day dawns and these two people have just passed through. In that last montage where we revisit the scenes, I like the locations. It has a rich feel that doesn't cost anything. The film's been designed already because of the physical locations.

There was no conscious effort to refer to Max Ophuls? I mean, it's a very romantic film.

Yes, *Letter From an Unknown Woman* was hovering, as was *The Third Man*, because we were in a lot of the same locations. But, hey, I really filmed on the large Ferris wheel. They used the studio. [Laughs]

It's romantic, but not sentimental.

I hope. I can't say that I'm a big fan of the genre. I don't usually go out of my way for overtly sentimental movies, just like a lot of teen movies rubbed me the wrong way. It's fun to get into a genre and try your own realistic turn on it. *Before Sunrise* was that. It couldn't have been more intimate: Julie, Ethan and me working in a hotel room for three weeks, rewriting the script, having new ideas.

This film evolved over time, and the characters took shape over time.

Yes, and we shot it completely chronologically, so they evolved even during the shooting of the movie. The end wasn't the exact end we wrote the first time. It was close to it, but it wasn't word-for-word. You evolve. I don't look at that as a frustration because it's not the same thing I imagined. I didn't imagine an exact thing. It was a process. I imagined an end result, an emotion or a feeling. You're at the whims of fate, and all these other elements, the biggest two elements being the people you choose for these parts. Ethan and Julie are immensely creative people: they're both writers, they've both made films, they both have extensive acting careers. They were active collaborators.

Was there any improvisation in the scene where Ethan and Julie ask each other questions on the tram, which lasts for at least six minutes.

Not really. We rehearsed the hell out of it. But there's always things that you can never expect as you shoot. I guess we did six or seven takes, but it was just the one shot, no coverage or anything. You find these wonderful moments, just these little things like her hair being out place, and Ethan awkwardly reaching over. Then the tram stops and they get off: perfect timing.

Are the characters preoccupied with death and time?

That's definitely an overriding theme, and the time element is most crucial. They have limited time, the clock's ticking, and they're outside of time. They talk about it specifically when he says, "God, you know, we're back in real time" in the morning when it's light. The rest of the night is kind of a dream. I like the way we perceive time as humans. Time has different speeds, even though on one level, it's the same. There's one clock out there that's the eternal clock. Time is pretty subjective, it's different at different places in the universe in different times. But with time passing, you get to mortality. Those are sort of interlinked.

Where do you think that Jesse and Celine are at the end of the film? Do you think they'll meet in six months?

I like to think so. I'm just enough of a romantic to think they will.

Do you see *Before Sunrise* as a big departure in your work?

Yes, it was. It was telling a real intimate story. Just these two characters, it wasn't an ensemble. It operates on a different emotional level.

It's a surprising film to come from the guy who made *Slacker* and *Dazed and Confused*.

I guess, but like I said, there's that part of me. You make a few films and people think they know you, but a film is often just one experience out of your life, or one thing you are interested in exploring. I put myself completely in my films, but before I could honestly say, "That's me, fully, I am my films," I'd have to make about one hundred films.

Do you know why the film was more popular in the rest of the world than in the States? Do you think that some of the fans of *Slacker* and *Dazed and Confused* were surprised by the film, or didn't get it?

Probably. The film isn't ironic, it has little relation to current popular culture. It had nothing to do with the world at that particular moment. When a film comes out, there's a pop culture moment it can either be a part of or not. *Before Sunrise* was definitely not a part of a specific moment. When it came out, it didn't have anything to do with early 1995. Maybe that's less a big deal in other parts of the world. But it's not like it was a big bomb in the states. It made back double its budget in its U.S. theatrical run.

I'll say this for sure, *Before Sunrise* was the biggest risk. It could have been really terrible. It was the toughest to make work on its own terms because its own terms are so limited. I was excited when we wrapped. I looked at Julie and Ethan and said, "I think we really got something here, guys. I can't wait to edit this movie." It was special. In the same way it's them out of time in the movie, the film is also out of time. But it's eternal because it's about people.

How did *SubUrbia* become your next film. I read that you were going to make *The Newton Boys* after *Before Sunrise*.

I was going to do *The Newton Boys* next. We were working on the script once I got back from Vienna but it just didn't come about. The cast wasn't set, they weren't quite available. I'd heard about *SubUrbia* in Vienna that summer, and that Steve Zahn was kicking ass in the Eric Bogosian play in New York. When I got back, I flew to New York to see it. I'm a big fan of Bogosian's and couldn't wait. It was a great experience, and it seemed like something I'd done in a strange way: one night in the life of a bunch of young people. It always stayed with me. Not that anyone asked me, but I was immediately thinking how would that work as a film? How would you make it cinematic and interesting? I was so attracted to those characters. The challenge was how to do this adaptation and make it work.

What was the collaboration like with Eric Bogosian on *SubUrbia*.

Oh, it was wonderful. Eric's a writer and actor, and he knows enough about film to know that it's a director's deal. As we worked on the adaptation, he was very realistic and quick to cut longer passages in the shaping of the screenplay. If we had filmed the play verbatim, it would have been three hours long instead of two, so the challenge was where to condense, where to cut, where to transform the characters a bit, where to add new scenes. The adaptive process was a lot of fun and we were both very active in that. Then I wanted him to sign off on the cast, so he was active during casting. At some point he was just like "Good luck, man. It's your thing. I know you're going to make a good film. I trust you one hundred percent."

Did you have to work a lot with the actors on their characterizations?

Yes, the same way I would work on most other things. We just started at ground zero and rehearsed for three weeks, and then on weekends during production. When they arrived at their trailers, sometimes I was there with new ideas about what we were going to do that night. It's a lot of sitting around and just talking about characters and reading through it a lot, finding new things. I like that process. To me, that's the essence of a performance. You have to listen to an actor's instincts.

The theatrical origins of the piece must have effected how you shot and edited the film.

I tried not to let it too much. I knew we were stuck in this one location. That would definitely be the feel. I wanted that, but I moved around. We used all different sides, front and back. We're inside the store at the beginning. We got to really define that space, we got up on the roof.

There must be a risk, though, of the material not coming to life, and remaining stage-bound.

That was the challenge. I thought about it for a couple of years from the time I saw the play to the time I was making it as a movie. A lot of plays "open up" for a movie, which means you can use the same dialogue from the stage but use a variety of locations. With *SubUrbia* I just wanted to leave it at the convenience store as much as possible, knowing the weight of that means everything. By nature, if you hang out at a store like that all night, you get kind of run off a lot. You see the character Nazeer [Ajay Naidu] come out a lot and run them off. So they end up in different places all around the store.

Did you think that was being truer to the material and faithful to Eric's vision?

Yes. It's a big deal when they do leave that space. They walk off but they end up at that burger place; they all drift back. All roads lead back to the convenience store. Jeff [Giovanni Ribisi] has his epiphany as he's walking, he gets separated from the limo and he walks all the way back across town to the 7-Eleven. I keep calling it 7-Eleven even though we named it the Circle-A, because I always considered it that.

Why did you use a fictitious suburban town, instead of locating it somewhere specific?

I liked the name from the play, Burnfield. It's kind of a play on Mayfield, which is *Leave It to Beaver* land, and then "Burn" is like a field on fire. [Laughs] It's really specifically any town, any suburbia, USA. I'd hate to make it regional. It's definitely not Texas. In reality, the Burnfield of Eric's youth is Woburn, Massachusetts.

One of the things I liked about the film is the silence of it. I like the fact that when we hear music, it's mostly source music. What was your thinking about not having more music?

Sonic Youth did a little scoring, but for the most part, it's that boom box they have. I did similar things in *Slacker* and *Before Sunrise*, where most of their music is all source. I think that's often my first choice.

It does go against the trend of a lot of films these days.

I guess so. But I liked not having music, and just hanging out in a parking lot. The only sounds are cars and traffic. That just seemed that more oppressive, non-expressive.

Did you always know Gene Pitney's "Town Without Pity" would go over the opening credits?

Yes, that one came to me pretty early on. It's a great mixture of romance and longing, and with the images, there's an irony running throughout the song.

It's also very dramatic and intense.

It's very dramatic and to me, it linked generations. From the same one that was torn apart with James Dean in *Rebel Without A Cause* to today. It sort of says "This is suburbia now, but it was suburbia then, too. And it's the suburbia of the future."

It also links the parents of these people with them.

And soon-to-be grandparents. It's the entire postwar era of fifty years.

Your work speaks to those millions of people who are very creative, but who never really achieve public recognition. Often it's just a quirk of fate why somebody becomes famous and someone doesn't, but it's definitely an issue that seems to be important to you.

Well, as a person who's always striving to create, my ideal is to live in a world where I can create. I know so many people whose life is basically a life of art and creating things. Jeff represents me at twenty, who wanted that, but was nowhere near knowing how to achieve it. When he replies to the question "What are you doing?" he says, "Oh, writing, mostly, short pieces . . ." His creativity has no form yet. It's just that he has a brain and he's trying to express something. And that was me at that time. I was writing, vaguely. People might say about Jeff, "Oh, that's very depressing. He's obviously going to be there forever. He's a loser." But I say, "No, he's only twenty." It's really a product of his lack of experience and lack of worldliness. Who knows? He could discover something new and put all his energy and passion and intelligence into something very specific and achieve something great.

He's also afraid to make that leap and declare something, and that's why he's jealous of Pony [Jayce Bartok], who probably has less talent than Jeff, except in this one field. That's how I felt about a lot of the people I've known over the years; that they're as talented and more inspired than people I've met who have "made it." Sometimes they don't possess what Tolstoy called the "necessary bad qualities" to be good at what they do. Tolstoy said his older brother Nicolai was actually the better artist, but he didn't have the bad qualities that made Tolstoy so driven. Whether it's ego, or something to prove to the world, or your family, or those that rejected you. Who knows what's motivating some people? Some talented people lack that burning motivation, where others are motivated by their abilities. There is a lot of art inside them trying to get out, and they won't feel complete until it finds a physical form of some sort.

Do you know what these kids are rebelling against, if they're rebelling against anything?

It's a vague feeling. And how actively are they rebelling, anyway? They're just living. They wouldn't claim to be rebelling against much, I don't think.

Are they politically aware?

I think Jeff and Sooze [Annie Carey] are. In their own twenty-year-old way, I think they're very politically aware. Tim [Nicky Katt], too. He's the one that's been out in the world. He was in the service and travelled. He pretty much came back a failure with his tail between his legs, and his cynical attitude, "Oh, the world's a scam." He realizes he's from the wrong class and he's given up. He gives in to a certain position for himself and accepts it in a bitter way. Other people could take those same circumstances and turn them around, and say, "Yeah, I'm from the wrong class, but I'm just going to work that much harder to prove myself." Tim's smart, though. I consider him a tragic character in that he's just smart enough to see the world, and his lack of place in it. He knows people very clearly: he's no idiot.

But he's very cynical.

Yes, and he's giving in to the lower instincts that the loser does, such as racism, and blaming others, and fucking with people. Yet, Jeff looks up to him, because Tim is a drinker and a brawler; he represents activity, and someone who's living it, whereas Jeff is passive. Tim is kind of a performance artist. The whole thing he pulls on Jeff at the end, about Erica [Parker Posey], is pure performance, just for effect. That Tim would go to such lengths just for his own amusement says where he is in life. He doesn't give a shit about anything. It's cruel when he does these things to Jeff, but he thinks he's teaching him his lesson. He's like the master who does something to upset the student ultimately for their own good.

The character types such as the sensitive, intelligent liberal, the misunderstood suicidal young girl, the right-wing loser, the obnoxious one, are fairly archetypal. How do impart individual characteristics on them?

Well, you take these types, and try to infuse them with humanity and make them real people, and not just archetypes. It works very well on the stage. Tim was a little more of an archetype. He was more extreme and more outrageous. It's very entertaining, and he gets his point across, but I didn't think that would quite work in the film. So it was a process of casting an actor like Nicky Katt who's nothing but real, and then we worked on it. That character transformed quite a bit. They all did these subtle shifts. I wasn't trying to change the play that much, because I really didn't. You look at Sooze and her performance, and say, "Oh, that's good. She's got a lot of energy." But, you know, she's arguably full of shit, too. She's idealistic in a very naive way, but it's kind of charming that she hasn't given in to cynicism yet. She actually thinks she's going to change the world, and that's great. She's probably going to go to New York and get a big dose of reality, but who knows what'll happen? She could end up another Madonna, too. She could impose her strong will all the way if she's crafty enough.

Do you think the darker vision is a product of Bogosian?

Well, it's definitely in the play. I mean, Eric had that. But I share that dark vision. I've always been a fan of his work, and I like the really dark areas he goes into. I thought they were really funny. I think *SubUrbia* is funny: dark, but it's a great combination of funny and just really, really depressing [laughs]. My favorite compliment is "I laughed all the way, and boy, do I feel miserable and depressed after."

I find Bogosian's writing can slip into a kind of sermonizing at times.

Eric is a moralist in a way. He sees bad and he thinks it could be better. He thinks that people could be nicer and more fair, and honest and moral, and all of these things, and you see it in his work. But I shared his dark vision. I wouldn't have done it otherwise.

Were you disappointed with the lack of commercial response to the film? Or did you expect it to be a very specialized film?

What your up against is that on the surface it's a youthful film and that will keep an older audience away. And on the other hand, most young people won't see it because it lacks the star power and action to attract them in the first place. A film like this building slowly through word of mouth is a thing of the past. There's no time and there are so many films lined up for the theater. If you don't somehow open big, you haven't a chance. Think of all the successful films of the past that caught on slowly. Today, they'd be out of the theater rather quickly and would find their actual audience somewhere down the road on video. It's really all about marketing, and if you make a certain kind of film, you have to acknowledge the reality of what you're up against and be practical, keep the budget as low as possible.

Was it sold badly?

It was a tough sell, of course. In the marketing, nothing about it seemed like something you hadn't seen before. A bunch of people standing around. There was no real edge or hook that made it stand out as something sexy.

In your own mind, are you satisfied with it as a film?

Yes, very much. It's funny. You do get your moment. *SubUrbia* was acclaimed when it showed at The New York Film Festival. It got a great *New York Times* review. Then it didn't do business, so whatever feeling people had for it just got drained out of it: "Okay, it wasn't a success, so now it's a bad movie." But for me, I make my peace with the film when I finish it. Good or bad, whatever happens to the movie, I know what I feel about it. Here was the challenge and here's what it was. I grew a lot as a filmmaker. I stand behind the film. I think ultimately it's underrated. I have people coming up to me all the time saying, "Hey, I saw *SubUrbia* on video and I really loved it." In the future, maybe it's the kind of film that won't get a theatrical release at all. It'll play on cable or something. To get people to buy a ticket in the current filmgoing environment for a film that isn't going to throttle them in the Simpson-Brukheimer sense, or feature one of the few actors they'll go see no matter what, is a real challenge.

The Newton Boys **seems quite a leap in terms of structure and ambition.**

Yes. Though there's absolutely no link or similarity between *SubUrbia* and *The Newton Boys*, I think doing *SubUrbia* geared me up for *The Newton Boys* in relation to drama and structure. *SubUrbia* is actually a very tight story, narratively speaking. It seems like a "hang out" movie, yet it was almost maddeningly structured. In the editing, if I cut one thing, the house of cards half-collapses. It was by far the tightest construction of a story I'd ever tried to tell, and that was Eric's doing. That's the dramatic structure of the play. It was really good for me to go into that world, which was more confrontational and more dramatic than I had done in the past. There were a lot of plot-points to sell emotionally. Jeff had to believe Erica was dead. It all had to work dramatically. I knew *The Newton Boys* had its share of that, also.

You adapted the script for *The Newton Boys*.

With Claude Stanush and Clark Walker, from an over-abundance of facts from their life and times, much of which Claude had chronicled in various forms for over twenty years. We also did a ton of original research and archival work. It could have been a five-hour movie, and I had scripts that were well over 200 pages.

Did you always see it as this fairly big production, with all these different locations?

Yes, that's the story, there was no way around it. The final movie is as scaled-down and inexpensive as the Newtons story could have been told, and told accurately and fully. Many period films have just a few major locations, but this was like a road movie. These guys rarely returned to the same place. It was important to depict the full spectrum, as much as you could, of what Willis [Matthew McConaughey] saw as his heyday, those eighty banks, those six trains. That *is* the story; where they came from and where they ended up. Most criminals have a period of time where they are fully in their groove. And that's also the period when he found the love of his life. I wanted to tell his story.

How did you decide on the structure of the film? Obviously the robberies help structure the whole piece.

You want to keep the robberies varied and not repeat the same elements too much, because basically they're doing the same thing over and over. Break in, nitroglycerin, blow the safe, get the money, go. We tried to focus on those details during different jobs. But the large structure was always clear: enter the life, bank robberies, the Toronto episode, and the big train robbery. Those were the cornerstones.

It's obviously a story that a lot of people in Texas know.

Actually, almost no one in Texas knows it. Even a lot of people in their hometown of Uvalde don't know about them. The Newtons are really obscure. They never hit the public record until the Rondout train robbery. In certain historical circles they're known, but they're not big-time folk legends or anything. You generally have to kill a lot of people to capture the public imagination and go down in history. I liked that they were the flip-side of most notorious criminals, and that their consummate professionalism kept them unknown. That's true success.

Was there something about their character that attracted you?

Primarily, it's a character study. It was the Willis Newton character that fascinated me. But I loved the other brothers too. Willis would be working all summer, he'd go scouting banks in the winter. His brothers would be hanging out in Chicago, because the city had two major-league baseball teams. They loved baseball and usually either the Cubs or White Sox were in town. Joe [Skeet Ulrich] stayed in a luxury hotel all summer and ran up a food bill that was close to $10,000! [Laughs] They were just blowing all kinds of money; they lived great. I just love the fact that they were these dirt-poor kids from West Texas, and suddenly, they're in three-piece suits, and going to the nicest clubs, hotels, with cars, women. A most extreme social mobility was possible in that day.

When you read the book about their life, was there something about how they were transformed by this sudden wealth that interested you?

It wasn't so much the wealth but rather that I shared their attitude toward life, for the most part. I shared Willis's ambition in a certain way, and I related to him personally. He's someone who saw the world as essentially unfair, and when you grow up poor and underprivileged, it's easy to have that view of the world. How you react to it is the important thing, and had I been thrown in prison at Willis' age for something I hadn't done, I could have ended up some kind of criminal.

What about in terms of genre? You're working in the Western and gangster genres. There are references to *Bonnie and Clyde*. Were there any other films important to you?

In a cinematic sense, it was more an homage to those genres. It starts off like a silent film, with a very Western feeling, and then by the end it's a gangster film, and more specifically, the subgenre of a heist film. We see the planning of the train robbery, the execution, and the aftermath. The film even looks different. We tried to drain the colors, make it more monochromatic. The lighting's different. That part was total gangster. But they're all very traditional forms. I wanted *The Newton Boys* to feel like a classical movie. The kind of movie you might've seen in the forties or fifties by Ford, Hawks, Anthony Mann, Nicholas Ray. I wanted to keep it playful though. That's why the opening sequence shows that the film's not going to take itself really seriously, in the same way that *Butch Cassidy and the Sundance Kid* is very funny. I wanted it to be light-hearted because I thought that was the right way. That was how the Newtons lived. They had a real sense of irony about them, Willis especially. They seemed like fun-loving guys. We did this research and they're in these towns with all these naked girls running around, and they were drunk a lot. I just thought their times were pretty wild and they jumped in and experienced it all to the fullest.

Did you feel confident doing this film with so much money riding on it?

I was confident because I always thought I was telling a great story. I didn't think I was spending too much for what I was delivering. When I did *Before Sunrise* for two million dollars, I didn't think I was spending too much, because if it worked, it could get its money back on video. And that's how I felt about *The Newtons*: if it works, it's a very entertaining movie with stars in it that can be sold. Actually it's a very frugal production compared to a lot of studio productions. We're in the age of the sixty- to seventy-million-dollar contemporary comedy. Where does it go? *The Newton Boys* was a hell of a deal for a studio. At the same time, I really needed thirty-five million dollars; it would have been the right budget for this movie.

And you had about twenty-seven million?

Yes. We had eighty-one locations to shoot in fifty-six days, so it was a real hustle. It was an almost impossible schedule. But you do what you can. The same with *Dazed*. I was completely squeezed on *Dazed* and *Newtons*. *Dazed* had thirty-six days and I really needed about forty-two to forty-five. There's a lot of things I could have achieved and could have done better, if I'd had more days.

On some level, *The Newton Boys* is a critique of corporate America.

It's a critique of that ambition for money, that kind of greed. It depicts a really corrupt time in history. I always say that Willis' doppelganger here would be Joseph Kennedy, who at the same time was running booze. And it's easily justified: "Oh, it's a dumb law. I might as well cash in on it. Nobody pays attention anyway. Now I've got my system in place, I can amass my fortune and then I can be a respectable businessman, and my son can be President." That would be Don Corleone's goal and that would also be the Newton's goal. Right before the train robbery Willis says, "This is so our kids and our grandkids don't grow up on dirt." And he means that. That's his goal: to be rich because that buys you respect, stability, and a lot of things that he didn't have.

Was it always clear that Willis would be the central character in the film?

Yes, it was always his story. He's the driving force, manipulating and lying to everyone around him to get them to do what he wants. He's the dark center, the black hole of the movie's energy.

Doesn't the film glamorize the outlaw life, in much the same way that *Butch Cassidy and the Sundance Kid* did?

I think it does. I think that if you make a film about something, it inevitably glamorizes it. You make a film about a sanitation worker, you glamorize it, just by depicting it. Film's a powerful medium.

You're certainly engaging in myth-making.

And going with it. By the end, when they're walking out of the court-room, the way I do those shots in slow-motion, it's a parade, it's

pageantry. I wanted to elevate it to myth, because I think the Newtons are worthy of myth, and they haven't achieved that because they
didn't kill people. They didn't get caught, really. But I don't pass
moral judgment on them. Willis is—and there's an irony there—just
a small thief stealing from big thieves. That was the code of the West
at that time. If you have the guts and the gumption to go after something, and you can get it without getting caught, then on some level
it's yours. That's the code of the United States, actually. His attitude
didn't come out of nowhere.

**Now that you've made a big-budget film, do you run the risk of
being co-opted by the studios and watering down what was quirky
and special about your work?**

Everyone almost naturally assumes, indeed, projects that on to it,
but I really feel whatever personality I have as a filmmaker is very
much in *The Newton Boys*. The biggest difference here is I'm dealing
with very different characters than before. They're not introspective,
they're not self-analytical. They're active. If there's any pent-up frustration or aggression or resentment, the Newtons are actively striking back at the society that oppressed them. It's what the characters
from my other movies would like to be doing, but these guys are
really doing it. I like that, because I have an active personality. Part
of my personality is introspective and passive, but there's this other
part that's kind of driven, ambitious and really active. It was fun to
hang out with those guys and make a movie about that. By the end,
Willis is somewhat transformed. His wings have melted and he's
come back to earth. He's just lucky he didn't die, or someone close
to him die. He almost lost what he had. I think Willis saw things
differently after.

**They actually got off easy. They beat the system in a way, because
they lived really well and got very light sentences.**

They did, like most white-collar criminals do. The Savings & Loan
guys in the eighties are living really well to this day. That's the triumph at the end of the movie. People love the ending to this movie,

and yet they're walking off to prison. So, how's that a happy ending? They got a slap on the wrist, and got to live to be old men. So that in itself is triumphant.

It's an unusual ending with the Johnny Carson interview material. Why did you put that there?

Well, my question was whether I should do it at the beginning or the end. For a while, in the script, I had it at the beginning. I wanted to open it with, "Oh, shit. This is all real, what we're about to see." But I thought it resonated much deeper to see it at the end with, "Okay. Wow. This was real." You can't get any more real than being on *The Tonight Show*.

You had some gorgeous images in *The Newton Boys*.

Yes, but only because it seemed right in the telling of this story. I learned a lot on this movie and think I grew as a filmmaker. I wouldn't have been up for making *The Newton Boys* five years ago, but now I can see how you could spend a larger amount of money. I haven't found a story yet that would require that, and I'm not at all looking, but I could do it if I needed to.

It wouldn't scare you?

No, it really wouldn't. When I discovered *The Newton Boys* story, I was so passionate about them as characters and trying to tell a story, the budget became an afterthought. It's going to cost that much, and so what? It's a good deal; it's so much less than the average. I realize I can do that on something else, because digitally, there are so many interesting things you can do now with effects.

Yes, but your work has always been character-centered.

Yes, that's what kept me on *The Newtons*. It's a character piece. I want people coming out of the movie thinking about the characters, the same way when I think of *The Newtons*. There's these explosions and robberies and fun stuff going on, but at the end of the day, it's about these people.

Was there any compromise on this film?

Our only compromise came from budget restrictions. There's a lot of things I probably could've done, but I don't think about that too much. This is the story I wanted to tell and the way I wanted to tell it, and we were pretty much under the radar.

Creatively, it's always better to be the small film in a big system than to be the big film in a small system. I know people who have been just totally boned by their financing entity on a $6 or $3 million film, because it represents the company's whole net worth. When I'm doing a $27 million film at Fox, they're doing $60-million to $100-million films, or that 200-million-plus film.

How many theaters will it get into?

1,600 or something, which is pretty big, but it's not 2,500 or 3,000, like a lot of films. So, it's getting a medium studio release of a film of that size. It's the first time I'll have been through that, but I don't draw any distinctions about what that says about the film. Some people are groping for definitions of independent and they just don't exist. I would say independent is private financing, and having absolutely no interference. Woody Allen takes financing, and he doesn't get any interference. I mean, what's interference? I think interference is them making you cast somebody you don't want to cast. That would be artistic interference. That's never happened to me. Reshooting things, like reshooting an ending to satisfy an audience. I've never done that.

Cutting it against your wishes?

Yes, I've never done that either. I've never had a bad artistic experience, like getting the film taken away from me. You hear about these things every now and then, but I think that's largely a thing of the past. Studios don't take films away from people. If you hear of a film being taken away, usually it's because it's not working or the filmmaker is truly out of control and they're trying to solve a problem. I've been lucky.

The industry's in a funny place where it's really hard to know what an independent is anymore and people can work for the studios and still retain a certain amount of independence. The lines are so blurred now.

Yes, and I don't know any filmmaker who says that he's only an independent, or that he's a studio hack. We're all looking for funding for our next film. Some people are getting hired to do sequels, and there's that kind of director who's just making a living, and they're okay to take their place in the system. It's a real freelance business; it's film by film. I mean, most films are independent in a way. They're produced by some company, they're funded by studios. With *The Newton Boys*, I'm sort of an independent contractor who delivered a product to them that hopefully they can sell. I made it in my own hometown, cast who I wanted, wrote the script. It's very much my company's film, and just because it's financed by Fox doesn't really make it my big studio film. I was hardly ever in L.A.

For you, what's the most difficult part of being a film director?

My least favorite aspect is what's going on right now with *The Newton Boys* as it's being released. After having all the control as far as the film goes, I realize I have zero control when it comes to marketing. You get to make suggestions, or review materials, but they really don't want to deal with you. If you have a strong opinion or position, they are likely to do the exact opposite. I'm at a low point right now because I hate what they are doing with the movie, the lame way they are putting it out there. The stupid poster, the MTV-style TV ads with contemporary music. They feel more creative if they can sell a movie as something it isn't. It's almost like they are afraid to be honest with the public. What happens is you alienate the true audience.

What about shooting and postproduction? How do you feel about those?

Oh, I love both. Most people will tell you they love editing, and there is something special about editing because you're in control, and it doesn't matter if the sun's out or not; the actors are all gone, you don't have to worry if they got in a fight last night and got a black eye. The danger's gone. It's just you and your images and that's very freeing. But to me the most exciting is rehearsing and production. I group those together because that's where it's really coming alive and where I feel the most creative, where I can have a new idea, and implement it. I like the process and for me, it never ends. I'm not at all of the Hitchcock school of production being simply the rendering of something that's already been fully constructed. Even though I storyboard and plan out everything as best I can, I still want to change things and I find new things.

What's the most crucial thing you've learned about film direction over the last few years?

I could go through every film and say where I grew or what I learned. I think *The Newton Boys* is a big leap for me. I can use more tools now, having worked so thoroughly designing a movie. My collaborators were very inspired people. I had a really good time working with the costume designer, my production designer, the director of photography. Working with the actors is always great. There's so much fun in making films. It makes up for all the rest.

ALISON MACLEAN

Alison Maclean is a young film director raised in New Zealand and now based in New York City. She initially gained international recognition with a remarkable short film called *Kitchen Sink*, which played The New York Film Festival. A weird reworking of the Pygmalion myth, *Kitchen Sink* recalls the murky world of David Lynch's early films. *Crush*, Maclean's first feature, is an extraordinary character study of a predatory American woman, Lane, played by Marcia Gay Harden, traveling around New Zealand, who is responsible for a severe car accident that leaves her female companion in a coma. Lane's encounters as she tries to come to terms with her careless action and, in particular, her effect on an impressionable teenage girl and her father, form the center of the film's drama, which is set in Rotorua, a strange resort town in New Zealand famous for its thermal springs.

Crush is an extraordinarily assured film debut which signaled the arrival of a major international film talent. It has been favorably compared to Pasolini's 1960s classic *Teorema*, and to the surrealist vision of Lynch and Luis Buñuel. This surrealism is visible in many aspects of the film's menacing mood and sense of dread, which recall both film noir and the psychological thriller. There is something off-kilter and slightly out of time in the world of the film. The remarkable images and evocative music score contribute to the film's intensity and help make it a totally compelling cinematic experience. The landscape itself also becomes a key character in the film. *Crush* has been viewed by some as an allegory of the relationship between

New Zealand, a country with a repressed, conservative history, and the U.S., represented by the brash American character of Lane.

Maclean's experience in the film industry after *Crush* is instructive for aspiring filmmakers. A frustratingly long period followed the making of that film where she was attached to various projects and wrote several feature scripts. As she says, "If someone had told me that I would write three more feature scripts before I got another chance to direct one, I'd have quietly gone off and slit my wrists." Lately, Maclean's tenacity seems to have paid off. Along with Susan Seidelman, Maclean directed several episodes of the highly successful HBO cable series *Sex and the City*. Her second feature, *Jesus' Son*, based on the short stories of Denis Johnson was recently screened in competition at the Venice Film Festival.

Alison Maclean is likely to continue making the kinds of serious, personal films that now, more than ever need to be made. She is a filmmaker of uncommon ability and talent who is only beginning to make her voice heard in the world of international filmmaking. Alison Maclean spoke to me from New York.

Can you talk about your training at school and how you started making films?

There isn't really a good film school in New Zealand, so I went to art school and majored in sculpture. I started moving into photography and doing installations and performance work. Then I got a job as a trainee on a feature film on one of my summer breaks, working in the art department and then as a second AD [Assistant Director], and that job really turned me on to filmmaking.

This would have been when?

This was 1982. It was a bit of a revelation in a way. And from that point on I decided that was all I wanted to do, so I decided to make a short film in my final year at art school. They were very resistant because there was no real equipment or facilities there, so I sort of made it in spite of them.

This was *Taunt*?

Yes. One of their conditions was I had to do everything myself, so I ended up shooting and editing it, doing the music, and even processing the film myself at the start.

Can you describe these short films?

I made four films and they're all quite different. *Taunt* was black and white, twenty minutes long. At that stage, I was reading a lot of film theory, like the English film magazine *Screen*, and I was interested in subjective camera and the idea of male and female point of view in filmmaking. *Taunt* had no dialogue. It was a chase situation, a man chasing a woman, with one actor playing both parts. He was a Maori guy with very long hair, and the only difference was he wore his hair tied back as the man, and as the woman he wore it out. The film kept switching back and forth between their two POVs. So it was more of an experimental film, kind of dreamlike. I was very into Maya Deren at that stage, especially *Meshes of the Afternoon*.

In some interviews, you've mentioned reading about films but not being able to see them. But you had seen Maya Deren?

Yeah, I had seen her films. But sometimes I think it's interesting to be inspired by your imagining of a film rather than the fact of it. That happens a lot in New Zealand, where it can be harder to see foreign films. Who knows, maybe it's better. I had a very mixed response to *Taunt* and, in some ways, it set me back in that it was perceived as being long and a little pretentious. So it took me a while to get my next film, *Rud's Wife*. With that film, I wanted to prove I could do more of a straight narrative. It was based on some situations in my mother's family. It's about the relationship between a recent widow, a woman in her seventies, and her favorite son, who's an All Blacks [famous New Zealand rugby team] rugby player. It's quite satirical, dead pan, just a dissection of this family in the course of a day.

And then I did a film called *Talkback*, which was about a woman who's thrown into hosting a late night talkback radio show on her own. It intercuts between her and these fairly eccentric people who call her up in the course of a night. When I developed the script, I drew on a lot of real calls and based some of the characters on actual callers that I met. At that stage, I was very interested in having the story evolve out of a more documentary base, though the finished film doesn't look like a documentary. It was a bit of an experiment for me and not a completely successful one.

And then I made *Kitchen Sink*. That was something very different again—a thirteen-minute horror film that was more mythical, I guess. A fairy tale. It's about a woman who finds a hair in her sink and pulls out this creature and it's this constantly evolving metamorphosis, with virtually no dialogue at all. For me, it was an exercise in visual storytelling. I was quite inspired by *Woman in the Dunes*, but also certain horror films like *The Fly*. In a weird way, it's kind of a Pygmalion story. That film really changed everything for me; it opened a lot of doors and indirectly got me to the States.

Were you consciously trying to work in different forms, different genres? Or did it just happen?

I guess I'm always attracted to doing something I haven't done before in a film, and I'm also very interested in genre. For me, there's a certain freedom in improvising within a prescribed, even rigid form. I enjoy studying the grammar, seeing how I can bend it, play with audience expectations.

Do you think some of the theory that you had read found it's way into your films?

Yeah, less so recently. For a while I was reading a lot of film theory, and then, at a certain point, I became irritated by it and I just went back to doing things more instinctively.

What are some of the formative influences on your filmmaking?

It really changes so much from year to year. There are certain directors who have been a big influence over the years. Kubrick is someone I admire hugely.

I noticed in an interview that you liked *Barry Lyndon*, which is one of my favorite films.

Yes, I adore that film. I admire what he did formally in his films. Each one creates such a specific, coherent world, and I like their formal rigor. He was such a brilliant filmmaker. And Scorsese, particularly his early films, and Buñuel. I saw several Buñuel films in a row around the time I was writing *Crush*, and that was a big influence. I was quite obsessed with Jane Bowles at the time, too. The tone I was after in *Crush*, a certain kind of deadpan, mordant humor, comes directly from her. She showed me a way to write dialogue, too, that was real but not quite real at the same time and very concise.

Were you particularly film literate in terms of your background?

Not wildly. I'm not one of those people who can quote endlessly from old films. And certainly before I made *Taunt*, I wasn't much of a filmgoer at all. I hadn't seen a lot of European films and festival films, and I've slowly caught up over the years.

Has your background in photography and sculpture entered into your work?

In the eighties, I was very interested in a lot of performance art. People like Vito Aconcci and Joseph Beuys, later on Cindy Sherman, photographers like Philip-Lorca diCorcia.

Where did the idea for *Crush* come from? Perhaps you can also describe the process of writing the script.

It had a long gestation. I started thinking about it on a trip to the States. It was my first trip back since I was ten or so, and I spent three months traveling around and a month in New York. The story grew out of thinking about the character of Lane; she was the catalyst for the whole story.

This would have been in the late eighties?

Yes. It was partly inspired by a woman that I met here who'd been a childhood friend. I hadn't seen her for years, and then we ended up traveling together a bit, and I was quite intimidated but also sort of enthralled by her. She was somewhat antisocial, just one of those people who doesn't really pay too much attention to what other people think of her. To me, there was a certain freedom about the way she behaved that was completely bracing and opposite to the way I am.

She was extroverted?

Yes, but also a real original. She had no interest in small talk. There'd be these long, disconcerting silences where she would never ask questions, and the conversation would just die. And when she came out with something, it'd often be very sharp, so it was kind of intimidating.

But you did have it in mind to write a feature length script?

Yes. I was slowly thinking about some ideas and I had this idea about an older woman and her relationship with a girl who's about fifteen who's infatuated with her. I mean, I've had those relationships in my life when I was younger. So then it started to develop along two lines. It was important that this woman be an American, and that it was about the relationship between a tiny country like New Zealand, which is very seduced by America and is constantly trying to define itself in opposition to it or else being completely suffocated. Basically eighty percent of our news comes from the States. The most trivial, middle America stories that have no relevance down there.

What about the shadow of Great Britain?

Yeah, that has obviously been a huge influence in the past but it's definitely waned over the last ten years. I think the embrace of American culture and TV is partly a reaction to the colonial thing. I don't think the English influence is particularly strong now at all.

So you were consciously trying to make a political statement in the film?

Yes. I didn't want it to be heavy-handed, but those things interest me. I thought there was a way to make the story work as a kind of allegory without being too obvious about it. I'm trying to think of other films that do that. *The American Friend*, which is a film I love, does that in a way. So it started with that relationship, and then, for some reason, I started with a car crash. I started thinking about what could happen in the wake of a crisis like that. And then I thought of Rotorua [New Zealand] because, I don't know, there's something oddly mythical and other worldly about the place—a town stuck in this strange kind of time warp, the 1970s. I guess I always thought of it as a bit of a fable, and so I wanted it to be one step removed and Rotorua seemed like a good place. Also, the fact that it's so unstable. It's considered to be a complete folly to have built a town there because the ground is so unstable.

What was the involvement of the Sundance Institute in the script process?

Actually, my agent sent them the script quite late in the process. I'd been battling away on it for two years. It took me a long time to write the script. I didn't really know anything about Sundance but it was good because it gave me the push I needed to finish it. It was ironic because, in a strange way, getting that American stamp of approval helped get it financed in New Zealand.

Who's Anne Kennedy, the co-writer, and what was her involvement?

She's a friend of mine who's a novelist. She hadn't written a feature, but she'd written scripts for television. I'd already worked out most of the story, but we spent several months working out the scenes in more detail. In the end, I wrote the actual scenes and she became more of a script editor, where I would show her pages every few days and she'd make suggestions. I've never managed to achieve that since. It was quite a special relationship and I really felt that she had the same film in her head. She helped me enormously. Writing a feature script was something that I never wanted to do; it really seemed like it was something beyond me. It was such a battle, that first script.

But had you been writing before?

No. I'd written small things, essays or whatever, but that's all. I'd co-written some of my shorts with other people, but it was a huge leap to write a feature script and invent the whole thing. For my other shorts, I'd developed this working method where I based the dialogue and the characters on real people or I did a lot of research. This was the first time I'd just invented the characters.

How prepared were you when you began shooting the film? Did you storyboard? Did you have a pretty clear idea of how each scene would be filmed?

Yeah, I did. I spent a long time with Dion Beebe, the Director of Photography. It was his first feature and we spent about five weeks going over the whole film, shot by shot. But, of course, once we got on set, half of it had to be thrown away. I felt reasonably prepared because I went back to Sundance for the director's lab. It was perfect timing because I was there for a week with Marcia Gay Harden [Lane], so it was very much a rehearsal for the real thing.

Was that the extent of the rehearsals or did you rehearse more later?

I rehearsed with the actors in New Zealand, but Sundance gave me extra time. It was great because I was petrified and they gave me a lot of moral support. It was great to be working on the scenes and have another director there; to be able to turn to them and say, "Now what? I'm stuck" or whatever, talk things through as they came up. I always think it's hard as a director; you never really get a chance to be an apprentice.

What was your experience with actors before this?

Well, just my shorts, that was it.

No training?

I just learned by doing it and making a lot of mistakes and, in some ways, I still feel somewhat inexperienced in that area. You need time, gaining experience by doing it. Luckily, with *Crush*, I had a really wonderful cast; they were very generous and smart. Although I didn't have a great time making *Crush*; it was difficult, but working with the actors was definitely the best part.

Did the film change much while you were shooting it?

Yes and no. I guess it didn't change enormously. We didn't do a lot of improvising. Donogh Rees, who played Christina, changed her character a lot. The way that character was written, she was more of a vessel, more childlike in a way, and Donogh brought this almost frightening stubbornness that took me by surprise. It was really interesting to see how that shifted the balance of the four characters. I think it makes the last third of the film more ambiguous, because, as written, it's more clearly about this younger girl manipulating a disabled woman who doesn't really know what's going on. But the way Donogh played it, you feel like there's possibly this other agenda going on, an old score being settled.

Was there any difference working with Marcia Gay Harden and the other actors?

Yes, in that compared to every other actor I'd worked with, she was very experienced and trained. She'd been through New York University and she was pretty assertive and very definite in her opinions. That caused some tension at times, but I also learned an enormous amount from her. She's a very skilled, sophisticated actor.

Can you talk about the shoot itself? You said it was not a very happy experience. Why not?

For all kinds of reasons. In some cases, I didn't get the crew I'd wanted. There's a very small pool in New Zealand. As the shoot went on, I didn't feel that we were a cohesive group, and some of the crew didn't quite get the script or didn't even necessarily like it. So I didn't feel that full support I'd had when I made *Kitchen Sink*. That was a completely charmed experience from beginning to end and this was almost the opposite. Also, I was terrified. The part I found hardest was blocking the scenes with the actors, choreographing their movements with the camera. You're trying to find an interesting, fresh way to shoot it under this enormous pressure.

So you felt that your inexperience was a disadvantage with the crew?

Yeah, definitely. I kept feeling that I had to prove myself.

And what about being a woman? Did that enter into it at all?

It's somewhere in the equation. I don't know how much, but yeah, it probably entered into it. There were some conflicts I had with certain people which were partly exacerbated by that.

I found the camera movements quite deliberate, very slow, and the look of the film seems very carefully worked out. Could you describe how you worked with the cinematographer and the art director?

I made a decision with this film to be guided by the actors more than I had in the past, and so the performances came first. But I was also very interested in the sense of place; I thought of Rotorua as a character in itself. I was interested in being a bit more removed than is common in many Hollywood films. So you're seeing the relationship between people in a room and you're seeing the space and the landscape. I tried to keep it simple, too.

Obviously the sense of place and the physicality is crucial.

Yeah, that was very important.

I get a sense that you wanted to put even more weight onto the physical and the objects.

Yes, that's true. I get impatient with many Hollywood films because there's this assumption that meaning or emotion is contained in those few square inches of an actor's face and I just don't see it that way at all. I think there's a power in withholding information, revealing things gradually, letting the audience discover things within the frame in time, in the way they stand. Take a film like *Safe*. That's a film I admire enormously and I think a lot of power comes from its restraint. If you're looking at the back of someone's head or their body, it's like your curiosity, your desire to see their face and know more, sucks you into the screen. You fill it up with your own feelings and imagination in a more powerful way.

Was *Crush* difficult to edit?

Yes, it was difficult. There were a lot of choices about the way the scenes could be put together, and it was fairly complex with the four characters.

How closely did you work with the editor?

Very closely, and we kept having screenings and getting feedback. It changed quite radically in terms of the structure, especially in the middle section, which was quite long.

The music and sound I think are very important in this film and quite effective. Are you particularly sensitive to that aspect of post-production?

Sound is incredibly important to me. It's one of my favorite parts of the process. I love working with composers and musicians. This was the second time that I'd worked with a band who had never done a soundtrack before. I had worked with a band called Headless Chickens in *Kitchen Sink*. This was a group called JPS Experience. They did a little demo for me, and I was very impressed because their music uses a lot of odd sound effects and is very atmospheric but, more importantly, they really know how to communicate emotion. I found it very direct compared to a lot of the more established film composers. I was also working with a young Australian composer who'd just come out of film school there who's very talented, Anthony Partos. It ended up being this unusual situation where he composed the opening titles and the end credits. He would send tapes over and I'd play them to the band, and then vice versa. They really had no contact with each other; they were just playing things over the phone. I was worried that the end result would be a total mish-mash but I think it works.

Were the actors clear on who their characters were? Did they have a good handle on them?

They're all very different. Marcia really got that character right away on a very deep level. I came over to the States to cast that part. I saw about a hundred women from both coasts, and Marcia was the one. It wasn't a difficult choice. She was just so close to the way I'd imagined Lane when I wrote her. She's very striking, very charismatic. It was amazing when she arrived on set, she just galvanized everybody, the whole production, with her energy.

But did they ever question their characters, what their characters did, and why?

Oh yeah. We'd argue about things all the way through, little things. Marcia was concerned about her character being unlikable, a little sensitive about being the ugly American. At the same time, she was brave and not afraid to appear unsympathetic. Donogh Rees, who played Christina, was incredible. She just completely threw herself into it, did huge amounts of research, spent time with people with head injuries and a physiotherapist. It was a very demanding part for her. I remember the day something changed, we'd been rehearsing for maybe a week or so and she just got it and you could see in her body and the way she moved that there was something wrong. It was almost uncanny, you know? But Donogh was so completely fearless: There was nothing she wouldn't do. She's completely without vanity, too.

Did you find your own understanding of the characters changing from your original conception?

They were just *more* of everything. More complicated. More alive and driven and real. You know you write certain things and you become slightly immunized to the more disturbing aspects of the characters, and then when you see an actor doing those things, it's a bit of a shock sometimes.

What does the title of the movie mean for you?

It's funny because I actually called it *Crash*, believe it or not, a long time ago, before I'd even heard of J.G. Ballard's book. And then I thought of *Crush*, which is a word that I'd never use in conversation, or didn't back then. So it was just there as a working title, and then the story kind of wrote itself into the title. I liked the double meaning of it, and more and more, that seemed to be the theme of the film: the idea of an infatuation that is quite intense and fantasized and doesn't have much basis in reality, that can easily flip the other way and be destructive.

Did you see Lane as a sexual predator?

Yes and no. That's kind of her currency. That's the way she gets what she wants in life. That is the source of her power and she knows it.

But there's more to her than that. I think there's a real heart there as well.

She's a real femme fatale. Were you considering working with film noir?

Yes, I guess, but hopefully fleshing her out and making her more human as well. Lane has a certain blunt honesty. Also, the fact that she's attracted to women as well as men.

I think Lane has more complexity than the other characters.

No, it's true. But it's hard in ninety minutes or whatever with four characters to make them equally compelling and interesting. But I guess I had more energy, more fascination with that character than the others.

What about the character of Colin [William Zappa]?

In hindsight, I think he came across a little too self-pitying. He didn't quite hold his own with the three women.

Were you satisfied with the other male character, Horse [Pete Smith]?

I'm very happy with Horse. He's a secondary character but he has a lot of vitality, I think. And he does this pretty bad thing to this girl, Angela [Caitlin Bossley], but you kind of like him anyway, in spite of it.

He has no pretensions about the world.

No. And I don't think he would see what he did as a violation. He'd say it was something she wanted to do and maybe he just pushed it a little. It's hard to completely condemn him because you can see he's basically a decent person. It's hard to explain, but he has a certain innocence.

Are there things in the film that make audiences uncomfortable?

Judging by some of the reviews I've had, yeah.

Could we talk about the sexual relationships between the women?
I know you wanted to keep that fairly ambiguous.

I wanted a hint of it. I think if you make it too explicit, suddenly it's a
film about a lesbian avoiding her sexuality or something, and those
kinds of things don't really interest me, those cut-and-dried definitions
of who people are. When you encounter people in life, you almost
never fully know those things about them. There are always areas of
contradiction or ambiguity. It's interesting to me to see that in a film,
and have to work it out for yourself the way you do in life.

The sense of how much we know about these characters, and how
we understand their actions, is very interesting in the film. Was it
difficult to determine how much to reveal about these characters?

It's true. I had a scene where Lane was alluding to her past, where
there was some hint of abuse there. I even shot it. Then we cut it out
because it made it too sordid, and I thought it was more interesting
if you didn't fully understand why she was behaving the way she was.

One of the striking stylistic elements of your film is your decision
to shoot in a fairly nonclassical style. Can you talk about your decision to shoot in a particular style like this?

I guess that kind of classical shooting style bores me because it does
all the work for you, there's no mystery. I prefer to withhold certain
things or reveal things as it goes along. I knew I wasn't making a
Hollywood film, it was going to be different from that. One of the
luxuries about working in New Zealand is that you're not quite so
accountable to the marketplace and its pressures.

Because of the financing of the films?

Yeah. Basically, *Crush* was entirely financed by the New Zealand Film
Commission. So you do feel a greater freedom. There's nobody
breathing down your neck. Our attitude was, if it got an American
distributor, if it got picked up in Europe, then that's just a huge bo-
nus. It's something you wouldn't necessarily be expecting. Now that
I'm working here, I'm much more aware of those other pressures,

because you just know that your choices on this film are going to dictate what sort of film you can do next. So you have to be much more canny, I think, try to stay true to your ideas but also do something that's going to attract a sizeable audience.

You often create menacing moments out of quite ordinary situations just by the way a scene is put together or the way sound is used. For example, in the scene when Angela and Lane go to the hospital to visit Christina, there's this camera movement down the corridor of the hospital and we see this bald man talking to a bicyclist in a room, and then the bicyclist talks to Lane later and he has some kind of medical condition, a jerky walk and a strange voice. I thought I was watching David Lynch in some scenes.

The scene where Lane goes to the hospital, you're with her, inside her anxiety. I guess I've had a lot of anxiety in my life, panic attacks, whatever. I'm just very sensitive to that very heightened state of tension or anxiety and the things you notice when you're in that state. Things become exaggerated that somebody else wouldn't notice at all. It's not a horror film, but it's verging on being a kind of psychological thriller.

Maybe you're a surrealist.

That's what I love about Buñuel. I think he is a brilliant surrealist.

It's a little hard to get a handle on some of the characters. I found myself disliking Christina a lot.

Well, you don't really get a chance to know her before the accident, and after that, her personality is completely transformed. She's driven by her needs and urges, and she's quite tyrannical really. I mean, it's not very attractive. But she has a childlike directness too, which is very disarming.

I think there's a sense in which Christina and Lane are archetypal characters as opposed to fully rounded characters. Does the film work allegorically for you?

I always did see it as a kind of a fable. Maybe they are archetypal but it's not like I could label them or define what they are exactly.

One of the resonant lines in the film for me is when Colin asks Lane, "So why have you stayed?" She furiously replies, "I've stayed, that's all it means, I've stayed." Her response says a lot about her character.

People do enormously complicated things to avoid things in their lives. You get the sense the affair she's initiated and everything else is all to do with Christina and not being able face the consequences of what she did.

Well, she doesn't seem prepared for the consequences of what's going on. She sets these things in motion.

Yes, but you feel that she just can't bring herself to go to the hospital. She can't face it, but she can't run away either, and you feel it's probably the latest in a long line of other casualties that are a direct result of her carelessness. I guess you could see the entire story as being the playing out of that transference.

Did you achieve what you wanted to achieve with the film? Is there any part of it that doesn't really satisfy you?

I guess I felt when it was done that perhaps it was too restrained, too controlled, that I hadn't let the emotional lives of the characters come to the surface as fully as they could have. I'm talking about the way it was shot and staged. That's an area I've consciously been trying to push myself in, to loosen up a little. I like the idea of this potentially overheated, melodramatic story married to a certain coolness.

How did audiences react to the film? Were there different responses to it in New Zealand and Australia as opposed to America or Europe?

It was very polarized. It did well in San Francisco, probably best of all, as well as England and France. It was received with a certain chilly incomprehension in New Zealand. There were definitely people there who got it and loved it. But the reaction was also more critical than anywhere else in the world. They thought I couldn't make up my mind what genre it was, and there was a definite defensiveness about the men in the film.

Did the *New York Times'* negative review bother you?

Are you kidding?

Such a terrible review.

I was really hurt, but, at the same time, it seemed a very personal response. He obviously couldn't bear Lane's character; maybe she reminded him of somebody he knew. He said things—of course I know it by heart—such as that he had no idea what the film was about beyond the contents of Lane's wardrobe.

It's just your luck that you got Vincent Canby at the very end of his run.

Yeah, two weeks before he retired.

What did you do in the period after *Crush*? Could you talk about that a bit? You had this Disney period, didn't you?

Yes. I had a brief Disney period. Nothing really came of it because we didn't see eye to eye on anything.

Did you actually work on *Up Close and Personal?*

I did! For a short time, I was attached there. In a strange way that brought me to New York because I moved here while I was working on that film.

It's such a bad movie!

I know. Potentially it could have been great. Joan Didion is a big hero of mine but I never got a chance to meet her. Disney and I didn't seem to agree on anything, so that took a year. Since then I've developed several other projects. If someone had told me that I would write three more feature scripts before I got another chance to direct one, I'd have quietly gone off and slit my wrists.

You also worked on the *Bedlam* script, didn't you?

Yes, I wrote that over two and a half years. I'm still trying to set that up. And another film called *Iris*, which Good Machine is producing, a horror film about false memory. There's another script for an action film set in Bangkok. Then, more recently, I got an offer to direct this film called *Jesus' Son*, based on a book of short stories by an incredible writer, Denis Johnson, and that's the film I've just finished shooting now.

Do you want to keep making films in North America or does it make a difference? Do you consider yourself an international film director?

I guess I do because my projects seem to be. In some ways, I feel like a foreigner wherever I am, so, yes, why not? I love New York, and I'd love to keep working here, but my experience in the last six years has been pretty sobering in that it's so damn hard to survive, let alone trying to make idiosyncratic films.

Do you think you can keep making this kind of unconventional film?

I don't know. I hope so. I have several projects now that I love, all quite unusual in their own ways and all a hard sell, but I definitely think there's an appetite out there for unusual films.

Absolutely. What qualities do you think one needs to succeed as a filmmaker?

Well, based on my recent experience, you have to be very patient and, at the same time, tenacious and bloody minded. And lucky, of course. You have to be pretty driven to deal with all the obstacles that come up, internal and external. You know, people make different choices and I guess my choice has been—and I literally pay for it on a daily basis, financially—but my choice has been to keep trying to work on projects I really care about. Maybe there'll come a point when I'm fed up with the struggle. There aren't that many films out there that really matter to me as a viewer, and those are the kinds of films I want to make.

JOHN MCNAUGHTON

John McNaughton's astonishing first film, *Henry: Portrait of a Serial Killer*, is one of the most compelling, if disturbing, films of the 1980s. In its penetrating treatment of a very violent subject, the film announced the emergence of a major directorial talent. *Henry* may be one of the most truly horrifying films ever made, yet it also offers a serious examination of cinematic violence and sordid human behavior. It does not glamorize, or make attractive, the depraved activities of its subject, serial killer Henry Lee Lucas (Michael Rooker). It is unsettling in its low-key, methodical presentation, even to viewers who have no interest in the horror genre. But to describe *Henry* as a horror film ignores its socio-economic concerns. Ultimately, the film is a courageous exploration of human depravity and one of the most original American films of the decade. Although the film is a serious treatment of an admittedly difficult subject, it took over eighteen months for the film to make its way into a few theaters on a very limited release. These early difficulties marked something of a consistent pattern for McNaughton in getting his work seen in the form it was meant to be seen, at least until most recently.

McNaughton's most interesting film may be the little-seen *Normal Life,* one of the few American pictures of the 1990s with any interest in the lives of real working people. It offers a devastating portrait of a volatile couple and their descent into a life of crime. What is extraordinary about *Normal Life* is how honest, realistic and sympathetic it is to its protagonists, extremely well played by Ashley Judd and Luke Perry. McNaughton's own background growing up in southside Chicago no doubt gave him insight into the plight of the working-class who were falling between the cracks in Ronald Reagan's conservative economic "revolution" in the 1980s. Once again, McNaughton experienced difficulties with his production company and the film went virtually unseen in theaters. Only after McNaughton voiced vehement complaints did the production company eventually play the film for limited runs in New York and Los Angeles. *Normal Life* was also given a modest international release. Most viewers have had to content themselves with discovering the film on video. It is, in my opinion, one of the most dramatically satisfying American films of the 1990s.

McNaughton has worked as an independent and for major Hollywood studios, but he claims that his experience with small independent companies offered him no more creative freedom and interference than he received with larger projects, such as *Mad Dog and Glory*, with its refreshing Richard Price script starring Robert De Niro, or his recent box-office hit, the Hitchcockian pastiche *Wild Things*.

In little over a decade, John McNaughton has carved out a unique place in the contemporary American cinema. Apart from the above-mentioned films, he has worked in a variety of genres such as horror/sci-fi (*The Borrower*), the concert/performance film (Eric Bogosian's *Sex, Drugs, Rock & Roll*), ironic spoofs (the hilarious *Rebel Highway: Girls in Prison*, co-scripted by Sam Fuller), the gangster genre (*Lansky,* from a David Mamet script), and *Condo Painting*, an experimental documentary about painter George Condo shot on video and blown up to 35 mm.

McNaughton is a filmmaker of great versatility and talent who seems only now to be coming into his own as an artist. In recent years, he has also tried to shake the unfair labeling of him as a "difficult" director, a label that seems to describe any artist in Hollywood who fights for the good of his work and merely wants to make films that will be seen in a form resembling their maker's original intentions. McNaughton has lately entered a very productive phase of his career and is now being offered projects which, earlier, might have gone to more high-profile directors. He is an uncompromising filmmaker of integrity who believes strongly in the power of cinema to touch people's lives and explore sometimes dark and troubling questions. I spoke to John McNaughton in Los Angeles.

Tell me about your background, and growing up in Chicago.

Chicago was a great melting pot and heavily industrialized, and for working-class people, postwar America in the fifties and sixties was an incredibly prosperous time.

How did you end up going into the fine arts?

The arts and music were the only things that interested me as a kid. I took an art course in high school. They also used to take two kids from every high school in Chicago and put them in a special art program at the Art Institute of Chicago in the summer. A friend and I were chosen. I also took piano lessons as a kid and got involved in rock-and-roll bands.

But you weren't particularly surrounded by art in your house?

Not really. But I gravitated towards it, and we had The Art Institute of Chicago, which was a big influence when I was in college. I spent hours and hours there. I also did two years at The University of Illinois studying sculpture. Then I transferred to Columbia College in Chicago and studied film, television, and still photography.

The other big influences on me growing up were television and movies. I was born in 1949. My father had a bar on the south side of Chicago, and he put in a TV in 1948, and naturally prospered. Within a few months of being born, there was a television in our house. I was an only child and I lived in front of it. I know all the television shows from the fifties and sixties. [Laughs] It's part of growing up in America at that particular time.

Did you see a lot of films growing up?

Yes. I remember when I was at University of Illinois going to see two films which really had an impact. One was *Blow-Up* and the other was *A Fistful of Dollars*. I remember seeing *Belle de Jour* back then. I also loved old movies on television when I was a kid. Of course, I went to current movies too. I was fortunate when I was a kid, seeing *Liberty Valence*, *Vertigo*, and *Psycho* when they first came out. Hitchcock and Ford were still alive and working.

So, you gravitated both to the American cinema and European art films.

Yes, and as I started to mature into my early twenties, I discovered the European masters: Bergman, Truffaut, Fellini.

Did you make any films at Columbia College?

I didn't really have money to. I went out and shot a bit of this and that, but I didn't make any real films until later.

What were your first filmmaking experiences?

I worked in an advertising agency for ten months. That's as long as I could stand. This was 1973 or 1974. Then my marriage exploded. I wasn't happy working in an advertising agency. I felt trapped in this life. I wasn't where I planned to be, or doing what I wanted to do at all. So, I took off with a traveling carnival and a 35mm still camera. It was fabulous.

How long did you do this?

Just one year, then I ended up in New Orleans. I was going to stay there for a couple of weeks and then head up to New York with the photographs I'd taken during the year with the carnival. But I ended up staying in New Orleans for a couple of years. Then I decided it was time to go back and do what I really intended to do, which was make films. I came back to Chicago in 1977 and pieced my way back into the film world. But it was very frustrating because I still had to work in the advertising business, which I hated. When we made *Henry* a few years later, we took a number of people out of that world.

Were you directing commercials?

No, I never did. I really had no interest in doing commercials. To this day, I don't do them.

How long did you work in advertising this time?

About a year. Then, I went to work for the MPI folks [the eventual producers of *Henry: Portrait of a Serial Killer*]. These guys had just started their little business. At the time, there was no half-inch VHS or Beta format, no theatrical films on videocassette. This was when they were running those Super8 loops in restaurants, things like old Chaplin pictures and cartoons. I would take those loops and circulate them from various pizza restaurants and stuff. They would also place 16mm projectors in conference centers in local hotels and rent 16mm films to old people's homes, a very early audiovisual business, but they got into the video business on day one.

When did *Henry* start percolating?

I was working for those guys, the Ali bothers, who eventually became MPI Home Video. Although the video business hadn't really taken off, I bought a bunch of video equipment and tried to freelance. I stumbled along like that for a couple of years, and then I happened to call the guys from MPI because, in the meantime, the video business did start to develop and they were making a fair bit of money. Early on, we had talked about how someday this video business was really going to take off, and how they'd make movies just for video, and one day we'd make a movie together. I went back to them and produced a couple of little documentaries called *Dealers in Death*, using public-domain footage. We just cobbled together whatever we could get for nothing. We hired Broderick Crawford for $2,500 to do the narration. Cash money, twenty-five hundred-dollar bills. Then we were going to do another one about professional wrestling, but the deal fell apart. I had been living in L.A. and I was in Chicago for a visit one day. I stopped by the office and Waleed—Waleed and Malik are the two guys who run the company—said, "You know, John, why don't we make that movie we always talked about." At the time, horror films were selling like hot cakes on video. I said, "Sure!" He said, "I'll give you $100,000 and you'll make me a horror film, and we'll see what happens." As I was walking out the hallway, I ran into someone I'd grown up with who worked for them, sort of a collector and connoisseur of the arcane and off-beat. He had this office stacked up with videos and books. I said, "Waleed just offered me $100,000 to make a horror movie. I have no idea what to make." He says, "Here, I want to show you something." He put in a video cassette, and it was a *20/20* television segment on Henry Lee Lucas. And that became the germ of the film *Henry: Portrait of a Serial Killer*.

What attracted you to explore this dark side in *Henry*?

Well, what attracted me was seeing the real Henry Lee Lucas on *20/20*, and how creepy he was. I was also a big fan of true crime and used to read a lot about it. I'd never heard the term "serial killer" before. At the time, Henry Lee Lucas claimed to have killed 350 people, and he would give these elaborate descriptions. He had an interesting manner about him. He had a glass eye, a weird-looking character, but he had a gentle manner about him. You could see how he could get close to people. He had a laconic, easy-going way of talking. It was fascinating that this man could get close enough to someone to kill them. He has since recanted and now says that he didn't kill anybody, but it appears that he killed his mother, for which he served time, and at least a couple of other people.

Did you do other kinds of research?

We didn't actually meet Henry Lucas, but we started reading articles and books. The idea was that this guy was able to drift after he killed somebody and cross the state line before the body was found. Statistics show that most murders are committed among people previously acquainted, so there's always some sort of motive, some sort of sense to it. Serial killers, on the other hand, are people who are so twisted out that they just randomly pick a victim and slaughter them, and then move on. It was a fascinating idea.

In terms of getting ready to make the film, did you have a clear idea of how each scene would be staged?

I always have ideas on what the scenes are supposed to look like, but specific staging, no.

No storyboarding?

Oh, yeah, always. In fact, *Wild Things* was the first picture I've done where I didn't do a complete storyboard. On *Henry* we didn't have enough money for a shot-by-shot storyboard, so we had one panel per scene. Frank Coronado, a guy that I continue to use, came in and did something like 110 frames that summed up all the scenes. It's interesting when you start out like that, I didn't know about union crews, it was just "Here's the work we have to do today," and we'd shoot until it was done. One time it was twenty-four hours of straight shooting. Everyone was doing it for almost no money. People were on a flat rate for the length of the picture. Thinking back, we knew so little about budgeting and scheduling. It was like "Here's $100,000. Okay. I'm going to make a movie."

Did you stick pretty much to the script?

Oh, yes. And we rehearsed for two weeks, which I have continued to try and do.

But not on location?

No. It was mostly table rehearsals and setting chairs in the room to simulate the set.

So, you're a believer in that process?

I think it's invaluable. The actors spend time together, and the director is with them, and when you hit the set, you're in the same movie. When we did *Mad Dog and Glory*, David Caruso was not cast till the day before we started shooting. Robert De Niro, Bill Murray, and Uma Thurman had two weeks' rehearsal together. David came in the first day, and he had a completely different idea of the movie than the rest of us. It took a few days to get in sync. Rehearsals are invaluable to get everybody thinking about the movie in the same way. They get comfortable with each other.

Was *Henry* a difficult shoot?

Yes. There was no money. For me, it was twenty-eight days without a day off. We shot till we were done. It was very difficult. The crew consisted of a cameraman and two production assistants.

What about the editing process? You've continued to work with Elena Maganini since then.

She did *Wild Things* too. She was editing animated TV commercials, working full-time, and we set up a 16mm flatbed editing machine in her apartment. We'd cut *Henry* on weekends. None of us had ever cut a full-length feature or been around one being cut. You're making it up as you go. I think we worked on it for six months. The first cut was two and a half hours, and the picture's now at eighty-three minutes.

Did you feel insecure shooting your first film?

No, I didn't. I refuse to feel insecure. I don't see the point. What's going to happen? I remember having to direct Robert De Niro, and of course I'd seen *Raging Bull* and *Taxi Driver* and all the great things he'd done. I'm going to go up to this man and tell him, "No, that's no good. Do it this way"? But you just walk up there and do it and see what happens. Fortunately, in his case, he was wonderful. But what are they going to do to you anyway?

Did you know what you were looking for when you were casting the character of Henry?

You never know until he walks through the door, which happened with Michael Rooker. When he walked through the door, I almost dropped to the floor. He came in character. He opened his mouth, sat down, and read. Except for his shoes, he was wearing the clothes that he would wear in the picture. He was perfect for the role.

What was your experience with actors at this point?

No real experience with actors, just presenters in commercials, basically. But what I did have was the years I spent building sailboats and making jewelry in New Orleans, on the road with the carnival, working in steel mills, working in factories, working in bars. I think I have a good understanding of human beings and class and type and behavior.

Were you particularly interested in understanding Henry's character psychologically?

I wasn't interested in trying to explain him. We presented a certain amount of information and let the viewer draw some conclusions.

When Henry talks about how he killed his mother, I'm not even sure he's telling the truth.

He's not. We had him contradict himself within the scene specifically to raise doubts. He's told the story so many times. When most of us tell stories, we tweak the details. We embellish and perfect them over time. Henry Lee Lucas would tell the same stories in different interviews, but the details would always be altered. I felt like there was a core of truth in there, but this guy is so far gone that he doesn't quite remember it either. Some of it's the truth, some of it's lies, some of it's embellishment.

There's a sense that you're trying to make him a human being, on some level, in that scene.

There's a line in Cormac McCarthy's novel *Child of God*, which goes "He's a child of God, as you or I." The character in that novel was similar to Henry, this white trash, Southern demented guy who murdered a bunch of people. Nonetheless he's still a person. I hate these wild, drooling villains most films present, they're so unbelievable.

Did you feel that you had an understanding of Henry?

Yes, and Michael did. Michael came from that same basic socio-enonomic culture. He was from a welfare family in Jasper, Alabama.

I remember talking to him once about character models and he said, "Oh, yeah. I have an uncle who's a lot like this guy."

When we see the first murders, it's very swift and physical. It sets the pattern for other murders in the film where we see stabbings, piercings, a man with the television smashed on his head. They're all very messy. You really wanted to get across the idea of just how much physical effort it takes to kill a human being.

Murder is messy, bloody, ugly, and repulsive. One of the big themes in *Henry* is violence as entertainment. Normally, the way you develop the theme is to set up a character to be a bad guy, have him do something that makes you dislike him, and then turn up the heat where you dislike him enough that you're happy to see one of the heroes slaughter him. And you get a great cathartic release. That's sort of what we did. In the scene with the television set, here's this big, fat, ugly guy who is repulsive to start with. We did everything we could to make him distasteful and repulsive. Unbeknownst to him, he's standing with the two worst guys in America, and he's insulting them. And we take it through the biggest, funniest, "Here's violence for entertainment the way you like it, folks!" This guy has pushed it over the line with the wrong guys. He's a complete creep. And we have him stabbed with a soldering iron, with the TV over the head, which is humorous in its own way. "Okay, wasn't that a lot of fun? Now, we're going to show you what it might look like to move in on an innocent family and just slaughter them randomly." It's about as ugly a thing as you're ever likely to see. "Now, how much fun was that?" To take the audience one way, and then show them what it might really be like. And then we pulled a double trick of going in the house and seeing that they've got a camera, and the camera hits the ground, and we cut! You think you're still in the room with them but, indeed, you're seeing the playback later on a TV screen, and they're now entertaining themselves with the record of their own mayhem. And you're sitting right next to them in a kind of complicity.

The film presents these morally reprehensible characters quite neutrally. You're very nonjudgmental in the film.

Certain filmmakers give you cues as to how to morally perceive the situation. I'd much prefer to show you the situation and let you make your own moral and intellectual decisions about the characters and what's going on. I also love to challenge. The convention is to offer hope, and there's absolutely none in this picture. You have to have a sympathetic character, and after a while, you realize that compared to Otis, Henry is somewhat sympathetic. You can't help but like the guy for certain reasons. Then, you've got an inner conflict. I like to challenge people in their beliefs.

Do you think Henry's really sympathetic?

I think that Michael Rooker as Henry has a great deal of sympathy. I think Henry is a terribly damaged human being, and really did go through some horrors as a child growing up, but he has his limitations. He has a personal code—"Otis, that's your sister!"—even though Henry killed his mother. Whereas once Otis gives himself over to the beast, it's complete. He just doesn't have the moral fiber to delineate any sort of code for himself.

Were there any models in your mind, at all, making *Henry*. It's fairly original.

I strive for originality.

Is Henry capable of love?

I think so, but he's so damaged that the minute he feels a sexual attraction, it expresses itself as violence, and that's what he's trying to prevent when Becky comes on to him.

I like the way you handled the killing of Becky at the end of the film. It's very discreet and imaginative: seeing him shave in the motel room in the morning and not knowing what happened the night before. You deliberately withhold narrative information until we see a suitcase dumped by the side of the road, and then we understand what went before. Was that how you'd always planned it?

Yes. We were telling the story of this guy who did certain things for a living, but his art was murder. That was his vocation. At the beginning of the film, there was a tableaux of his killings. That was his artwork, his pieces, so to speak. In telling the story of a man, then two men, who murder other human beings, we tried to show the aftermath. At one point or another, you have to show the whole act, but if you show the whole thing every time, you're just going to numb the audience. They won't be able to deal with it. After we saw the killing of Otis, you just couldn't see Becky get killed. She was the only decent thing in the whole picture. You just couldn't do that to an audience.

You had a very difficult time getting this film released and shown.

Yes. The original intent of the people who funded it, from their corporate point of view, was to get it straight to video. If they could make a film for $100,000 and own it, there's no way they could lose money. Once we started shooting, and I saw the dailies, I thought it could play in theaters. I could have had some fun with horror B-movie stuff, but it wasn't what I was aspiring to. *Henry* stylistically took some of the gore effects and stuff from B-movies, from horror films, but we also took from Cassavetes. It's an amalgam of high and low art.

It never got a theatrical release, did it?

It did, but very limited. In Europe, it did well. It did two million dollars from cinemas in Spain. When I read that, I thought, "Wait a minute. How come I keep getting these royalty statements about it losing money?" For years this film has been "losing money," and it was made for $100,000.

You still haven't seen money from it?

We saw a little money from the first video release. Ever since then, it's being losing money hand over fist. I can't quite figure it out.

How did audiences react to *Henry*?

The first time it was shown at The Chicago Film Festival, it was projected on video, so it looked pretty rough because we didn't have a print yet. The first time I saw a print projected to an audience was at the Telluride Film Festival. I'd say, during the scene where the family is slaughtered, we lost about fifteen percent of the audience. They were flying out the door. But the next screening, when word got around that it was an artistic film, we lost only one person.

Your next film was *The Borrower*. It had a very troubled history. How did that film get made?

After *Henry* was completed and not released, it was pretty hard to base a career on a film that nobody was seeing. There was a really good transfer lab in Chicago where we did a one-inch master, color-corrected video before we ever printed *Henry*. So I was able to order videocassettes of a very nice quality and circulate them. But I went eighteen months, basically, with no income whatsoever.

You finished *Henry* some time in 1986?

We finished around June 1986. Eventually, I got an agent, and *Henry* was seen in a couple of festivals. It was seen at Telluride, it sort of broke open. A lot of people wrote about it. My agent sent me every bad horror-film script that was doing everything we tried so very hard not to do in *Henry*, all the obvious crap that you've seen a million times. I couldn't bring myself to do any of them. Eventually, the script to *The Borrower* came through. It was a picture that was budgeted at around six or seven million dollars, but there was no way that company was going to spend that.

Which company was this?

At the time it was Kushner-Locke and Atlantic Releasing in partnership. So, I read the script. Many of these horror-film scripts had a stock story, and they'd plug in seven special effects scenes that really didn't need to be there, very gory. They'd cut somebody's heart out, just so they could stage this stupid special effect. The thing about *The Borrower* was that the whole conceit was integral to the character. The main character was a different form of life who was transformed into a human form. He lost his head so he had to go and get these heads. It wasn't gratuitous. Also, I loved the metaphor where this creature goes and takes the head, the life, the mind of another human being and then inhabits it. So, you have a chance to explore class, different types of people, male, female, et cetera. It's sort of a metaphor for what an actor does. They take another person's character and become that person. There was something interesting to the basic concept.

What was the process of working on the script like?

That script went through so many rewrites and writers the company insisted on using. Our original draft had the cops do very little. They were just a couple of dummies that were always two steps behind the action. Part of the conceit was that every time someone would come forward with these stories, "I saw him rip the head off this guy, it put it on his head . . .!" it was like, "Send him to the drunk tank. I don't believe in creatures from outer space. This is nonsense, it's just some maniac."

I learned a lot of lessons on that picture. Part of the reason we were getting financing was because Rae Dawn Chong, who played one of the cops, was in it. Now, I do not think actors are meat puppets. I do not think they are talking scenery. I get along wonderfully with them. What they do, I think is miraculous, and I love working with actors. There has only ever been one that I just didn't like—and she didn't like me—and that was Rae Dawn Chong. She was impossible, and she didn't want to be in the picture. She did it for the paycheck, and acted like it. And we did not get on. The script had to be completely rewritten so that she would be the central character. Up to that point, in our draft, the monster was the central character. The cops were just a couple of bozos, very inconsequential characters.

The film is pretty funny in places.

I watch it occasionally. It was supposed to be like a rock-and-roll horror film that was funny. I still laugh; I think it's funny. Antonio Fargas was a bright spot. He was wonderful to work with. Tommy Towles was really fun to work with.

How much of the film represents what you wanted to accomplish?

It's a tribute to a certain genre of horror films from the seventies. Making it was just nightmarish. The company was going bankrupt, there was a lot of personal animosity among different groups on the set. It was the most difficult film I ever had to make. Eventually, it was taken away from us in postproduction. It was completely shut down when the company went bankrupt. The completion bond company tried not to pay people and we had to threaten to throw the negative into Lake Michigan. It was really a trying experience, but I have a fondness for the picture because it makes me laugh.

Did you have problems with the crew?

We were going to shoot in Chicago. At the last minute, Atlantic Releasing was getting into financial trouble. They had a building on Sunset Boulevard, with all these executives with nice cars, and they only had one movie in production, which was *The Borrower*. We didn't know if the unions were going to give us a break or not, and, more than anything else, the executives wanted to have something that they could get their hands on so that they could justify their jobs. So they moved the whole picture back to L.A. I started out with a pretty decent crew, but through a lot of ugliness on that shoot, they wound up firing my whole camera crew and bringing in another crew. There were a lot of people on the replacement crew who really soured me on working in Los Angeles. The best people in the world are here, but so are the worst.

We had no rehearsals on that film and it shows. There was an insane person in charge, who said, "What are you? A film student or something? This is Hollywood! You don't rehearse here."

How did *Sex, Drugs, Rock & Roll* come about? Were you a particular fan of Eric Bogosian?

I'd seen *Talk Radio* and liked it. After *Henry* was finally released, I got three fan letters: one from John Waters, one from David Mamet, and one from Eric Bogosian. After *The Borrower*, I was in New York—this was 1991—and we were about to make *Mad Dog and Glory*. I had gotten a phone call one day and it was Martin Scorsese's assistant saying, "Marty's going to call you in five minutes. He wants to talk to you about making a movie for him." First, you think, "Who is this, really?" Anyway, we wound up with this beautifully written piece by Richard Price that we were prepping in New York City. We had already cast Bob [De Niro] in *Mad Dog and Glory*. Then De Niro got taken away from us to make *Cape Fear* for Scorsese. We were left hanging with no film.

In New York, I thought I'd use the time to have some meetings and see what else was going on. I figured I'd meet Bogosian, tell him it was nice of him to send that letter, and just say, "Hi." So, we set up a meeting and Bogosian came in and said, "*Henry* is my favorite movie." He said, "You know, we're making a movie of *Sex, Drugs, Rock & Roll*," which I had never seen. Even when I was absolutely starving, I couldn't take material that I just didn't like. Someone had videotaped the show, and Eric gave me a cassette of the stage show. I watched it and thought it was brilliant. I think they were negotiating to have Haskell Wexler do it, but it didn't work out, so I got the job.

They reset the play for a couple of weeks in New York so we could study it. Then we took it to Boston because they could get a bigger theater. It had 1,100 seats so we could get all our cameras in. We wanted the experience of the movie to be big. We didn't want to shoot in a small theater, which we would have if they had stayed in New York.

You thought it could be cinematic?

Yes. There were originally twelve monologues—one was eventually cut out of the film—and each character had a different personality. We tried as much as possible to work with a live audience. Of course, they were selling 1,100 seats per night. Eric has to have an audience, otherwise he doesn't live. But we couldn't really bring cranes over the audience's heads, so it was very difficult. We tried to shoot each character in a slightly different style of camera work suited to that character. To some degree, we were successful, though not entirely. But it was tremendous fun. It was like shooting a Super Bowl. Once it starts, it's going and you can't call, "Cut." Ernest Dickerson shot it, and we had three cameras. Often we had a fourth just locked off and running, with no operator because we couldn't afford another crew member. We shot four different performances. Then we shot some inserts in front of a couple of hundred people that we'd invited, so we could move cameras around.

Are you happy with the result of that film?

In many ways, I was; in some ways, I wasn't. The production company was going bankrupt and we had a lot of problems in the audio postproduction. We had a hell of a time getting a mix pulled together on that picture. We had some bad sound cutters. They cut some laugh tracks in backwards, and they were just slovenly and horrible. We had a problem with one camera, the focus-puller was not pulling correctly, and one of the things I regret is we're missing the left camera a lot, because it was often out of focus. But, again, you always have these grand ideas of perfection before you do something, and then you're faced with the reality of doing it.

Did the film get much of a release?

They went bankrupt. I think they planned 200 theaters, and maybe we got it in eleven. They had no money to promote it.

So, then you went back to *Mad Dog and Glory*?

Yes. And, of course, there was a strike in New York, so we had to move it to Chicago, even though Richard Price wrote it for New York.

What was the budget on that?

I think it was between seventeen and eighteen million. I think it was actually twenty-one, and we came under about two million dollars.

So, that's your first big studio picture. Did you have much input into the script or was it pretty much the way Richard Price wrote it?

Pretty much. It was a really good script. I sat with Richard, and I always make notes and stuff, but I probably had less input into the script than anything else I've done. Richard had worked on it a long time. It's interesting when you have actors read. Richard sits there and he keeps cadence. He writes that stuff in a very specific cadence. He has an amazing ear for it. If he knows you for a couple of days, he'll be able to mimic your speech. He just has a gift for the rhythm of language. He does what David Mamet does, but without taking it to the same level of abstraction with language. He has the choppiness of everyday speech, the inversions of words. I found, especially with his dialogue, actors wanted to change things. Normally, I would say fine, but on that, it's almost like verse. If you alter it, you destroy it.

There were no problems on this film?

There were problems later with the studio.

What was your working relationship like with De Niro?

It was great.

Did the two of you have similar ideas about the character? What kinds of discussions did you have about that character, and did you do much research?

We had a lot of similar ideas. We spent time with the actual New York City crimes-scene police, going out with them to homicide sites and watching them do their work, riding with them, and hanging around the station. Mostly, these guys hang around the station. They eat and they wait. If it's night time, they sleep. Technically, it's against the rules, but no one cares. When the phone rings, it means someone's been murdered, and they get up and go do their jobs.

Whose decision was it to use Robby Müller as cinematographer?

It was mine. What can I say? It was a bit like Rae Dawn Chong. I think he did a good job, but we did not get along. He's a very unhappy man, and he makes sure those around him participate in his unhappiness.

He did the job, though.

Yes, he usually does. He's a Dutch painter, you know? He can tweak it.

Was it a happy experience working with Scorsese as a producer?

Yes. He wasn't around a lot. He's got a tremendous sense of humor. Marty's mind runs double speed, and he's very funny.

But he didn't have much involvement?

At the beginning of the planning stages, yes. He'd call in every day while we were shooting, but once we got into postproduction, he was off on *The Age of Innocence*. He was finishing *Cape Fear* when we started, and he was starting *The Age of Innocence* as we were finishing. Once he went off to do *The Age of Innocence*, he was consumed.

What style were you going for in *Mad Dog*?

Since we were using Robbie, the shooting style was a little more European and not at all slick. Simple and elegant, but not slick and flashy. The story, at its core, was about an ordinary human being, a.k.a Mad Dog. To me, this film is about the heroism of the common individual. The guy working a cop job, living in the world of the dead, basically, and through an act of courage and heroism and love, can be a hero, in a different sense, of course, than Rambo or the *Die Hard* movies. I liked that idea. It wasn't meant to be flashy in any way. It was meant to be simple, but not in a negative way.

This low-key, understated quality is quite refreshing.

Well, Universal Pictures didn't see it that way. [Laughs]

It obviously needed careful handling, because of people's expectations. I guess you got the Bill Murray crowd?

Again, I think if a director's picture doesn't do really well, the first thing they say is the marketing department screwed up, and sometimes they do, and sometimes they don't. In this particular case, it was a very difficult thing to sell. What the big studios know how to do is market genre. They know how to market an action picture. They know how to market a love story, a comedy, or a buddy picture. But *Mad Dog and Glory*: "What is it? Is it a cop picture?" "Well, it's about a cop, but it's not a cop picture." "Is it a love story?" "Well, there's a love story in there, but it's not primarily a love story." "Is it a comedy?" "Well, it's funny, but it certainly isn't a straight-ahead comedy." "So, how do we market this?"

But you were very conscious about mixing genres?

I have no interest in doing what's already been done, in a formulaic way. In some ways, we switched the roles from what people expected. We did a full-stage reading with De Niro in both roles. He could do the gangster role in his sleep. He's done it over and over. Bill Murray has played the nerdy guy a lot. He would have been the expected choice for the role eventually played by De Niro. The problem was in the selling of the picture. What they did for our film trailer was misguided. "We have Bill Murray. He's the most sellable thing in this picture." "How do we sell Bill Murray?" "We show all the funny stuff he did in this movie." So, everyone's watching the trailer and saying, "Ha, ha. Look at Bill playing a gangster." Then you put down your seven bucks and walk into the theater, and see this drug dealer blow away two kids in the first scene.

But you also have a very sweet romance going on.

Yes. I'm perfectly willing to admit when my films aren't successful, you can't always blame marketing. But in this particular instance, a month after our picture was released, they fired the head of marketing for incompetence. I felt vindicated.

But you were happy with your work on the film, with the finished product. You felt that you'd accomplished what you wanted to accomplish?

There were problems with the ending. We were accused of softening it. Actually, we made it a little less soft than was originally written, more bittersweet. It was originally a very happy ending. It read nicely, but it didn't play. We reshot the ending, and of course the word went out that we'd sold out the picture with a cute ending. I thought Bill was really quite wonderful. And Bob, and Kathy Baker is just a genius to work with.

How much business did it do?

Twelve and a half million dollars, or something. The film came out in early March. And that weekend there was the biggest blizzard to hit the eastern half of the United States for a hundred years. So, that weekend was completely mediocre, and that was it.

I was really happy to see *Rebel Highway: Girls in Prison*, by the way, which I'd never seen. I'm a big fan of *Shock Corridor*.

That was shot in twelve days.

No kidding?

We were on schedule, too. We made it in twelve. It was shot by Jean de Segonzac, who I had worked with on *Homicide* and is quite amazing. He also shot *Normal Life*, and now he's directing. It's unbelievable, the amount of work that guy can do.

Certainly, it's one of the more stylized films you've done.

As a kid, I was very fond of those drive-in, B-pictures that they cranked out in the late fifties and sixties.

This was actually better! [Laughs]

[Laughs] Yes, you go back and look at those originals sometimes, and you wonder "What did we ever see in that?"

Did Sam Fuller have any other involvement? Was it a script that he had written earlier.

No. Lou Arkoff, who is Sam Arkoff's son, produced it. He pitched the series of ten films to Showtime. His father has a library of 700 titles, and they picked ten or fifteen and offered them to various directors. You could basically do whatever you wanted. You could shoot it frame for frame the way it was or you could just take the title and throw the rest out, which is what most everybody did. The original was pretty crappy. [Laughs]

Did Fuller work with the original at all?

No. After *Mad Dog and Glory*, I had this period of what they call "movie jail," you piss off enough of the right people, and all of a sudden you are persona non grata.

Had you started working on *Homicide*, or was that afterwards?

I think I did one *Homicide* and then I did *Girls in Prison*, and then I did four more *Homicides*. But I went about a year not doing anything, just trying to pull some projects together. I wasn't that popular at the time, especially in one or two of the agencies where you need to be. If you need actors, you've got to have somebody in there to help you, and I wasn't being helped. Anyway, I was invited to the Brussels Film Festival to be on the jury. Whenever I'm not working, if I can go to a festival, I always do. I enjoy it. So, they convene the jury members, and it turns out that the chairman is Sam Fuller, which no one had told me. And I thought, "This is great!" We became pals immediately and just had a lot of fun. He was quite a character. He was eighty-three years old. So they asked me to make *Girls in Prison*, which didn't pay particularly well, but it did offer creative freedom. So, I said, "I'll tell you what. I'll do it if you let Sam Fuller write it." They said, "Sure." He wrote it in Paris and sent in a draft. Interestingly, the draft was a pile of ideas, very loosely organized, but the ideas could only have come from Sam Fuller. They were wonderful, like the potato sack race in prison. [Laughs] First time I read it, I said, "Sam, we can't do this." And then you think it's like a Zen thing; in its way, it's the perfect thing. Same with Lou Arkoff, "We can't do that." But, I said, "No potato sack race, no McNaughton!"

Did you work on the script?

Yes. But, like I say, I never could have come up with that stuff. I organized it, but the ideas pretty much came from Sam and Christa Lang. I don't know who did what, but I'll bet a lot of money that Sam came up with the potato sack race. [Laughs]

The style of the film is hyperbolic, a very ironic style.

Again, I tried to homage Sam's movies with the wildly dramatic camera moves.

The camera moves are pure Fuller. The production design and the costumes were really quite good. You worked with good people this time.

When I came back to do *Girls in Prison*, I had a lot of trepidation about working in L.A., especially on a low-budget film, because of my experience on *The Borrower*.

What was the budget?

1.3 million, and I think I was the only one in the series who made the budget. But I had a fabulous crew. It completely changed my opinion about working in Los Angeles. I liked Lou Arkoff and Debra Hill. They pulled together a really great crew; it was a pleasure to work with them. And the fact that we got that thing done in twelve days!

I think, with material like that, which is so ironic, the only way it's going to work is to treat it with respect. If you condescend to it, then it becomes cheap.

Working with the actors, I told them, "You have to play it as straight as you possibly can. I know this dialogue is insane, but you have to play it." You watch Sam Fuller's pictures; they're just straight delivery. They're not camping it, because it'll turn to shit immediately. Say it as if you mean it, straight from your heart, and it will work.

Did you prepare yourself by screening Fuller's films?

Oh, yes. Fortunately, in Chicago, I live very close to Facets Multimedia, and they have a lot of Fuller's pictures.

The attack on Tom Towles reminded me of the "nymphos" scene in *Shock Corridor*. [Laughs]

That's exactly it! [Laughs] It was a lot of fun and a very good experience.

A lot of the scenes are quite energetic.

They had to be. We were in a hurry most of the time. [Laughs] And of course, did you notice Anne Heche in there?

Yes, she's terrific!

Some people just have that gift. She's magnificent.

How did *Normal Life* come about?

Normal Life was very interesting. It's a true story. It happened in Chicago. I remember when it happened. There was a big piece in *The Chicago Tribune* when Chris Anderson, the convicted killer, was trying to break jail and was gunned down. My business partner, Steve Jones, was reading it and said, "This is such a great story, we should option this piece and make a script." We couldn't find the woman who had written the story. Then, about a year later, a script gets sent, and it's that story. The script was written by Peg Haller and Bob Schneider out of Brooklyn. They met the various family members, did a lot of research and wrote a draft. We were supposed to make the film for October Films with Kyle MacLachlan and somebody else, and two weeks before we started prepping, October killed the project. It eventually came back around, with Spelling and Fine Line. It came together quickly, and we only had four weeks to prep and four weeks to shoot.

What was the budget?

The budget was 2.75 million. Again, I brought in Jean de Segonzac, and we came in under budget.

***Normal Life* is a very melancholy film. Again, it has a kind of realistic style. It's almost a response to the romanticism of *Bonnie and Clyde*.**

It was very anti-Hollywood in its deglamorizing of outlaw life. I guess the economy's improved these days, but what was fascinating about the story of Chris and Pam was there was that period in the late eighties when the middle class was just falling off the map, being raised to strive for the American Dream, but unable to achieve it. It started when Reagan broke the Air Traffic Controllers' Union. The unions, which sometimes become cumbersome and not very productive, were just being blown off the map. The working people didn't have a chance. It was so touching that these two, in order to achieve their idea of the American Dream, took to these small bank robberies. Instead of leading this outlaw high-life, he opens a bookstore. They had their little house and dog. It wasn't that they were trying to be outlaws on the road with machine-guns.

It's such a shock these days, to see a movie about people struggling to make a living. Hollywood just isn't interested in movies about people who work.

No one's paying attention to these people, regular, middle-class human beings, who are trying to make a living and have a normal life, but can't because the government has redistributed the wealth.

It's definitely your most political film.

I think it's very political, and that's a reason why, instinctively, Fine Line killed it. Not because they misunderstood it; they hardly watched it. If you're making a movie for $2.75 million, and working for Spelling International and Fine Line—two entertainment corporations interested in making an entertainment product they can sell and profit from—like all corporations, they don't want to change the basic structure of the economic model, because they're doing great. For me to come in with this critical point of view and say "Things are really wrong here, and wealth is not distributed so that the average person can have a break." They're all having a great break in their executive offices. Basically, it's very difficult to make a film that is truly critical of this socio-economic system, because the people financing the films are precisely the people benefiting the most from the system.

Did they give it a release at all?

They released it after I went to war with them. It was a golden day for me the other month when I read that Ruth Vitale was no longer head of Fine Line, and Chris Pula was no longer at New Line. Pula sat through the entire screening of *Normal Life* talking on his cell phone, running outside the door, and didn't pay any attention to the movie. They called me one day when I was out here, riding from the airport to the hotel. "It's Ruth Vitale, John. Mitch Goldman and I want to talk to you. We've decided not to release the movie." I asked why? "It's for your own good." I said, "Listen, you can tell me it's a business decision. That you've decided it's not going to make money, and there's nothing I can say. That's life. But if you tell me it's because the film isn't good, I will fight you till I die." And that was basically what she was telling me.

I went on a rampage and called a lot of people I know in the press in New York and Chicago and Los Angeles. Then I talked to the William Morris Agency. I became a William Morris client because they had worked so hard to pull together such a little, tiny film. Usually it's not worth a big agency's time to pull together a three-million-dollar film when they could be pulling together a thirty-million-dollar film. But they had just signed Luke Perry, Ashley Judd had been a client, and they put us together and found the financing, so I became a client of theirs and am to this day. I went to them and said, "Listen. You've got me, you've got Luke, and Ashley. You've got three clients, and they're insulting us." And Fine Line was forced to release it, but they would only release in New York and Chicago. If you don't release in Los Angeles, you're not eligible for Academy Awards. The worst thing that can happen is for them to say the picture's no good, and then have all the critics say the picture is good, then their bosses look at them and go, "Well, why did you bury this picture that everyone says is really wonderful? Isn't it your job to make money with things like this?" So, they did not release in L.A. for that very reason. But Roger Ebert called it one of the best films of the year.

The film feels very real. The location work is very good.

The writers interviewed the mother and brother of Luke Perry's character. The family of Ashley Judd's character would not cooperate, but there was enough information from people who'd met them and people who lived next door to them. So the parking lot scene was shot in the parking lot where it actually happened. We used many real places, and the real vicinity is very interesting. It's out by the Chicago airport. In 1960, none of that existed. Until that airport was built, it was farm land. I find that the ugliest part of Chicago; the worst ghetto has a charm compared to that area, which is incredibly bleak. They build these big apartment complexes that are holding pens for the proletariat. They go to their jobs in these big, boxy places. They go to the malls, where they spend what they're programmed by TV to want to buy. They're just in this endless cycle. You make your $700 a week, go home, watch TV, and spend your money. It's very depressing.

The film has a very low-key style. The material is so downbeat. I don't think a flashy style would have worked well. It's almost documentary-like.

Again, it was like "Okay, we're going to take you into this little apartment. We're going to throw you in with them, and we're going to close the door behind you. You're going to be in these people's lives on a moment-by-moment basis."

How did you see Pam and Chris?

It was very interesting doing the research on these people. There's no doubt that they deeply loved each other, which was touching, because they were completely wrong for each other, unable to connect to the world in any sort of healthy way. He was very close to his family. They were in Boy Scouts, they went camping together. She had a very troubled life, and unfortunately, the legal department at Fine Line made us take out a couple of scenes with Pam's mother, because her real mother was not cooperating in any way. Pam was an orphan, and she was adopted into a Jewish family, though she wasn't a Jewish kid. When she was twelve or thirteen, there was a long and bitter acrimony between her adopted parents, which eventually led to divorce. Although Pam had relative affluence, she had a very difficult time and was a pretty wild kid. He, on the other hand, had a very close family.

I have to say that Luke Perry totally surprised me. I didn't know what to expect from him.

He's a good actor. It's funny because I'd never seen his TV show [*Beverly Hills 90210*], although I knew who he was, certainly.

Did you have anything to do with his casting?

Well, William Morris said, "What do you think about Luke Perry for the role?" I said, "Are you nuts? This heartthrob kid?" They said, "Well, you should meet him." One thing I've learned is that you really should meet actors. It's a mistake to identify them with the roles they've played. If you meet them, it's amazing how often they turn out to be really bright, good actors. So I met him and liked him immediately. He didn't go to college. He went to New York, got into modeling and then started acting in soaps. He's incredibly smart. And I'd already met Ashley a couple of times when she was on her way up.

Had you seen *Ruby in Paradise*?

Yes, I loved it. It was just so natural. Luke related to the character, since he's from a small town in Ohio. Ashley's from Kentucky originally. She was very convincing, and they got along really well. There was a good chemistry. They had a sort of country thing going on together. Again, we rehearsed intensely for a couple of weeks. And one of the great regrets to me was—Fine Line, those scoundrels who wouldn't release the picture here in L.A.—but that was a hell of a role, and Ashley is nothing if not fearless and she might've had a chance at an Oscar nomination.

You got quite a performance out of her. It's hard to sympathize with her exactly. Yes, she's fucked up, but what's challenging about the film is that it's uncomfortable for the viewer. It's hard to know how to react to the characters.

It's a very confrontational film. In a sense, after that picture, I realized, if you want to see how tough life is, just walk out your door. Although I'm very proud of *Wild Things*, and I feel it's a very uncompromised picture, it's certainly more of an entertainment.

But you're definitely bucking a trend when you make a film like *Normal Life*.

Well, somebody's got to. [Laughs]

What is your feeling now about working in Hollywood.

Everyone's talking about independent cinema, but show it to me! It doesn't exist. New Line is independent? Of who? Warner Brothers? I don't think so. Miramax? You know, I've not worked for those guys. I've met with them on a number of things, and there's many things to be admired, and certainly their company has cranked out a lot of wonderful films. But independent? I don't think so. October Films? MCA just gave them a pile of money. Two of the independents I worked for went bankrupt and the films were hardly seen. My experience with Universal [on *Mad Dog and Glory*], until we got down to the end, was pretty good, and my picture *Wild Things*, for all practical purposes, is done. I feel it's okay; we may have changed a line here or there. But it's pretty uncompromised, and in many ways I would rather work for a studio than an independent. They're going to be there next year; they're going to be there to distribute your picture. My experience with Fine Line, an independent, on *Normal Life* was such a despicable experience. I found them arrogant.

Are you bitter about things at all?

No. You really have to understand that often in life, the joke's on you, and you have to have a sense of humor. No, I'm not bitter in the least, I've had a pretty good time.

I found *Wild Things* something of a departure for you. Can you talk about how this project came about.

After doing *Normal Life,* and the disappointment of working a year to make a picture that Fine Line decided not to release, it occurred to me that it had been a long time since I made a big movie and it was time that I do it again. I felt that if I spend thirty million dollars of someone's money, they are probably going to release it. And I had also recently changed agents to the William Morris Agency, since I had burned a lot of bridges with agencies in Los Angeles. I decided I should really try and work with them and show that I was a good boy and willing to make an effort. So I was looking for a studio picture to make.

You saw it more in terms of a career move than being interested in the property itself?

I never think career first. But it had been a long time since I'd done anything that anybody had heard about. And that's not good, because eventually, you won't be able to make any movie. So in one sense, yes, I had to think about making sure I made a movie that would be seen.

What was attractive for you in terms of working with this neo-noir, Hitchcockian material?

The same thing that always attracts me: a good story. Normally, I'm not that interested in thrillers. I find that nine out of ten thriller scripts are written by first-time screenwriters who are pastiching other successful movies together in a way that they think is going to get them a big payday. So, usually, I'll read the first five to ten pages and the last few. Almost always there is no surprise: I can tell you what happens in the middle part. They sent me *Wild Things*. I read maybe thirty to thirty-five pages and I was getting very tired, it was late. So I thought, I'm going to jump ahead and read the end, and I had no idea what could have possibly happened in between. So I went back that night and stayed awake and read it through. It was based on what I thought was a really good plot. I met with the people at Mandalay, and they had their reservations about it and so did I. I told them what I thought needed to be done to that script to make it a good picture and they agreed. So we brought in another writer, Kem Nunn, and we worked on several drafts.

This film strikes me as much more plot-driven than your other work, which is very character-driven. This is something of a change, don't you think?

Oh yeah. It was the first time I ever worked on a piece that was story-driven. It sort of started out as big breasts and high school, and I thought, "Yeah, yeah, I've seen this before." Then it turns into this issue movie and rape drama: "Did he do it?" Yeah, I've seen this before, but each time it turned into something I didn't expect. I thought it was really great plotting. I thought I could make a commercial film that I could be very satisfied with.

The style of Wild Things seems more classical, more accessible than your other work. Did you feel a need to alter your style for commercial reasons?

You know this business is art *and* commerce, and they're so closely entwined. Is *Wild Things* a commercial film? I hope so, but what the film is about is the difference between what's happening on the surface and what's going on for real underneath the surface, the difference between what people say and what they do. After making *Normal Life*, I came to the conclusion that I'm not that anxious anymore to go to the movies and see how horrid things are, and what a shithole everything is.

At any rate, the material is completely dark, there are no sympathetic characters in *Wild Things*. So I'm dealing with extremely dark material and my thought is to make the surface of this picture as lush and beautiful as it can possibly be. So, is it commercial? Yes. But is it thematically interesting? Absolutely. And it's an artistic choice as much as a commercial choice. I wanted to make a really beautiful picture.

I think the narrative structure was pretty interesting, especially the stuff at the end, after the end credits, when those scenes come on. That was a real surprise. Was that in script?

Yeah, that was in Stephen Peters' script. He also had a series of flashforwards at the beginning, but we wanted a more languid beginning, and I felt that somehow the ones at the beginning were more conventional, whereas the ones at the end weren't.

The film has done very well.

It did quite well and it continues to do well. It was the number one picture in France for three or four weeks. It's doing well around the world.

They did right by you in terms of the release and everything else.

It's the first picture in my career where I can say that the studio worked really hard.

***Condo Painting* is obviously the most unusual film that you've made. You've never made an experimental documentary like this before, have you?**

I had worked that way before, although nothing that really went into the market place. It's strange, I worked that way early on, but the technology didn't produce particularly wonderful pictures. With *Condo*, we did a bit of trailblazing in the technical area of filmmaking. We used a digital camera for some shots. We had one digital camera, but, unfortunately, I was not very comfortable using it. I must say it looks very good and it's more stable and less noisy, but what I loved about the Hi8 was how easy it was to handle because of the LCD screen. The quality of the Hi8 in transfer reminds me more of the old Kodachrome film stock. It's a little more exaggerated, a little more garish, a little more family-on-vacation, a little more amateurish but more colorful than the professional stock like Ektachrome. So I don't regret it. But now they're getting high-definition cameras down to the size of news cameras and the little digital cameras are becoming much more flexible, and they're pretty amazing in the quality of image they produce.

I only saw a videotape. Have they struck any prints yet?

There is one print. We had the premiere in Monte Carlo in May, 1998.

How did that go?

It went really well. I have to say it was one of the best days of my adult life.

It seems like a strange film for this kind of an audience.

Well, it's interesting because George Condo is a friend of Princess Caroline and she sponsored the screening during Cannes, which was on the same day that they open the ballet. George painted the curtain for the Ballet de Monte Carlo, the same curtain Picasso painted for Diaghalev. There's a tradition of having someone come in every year to paint the curtain, and this was George's year. The princess, an incredibly sophisticated person who is very current in all the arts, made a day of it. There was a cocktail reception at the ballet followed by the première of the ballet and the film, and a big dinner that evening with people from the ballet, people from the film, people from all over the world. It was really quite a wonderful day. It was nice to cross the bay there in Cannes. It was like movies aren't the only thing in the universe.

Was the reaction to the film interesting?

The reaction was really great. Helmut Newton and his wife were there. Ringo [Starr] was there, who is a friend of George's, and Princess Caroline was there and various other luminaries.

Quite a rarefied atmosphere.

Yeah, it was quite a day and night. Bernard Picasso—who's in the film—was there with his little entourage. It was quite an evening.

Why did you make *Condo Painting*? Was George Condo your friend?

He became my friend. I met him over the project. I was introduced to him by someone from the Pace Gallery. I did not know him or really know his work. We shot the film in New York and Chicago, and I did postproduction on it simultaneously with *Wild Things*.

Why did you want to make a film about an artist?

The idea came from the Pace Gallery. They were experimenting with the idea of a short video piece that they could use in place of a catalogue at a gallery show.

Did they know it was going to be feature-length film?

Well, we shot for two weeks. We had a two-week period where we could take the time and George was going to paint a painting. He had painted the first third of the painting. He and I decided early on to give them their little fifteen minute promotional piece but we were going to make a longer movie.

Are you familiar with the American avant-garde movement? Have you seen any of those films?

I saw a lot of that stuff; I'm a child of the sixties. There was a very progressive place called the McKinley Foundation in Champaign, Illinois, which is a Unitarian Church. All the bohemian kids hung out there, and they would have Underground Film Night one Friday every month. It was just not to be missed: Maya Deren, Stan Brakhage, Kenneth Anger, the Mekas Brothers, and on and on. I saw all that stuff.

What is your feeling about working in video as opposed to working in film?

I started out working in video. I love it. I love the way we worked on the Condo film. There was myself and George, and perhaps one or two assistants. His wife would often be there, and one of his assistants from his art practice. It was completely informal. We ate well, drank good wine, smoked cigarettes. It was a very different approach, but we often worked sixteen hours a day. It was a complete joy. With the little camera, it was so intimate to be able to get two inches from the paint brush. You know, in big-budget Hollywood filmmaking there are rules and when someone gives you thirty million dollars it's difficult to break the rules and start making jump cuts and things like that. The great thing about the Condo film was whatever the rule was, we ignored it: jump cuts, crossing the line, who cares, nobody will care.

George Condo is a very interesting, provocative guy, and he's got a lot of interesting ideas. He's almost a Dadaist. You're referencing a lot of modern art traditions in the film, like the beat tradition and the surrealist tradition.

George is very intelligent, and a well-read, well-educated fellow. He's studied the history of art, the technique of the masters, different styles and periods. Also, he's nine years younger than I am, but both of us are complete products of American middle-class upbringing. One of the quotes in the movie is, "I knew who Andy Griffith was before I knew who Andy Warhol was," which is pretty much an American education. It was fun playing with those TV characters, like Jethro and Grannie [from *The Beverly Hillbillies*]. How archetypal they've become not only to America but to the world.

Certain people I work with have very strong personalities, and I find they influence me. Robert De Niro is an example of that. George Condo is another. We actually started shooting *Condo Painting* before I started shooting *Wild Things*, and it very much made me come back from the cinema of the ugly, rubbing people's faces in how horrid things can be. He's not that type of artist. He's still very much in the tradition of trying to make beauty, and I think that was very influential on me, to try and make something that was beautiful to behold even though there are other things going on.

Will there be an audience for this kind of film? What kind of a release is October Films planning?

I really don't know, and the good news in terms of career is that I seem to be reasonably in demand and working all the time. The fact that that the film even exists today in the form that it does is amazing. And it has an incredible soundtrack. I don't believe your tape had music.

No.

We got six pieces of original score from Danny Elfman. We have an original song from Beck that exists nowhere else but in our movie. We got an original song from Julianna Hatfield and twenty-one pieces of music from The Residents.

That's great. I'll be anxious to see it on the screen.

It sounds really good. The fact that a beautiful 35mm print even exists, transferred from Hi8 into the Avid, from the Avid to the digital Beta, from the digital Beta to a high-definition tape to the 35mm film with a full-surround Dolby track is really a miracle. It's born. When we did *Henry*, I had nothing else to do but fight for that film, which I did for a year and a half. And people always said, "Who is going to want to see this?" I think for $112,000, plenty of people are going to want to see it. The same thing with *Condo Painting*.

So in this *Lansky* film you are now doing for HBO, Richard Dreyfuss is playing Meyer Lansky?

Yes. David Mamet wrote the script, Anthony LaPaglia is playing Lucky Luciano. Beverly D'Angelo is going to play his second wife.

Have you had much input into the script?

Yes. More than I wish I'd had to have, but we just had a script that was much bigger than we could afford to shoot so the script stage has been a difficult process. We had to cut fifty scenes. Mamet had 165 scenes at 142 pages and we have 110 scenes in 106 pages.

What kind of film can we expect?

Well, HBO has finally seen my latest draft. If I get to make it the way I want, I think certain people will find it confusing. It's very much about memory told from the point of view of Lansky as an old man, from the day they're kicking him out of Israel. He will then go on an odyssey from country to country, getting refused until he is forced back to America. But during this period, he reflects and remembers the story of his life. Mamet's script is very non-linear, as memory is, and HBO is worried about that. And the character goes from age ten to age seventy-six. We have four actors playing Meyer Lansky, we have three actors playing Benny Siegel, and we have two actors playing Charlie Luciano. The confusion that may add, along with the non-linear aspects of the structure, are a real challenge. But I wouldn't do a gangster movie just to make a gangster movie like any other gangster movie. His last day in Israel is more or less what we call real. But when we go into his memory he can remember it any way he pleases. So it's really fun. Those are the ideas that interest me. I've been reading Nabokov's *Speak Memory*.

How do you feel about your career as a director? You've had a rough ride in some ways. But you seem to be at a pretty good point now. Do you have regrets about anything?

No, no regrets. Someone once asked me, "What would you have done if you had had more money to make *Henry*?" I really thought about it seriously, and I guess I would have paid people more and that's about it. Same with this thing. In a sense I wish we had more money, but we're so squeezed it's like being in the depression: Everyone grows close. I have no regrets whatsoever.

What are some things about directing that you dislike?

The toughest part for me is the actual day-to-day on the set because you're just so at the mercy of things you can't control. The weather, the sun, somebody with the camera truck runs into a lamp pole, the actors, whatever. When they're words on a page and drawings on paper, they do whatever you want them to do and when you get to the cutting room they pretty much do whatever you want them to do. During the shoot, you're always racing the clock. One of your biggest enemies is the sun, the giver of life. It either wants to come up when you need it to stay down or it wants to go down when you need it to stay up. It's always rushing you.

I think of the Dorothy Parker quote: "I hate writing. I love having written." Sometimes it's pretty great out there. It's sort of like taking an army out to do something peaceful, but it's the same sort of *esprit de corps* and commitment, and slogging through hell. It's physically taxing. *Wild Things* was incredibly taxing physically. The heat was horrendous, the weather was awful, the insects were constant. You'd come home every day, cooked by the sun, dehydrated, exhausted, covered in insect bites of varying types, and fall down, and get up again and do it the next day.

Something must drive you to keep doing it.

I don't know. If you don't do it you go insane. You realize what you love, that it's just addictive.

MICHAEL RADFORD

Michael Radford's most commercially successful film was the hugely popular Italian film *Il Postino*, starring the late comic actor Massimo Troisi. It was remarkable for several reasons. Apart from its extraordinary commercial success, it was also unusual in that it may have been the only Italian-language film ever released in Italy with Italian subtitles because of the Southern dialects used by its actors. It was also notable for the death of its star at the end of filming. Troisi was dying during the filming, and this necessitated the use of a double for at least sixty percent of the shots. Because of the unusual production circumstances, Radford could only use his main actor for one or two hours each filming day, and could count on getting one or two takes of each shot. Radford calls the film "a real cut-and-paste job," although the finished product feels seamless in its construction. It is also one of the more human films made in the 1990s.

Radford's work is noteworthy for its wide-ranging subject matter. His first theatrical feature, *Another Time, Another Place*, was an intimate portrait of Scottish farm life and the effect a group of Italian prisoners-of-war has on the tight, repressed community. The film recalls Italian neo-realist classics of the 1940s in its truthful portrayal of human behavior and contemporary Italian masterpieces such as Olmi's *The Tree of Wooden Clogs* in its accurate view of rural life. Radford followed his low-budget realistic drama with his acclaimed version of *Nineteen Eighty-Four* starring Richard Burton and John Hurt, a film which, stylistically, seems light years away from the realism of the Scottish countryside of his previous film. *Nineteen Eighty-Four* inevitably painted a grim view of the Orwellian future, although one would be hard pressed to do otherwise and remain faithful to Orwell's vision. Radford's last film in the 1980s was *White Mischief,* his corrosive treatise on the useless lives of upper-class British colonialists in Kenya during the dying days of the Empire. The film was so harshly received and misunderstood by the British press that it almost made Radford give up filmmaking for good. As Radford states, the film "wasn't meant to be like *Out of Africa,* the cinema of waxed furniture. I was trying to make something much more decadent." It would be another seven years before Radford finally succumbed to Troisi's annual entreaties to make a film together and agreed to make *Il Postino.*

Radford's films are always elegantly constructed and feature strong performances. Their stylistic sophistication, however, is often overlooked because they operate in fairly classical ways. His characters are always deeply empathetic. Radford is unquestionably a moralist, yet he always manages to present his characters in a nonjudgmental manner. They are also strongly connected to their environment. From the small island setting of *Il Postino,* to the modern-day London of *B. Monkey,* his recent sophisticated thriller, Radford's characters always lead lives deeply rooted to their physical world. I spoke to Michael Radford in London.

Radford

Can we start with your background. Where did you grow up? You were born in New Delhi, weren't you?

Yes. My father was in the British army, the Indian army actually. His family had been in India for 100 years. My mother is an Austrian-Jewish refugee whose father decided to get his family as far away from the Nazis as he possibly could, and so he got a job as a doctor in Bombay. That's where my mother met my father; quite amazing really.

How long were you in India?

Oh, not anything that I can remember. We moved around every two or three years. Wherever the British Empire was collapsing, that's where we'd move to, coming back to Britain for my education.

Were your formative years during the fifties and sixties mostly spent in England?

Sort of divided up between the Middle East and England through 1961, then until 1965 we were in Germany. We came back for little spells, and were in Scotland for a couple of years at some point in the fifties. Then we came back to this country when my father retired at the end of the sixties.

Did you see many films growing up?

I had a strange film upbringing because I hardly saw any movies when I was a kid. We weren't allowed to watch them at school, and when I got abroad there were just no films, not that I could go and see anyway.

What about the European art film explosion of the sixties?

Well, the interesting thing was when I got to the sixth form at school in Bedford we were allowed to go to the Bedford Cinematographical Society, where they showed films with subtitles on them. Films with subtitles were considered artistic, which is what turned us all on to going to them. That, and a good smoke in the back row on Sunday afternoons when the lights were down. And there I saw my first swatch of movies, which started with—and I remember this very well to this day—*Shoot the Pianist* by François Truffaut. And then I saw about thirty movies, ranging from things like *The Seventh Seal* and *The Silence* through to *L'Avventura*, Eisentein, *Les Amants*.

How old were you at this time?

I was about sixteen. And that made a great impression on me, but it never occurred to me for a single moment that I would be a film-maker, but I got a great taste for movies with subtitles. At that time, I wanted to be an actor because I had just been in school plays and stuff and thought it was a gas.

Is that what you pursued?

I did. I left university with a degree in politics, philosophy, and economics and I actually became an actor for nine months and, during that time, discovered I was not cut out for the acting profession. It had nothing to do with me wanting to be a filmmaker. I gave up acting and became a teacher of liberal studies in a further education college in Scotland. There I picked up a film camera which nobody knew how to use. It was a 16mm Bolex. I started making an improvised movie with some kids and the extraordinary thing was, it had a real power to it. I felt like St. Paul on the road to Damascus. I just felt this was really what I would like to do with my life. I was about twenty-five.

Were there any other films or filmmakers that had a particular impact on you?

Throughout my university time I just went to the movies literally all the time. The movie director that epitomized everything that I loved in the movies was Ingmar Bergman. There was a cinema just down the road from my college that showed only Bergman movies. [Laughs]

This was in London?

In Oxford. I went to Oxford for my degree. There was a film society in Oxford where they made movies, but I wasn't involved in it because it never occurred to me that I could actually do something like that. It just wasn't in my frame of reference. All I knew was that I loved films. And, indeed, when I did start making these improvised movies with these kids, all I ever really wanted to do was improve the standard of educational documentaries. I used to show these documentaries to the students and I would think, I can make something better than that. They were so badly made.

What was the experience at film school like? You were in the very first class at the National Film School, weren't you?

Yes, it was pretty fantastic. First of all, I bumped into a bunch of other people who were much more sophisticated than I was, guys who had been struggling away in the BBC, independent filmmakers, people who really knew what they were talking about. Above all, I met this bunch of Godard freaks who influenced me enormously and I became a devotee of Jean-Luc, and still am in a certain sense. I had a great time there because it was an institution founded in the wake of the sixties, so it was a radical institution. There were no teachers. There was enough money to make three short movies on your own. You had a budget where you could go to the film industry and ask somebody to come and tutor you and you'd pay them.

Everybody got to make three films?

Yes, everybody. After the inflation of the seventies, that budget never came back.

You made documentaries?

No, I made no documentaries at all, I made only fiction films. I discovered that I had one thing over all the other people. I'd been an actor for five minutes, so I knew about actors. I wasn't afraid of them. I understood the process to a great extent. I had read my Stanislavsky and been actively involved in drama at university. And I'd done nine months in rep in Scotland. So I knew what they felt like. To this day I do.

The film school was a great institution. From my point of view, it was the perfect thing. I was old enough to not want to be taught. I didn't want to hide behind anything. I had plenty of ideas and I was going to make movies whatever happened. I was highly motivated.

Did they bring people in from the industry?

Yes, basically. But anyone who wasn't highly motivated just sank. And, of course, the system has been radically revised since, and now it's like any other place. You get diplomas. There were no diplomas then; there was nothing. You just came out into a hostile film industry. And there wasn't much of a feature industry. You either went to work in television or commercials or you went abroad.

You ended up making a series of documentaries?

They're quite good actually. Two of them at least. *The Madonna and the Volcano* and *The Last Stronghold of the Pure Gospel.* These two films on religion were really quite radical for their time. There was a very strong documentary movement at the film school. Colin Young had been very active with people like Leacock and Pennebaker and the observational, anthropological documentary guys like Jean Rouch. He felt that everyone should have an understanding of that way of making documentaries. Of course, by osmosis, we took that in but I immediately put it into practice the moment I arrived in making documentaries for television. No commentary, no script. They just freaked out at the BBC.

But you still wanted to make a feature, I take it?

Yes, all the time. That's really where my heart lay. As far as documentary was concerned, I hated the fact of interfering and having so much power in people's lives.

How do you think the experience of making non-fiction films affected your later work?

Well, it taught me a number of things. It taught me to think on my feet because one of the precepts of observational documentary is that you don't act things out. You have to be very nifty about catching moments, and you learn that people have a kind of an essence that reveals itself, whatever they do. If you're patient enough, you'll see that revelation and you'll be able to put it together. I think documentary is the real pure art form, pure cinematic form. It owes no allegiance to anything, whereas fiction filmmaking owes great allegiance to theater, to literature, to acting. The thing about documentary for me was the capacity to read a situation and adapt myself to it. These days people say to me, "That movie was very well cast," that kind of stuff. I think it's because, having chosen an actor, I tend to use the person in front of me rather than try to impose the character on them.

Let's talk about *The White Bird Passes*, your first television feature for the BBC. How did you meet Jessie Kesson?

You're always looking for a way of getting from documentaries into feature films. I went to BBC Scotland to do a mountaineering film which my girlfriend had been asked to do and didn't really want to do. So I went to do this documentary and, while I was there, they were so pleased with what I'd done, they said, "Would you do this documentary about this writer who was completely forgotten?" So I started reading her books and got the idea that I would do a film about how a writer translates her life into fiction. Her books were very autobiographical.

It was to be a long documentary with dramatic inserts of ten or fifteen minutes. They were happy with that idea. Then I just went away and I wrote a feature film and gave it to them. They liked the script so much, they commissioned it. I ended up doing it and it was a huge success. What I think struck people about it was that it wasn't in that sort of British realist or naturalistic tradition. I just wanted to try and express the imaginary world of a child who could actually live through this difficult stuff and somehow survive and grow and flower. I tried to put into it a couple of poetic moments. So, although the wigs are a bit ropey and some of the lighting is not that great, that film really enabled me to do a feature film. It was received very, very well.

Was it daunting to take on a feature?

Not in the least. The BBC in those days was really quite a well-funded organization. They gave me enough time to make it, enough equipment, a rep company of Scottish actors, some good, some not so good. They treated me wonderfully well. And because I had made three or four films at film school, I had no problems with how to make a feature film.

One of the things that struck me about it—and I realize it's a strong characteristic of all your work and plays such a key role in defining who they are—is the connection of characters to their physical environment. What are your thoughts on that?

I've always thought of the physical world as a metaphor for the interior world of the characters. I've never subscribed to orthodox views of what something beautifully shot is. I don't find commercials beautiful because there's no interior life. I find Ozu movies beautiful because there is an interior life. The physical environment isn't just something that defines a character, but the character defines his own physical environment when you're actually making the picture. That's from the creative standpoint. I always try to find the shot—and there are usually only about five or six of them in a movie—which absolutely sums that up.

It seems to me your work is concerned with our own memories of childhood and our past and how we use that in the present.

I think it's quite legitimate in the cinema because it is true that we make the past our own. I call it the science fiction of the past. It's as though you create a landscape in order to inhabit yourself, and construct your internal reality in order to proceed. To me, that's beautiful if you can actually show that on film.

Did Jessie Kesson like the film?

Yes, very much. We instantly decided to collaborate on another one which wasn't an adaptation of her book. It was actually an attempt by her to write a screenplay, but she couldn't write one. So she just sat down and drafted a novel instead. About a year later, I got hold of the draft novel and turned it into a screenplay.

All your films, from *The White Bird Passes* through to *Il Postino*, seem quite interested in the issue of how one maintains humanity in the face of adversity, how we can make something extraordinary or poetic out of our daily existence.

I think it's the capacity to dream which keeps us going. Also, the capacity to reshape our own past into something that can be told. One reason I became a filmmaker, subconsciously, was that ever since I was very little, I've had very strong feelings about places in ways I just desperately wanted to express. I found that I couldn't express these sensations through painting or writing or still photography.

White Bird Passes **was well received when it was broadcast on TV.**

It was hugely well received. It prompted Channel Four [*Film on Four*] to ask me if I wanted to make a film for them, and we proposed the idea of *Another Time, Another Place*. We didn't have much money. We shot it in Super 16mm for about £300,000.

Did that film change a great deal from what you had written?

Yes, it did. I was very influenced at that time by Ermanno Olmi's *The Tree of Wooden Clogs*. I wanted to make that kind of European picture in the U.K. I'd written something that was about three-and-a-half hours long. You know, Agriculture in Northern Scotland, Part Two. It was vast and sprawling; lots of scenes of Italians digging roads, getting to know the local community, all this kind of stuff. The film was told from two different points of view: the girl's and the Italians'. It became very clear about two weeks into shooting that we were never going to make that movie. We didn't have enough money. My producers came to me and said, "You've got to cut it down." I had the ghastly experience of literally ripping thirty pages out of the script overnight and trying to rewrite it into something new. The trick was to base everything on this girl [Phyllis Logan]. As I was filming her, I realized how extraordinary she was. Then I deliberately decided to see everything from her point of view, so nearly everything is shot from over her shoulder. Physically, it was phenomenally difficult. We'd put all the actors in a bus and wait to shoot. The weather used to change every five minutes, so if it wasn't raining, you'd get out and shoot either a summer scene or a winter scene, depending on whether it was sunny or not. We were constantly keeping one jump ahead of total disaster. I would shoot half an interior scene and then we would make the decision to go out and shoot another scene and we'd manage to get a quarter of that done. Then the rain would come down, the weather would change, it would snow. Because we had no movie stars, all the actors sat in a bus all day, every day, waiting to be pulled out and to perform. It was an absolute nightmare, really unpleasant.

In terms of preparing that film, did you work with the actors much beforehand?

Not at all. In fact, I was trying to fire one of the Italian actors in the first week. Giovanni Mauriello, who played Luigi, was a singer. I also had one Italian actor and a guy who I found in the street in Rome. I didn't know what I was doing. I didn't know how they were going to be. Indeed, Giovanni was terrible at the beginning. He'd never been in a movie before and he was ashamed of his Neapolitan accent so he put on an ordinary Italian voice. Then he thought because he was in the land of Shakespeare he had to gesticulate. I couldn't get through to him. Finally, I had this screaming match with him, and Phyllis went off in tears. I finally got through to him that he should just throw away the script and be a Neapolitan and just invent it all. From that moment, he was fantastic. We threw away the Italian version of the script and just invented whatever it was as we went along. We would invent locations according to the light. The light dominated everything.

Did you invent scenes that weren't in the script?

Well, they were indicated. A scene might have been in a field. But what they were actually doing, where it was, was not decided until literally minutes before we shot it. We'd drive around in a truck. I don't think the island had ever had any filmmakers on it before, so they were kind of "Yeah! Dig some cabbages here, cut the corn here." The last day we did thirty-two pickup shots in thirty different places. It was amazing.

Did you have to do much research for this subject?

No, I didn't really. I don't believe in that kind of research because, once again, you're talking about the science fiction of the past. Yes, I have to make sure that people's clothes look reasonably alright, but if you watch *Jules et Jim*, they're all wearing sixties' sweaters. Who cares?

Your style is very unhurried. I noticed this also in *White Mischief* and *Il Postino*. There's a sense that you want to give the viewer time to contemplate things, to get to know the characters, but also just to think about things. And you certainly notice it in *Another Time, Another Place*.

Another Time, Another Place is the classic movie of mine. I think *B. Monkey* is probably going to be the same. It was loathed in the United States by the critics and loved in Europe. Jean-Luc Godard wrote me a letter, Bertolucci rang me from Rome—all my heroes, all the people that I'd wanted to emulate. *Cahiers du Cinéma* devoted a whole series of articles to it. It became *the* European movie at a certain moment. In America, I remember my first review somewhere in New York, which was "*Another Time Another Place*—go see another film." Not everybody disliked it. I remember the head of Warner Bros. International saying to me, "This is a gem of a movie. We aren't going to distribute it, but it's a real gem of a movie."

Do you think it's because of the pace or the subject matter?

I think it's to do with both the subject matter and the pace. I think that Americans like their logic very clear: They don't like ambiguity and they like their transitions to be fast. Once something's been made clear to them, they want to get on to the next thing as quickly as possible. Whereas Europeans tend to like the ambiguity, to soak it in a bit, and the transitions are slower. I realize now that when I'm working on a script, I tend to move like a game of chess, with the same kind of contemplation, the same sort of thought, and the suspense is the game plan, if you like.

One of the things I like about the film, and all of your work, is its lack of sentimentality. In that film in particular, you cut scenes off before they slip into melodrama. The scene where Phyllis Logan makes love with her husband, which follows the exuberant Christmas scene, rang very true.

Exactly, and I was criticized in Scotland, where they said she would never have taken her clothes off. [Laughs] I said she gets into bed naked there probably for the first time because she's just been let free.

Phyllis Logan is terrific in this film. Can you talk a bit about working with the actors on their characterizations or working with an actor on a particular scene?

There are two things that I do. I tend to look for what we used to call "a tingle" when I was teaching at Sundance. I tried to define it and Denzel Washington was there and we decided to call it "a tingle." It's when you just feel the scene happening. If I don't get that, I get very disturbed. I don't like rehearsal much because the nature of rehearsal is to think it out, but you really need to have the camera, or one of these viewfinders which has lenses on it, and I tend to work with that very, very strongly, just walking it through and feeling the drama of the scene and the actions as well as the delivery of the lines.

I also tend to shoot the subtext of things rather than the text. I don't need to shoot the lines because they're delivering the goods. So what I'm trying to do is shoot something else. It may be a closeup of something or it may be just a way of framing which will tell you something more about what is on the surface.

Isn't that something you bring out in the editing as well?

Yes, but I'm not a great editor, actually, and so I try and shoot it first, to find a shot that will somehow sum that up. Working with the actors, first of all, I tend not to do too many takes because I think it's useless to do that. I learnt that most strongly with *Il Postino* when Massimo [Troisi] could only do one take anyway, so I realized we were doing fine with just one take. You spend hours doing lots of takes and then you sit through them and you think, why on Earth did I do them all? I can't tell the difference between them. I think a director shouldn't impose himself on actors because what you are trying to do is draw from them the essence of themselves, and they need confidence and space to do that.

But you must discuss the character in advance, what your take is on it, what their take is on it.

Yes, of course. What the character wants, where they're going, what they're doing in this particular scene, of course.

What impact do you think the Italians or Luigi in particular had on Phyllis Logan's character? How did she change because of this experience?

Well, here's a girl who wanted to live out a dream. She was prepared to go to that point. Everybody was dreaming about those Italians in one way or another, but she was the one who went for it. Having done it, she discovers the pleasure of living out that dream, and she also understands the pain of it. She understands that her life will never be the same again. It's at this point that Hardy's *Tess of the D'Urbervilles* begins. That's when I finish my movie. There's a big melodrama about a girl who did something like that and what happened to her, but that wasn't what interested me. What interested me was her understanding that her life will never be the same.

You wrote that *Another Time, Another Place* was your most satisfying experience as a filmmaker. Why do you think you said that? Because it was your first theatrical film?

Because it was my first theatrical film. I mean, it was a nightmare. I literally tried to run away from the movie in week two because I thought that Giovanni was never going to get the role and I was so committed to him. I just didn't know what to do. I was praying that some disaster was going to happen and that I wasn't going to have to finish this movie. I was so wound up that everything had to be perfect, everything had to be right. That I'd chosen the wrong locations, that I'd chosen the wrong actors—I was obsessed by that.

I remember Simon Perry, my producer, saying to me, "Look, if we finish this movie and it's a dog, chances are we'll get to make another one; but if we don't, we'll never get to make another feature." [Laughs] That was the best piece of advice I ever had. For me, it was the most satisfying movie because I made it according to my own lights. In other words, nobody told me what to do. I made the movie I wanted to make. Apart from having to tear thirty pages out of it, nobody tried to cut it down, nobody tried to change it, nobody tried to make it into a different movie, nobody tried to interfere with it while we were making it. Everybody trusted me. I ended up with a movie which is the way I wanted it to be.

Did you have a sense after you made it that "I am a filmmaker now"?

No. I thought I'd made a dog, I really did. It was only when people came out of the cinemas, where they'd been watching the rough cuts, that people started to treat me with a new-found respect. It's like realizing that the girl you are in love with is in love with you. You don't realize it at the beginning and then, suddenly, there she is, she's actually in love with you and it's unbelievable.

Nineteen Eight-Four seems like quite a departure after Another Time, Another Place.

Well, it was and it wasn't. It was certainly a big picture. The interesting thing about it was I did it because nobody else was doing *Nineteen Eight-Four* in 1984, and that just seemed ridiculous to me. It was something I had always wanted to do. In fact, when I was at film school, I used to say to myself, "If I could make *Nineteen Eight-Four* in 1984, I know I'll be alright." And there it was, ready to be done, although I was obliged to do it without special effects. We didn't have time or the money so I had to shoot it all for real, which was quite a challenge.

You mean all the images on the television screens are . . .

Back-projection, or front-projection much of the time. I did some preshooting: I shot all that material and edited it. There was no digital editing in those days. I wanted to degrade it and eventually we transferred the editing to video, went to a video-editing suite which was really big and cumbersome, and then edited it like a sound edit. We had charts. Finally, we produced a film that looked like 1940s newsreels. That took three weeks to do. Then we started to shoot the film and project these things on the background screens.

What was the most challenging part about adapting the novel?

The real key was to make a parallel science-fiction world. In other words, make a universe as if it had been conceived in 1948, which is when the novel was published. From then on, it was a question of looking at things, getting the philosophy of INGSOC, which was fundamentally that machines were there to make your life more difficult. The other thing that I wanted to avoid was making a rather crude, communist-bashing film. I wanted to make a film that took all totalitarianism and examined it like a Greek fable. When I look at the movie now, what I love about it is the fact that it feels like a kind of meditation. It doesn't have any great ups and downs of melodrama. It has this rather quiet terror in it. It's almost like this man's dream which is just slowly disintegrating. I like it for that. It's inhumanly depressing. And, of course, when you put them on film, all those ideas grow in magnitude and become almost unbearable, like the rats and torture and stuff like that. But that's the nature of the piece.

Did you feel like you needed to make it relevant to a younger audience?

No, and the curious thing was, it was phenomenally popular with the young audiences. It was actually not popular with all the people who theoretically should have found it appealing. The audience was almost entirely under twenty-five.

In terms of making it relevant for 1984, what were the big issues for you?

Identity, more than anything else. Identity in a world that is more and more confusing for people. What I discovered incidentally was that Orwell knew very little about television. For him, basically radio and posters were the items of propaganda and by the time I came to make it, I was making a film fundamentally about television. Not just about television, but about television and its pervasiveness, and its ability to strike at the heart of identity. In the old days, artificial imagery represented about five percent of people's existence, and it was a way of referencing the world around them. Now you'll find that artificial imagery is about eighty-five percent of people's existence, and it's the other way around: The world has become a way of referencing that imagery. In order to understand what you see on television, you look for clues in the world outside. It seems to me that that's just one area of the loss of identity. And really, where is your identity in the universe? It's there in your head, it's there in you dreams and your past and the thing that unites you to the child you once were and to the adult you're going to be, from your birth to your death. That's your identity.

There was a lot of anticipation about the film. People were expecting you to be more faithful to Orwell's vision than the 1950s version. It was a big production. The set design is incredible. And John Hurt and Richard Burton are amazing in the film. Yet there was some criticism that you were actually too faithful, and that the Winston/ Julia relationship was emotionally cold.

Yes, some people said, "Why isn't it about Mrs. Thatcher?" But the movie was reasonably successful, although in the United States it was sold to a bunch of crooks who just sold it off to video and didn't even release it in 1984. It did very well in most countries, particularly countries which had suffered totalitarianism, places like Germany and Venezuela and South Africa. I was mortified by the criticism of it. I was accused of being academic by *liberation* and *cahiers du cinéma*, who had supported me so much. That was a real blow to my self-esteem. But I realize it's the old thing: They build you up and then they want to knock you down. I think now, with a bit of hindsight when all the pressure's off, it's a pretty good adaptation of a classic book. I wouldn't do that lightly again; but I'm really rather proud of the movie.

But the experience of making it must have been quite different from making a small film in northern Scotland.

Yes, except that it was a gas. Shooting big stuff isn't difficult. People think that it is but it isn't because you have bands of assistants. All you need is time and money.

Those rally scenes are great.

And I didn't even have any storyboards. These days I'd have a storyboard, all these cameras and stuff and 2,000 extras. It was great fun to do.

You shot some of it in Battersea Power Station?

No, there was a scene with Battersea Power Station in the background. I shot it all on location in Mrs. Thatcher's London. I shot some of it in an old disused gas works called Beckton Power Station, which was immediately then used by Stanley Kubrick for *Full Metal Jacket*.

Were there any particularly cinematic influences on the film? I was thinking about German Expressionist films like *Metropolis*.

Not consciously, no. We developed a film process called bleach bypass. [A laboratory process which desaturates the color in an image. A similar process was used by Terence Davies in *Distant Voices, Still Lives*.] Certainly, that was the first time it was ever used. In fact, we invented it at Kay Laboratories.

The issue of point of view is crucial to this film because it does seem like Winston's subjectivity is driving the film.

When you start to adapt the novel, you realize that it's really not a very good novel. It's a great book, powerful and dramatic and forceful and significant. As a novel, it's a bit of a tract. He's a bit of a preacher, Orwell, and he doesn't let you off the hook much. The real problem is that Winston is a member of that society but also he looks at it from the outside, like a Martian. Because Orwell is an essayist, he takes this society and analyses it as an essayist would, but he does it through the eyes of a man who is actually a part of that society. What I tried to do was to make all Winston's identity, all his dreams and ideas, part of everything that existed there. How could his relationship with Julia possibly be loving since he comes from a brutalized society? These images of the golden country actually come from propaganda movies he's seen.

You realized that it had to have this strong point of view when you were writing the screenplay?

Yes, and he had to be a man who was, to a certain extent, ignorant of himself, because you couldn't allow him that degree of self-knowledge.

Is Winston capable of really critiquing the situation?

I made a documentary about extreme Protestantism in the north of Scotland in a community on the Outer Hebrides, all of whom were "We Free" fundamentalist Calvinists, except two or three who were poets. These poets railed against this fundamentalism but were still a part of that society. In other words, they saw fundamentalism in its own terms. They weren't people from outside looking in and saying, "Well, isn't this crazy?" Their brothers were part of it, and when they criticized it, it was from the inside. It was like somebody struggling to get out but using all the language and the imagery of the very system they're trying to escape from.

So, ultimately, it's ineffectual?

No, it's not ineffectual because Winston is a man with his identity. It's just different. He's not actually a Martian suddenly having to live in this society. He is a fundamental part of it. He's grown up in it. So he's going to assimilate. What you have to do is create a believable character whose vision of love is brutal because it's been brutalized. He's slowly discovering that you can make dreams out of anything. He criticizes it but he's kind of picking his way through.

But there is a sense where you feel very powerless because of his failure. It puts the viewer in this powerless situation.

I know. But that's the nature of the novel. You know famously in the novel that Orwell gave him absolutely no outs whatsoever. Right at the end, when he writes two plus two equals, Orwell put five in the book. And the famous story is that when the book was printed, there was a gap, there was nothing there. It's said that one of the printers was so outraged that he left it blank. [Laughs]

You had some kind of conflict about the soundtrack?

We went over budget and Virgin tried to impose The Eurythmics, which I didn't mind except that I didn't like what they did very much. So Virgin let me off the hook, but they wanted to produce an album, and then The Eurythmics insisted that their music go back on the movie. I felt that wasn't right and Virgin withdrew all the prints from the cinemas and put The Eurythmics music on it. I don't mind the music now, but, at the time, I was really, really upset by that and I said so publicly. Nobody expects you to do things like this, and it probably accounts for a lot of my troubles, but I stood up and said, "The film I'm getting this prize for is not the film you are seeing in the cinemas."

What is the relationship of *Nineteen Eighty-Four* to the present moment? There are different issues than Orwell imagined.

Yes, because the era of totalitarianism has passed. You only have to read Suetonius' *Twelve Caesars*, which is one of my favorite books. Society kind of doubles back on itself. Every two hundred years there's another self-righteous, right-wing, puritan fundamentalist regime that comes in. Nobody's allowed to have sex and then it slowly disintegrates into a decadent society of orgies and then another right-wing regime comes in.

Where are we now?

I think we're in an era that is fundamentally looking for idealism. Idealism has been so disgraced that suddenly we find that we have nothing to believe in. I think you need something to believe in. In terms of doublethink, come on: you only have to look at the Labour Party in Great Britain now spouting Margaret Thatcher's ideas and saying, "We're a Labour Party." It's just wonderful to watch.

Power has a way of doing that.

Absolutely. You know, *Nineteen Eighty-Four* is a fable and you have to take it that way. It's about the dangers of power.

I'm curious about how you worked with Richard Burton. He is incredibly understated in his performance. It's beautifully modulated, but it is a bit of a departure for him. He came in late to the production, didn't he?

Yes, he did, and I couldn't imagine doing that these days. We'd been shooting for six weeks before we cast him. We'd cast a number of other people, all of whom for one reason or another couldn't do it.

I remember reading an article, "Rod Steiger is rumored to. . ."

Rod Steiger was definitely one of them. He had a facelift which collapsed and went horribly wrong. We got this wonderful telegram saying, "Mr. Rod Steiger's facelift has fallen. He cannot do this role." Alan Bates was going to do it at one point. Paul Scofield was going to do it but broke his leg. He was the first choice. Marlon Brando wanted a million dollars a day.

Burton was a bit of a coup wasn't he?

Well, in a way he was the forgotten man. Nobody really knew what he was like. And he came and was a pussycat. He gave up drinking for the duration of the movie. He was quite honestly unwell. It was my second movie, I was thirty-six years old, we were all young and he'd gone off it all. He had been working with these old hacks for so long that he'd just had enough of it. He wrote to me, saying, "Of the seventy-two film directors I've worked with, you are only the eighth that has given me any new dimension," which I thought was really great. But people were terrified of him, and I wasn't. I felt strongly that he had too much presence in the cinema. It's funny to say, you always look for screen charisma and here was a man with *too much* presence. You had to pull it right back. I never thought he was a gifted cinema actor. He was wonderful on stage, and he didn't have to do much. He had this rich voice and this incredibly handsome face. He was the most extraordinary actor I've ever worked with because he didn't give two seconds for the psychological interpretation of the character. You'd just give him an adjective, say "slower" or "more charming," and he would remodulate his entire performance. He could read the telephone book and make it into a performance, just amazing. He was like an oven—you turned him up and down to cook things.

Did you do a lot of takes?

Yes, because he could never remember his bloody lines. He was a man with a legendary photographic memory and he couldn't remember a single line. He would play all kinds of tricks on the set to cover for his memory. He'd say, "Sorry, I thought I heard a voice," or "I thought I heard someone say cut." [Laughs] And he'd regale us with stories. He was absolutely great.

Seeing the film now, do you feel it was an honest effort?

I feel more about it now. I'm amazed at how much poetry is in it, in the *mise-en-scène*. Forget the story, just in the *mise-en-scène*. I'm really quite amazed by it. I didn't think that it was so good. That's honestly what I feel. But I now think both that one and *White Mischief*, the two movies that people kind of attacked, are much better than they were given credit for when they came out.

I was quite shocked by all the negative reviews of *White Mischief*.

It almost ruined my career. It stopped it in its tracks.

Was *White Mischief*, the book by James Fox, well known?

Yes, it was pretty well known over here. It was a document. There was a lot of it in the newspapers. It became a kind of cause-célèbre once more as he tried to solve this crime. It was glamorous tittle-tattle.

Do you think it's an accurate portrait of the real Happy Valley crowd and those events?

Yes, I do. You see, I grew up to a certain extent amongst people like that, with that colonial atmosphere. I think it was difficult for critics because Britain is obsessed by class. It wasn't done to make a film about upper-class people. I think people were expecting one of those James Ivory films or *A Passage to India*. In Europe it was called *The Road To Nairobi*, which made everybody think it was a Bob Hope movie. It wasn't meant to be like *Out of Africa*, the cinema of waxed furniture. I was trying to make something much more decadent.

It is a particularly devastating portrait of the end of the empire, of this class of people, and you were heavily criticized for it.

I think I was heavily criticized because the story is a bit weak, but I actually think that people missed the point of it, largely speaking. It was supposed to be a subtle critique of the end of empire. I didn't shoot it at the golden hour. I shot it in the middle of the daytime with this harsh light quite deliberately. I concentrated on the costumes because I felt that to put these extraordinary Chanel dresses in the middle of Africa would be even more extraordinary. You just get a sense of the absurdity of this whole process and the fact that you can't own Africa in the way they thought they could.

All of that gets through, I think.

Yes, but it wasn't considered particularly interesting. From my point of view, I found that melancholy decadence very touching. A lot of people loved the movie. It's become sort of a cult in the United States.

Did you feel an obligation to some kind of historical accuracy because it was so well known and because some of the people were still alive?

It's the $64,000 question. When does history become fiction? With *Elizabeth* you can rewrite history completely. Can you rewrite history when it's within living memory? You have to, because, as Aristotle said, "Because the Trojan War happened doesn't make it interesting."

Did you feel a certain freedom to play with history?

Well, I felt a *certain* freedom. But I also felt constrained by a number of things. I think it might have helped had I been able to make one of the characters slightly more likable, probably Joss Ackland's character. He was sympathetic, even though in real life he was an absolute scoundrel. In a way, the film is about two people who make a pact with the devil. One of the problems with the film was that we ran out of money in the middle of it, and Columbia Pictures came and bailed us out. In the process of doing that, the pound and the dollar had changed and we lost about $800,000 of the budget. There was supposed to be a week of shooting in England that was all prequel to the movie as it now stands, which would have set things up. As it was, I had to set things up in one scene with Hugh Grant's character. The pact that Greta Scacchi's character makes with Joss Ackland was much, much clearer. Here are two people agreeing to sell something to each other and it doesn't work. It was a shame to lose that. Producers always say, "Oh, you'll lose that but it'll be fine." It wasn't fine. I needed those scenes.

It is a touching film. Sarah Miles's character is a very sad, pathetic character and Joss Ackland's suicide scene is powerful. It's so sudden when he turns the gun on himself. Was that created on the set?

Yes, it was pretty much. I didn't quite know how I was going to do it.

Trevor Howard looks like he's close to the end. It must have been difficult to direct him in those three scenes.

Pretty difficult. He didn't really know where he was. But he still had great comic timing. [Laughs]

Was he your choice?

The part was written for a man much younger but just the thought of putting Trevor Howard in the movie was too much to pass up, really. I remember when we were sitting in the African bush and we were watching *Brief Encounter*. There's the old boy snoring in the tent and the rest of us just looking at him in his full glory.

John Hurt's character reminded me of Trevor Howard's early character roles. Did he model himself?

I don't think so, no. John's such a supreme actor, he just kind of made it up. I like him in that. Sarah Miles was different from the other actors in the sense that she is somebody who has no self-discipline whatsoever. She just fires in all directions and says, "Oh well, you'll find the best bits in the editing room." She absolutely knows the situation. You think, my goodness me, this person can't act at all, and slowly, as you put the film together, you realize that she's been really cunning. I've never come across anybody like that.

Is it because she really understands the filmmaking process?

She understands the process. She also understands that her technique is lousy.

So she gives you different things on different takes and expects you to put them together?

Her interpretations of lines will be wildly different. But because she's so magnetic on screen, she can get away with that stuff.

For you, what was the most interesting issue to explore in that film? Was it this sense of useless, wasted lives?

Yes, that was it. Everybody has this huge nostalgia for that kind of lifestyle. All these movies and television programs had been coming out about the glorious imperial past and all the rest of it, and how wonderful it was. I wanted to show these people trapped in this terrible melancholy.

But the film didn't do well?

No. It lost money and effectively stopped both Simon Perry and myself in our tracks. We had to dissolve our company.

But that's not why you left England? It's not really because of the failure of that film?

It actually was because it really got to me psychologically. I began to look at myself and wonder why I was making films and what I was doing, who I was trying to be. Should I be in the United States or should I be in the U.K.? I just couldn't figure any of it out. Then I started making this picture called *The Slow Train to Milan*, which fell apart after nearly two years of working on it. Quite rightly: It was a bad script. Then I got married and went to live in Italy, and suddenly there were no more films. I went through everything I had and I was literally broke. All this time nobody asked me to make films except this Italian actor who rang me up every year and said, "Let's make a film together," and I would say, "No." Then suddenly, I said to myself, "Why on earth am I turning this guy down?"

Massimo Troisi was a director too wasn't he?

Director in the sense that he made provincial, low-budget comedies which were loved in Italy. But they were no great shakes as movies.

But he had a big following as an actor.

Yes, huge. As a comic, really.

What did you do before you got to make *Il Postino*? Did you do any other work?

I wrote scripts. Actually, the gap was smaller than it seems, although it's six years from *White Mischief* to *Il Postino*. There's always a year and a half after a movie where you're promoting the movie and stuff like that, and then there's time preparing the next movie. So there was effectively about three years where I did nothing, really. I wrote scripts and shot commercials.

That's something you said you never wanted to do.

I didn't want to do it. I found myself doing it. It kept body and soul together.

Did you feel that you had abandoned the U.K.?

Yes, I thought I had actually, and I thought I was never going to make another film. I didn't know really what I was going to do. I came back to teach at the National Film School. That was rock bottom. I was literally earning 200 quid a week, wondering how on earth I was going to pay off my debts.

So then *Il Postino* happened. You finally agreed to get involved with Troisi?

Yes, and we decided on this subject together.

He kept calling you up because he liked *Another Time, Another Place*?

It was his favorite movie. It was really successful in Italy. It's considered a classic there.

Was he dying at that time?

No, he wasn't dying at that point. He'd always been ill because he'd always had a heart complaint. He had rheumatic fever when he was a kid, so he had a weak heart. But he took pills and everything was fine when we started this project. What happened was we decided we would get Italy's best known screenwriter to write the screenplay and make it a real prestige thing. So we got this guy named Furio Scarpelli, who wrote *Big Deal on Madonna Street*, and he turned in a piece of shit. I mean, literally, it was so bad we just chucked it in the bin. They [Scarpelli, and his son Giacomo] actually accepted to get nominated for best screenplay at the Oscars. I was hoping that we weren't going to win because I couldn't believe these guys were actually going to step up on stage.

Aren't there five or six screenwriters credited with the script?

Yes, but there really weren't. These guys didn't do a thing. They wrote this first draft, but they had it in their contract, so they got credit. There's not a line, not an idea, nothing of their first draft in the final film.

It was basically you and Troisi?

No, actually, the screenwriter Anna Pavignano played a large role. I can't write a screenplay in Italian.

But you could write and have it translated.

I structured the screenplay, which is what I'm really good at. Anna then took my structure and wrote the dialogue for Massimo, and then Massimo would come in and improvise a bit more and we'd work it through. It was basically the three of us. We worked out the story of the film and all that stuff.

When did Troisi get really sick?

We went to L.A. to write the final draft of the movie. Then he said, "I'm going down to Houston for a check-up because I haven't been there for ten years." He went down there and they told him he was about to conk out. It was one of those things: Once he knew that, he started to conk out. They tried to fix him up, because he said, "I want to make this film first." They said, "Your heart is about to explode. You need a transplant." But, actually, he deteriorated from that moment on, rapidly. We first thought it was psychological, and we started shooting. About two weeks into shooting, he collapsed and we realized he was in dire condition. At that moment, I thought the film was over.

So you shot the film knowing that this was going on and he was only able to work a couple of hours a day?

Yes, that's right.

With doctors on the set?

Yes, there were. There were cardiac specialists.

That's when you decided to shoot it in a different way?

Basically, I was told I could shoot him in closeup and that was it. I used a double for most of the movie, sixty percent of it. Then our schedule went up the creek and all the actors couldn't meet their dates. I remember shooting part of the wedding scene with seven doubles for the different actors.

This is a film that could easily have become quite sentimental, I think. Did you feel yourself resisting that?

Absolutely.

Also, it seems to be paying homage to Italian neo-realism.

Definitely.

Did you and Troisi have discussions about the feel of the film?

Not really, he left all that to me. By that time, he was too sick. It was during the casting process that we had most of our discussions. I found it incredibly hard, although I speak fluent Italian, to grasp the nuances of the culture. So he would help me with that and with the actors, if they were being genuine or not. By the time we got to shooting it, he was too sick to really involve himself, and I wouldn't have let him. What did happen was the crew didn't listen to me at all when I said what kind of lighting I wanted and different things. You can't imagine what the first days' rushes were like. The lighting was horrible comedic lighting, so you could shoot a midshot all around the room and nobody would have to worry about hitting their marks. The make-up, the costumes, everything was just diabolical, and I threatened to fire the entire crew. That's the one moment I went to Massimo and said, "Massimo, listen. They are just doing what they think will please you. They're not paying any attention to me at all. Unless this stops, I'm getting out of here." The next day everything was different.

Does the film look and feel the way you intended?

In parts. There are moments where I am just grabbing things. It's a real cut-and-paste job. There's a particular scene where Massimo quotes poetry to Maria Grazia on the beach. Massimo was never in that scene or anywhere near a beach. I had to shoot that scene with her, a double, and then Massimo saying the words in closeup at Cinecitta studios standing on a rostrum reshooting his face. Do I look at that and see trees in the background and wonder if the light matches? Yes, I do. I see it every time. But was I able to do certain things? Yes, I was.

Does the film communicate what you want it to communicate even though the conditions were not ideal?

It appears to, yes. I wanted to make a film about poetry and the importance of poetry in people's lives. And how poetry doesn't necessarily mean verse. I think, for me, the best thing in the movie is the constructed scene of them doing their recording of sounds. Again, that's not Massimo doing that. I just sat him down and had him read all these things for shots that I'd pinched. And *everybody* understands that he's found the poetry in his life in some kind of way.

It's a lovely idea. Do you believe that? Is there a poetics of the everyday world?

I think it's about people coming to terms with who they are, actually. He's not a great poet, this guy. He's never going to write a poem. He's never going to be Pablo Neruda but he's come to terms with who he is. That happens to all of us. We have mentors, we have ideas, we have dreams. And, finally, we come to terms with who we are.

The idea of living the authentic life?

A man who is fulfilled in himself because he's come to terms with who he is, and he's going to live it, he's going to fulfill it.

You have Neruda telling Mario [Massimo Troisi] that some people, through a force of will, manage to change things. Did Mario change the world and the people he encountered? Did he change Neruda?

Yes, I think he did. One of the nice things about it is I did no research on Neruda at all and everybody in Chile said to me, "This is exactly how he was."

It's also a mark of Phillipe Noiret's skill as an actor.

It's a mark of his performance and also human psychology. Here's a man who speaks to the people but he can't be dealing with them everyday. So he comes across as being a bit of a shit.

What about the experience of making *Il Postino* and working with Troisi? Did that change you?

Yes, it did. It was the first time I'd worked with a really great comic, and I realized how much that can bring to a movie. It must be just a pleasure to work with Roberto Benigni or Woody Allen or Steve Martin or someone like that. They just really bring something to a movie.

Are you saying that your work had been too serious before this?

No, it's just something new. I learned a lot about simplicity because, of necessity, I was obliged to be simple. I learned a great deal about the magic of cinema because I had to wing it, day by day. I learned not to be too precious about everything. I also learned, which I've always known really, that if you having a fucking good idea, it's hard to fuck it up. There are people who do fuck it up unfortunately, but if you know what you're doing and you've got a good idea, it's really basically that. And it was a good idea for a movie.

Was the ending the same as we see it, with Troisi's character dying at the rally, or was that pasted together?

No, that was how we wrote it. Absolutely. People thought we added it on, but it wasn't at all that, it was very definitely him.

The film was an amazing financial success. To some extent, it's the power of marketing. Miramax really did push it, didn't they?

They really did. But having seen other movies of mine being let down by distributors, I felt that somewhere along the line I was owed one.

Of course, you have to sell anything in this day and age. I don't think Miramax would have sold it if the word-of-mouth hadn't been so strong, if it hadn't just grabbed hold of people.

I find it surprising that it struck such a chord. It's no more an accomplished film than your other work.

But it did, and it was quite evident that it had. It was really at the Toronto Film Festival where I understood that the movie had a real force, when I saw a friend of mine, Christopher Hitchens—who's a real left-wing, cynical journalist—come out of the movie in floods of tears, and he just said, "I can't speak. I can't speak." Then I saw that the whole audience had remained in the cinema for about ten minutes after the movie had finished.

It didn't have to do with the reality that this actor had actually died?

No. Nobody knew who he was.

It was just the film working on its own?

That was it, really. It had that effect on people. Miramax, of course, milked it mercilessly, but that's their job. I don't think there is a movie around that isn't sold and hyped; you have to in order to make a successful movie.

It must have been huge in Italy, I would think.

Yes, but that was expected because Massimo died and he was a big star. Where it was really huge was in Argentina; it was unbelievable there.

What about Chile?

No. In Chile, they're fed up with Neruda.

How do you feel about the different stages of filmmaking: preproduction, shooting, postproduction. Which is more satisfying for you?

Shooting, unlike a lot of directors, who like to get into the editing room as quickly as possible, I love shooting a movie. I love standing out there in front of all these people not knowing what I'm going to do and having to think of what to do. It's the tension of it. When I write and I have to make decisions on my own, I can be incredibly slow because I proceed in doubt. So when the juggernaut is right behind me and it's about to roll over me and I have to keep going, I love the camaraderie. I love the stress, the invention, the torment of it. I love it.

Do you consider yourself a part of any particular British film tradition?

I don't think I do, really. They're not really very British, the movies I make. *B. Monkey*, a British movie set in London, looks like an Italian or a French movie. I feel really European, I speak four languages and I've lived in Europe. I mean, I am English and proud to be so, and I like British cinema though it is fashionable to decry it. I love Ken Loach's work and I love Stephen Frears' work and everybody else. I think there's a real creative surge going on here. But the things that I esteem in cinema, the *mise-en-scène*, that sense of atmosphere, of tone and feeling that you get more to the fore in French, Italian, Japanese movies, that to me is my reference.

Did you have any doubts that you were doing the right thing making films?

Yes, I did. I spent that long period not making films at all. It was partly a series of unlucky circumstances but partly also a sudden thrust into confusion, a confusion of identity about who I was. Was I a European filmmaker? Or was I an Anglo-Saxon filmmaker with one foot in Hollywood? I haven't really ever resolved that, and sooner or later I'm going to have to go to Hollywood or it will be too late. Because it's Hollywood, curiously, that has given me my biggest shot, that embraced *Il Postino*.

Are you saying that because of the success of *Il Postino*, you needed to capitalize on it?

I needed to, but whether or not I still can, I don't know. When you are one of the five Oscar nominees . . .

That opportunity may not come around again?

I think it's always there. I'm a proven director for the studios. I don't have too much trouble. My name still means something worldwide because it was a financial success. But I think, in a way, I can't keep refusing Hollywood, otherwise they will just go away. And I don't want to; I want to see what happens. Making a film is a long-term experiment; it takes two years.

How do you feel about the current state of the British film industry? Do you think it's in a bad place now?

No, it's in a better place than it has been for years, just given the number of pictures that are being made. I think last year there were 125 pictures being made in the U.K. When I left England, it was twenty-five.

I wonder if that's a good thing that so many films are being made. If there's more mediocrity out there, is it really such a good thing?

Yes, there's always going to be a lot of mediocrity out there because that's the nature of filmmaking. Originality, well that comes and goes. Originality is not something that I seek. I think that's a turn-of-the-century vision of art, that the only good art is that which is at the forefront of invention, and perhaps it was true in the sixties in cinema as well. I personally think that what's important is that the filmmaker has a point-of-view and that you come out of a movie thinking, "My goodness me, the plot might not have quite worked or whatever but I see the world in a slightly different way." If I look for anything in a movie, it's the people saying, "I couldn't stop thinking about it." This is why I hate these preview tests of audiences, because they are obliged to respond immediately to the movie. Actually, I think that my movies tend to appeal to people three or four days afterwards. They wake up and they think, oh, I haven't stopped thinking about those four or five images in that movie which really mean something to me.

I think what happens is you get companies like Miramax who base their reputations on pushing art movies, and then they grow, find a niche market and start to get instantly more conventional. To the point where *B. Monkey*, which is actually quite an elliptical, strange movie with a real elegance to it—probably the best movie I've made—just got completely cut to ribbons. It's twenty-five minutes shorter and the soundtrack is completely different.

What was the cut shown at the London Film Festival?

That was the Miramax cut.

They wouldn't show your cut?

No, it doesn't exist except on tape.

What was the reaction to that cut?

Okay. People liked it. But I didn't like it. I can't. It's like a kind of abortion of absolutely everything that I believe in about the cinema. Everything is sacrificed to so-called clarity, so-called storytelling, and being hip. I created a character, a woman who was ambiguous, strange, maybe likable, maybe not likable, all sorts of things, vulnerable. They've absolutely taken the ambiguity out of her, blanded her out. She was extremely dangerous, but they took all of that out and then thought, "Oh my god, how do we now make her conventionally dangerous? Let's put rock music all over it," which will instantly date the movie. I had this wonderful, elegiac jazz score running through the movie, which was kind of melancholy and about London and I'm sure it wasn't going to date. Now I don't know. People say that it's okay.

So you fought the battles and lost some on this one?

I don't know. I'm actually very collaborative. I don't believe that other people can't have a point of view, and it's true that it's a good cold shower to show your film to an audience for the first time. But I was unable to convince Miramax, and in the end, they had final cut and they produced the movie. It was a question of: Was the movie going to go out, or was I going to take my name off it?

But it's been finished for a while, hasn't it?

Yes, it's been finished for two years. This film was not a film in trouble; it was a film people really liked. It's an art movie, and it isn't what they thought it was going to be, which is a $100 million youth movie. There are other people who are really good at that kind of stuff: Don't get me to do it. I produced this movie which was basically a French movie set in London and they just changed everything. It started off in a really explosive way, with two people fucking on the tube—explosive, explosive, and they cut it all out.

So they took the edge off?

I think they have taken some of the edge off.

For you, what's the hardest part about being a filmmaker? What's difficult about it?

It's actually the waiting. I don't know how some filmmakers seem to be able to make a film every year or year-and-a-half. I don't seem to be able to make a film more than once every three years. Somehow or other I find myself in situations where I'm either in trouble at the end of a movie or in trouble before I start. On *Il Postino*, Massimo fell ill. *B. Monkey*, I made straight away but we spent two years in the cutting rooms. *The Swedish Cavalier*, the film I'm making now, I spent a year setting the damn thing up. I was talking to Ken Loach about this and he said, "You've got to have three or four movies on the go." But if I've got three or four movies on the go, I just waste time thinking about this one and thinking about that one. So that's the most frustrating thing. I've been in the movies fifteen years and I've made five movies which is one every three years; not a great track record.

What gives you the most pleasure from being a filmmaker? Are you still committed to it?

Oh yeah. You know what really gives me the greatest pleasure? I'm in my early fifties now and I feel like a young man. I feel like I'm right at the beginning of my career. You know what I'm saying? I'm not at the beginning of my career, but I'm certainly not even halfway through it, and in what other profession can you say that? All my friends from university are thinking about their pensions. And here I'm thinking about the next ten movies I'm going to make. I feel immensely privileged to be doing what turns me on for a living, and I love the glamour of it. I'm not like Woody Allen, I really do love going to Hollywood and Cannes. I love the different stages of making the film. Thinking about it, writing it, preproducing it, making it, and then thinking about it again. I find that very satisfying as an activity. I can't think of anything else I'd rather do in life.

Do you feel optimistic about the film industry?

I do, in a certain sense. It's very hard to know. Listen, we've been through an era of such great pessimism that relatively, at this moment, it's a period of optimism. There are more cinemas opening. We seem to have troughed out at the bottom. There's a great demand for product. I do fear for the art cinema; I fear for the next twenty or thirty years. I think we are going to find ourselves trapped in a cinema of consumption.

I think there's a European cinema about to happen. There was a European film awards the other day which I thought was going to be a real trashy event and, as it turned out, it was wonderful. There were no American movie stars there. It was just all the European movie stars—French, Italians, Germans, British—they all came. And you suddenly felt, yes, there is an identity here somewhere. There is an economic power and you can construct something.

PHILIP RIDLEY

Philip Ridley is an artist whose sheer breadth of creative activity is astounding. He is a screenwriter and filmmaker, playwright, children's book author and novelist, painter, and songwriter. His plays, novels, and films have won worldwide acclaim and numerous awards. He has won both the Critics' Circle and the *Evening Standard* Award for Most Promising Playwright for his play *The Fastest Clock in the Universe* and was shortlisted for the Whitebread Best Children's Novel Award for his children's novel *Kaspar in the Glitter*. *The Reflecting Skin* has won awards at the Locarno Film Festival, the Stockholm Film Festival, and the Birmingham Film Festival, among its numerous accolades.

Ridley's first foray into feature filmmaking was his superb script for *The Krays*, a film directed by Peter Medak. One of the best British films of the 1990s, and a huge commercial success, *The Krays* went on to win the *Evening Standard* Best Film of the Year Award. This screenplay, the short films that preceded it, and Ridley's artwork illustrate some of the qualities of Ridley's own features: a propensity for mythical, fantastically non-naturalistic images and a commitment to using the basic grammar of film, such as image and light, sound and music, composition, framing and editing, to create a unique, visually (and aurally) intense film experience. Philip Ridley's films are nothing if not total cinematic experiences.

His first feature, *The Reflecting Skin*, features striking imagery as it weaves a fantastic tale of gay, pedophile, serial killers in the wheat fields of what looks to be the American midwest. The film feels like it might be set in the 1950s, yet it is not set in any identifiable time or place, lending it an hallucinogenic, dreamlike quality. Ridley's second feature, *The Passion of Darkly Noon*, continued his obsession with dreamlike imagery and experimentation with genre and non-naturalistic form. It invokes the fairy tale and romance and horror films and weaves a hypnotic spell that culminates in a violent orgy of images Ridley has variously described as *Apocalypse Now* meets *Beauty and the Beast* and *Psycho* meets *Aladdin*. The final twenty-minute sequence features an amazing montage of images, and by Ridley's own estimate, "800 cuts."

Ridley's film work is striking in its formal investigation of the medium, as well as its thematic inquiry into the dark side of human behavior. His films have frequently been compared to the work of David Lynch, and he is surely one of the most imaginative, inventive filmmakers to have emerged in the 1990s. I spoke with Philip Ridley in London.

What was it like growing up in East London in the 1960s and 1970s?

My background is typical East London, working-class, really. We were quite poor. We lived in a couple of rooms: me, my parents, my brother. My dad was a long-distance lorry driver. My mum worked in a supermarket. My nickname was "Alien." Nothing to do with Ridley Scott's film. It was because, well, I never really fitted in. I was always the outsider. This has a lot to do with my asthma. I was chronically sick as a child, bedridden for months at a time—oxygen tent, no visitors allowed, the whole damn thing. As a result, I developed a very strong interior life. I devoured books, comics mostly—*X-Men*, *Spider-Man*—and I started to write my own stories and illustrate them.

So the writing and visual art started together?

Well, I was drawing before I wrote. My parents have still got all the exercise books I did when I was two to seven years old. Each one is cram-packed with sequences of drawings. Little stick people, birds, crocodiles, monsters, trying to tell stories without words, a sort of infantile hieroglyphics. So writing and drawing have always been part of my life.

Were you interested in film as well?

Oh, yes. Absolutely. I can remember a moment that changed the direction I was moving in or consolidated my interest in film. It was one summer—I must have been about nine or ten—and the BBC was showing a season of Alfred Hitchcock films. I remember begging my parents to let me sit up late enough to watch *Psycho*. The first thing I remember being interested in was the music, the shrieking violins. I remember being absolutely haunted for months, trying to get my mind around how a director, how this man called Alfred Hitchcock, worked out those sequences. Where did the imagination begin to do that speed of editing in the shower scene? I remember being absolutely possessed, going to the library and devouring books on film, then sitting down and storyboarding imaginary films. I used to do pages and pages of these things, writing the script, and then storyboarding it.

You eventually went to art school. Had you thought about going to film school?

It did cross my mind. The school I eventually chose, St. Martin's School of Art, did have a film course. This was at the beginning of the 1980s, when the barriers of what was defined as painting were breaking down in the academic world. I mean, they'd been broken down in the wider world for years and years. But now multimedia courses were starting up. St. Martin's had the reputation of being the most avant-garde of the London art schools. So, I thought if I went to St. Martin's and said I'm studying painting, I could stretch what that encompassed. When I went into that painting course, there were very few people actually putting oil paint on canvas figuratively. I mean, this is the generation at the School who were in the Sensation Show at The Royal Academy, people who were pickling goldfish and juggling with monkey heads. So I was able, within the confines of the art school system, to do my visual work, but also get into photography and video. I made lots of video films, and also started using their Super8 and Super16 equipment.

What are some of the cultural and aesthetic influences on your film-making?

In terms of other filmmakers, I've always been attracted to those people who *use* film, in other words, explore what is specific to the language of cinema. What can film *do*? Why am I making this as a film and not a novel or a stage play? Obviously, that puts Hitchcock at the top of the list. And Kubrick, DePalma, Tarkovsky. All those wonderful wizards who create magic out of film. The trouble is we live in a literary-based cultural environment. People still talk about film in terms of plot. What *happens*. Critics are especially guilty of this. I've had whole reviews of my work that just retell the plot. Whereas, in truth, the plot is the least significant thing. My big influences have always put images first. Some of the big blockbusters I saw as a young teenager did this brilliantly. I'm thinking of things like *Alien, Jaws, Carrie, Star Wars*, and *Close Encounters*, all of these things which we look back on now as being, yes, pure commercial cinema. But my God, were they great pieces of filmmaking. I was also influenced by painters like de Chirico, Paul Klee, and the English artist Cecil Collins, symbolist painters and hyper-realist painters who were able to take everyday reality and give it some kind of menacing, dark, surrealist edge. Also writers like Ray Bradbury—*Dandelion Wine* is one of the greatest books ever written—and Robert Bloch, Richard Matheson, William Burroughs, Patrick White, Tennessee Williams, Sam Shepard, and, of course, Philip K. Dick, who is my favorite writer.

So I take it that it's the more commercial cinema you were interested in.

When I was young, yes. There weren't many opportunities to experience "art" cinema in the East End of London. In fact, if truth be told, there weren't many opportunities to experience cinema at all. Most of the local cinemas had closed down. So if you wanted to see a film, you had to catch a bus to the West End and, for an East End boy, that was a pretty big deal.

What about music?

That was a huge thing in my life. David Bowie and all these art-based pop groups, Roxy Music. Brian Eno's ambient stuff and soundtracks. The only music I bought apart from the things I've mentioned were film soundtracks. I was never really into pop music like my mates.

I've still got memories of us at the age of fourteen going into big megastores to spend our pocket money on the latest album, and them all buying their new favorite groups, and me desperately hunting out the new Jerry Goldsmith or Lalo Shifrin or John Barry score. I remember these huge arguments: "Oh, how can you buy that? It's only twenty-four minutes' worth of music, and it's just the same tune over and over again." But for me, they were, and are, pure magic. I still get so excited when I see the new Jerry Goldsmith score or the new John Barry score. I would buy soundtracks and put them on to the films and videos I'd made, just image and sound. Very hallucinogenic for a fourteen year-old.

Can you talk about your short films?

It really divides into three stages. There's all the film work that was stemming out of photography that I did from the age of about twelve up until fifteen and I exhibited. I had my first one-man show when I was fourteen years old, mainly consisting of drawing and photographic collage stuff and still photographs in sequence. They were kind of like Duane Michaels with sequences of three or four photos. It was as close as I could get to moving images without actually having a moving image. A lot of those were self-portraits of me ritualizing everyday events and photographs of my friends doing certain things. I was always trying to persuade my friends to take their clothes off and do pornographic things in front of the camera. So, you've got all those still things, which I would still refer to as being film, in the sense that they were in sequence.

The stuff that I did from sixteen or seventeen, and the first part of going into St. Martin's, were experimental films, some of them lasting thirty seconds, some, a few minutes, and primarily on video with some Super8 and some Super16 works. But they were films for the art galleries, and were shown as part of the paintings and the drawings. Again, there are films of my friends and of me doing things, but they're in the tradition of art-house filmmaking.

After that, it begins to change. Not consciously, but because my writing was getting more narrative. I was starting to write stories and certain themes were beginning to emerge. There was the fascination with childhood, communication and alienation. I made a film called *Visiting Mr. Beak*, which is really where it begins to change. *Visiting Mr. Beak* was a very ambitious student film. Up until that point, I'd always been regarded as this quite abstract, experimental filmmaker. My favorite artists at that time had very much to do with the American avant-garde. But *Mr. Beak* had a stronger narrative. It was still surrealist, but it had a beginning, middle, and end. It had people wearing clothes. It wasn't just somebody against a brick wall, jerking off. This was a *huge* development, believe me. I got a group of people together, I wrote the script, drew the storyboard, and cast it. I shot it on 35mm. I managed to persuade these film companies to hire me all this equipment for two days. It's twenty minutes long. I put this film together and put music on it and, at that point, people started to take an interest. British Screen in England got hold of a tape of the film, and that lead directly to the next thing I did, *The Universe of Dermot Finn*

Did *Visiting Mr. Beak* get shown?

It had its first public screening at a festival in Cologne only recently.

But basically, it didn't get shown much.

No, none of the films before *The Universe of Dermot Finn* have been shown. I've got shelves full of videos that were all shown in galleries, but that's it.

What was *The Universe of Dermot Finn* like?

It's narrative. It's surrealist. I always admired certain animated work, particularly the Quay brothers and Svankmeyer. I was watching all of that at the time. It's set in East London, but it's a very stylized view of East London. It was financed by Channel Four and British Screen, and went out with *Robocop*. It was screened at the Berlin Film Festival with *Mississippi Burning*. It's been screened on television and umpteen film festivals. In fact, when the Scala Cinema was open here, it was a regular favorite. It was the beginning of this connection with my work and David Lynch's, because they always showed *Eraserhead* and *The Universe of Dermot Finn* together.

What kinds of things did you learn from making the two short films?

Oh, lots of things! The ability to describe to other people what I was trying to achieve for one thing. Up until that point, I'd basically done it all myself: I hadn't had to vocalize a visual look because I'd done it all. Suddenly, I had to work out concisely what I wanted.

Before we get into the features, it's interesting that you're involved in so many things. You write children's books. You're a painter and visual artist. You're a playwright. You even co-wrote the songs for *The Passion of Darkly Noon*. And you direct films. Can you speak about working in these different media?

It's very difficult to answer that because I've never really seen them as different things. As a child, I would write short stories. They were invariably dark fables and fairy tales. Then I would do illustrations around them, so it almost became like a medieval illuminated manuscript. I've always told stories and drawn pictures. And then each thing blossoms into something else. Sometimes I'm writing and I think that this idea is becoming a novel or this idea is becoming a screenplay, but I'm just doing this thing called "my work." What has made it difficult, particularly in this country, is that they've had to reinvent what they think I am every eighteen months. If you look at the press on me in the mid-1980s, I was just "a punk artist." Then I became "painter-turned-short-story-writer." Then I was "short-story-writer-turned-novelist." Then "novelist-turned-scriptwriter," then I was "scriptwriter-turned-film director." Then "film director-turned-playwright."

Do you prefer one to the other?

No. In fact, if I did, I would probably be further ahead, because I could concentrate. The advice I always got from people after *The Reflecting Skin* was to concentrate on film, to get my next film out quickly. And, of course, I didn't because then I'd made a move into working in the theater. I worked on two stage plays and consolidated my children's novel writing. Then I went back and did *Darkly Noon*. So I've never really followed it along as perhaps I should have in terms of—oh, that awful word—a career. I've never seen it as a career, anyway. All that's bullshit. I'm just doing my work.

In terms of your work as a painter, one can see how that informs your filmmaking, since your sense of the visual is so strong. How has the playwriting informed your filmmaking?

Well, I don't know yet. *Darkly Noon* and *The Reflecting Skin* were ostensibly written before I'd done any stage plays. I wrote *The Reflecting Skin* in 1989. I'd done the treatment and the first draft of *Darkly Noon* while I was shooting *The Reflecting Skin*. It was only then that I started working on the stage plays. The new screenplay—as yet untitled—is the first complete screenplay that I've done since I got involved in writing the stage plays. So we'll have to see how that turns out.

So, perhaps the filmmaking informed your playwrighting.

I think it did, but not in ways that you'd think. If you think about what a cinematic stage play would look like, you'd imagine lots of quick changes and all of that, whereas what happened with my stage plays was that they became cinematic in their desire to make the images and sound and music tell their own stories separate from the narrative. It's something that really excites me about David Lynch's work, particularly *Lost Highway*, where the images are separate from what you think the linear narrative of the story is. It's much like a dream, where describing what happens in a dream is not what the dream is about. That was something that I was very conscious about in *The Reflecting Skin* and even more conscious of in *Darkly Noon*: the moment of image. An "image-aria," if you like, where everything you've been experiencing—both consciously and subconsciously—climaxes in a visual epiphany, an image experience so intense it's tattooed to your eyelids. In terms of cinema, I can think of several examples: Sissy Spacek covered with blood at the end of *Carrie*; the chest-burster scene in *Alien*; the exploding head in *Scanners*; the appearance of the mothership in *Close Encounters*. And if you're wondering why so many of the moments are violent, well, violence is a very cinematic thing. Violence, spaceships, monsters, tall buildings, following someone, anything burning, anything screaming, anything in pain, people laughing: All this is cinema.

Much of your work seems to come out of dreamwork or the unconscious. In fact, you subtitled the two features *American Dreams*. How are they dreams?

Those two films were conceived from the very beginning as separate from the rest of my work. *The Reflecting Skin* and *The Passion of Darkly Noon* try to do lots of things. They're trying to create an hallucinogenic reinterpretation of what I imagined America to be like, in much the same way that Kafka wrote about America even though he'd never been there. He just imagined the skyscrapers and what everyone was like. They're an America of the mind. So, the references are all from comic books, Andrew Wyeth, Edward Hopper, this whole melting pot of what I imagined America to be—an East London boy's dream of America.

Do you consider your work transgressive? Are you out to shock?

I've never deliberately been "out to shock," actually. But that's something that's been said to me since I was fourteen years old, drawing and photographing my mates jerking off, people saying, "Oh, you're out to shock," when I wasn't. I was just exploring what seemed perfectly natural to me. I'm more shocked by people wanting to photograph fluffy kittens in big boots or cuddly babies. Now, for me, that's disgusting. It's tricky to set out to shock. *The Reflecting Skin*, if you read the script, is about a bunch of highly sexy, good-looking, gay, pedophile, child-killers that cruise around in a black Cadillac obviously killing young boys. Now, this was a huge problem to everyone when the film was coming together, particularly because it was a BBC film. There was this debate in the press at the time about children and sex and violence, and suddenly there was this film with pedophile child-killers. The film comes out and that's never been mentioned. The only thing discussed—the only shocking thing—is the exploding frog. All I'm ever asked about is, "Was it a real frog?" And none of us, in any of the previews, batted an eyelid at that sequence, so you can never really tell. If it shocks, it shocks. I'd rather be shocked than bored.

You often have characters, in both your films and plays, that are very cruel to one another. You seem interested in exploring the limits of human behavior.

That's just the sad, fucked-up human being I am, really. I always get nervous about artists who can explain so clearly why they're interested in certain things. Because I don't know. I suppose I've had a long history of endlessly fucked-up relationships, and I'm not happy and married with two kids, so I'm not writing about that. I grew up in a very violent culture in terms of gangs and street violence around me in the East End of London. I suppose all of this becomes part of you. I have always been attracted to dark things. I mean there are very few healthy relationships in Hitchcock. The apotheosis of that is *Vertigo*. You dissect that relationship, and it's probably one of the sickest relationships ever put on screen. It's surprising how cinematic sick things are. Healthy situations rarely inspire empathy. Things going wrong are what grab our attention. Bodies out of control, emotions out of control. A volcano is only interesting when it's erupting.

How did the script of *The Krays* come about?

Primarily because I'd written a novel called *In The Eyes of Mr. Fury*, a mythical love story set over three generations in East London. I was also working at a film company to earn some money while I was at art school. I did the storyboard for some pop videos and contributed ideas and generally helped out, swept up and made the tea, that sort of thing. Gary and Martin Kemp had their Spandau Ballet videos made there and they wanted to make a film of the Krays. They saw it as a vehicle for themselves. Gary and Martin were actors before they became singers, so it wasn't actually as bizarre an idea as it sounded. They both had studied with Anna Sher, an acting teacher here in London.

One day we were talking about it, and I said, "I think there's only one way this film can work: You should take a mythical approach, because so much about the Krays has become a cliché. I think you should take a mythical approach, and treat it as contemporary folklore." I gave them a copy of *In the Eyes of Mr. Fury* to read. They liked it, and asked me to write a draft. I said, "If I do it, I'll treat it like fiction. I'll just bring all my themes to it: mythical East London, childhood, strong women, overbearing mothers, fucked-up relationships, homoeroticism, violence." They said, "Fine by us." I wrote the first draft in a few weeks. I gave it to them and they loved it. Financiers were not so enthusiastic. It was turned down by nearly everyone in England. But what got the film going was, well, word-of-mouth, in a way. Every actor who read the script wanted to be in it. Before long, we had a cast to die for, and the actors kept talking and talking about it. Their enthusiasm was phenomenal.

You said it wasn't very accurate.

Historically, it's not true at all. Although, strangely enough, in England people seem to remember the story of the Krays more from seeing the film than from what really happened. Everyone's convinced the Krays had this one night where they killed Jack the Hat and Joseph Cornell. In reality, of course, those two murders are separated by years. But I needed two murders at the end of the film. I took all the facts, like the suicide of Francis, these twin brothers—one straight, one gay—the dominating mother, the murders of Jack the Hat and Joseph Cornell, and juggled them around to make something that, structurally, made emotional sense for me.

So, you were satisfied with the film of *The Krays*?

There's obviously whole areas and whole sections that I would have done differently. But you have to kind of let go. I did my job, which was to write the screenplay and set out what kind of film it was. What Peter [Medak, the film's director] did was completely cut through a lot of art-house elements in the screenplay and open it out into something more populist. I think that was a phenomenal achievement. It was the number-one film here in London for like seven weeks. There were queues going around the block in Leicester Square. That feeling of being associated with a popular piece of filmmaking was so weird for me. It's like a place I'd never thought I'd visit. I used to stand in Leicester Square with a friend of mine and look at the queues, murmuring, "Scary, scary." And it was. I couldn't help feeling I'd done something wrong.

You were working on *The Reflecting Skin* at the same time.

Exactly the same time. I was in Idaho while they were shooting *The Krays* here in London.

Where did the idea for *The Reflecting Skin* come from?

It came out of a series of paintings and drawings that I'd been working on while at St. Martin's. They were called "American Gothic," and it was basically little *Psycho* houses and wheat fields. It was an ongoing thing: pencil drawing, etchings, paintings. By the time I got to the end, it comprised something like 800 different works. Halfway through this series I invented this child called Seth, a little boy with black hair. People kept saying to me, "Is it America?" I'd say, "Well, I think what's happened is it's the year 2020, and somebody's taken an hallucinogenic drug that's making them hallucinate what they imagine 1950s America was like." So all the men look like Elvis Presley and all the women look like Marilyn Monroe and all the landscapes look like Andrew Wyeth. It became this playground puzzle of images. All the cars were Cadillacs. Women were walking around with huge *Psycho* knives by their sides. I used all this American iconography. There were whole sequences of this Seth character with his mates, torturing animals and blowing up frogs. When it got to the situation where British Screen said, "Have you got an idea for a feature?" It was a painter friend who suggested I use those paintings as a storyboard. And that's exactly what I did. I went through all these images of the American Gothic series, and I chose the exploding frog, the black Cadillac, the wheat fields, the blue sky, and the character of Seth to link it all together. The first draft was called *American Gothic*. Even while I was shooting the film, it was called *American Gothic*. It didn't become *The Reflecting Skin* until one day before we were due to shoot the titles.

Was it a difficult shoot?

The Reflecting Skin was shot in six weeks, and it was a nightmare only because of the weather. We'd established this very sun-drenched, blue sky, golden wheatfield look, and the first two shooting days we had the most glorious sunshine. All of the sequence in *The Reflecting Skin* where Seth [Jeremy Cooper] is approaching Dolphin's [Lindsay Duncan] house to apologize with all that choral music was done on the first day. The next day, when we saw the rushes, they were mind-blowing, exactly what I wanted. But often we'd set up to do these complicated situations that we'd rehearsed with the kids and suddenly the clouds would come over. *The Reflecting Skin* had this late-afternoon, "magic-hour" look, with long shadows and sun setting. We developed a system of working whereby we'd turn up in the morning and thoroughly rehearse the scenes we were going to shoot and all the camera moves. Everyone knew their marks and we would sometimes do two or three scenes. Then we would break for lunch and then shoot like crazy. I'd done a pretty meticulous storyboard. So people could read the film like a graphic novel. That's not to say we didn't improvise. We did, but always within the structure of the storyboard.

The music and sound are effective in that film. Both films, of course, have very intense, evocative musical scores. That, to some extent, stems from your sense, growing up, of how important music is in film.

Absolutely, yes. Music has always been a huge part of my life. But, in a way, it's more than just the music, as you said. It's the sound as well. The music is important and it's played very up-front. But what's more innovative for me is the use of sound and a lot of people completely overlook it. In *The Passion of Darkly Noon*, the soundscape is wonderful, I think. The whole film is about experiencing this kind of sub-bass score and sound echoed through every speaker. The film becomes a totally sensory experience. It achieves a kind of alchemy in the auditorium. Pure cinema. It's not about plot or character: It's about percussion and the color red.

The Reflecting Skin **doesn't fall neatly within any particular genre. It seems a pastiche of several forms, part coming-of-age, part love story, part horror. Were you fairly conscious of subverting codes or mixing genres?**

Well, yes. But I strongly disagree with the use of the word pastiche. The emotional content is too honest and true for it to be pastiche. It's more like this modern art term of "appropriation," of taking something from one form and turning it into something else, like Andy Warhol did with the Campbell's soup tins. His prints are not *pastiche.* They're something else entirely. It's the same with the images and the language in *The Reflecting Skin* and *The Passion of Darkly Noon.* It's taking other genres—horror, shlock, love story, fantasy— and rendering them into something new, a dreamlike vision, an experience of dreaming, an acid trip, if you like. The lonely house in the middle of the woods is treated with the same iconographic significance as the stable in Bethlehem.

The Reflecting Skin **is very painterly. Some of the images like Lindsay Duncan's blood splattered . . .**

That's my favorite image!

. . . face and dress is an example of a very painterly shot. I think the whole film highlights its pictorialism. Were there any filmmakers that influenced your style?

I've never been that interested in the social-realist, kitchen-sink school of cinema. Unless you can show me something extraordinary in the cinema, don't bother showing it to me at all. What we were saying earlier about these seminal big films from the 1970s had a huge influence on me. The opening of *The Reflecting Skin* is straight out of the prom sequence from *Carrie*. It was something that I talked about with Lindsay Duncan. We went to great pains to catch this closeup when her face is splattered with that blood and you have the blue behind. Now, that blue behind is not the sky. The wider shots were done on location, but the closeups of her screaming were actually done in the studio six weeks later because I couldn't get the right quality of blue behind her. I wanted this very pale, hazy blue. I wanted her skin to be whiter than it was on location. I wanted the blood to be more red. And she's wearing black. I remember saying at the time, "This is Sissy Spacek, and the bucket of blood has fallen on her," which is still one of the most beautiful images in the whole of contemporary cinema. It's the Mona Lisa of the horror film.

In *The Reflecting Skin*, you use a lot of crane shots. There's this very fluid style. Those crane shots add a tremendous emotional weight to some scenes.

They also make the epic quality of the film punch home. It becomes a much bigger thing, especially shooting in the outskirts of Idaho like we were. That crane had to be ordered three months ahead of time so I had to be very specific when I needed it. All those crane shots were done in one day, every one. The biggest one is the one that opens the film, with Seth appearing in the distance. We got the frog in, with Seth in the background. We made four attempts to get that right. It's quite a complex shot. You've got a child, not a trained actor who can hit his marks. If you look very carefully at the film, you'll see the trail lines going through the wheat of the three previous takes. So we did the opening shot of the film, and then we said "Okay, let's get him running out of the house!" So we drove all the way over with the crane, and got him running out of the house after he sees Dolphin make love to Cameron [Viggo Mortenson]. All day was like that, totally crazy.

Did you have doubts about any aspect of the film as you were making it?

Every day. But you do that with everything. The thing that intrigues me about creating anything is not only is it part of your journey, but it's a record of how you were working at that time. I'm not one of these people—in terms of the books and stage plays—who endlessly rewrites every time a new edition comes out. I think part of the journey is to see what I did then. There were certain things that I did wrong on *The Reflecting Skin*. But then you think that if I actually changed them, it would be a different film. I was doing this very hallucinogenic, dreamlike thing, seen through the eyes of a child, so my thinking then was that everything had to be bigger, brighter, louder. The wheat is as golden as a childhood memory of what that wheat looked like. The sky is bluer than it could ever be. The mother [Sheila Moore] is more of a caricature than she could ever be. The interior designs are almost operatic, because it's how a child perceives it. That ricochets through the performances. My belief was that having set off this landscape, getting the set direction, getting the costumes, I couldn't then have everyone act like they were in a Ken Loach film, because that would have been even more jarring. Once you've made the decision that all the knobs are going to be turned up, then performances have to be turned up as well. I think it's quite a cinematic ride. It's stylized to the level of Restoration comedy, in a way. Of course, there were doubts every day; there always will be. But you can't think about them too much, otherwise you'll go mad.

When I watch *The Reflecting Skin*, it seems like it's a film out of time and out of place. I mean, it's supposed to be the 1950s, but there's something not 1950s about it.

It's never said in the film when or where. It never occurred to me to specify it until we had to do press releases.

Was that part of the dream aspect?

It's part of that dream eclecticism that the film has. I wanted to say that it was set on Mars for the advertising. I wanted to say it was like *The Martian Chronicles*. I remember saying when we had the first meeting with the publicity people, "No, I want to say it's the first Martian colony and they want to recreate America on Mars." We were playing around with lots of ideas like that. When the child is screaming at the end, there was a moment where I was going to cut to him screaming at Earth in the sky, and you suddenly realize that you're not on Earth, but on another planet, and you'd see not the setting sun, but the planet Earth in the background.

It seems to me, you didn't want to go into character motivation at all.

No, not with *The Reflecting Skin* or *The Passion of Darkly Noon.*

It's part of the anti-naturalism?

Well, it's just not what the films are about. You really couldn't do that with those scripts. It would become redundant. Both films are archetypal fables, especially *Darkly Noon*. To read too much character motivation into them is irrelevant. I mean *Darkly Noon* is basically a fairy tale for grownups. The symbolism is very basic, at least, a mixture of the basic (blood on bible, crucifix poses) and the more obscure (barbed wire bird, silver shoe). As a result, the character motivation is pretty basic. It's all part of the language of the piece.

How did the script for *The Passion of Darkly Noon* come about?

On the way out to do the landscape work for *The Reflecting Skin*, we had to take a long ride in a mini-bus, about a two-hour trip every morning. We went past a religious commune, a small thing that was partitioned off with barbed wire. I started to make up this story, "Well, perhaps there's a guy who . . ." It was like a modern fairy tale to entertain the kids. By the end of shooting *The Reflecting Skin*, I had the basics of *The Passion of Darkly Noon*. I was already talking to Viggo about that being the next film.

How did the three actors, Ashley Judd, Brendan Fraser, and Viggo Mortensen get involved?

Viggo had been there from the beginning. I sent the script to Brendan. He liked it—and was an admirer of *The Reflecting Skin*—so I was thrilled to have him on board. Ashley auditioned for the part, and she was just, well, incredible. She had this elusive, strange ethereal quality. I knew she was just absolutely right.

As you say, the film plays with the idea of fairy tale. Ideas such as the house in the woods, the golden princess, the dark stranger, the temptation of the innocent. How specifically did you want to work with such elements and structures?

You can go through the whole of *The Passion of Darkly Noon* and pick out the quotations from horror films and the quotations from fairy tales. It's all the way through the film. The house in the woods, "Rumpelstiltskin," "Snow White," "Beauty and the Beast," *Halloween, Friday the 13th, Psycho, Carrie*.

There's a real erotic quality to several scenes involving physical pain, especially the scene where Darkly [Brendan Fraser] wraps his body in barbed wire.

Yes, we had fun doing that. It runs all the way through. In terms of the fairy-tale aspect, Darkly has always been told that sex is wrong and he should be punished. When he meets Callie [Ashley Judd], he begins to subvert sexual passion with pain. In the sequence at the end, the attack on the house (or the "Wrath of God finale" as the critics describe it), Darkly attacks the house as if he's making love. It becomes a very sensual, dreamlike, almost erotic attack, in much the same way that Hitchcock said he shot his love scenes like they were murders and he shot his murders like they were love scenes. By the end of the film, violence has become sex, and sex has become violence. But one can only talk about that in terms of a fable.

There's also a strong tension as the film goes along, an atmosphere of dread.

There's a real foreboding in the film, and that's something we talked about right from the beginning. I kept making references to *Carrie*, the structure of which has always fascinated me. A lot of people misunderstood *Darkly Noon* when they said, "We can see the end coming." The point of the film is *knowing* that something terrible is going to happen. That's why I have the days count down to this nightmare at the end. The three lead performances, which I'm really pleased with, also contribute to that. It's very difficult to get the tone right on a film which is such a stylized piece. Obviously, Viggo had a headstart because he'd done *The Reflecting Skin*. But both Brendan and Ashley have this incredible ability to play it for real. Yet they're doing these strange, hallucinogenic, dream-time performances that allow you to be engaged with what they're saying, and be interested in what's going on, while sustaining the fairytale, fable quality.

The image of the giant shoe is very compelling.

If I had one moment where all my work has been heading, it's the silver shoe in *Darkly Noon*. It's about image, music, magic realism, symbolism, more tongue-in-cheeky than tongue-in-cheek. You don't know how to react to it. It's the quintessential moment. Once I'd done that sequence, I felt like I could move on to something else in my next film. I don't think I could ever do a sequence like the floating silver shoe again. And the thing's provoked such reaction! I remember an audience in Germany who were really insistent that I tell them its meaning. They were quite angry that I couldn't explain it. It happened in Japan, too.

I thought the scene with Quincy [Lou Meyers] was sort of interesting because it's very elaborate. It's a very long take involving a lot of choreography.

All on Steadicam. It was a day's work to do that. It's another example of where something else is beginning to happen, in terms of the way I'm directing and my work with actors. The actors play around a bit more in that scene.

You've described the last sequence of the film as *Apocalypse Now* meets *Beauty and the Beast*.

[Laughs] I've described it in lots of ways. It was *Psycho* meets *Aladdin* at one point.

When you were shooting the film, and the complex final sequence, did you have a sense that it would be this elaborate in its final shape?

Yes, right from the beginning. In fact, the end sequence was meticulously storyboarded. It had to be. Every time something exploded, it cost me fifty pounds. Every time you hit a wall and a spark happened, it had to be budgeted for because I was under a two-million-pound budget. Then we played around with it in the editing. I worked out the basic structure. We shot everything from three cameras, so we had a variety of shots to play with. It took as long to do that final section as it took to do the rest of the film put together.

I think what's noticeable about *Darkly Noon* in relation to *The Reflecting Skin* is how much more elaborate the editing patterns are. Throughout the film, as Darkly's madness intensifies, the editing patterns become more radical and experimental.

Well, the film breaks up.

I was thinking of that scene between Darkly and Clay that had radically elliptical editing patterns. The "pain in my heart" scene.

Oh, where the jump cuts are? I was lucky to get away with that. A lot of financiers wanted that scene cut because they thought it was going to be too hard to understand.

Really? It's one of the key scenes in the film.

Well, it is. The film doesn't get interesting to me until Darkly starts to go mad, with those jump cuts and those scenes where he suddenly disappears from the shot, or the way the soundtrack and music start to get really bizarre. All of that is what the film is about. I'm so proud of the last fifty minutes of *Darkly Noon*. Lots of things are happening that I haven't seen done before.

You have a lot of experiments with sound and overlapping dialogue in the film. Formally, it's a more complex film than *The Reflecting Skin*.

Yes, I agree. It's more confident than *The Reflecting Skin*. There's a lot of experimentation in terms of the editing, the way music is used, the way songs are used, the acting style. The first third of the film is all done on tripod and tracking shots, and as he goes mad, you have a transition through Steadicam. The last third of the film is all hand-held. But, as I said, people don't review films in terms of film, they review films purely in terms of story.

The scene where Darkly prepares himself with red paint seems almost to be about the color red?

Well, the whole film is a battle between red and silver.

And that scene is intercut with that rough love-making scene between Callie and Clay. It's a fairly ambitious sequence.

It lasts something like twenty minutes, from beginning to end. There's something like 800 cuts.

Some of your music choices are also interesting, like the percussive tracks, and you collaborated on the two songs. How closely did you work with Nick Bicât?

Very closely. Nick had worked with me on *The Reflecting Skin*.

Did he know what you wanted?

We'd done a lot of the music before I started filming, so I established that I wanted basically three main themes. The opening echo theme was going to run through the film. Then I wanted one other thing, which was going to be the silver shoe theme, and becomes the love theme for the piece. Then I wanted the percussion to gradually take over the film, so that by the last two reels, the attack on the house becomes like a percussive ballet. All of those were established. And I took a lot of the music out there with me. The actors were acting to the music.

Do you write music?

No, but I used to be in a band. Everyone at art school was in a band. So I had an idea of how I wanted it to work.

There are some images that seem to specifically echo *The Reflecting Skin*. I was thinking of Callie's blood-splattered face echoing Lindsay Duncan's face and dress.

Yes, and the bandaged hand.

Did you achieve what you wanted to achieve with *Darkly Noon*?

Yes. In fact, it's more what I wanted than *The Reflecting Skin*. There are fewer scenes in *Darkly Noon* that I would go back and change.

I think it is quite a leap, actually.

And it's widescreen. I mean it *really* uses widescreen. It's not widescreen like most films with the actors in the middle and blank spaces on either end. That's another thing that freaked people out about distributing the film. There are big problems in going through to video because there are whole scenes where you just see trees. I've put Brendan and Ashley on either side, and you can't see them in a full-screen video. The saddest thing about *Darkly Noon* is that, because it came and went from the cinema so quickly, few people have experienced the film as it should be seen. The only experience that you can have with *Darkly Noon* that makes sense is to see it on the big screen with the sound turned up very, very loud.

What current films excite you?

Anything that uses the language of film. Subject matter is irrelevant. It's just a shame that most films are, well, just filmed novels, worse, filmed radio plays. I leave the cinema and I can't remember one *image* from them. Not one. There's no love of cinema. No desire to express a vision through light, color, camera movement, editing, music. There's no desire to dare. To be remarkable. I want to go to the cinema and see remarkable things.

BENJAMIN ROSS

Benjamin Ross is a young British filmmaker who directed one of the most imaginative films of the 1990s, *The Young Poisoner's Handbook*. The film is brash and vibrant and an example of in-your-face filmmaking. Relentless in its driving narrative rhythm, it tells the tale of real-life criminal Graham Young, who not only poisoned members of his family, his colleagues at work and girlfriends, but kept a journal of his crimes in an almost clinically scientific way, monitoring the poison's physical effects and ultimate gruesome results. One of the strongest aspects of Ross's film is the almost tactile way in which it captures the physical effects of the various poisons. It is one of the most energetic debuts of the decade and clearly announces the arrival of a major filmmaker. The film has a clever, witty soundtrack of songs from the early 1970s, a carefully worked out color scheme and art direction that takes its clear inspiration from pop art and key films of the period, such as Kubrick's *A Clockwork Orange*. It also contains a remarkably sympathetic portrait in the leading role by the hugely talented Hugh O'Conor, as well as a rigorously constructed first-person, subjective presentation. The camera is very much at the center of the film's presentation, and the visual distortions and swooping camera moves all seem to be emotionally integral to its point of view. They never draw attention to themselves in the kind of showy, excessive way one finds in such recent films as *Elizabeth*. Every element of the careful design seems emotionally necessary to the film's subject, and its attempt at getting inside the main character's head.

Ross's struggle to get *Poisoner* financed and made without compromise is an example of the tenacity needed in the current climate of filmmaking to get that all-important first feature made. The interview is revealing in the way Ross describes in detail his process of making the film, and how prepared he was on virtually every aspect of its look and design. Yet shooting it was still a remarkably unsettling and scary proposition for the young director. As he states in the interview, he "never anticipated that it would be so hard" to make a feature film. After the film was finished, the process of promoting it at festivals and trying to get people interested in seeing it consumed another two years of Ross's life. It seems that for many young filmmakers, making their first film is only the beginning of what can often turn into a difficult and frustrating period of struggle.

When we spoke, Ross was about to go into production on a film about eighteenth-century gangsters in London. It eventually fell apart, although there is still optimism that it will someday get made. Finally, after not being on a set for four years, Ross was hired by HBO to make *RKO 281*, one of the most talked about scenarios of the decade, which describes the making of *Citizen Kane* and which several other directors have tackled without success. John Malkovich stars as Herman Mankiewicz and Melanie Griffith as Marion Davies.

One of the realities of the film industry is that it is constantly in crisis. There are no guaranteed formulas, and if one truly wants to make personal films, the road is incredibly difficult and fraught with innumerable obstacles. Ross is such a talented director that I am sure he will be making films for many years to come, and they will undoubtedly be imaginative, rigorous, and hugely entertaining. I spoke with Benjamin Ross in London.

Where did you grow up?

I have a middle-class, Jewish background, suburban North London.
My dad's a lawyer. My mum was a teacher of French and a librarian.
A nice family.

When did you first get interested in films?

I was watching and thinking critically about film from a very young
age.

You were a movie fanatic?

Yes. I think I was. More then than now; the films were better.

Can you talk about how you made the leap to making films?

I never seriously considered doing anything else. I was making short
Super-8 films from a young age. My aunt got me a Super-8 camera
for my bar mitzvah, and I sat and watched it for a year or two, scared
to touch it. But by the time I was fifteen or so, me and some friends
were shooting quite regularly, and I compiled quite a lot of crappy,
unwatchable Super-8 footage before I ever seriously considered doing anything with it.

Did you go to university?

I had wanted to go to film school. I wrote to The National Film
School at the time, and they told me to come back in ten years. There
was no way that my parents were going to pay for me to go to a film

school. So I went to Oxford to study English, where I was told there would be all sorts of film activities I could get involved with, and that I wouldn't have to abandon my ambition. I was quite upset about it, actually. In the end, it was fine, I got to read for three years.

I had originally wanted to go straight to film school but I went on a little diversion first. My aunt, who had given me this Super-8 camera, worked in the film business in New York, selling advertising for Screen International and other magazines. She had a lot of film contacts, and she introduced me to some low-budget outfits in New York. I started to get work on holidays when I was a student at Oxford. I went to work for Troma, who did *The Toxic Avenger*. So I started to get the hands-on experience of low-budget filmmaking. It wasn't for long stretches but for summer holidays.

What sort of cultural and aesthetic influences did you have growing up?

I was always a classicist. I liked reading Dickens, Conrad, Dostoevsky, and Tolstoy. They were my favorite writers. I like classically structured works.

Any painterly influences?

Since I've started making films, I've started taking an active critical interest in the visual arts, which I wasn't very aware of when I was growing up. Then I was just interested in the cinema and books. *Taxi Driver* was a key film for me when I was thirteen. Scorsese and Kubrick were big for me as a teenager. But I'd been into movies for a long time before the mid-seventies, movies that kids would be interested in, horror movies, Tarzan movies, Western movies, Robin Hood movies. But around 1976, 1977, movies started to get very good. *Taxi Driver* and *One Flew Over the Cuckoo's Nest*. I was reading that sort of literature at the time: Kesey, Tom Wolfe, and Kerouac.

How old were you when you discovered Stanley Kubrick?

Young. I used to read the film guide books. I used to read about the films before I got a chance to see them, and the books would rate them. So I knew about the films before I'd seen them, and then they'd be shown on TV. I must've seen Kubrick and Lindsay Anderson, and all that stuff, around the same time I saw things like *Cuckoo's Nest* and *Taxi Driver*. These films were coming out in the cinema around the same time I was catching up on the really good cinema of the late sixties and early seventies. For me, it was an explosion of great movies that were contemporaneous with my life. Altman, Lina Wertmüller, I used to go see everything, and because we were in North London, I was near The Everyman, and I went to The National Film Theater. There was also the old Scala theater.

Did you decide to go to Columbia University to study film because of your connections to New York?

Probably, and because I loved the city. I loved it from movies, and I loved it from living and working there. I was willing to do anything to get to America, because I was convinced—as I still am a bit—that that's where you have to be, if not for real, at least imaginatively.

What was your experience at film school like?

It was great because it got me into making films competitively and publicly. I'd been doodling up until then, and all of a sudden, it became a serious business, with a lot of pressure and competition. I had good teachers. I met Kusturica, who I found inspirational. He taught me a lot of what I needed to find out as a filmmaker. Whatever you think of his films, Kusturica has this fantastic sense of himself as a director, what it means to be a filmmaker in the old sense. I find that very nice. It conforms to what I always wanted from film; something heroic. Ralph Rosenblum was also inspirational for me. It was a lovely time for me.

I read that your student film didn't quite work out.

[Laughs] Mine was pretty bad. I have no hesitation in admitting that, though it was a very good learning experience. I used actors who were not good. All the things that can go wrong with a production, over which you have no control because you have no money, went wrong. I was also wildly overambitious. It was set during the Holocaust in 1940s Poland. It was potentially a good story, but my eyes were bigger than my stomach.

You decided to come back to London after film school?

I had to because my visa had run out, and I was writing a script which, as it turned out, was the first draft of what became *Young Poisoner's Handbook*. It was about growing up in North London. There wasn't much point in being in New York writing that. I had gone to New York thinking that somehow I had to make myself American because all my influences were American. In fact, when I got there, I found myself thinking about home and who I was. The experience of being dislocated somehow made me realize what I had to write about, which was what I knew. What I learned from that disastrous student film is that you have to make films about what you know, at least on some basic level.

How did *My Little Eye* **come about?**

I came to England pursuing the draft that later became *Poisoner*, and there was a Channel Four/British Screen scheme to make short films, the *Short and Curlies*. So I got this short film to make with Channel Four, and they introduced me to Sam Taylor, who was an up-and-coming producer at the time, and we started to work together on that. In fact, we've worked together since on *Poisoner*.

It feels very personal, the short film.

Yes, it was. It was a leap from what I'd done at film school. I think it's successful. It was the first thing where I thought I expressed myself on film, where I felt I knew what it was to direct a picture.

It's a good discipline to make a short film that realizes its ambitions. I think it's hard to do.

It's very hard. And I think they can be very gimmicky too, these short films that end with a twist.

You learned how to tell a story, how to direct actors, how to work with a crew, to a certain extent.

Yes. It was a very hard week when we were filming it. It felt terrible, and I thought it was a disaster while I was doing it. That was another thing I learned. You don't have a clue what's happening; you don't know, because it's all going so fast. The simple pressures of filmmaking force you to respond because you've got so many decisions to get through. You're responsible for your scheduling and for your shot plan. You are essentially responding on a very instinctive level all the time. The trick is to trust that.

Did you feel overwhelmed by the shoot?

Yes. It was terrible! It always is. I didn't really start to enjoy it until half way into *Poisoner*, when I realized, oh, I can really do this. It's been three years since I've been on set because it's taken me a long time to get this last project together. I've been writing, trying to raise money, storyboarding the new film, editing and promoting the last one. I've had a lot of time to think about what it is to direct a picture. It's certainly an absurd way to move through life. But it's better than a job.

You're also so vulnerable as a filmmaker. If you're trying to make good pictures, it's practically impossible. In statistical terms, it seems to me that a good film is a very hard thing to come by. There are many elements that go into making a film, and it's a hugely complex, multifarious beast. Any film undergoes a series of complex metamorphoses from one form to another, and the real skill is in being able to keep it coherent and true to itself, to protect its character through those different transformations. You have to be able to see the essence of something and then fight for it. It's a very strange job, and I'm sure it's different for everybody who does it.

Let's talk about *The Young Poisoner's Handbook*. Where did the idea for the film come from?

I had known about Graham Young for a while because his story had taken place very close to where I lived as a kid. We lived just off the

North Circular. He was a sort of minor celebrity. He was pretty notorious because he was only fourteen when he was sent to prison. I knew about him from 1972, which was the second time he'd been released and had re-offended. I remember reading the newspaper and seeing the famous picture he'd taken of himself. He was all over the press at the time. The big scandal was that he'd been released by the Home Office and sent to a place where he could get his hands on his favorite poison. All these quite farcical elements made it an issue of national importance.

It also turned out that I knew people who'd known him. There's a family connection because my mum went to interview him in prison. She had worked for my dad's firm, and Graham Young got in touch with my dad's firm, looking for legal representation from inside prison. Someone who'd been his cellmate had been released and was selling paintings he claimed were by Graham Young. Graham had got into painting portraits of himself as Hitler and all sorts of weird things at this stage. He claimed that these paintings weren't his and this guy was making money falsely off his name. Graham wanted to sue him and was looking for a lawyer.

What was it about the story that drew you to it?

Years later, when I'd been in America for a couple of years, and I'd done this failed student project, I was thinking I have to go into myself and look at the familiar, and try to find a way to turn that thing into dramatically entertaining or interesting material. The idea of Graham just came out as a way of doing that. But it was an obscure biography for me. It had nothing to do with my life. It was a platform, a way to explore cinematically things that I knew and cared about, an attitude towards a certain type of life, lower-middle-class life, really.

What themes did you want to explore?

Well, whatever's in the picture. [Laughs] To be honest, I never look at subject matter and say, "Oh, that interests me because of its theme." It's a purely instinctive thing for me, more like, "Where do I want to put myself for what's likely to be the next two, three, possibly four years of my life?" That's how long it takes me to make a picture. I realize that now. I write solely for myself and then get another writer on board. It's a long haul. The themes emerge from the process of debating and living with the characters and their world. I would never go into a project with an overbearing idea of what it was that I wanted to say. It's something personal that I felt instinctively visually.

You said you worked on the script with another writer?

I wrote the first draft on my own, and then I met a writer called Jeff Rawle, who is also an actor. He was researching the same story around the same time as I'd written my first draft. Graham had recently died—he'd killed himself in prison—so he'd been in the news again in 1990. I'd started writing it a few weeks before he killed himself, quite by coincidence. Jeff and I wrote the subsequent drafts together, and the thing expanded over a couple of years. We were given money by British Screen to support ourselves. At the same time, this was when I had the short film from Channel Four, which enabled me to go out and promote myself a bit.

How was *Poisoner* ultimately financed?

It was complicated. Sam Taylor produced it and put together a three-way, European co-production between England, a French co-producer, and a German producer. Then we applied to Eurimages. Because of the German money, we were able to apply for German public funds through our German co-producer. So, we had Bavarian national money.

How prepared were you when you began shooting the film?

Very. I knew everything.

Did you storyboard?

Yes, I did.

Was your script really detailed?

Yes, in my mind it was, at any rate. I try to know everything and then improvise. Then it all changes and you have to try to be open to that. That's the challenge, I suppose.

Some people are more open to improvisation.

I like to keep things terribly technical. I'm very happy if my DP says, "A little to the right. A little faster." Very simple things. You know, "That sort of frame, please." And if that's all I'm talking about on a given day, "Can we have a 32-millimeter lens here?" I'm very happy if I can keep it to things like that. Everything else comes on its own. You don't want to sit around and talk about stuff too much.

Did the film change a lot from what you had written? Did you shift scenes around a lot?

All the time. And of course, shots. It's a huge mosaic, and the meaning of the thing changes every time you take one piece out or move it around.

Was there stuff you shot that didn't make it into the film?

A lot. Twenty-three scenes, shot and cut, and some mixed. Then we were selected for Sundance in 1995, and it was the first public screening of the film at 106 minutes. I sat and watched it with a couple of audiences. It was very popular. I realized that I didn't like the cut. I hadn't been able to see that until I'd seen it with an audience. I realized I needed to be very strict and brutal with myself about when it lagged and when it didn't. I begged the sales company who worked for the co-producers to give me the money to go back into the negative and into the mix. It wasn't fine-cut for me, it wasn't fine-mixed. It was all temporary, and I hadn't realized it. Luckily, we came up with £50,000 and I was able to go back and cut it down to ninety-nine minutes. We remixed because there were things that I didn't like about it. I hadn't been able to tell until I felt it with an audience. Your final film has to be for them. It has to deliver. That's what I want for my films: I want to be clear.

What if the audience steers you wrong?

Of course, you have to judge it. The film needs the weight, the ballast, the clean emotional response, and after three or four audiences, you get a sense. They're all different. Some of them are wildly different. We went to Park City and showed it to a group of Mormons, as opposed to the sophisticated Hollywood crowd who was watching it at Sundance, and their response was totally different. Actually, it was much warmer. Who can explain these things? I watched the film with Kusturica in Hamburg with a very dry, German audience that didn't laugh once. I turned to him and said, "Oh, God. They're not laughing." He said, "The audience is shit. Never mind audience. Film is good." You have to believe in the film. It got to the point where, at ninety-nine minutes, I believed that it was a living, breathing pitbull of a film that could survive, and I still think so.

Did the film stick pretty closely to the facts?

No, we took big liberties with everything. It was very much dramatized. I used the facts as a springboard.

How did you decide on Hugh O'Conor for the lead?

The obvious thing to do was to cast a very evil-looking boy. That seemed to me totally wrong. What distinguishes the film is it's a vision of evil from the inside, how the world looks to a skewed and gifted personality. You can delve into a moral and metaphysical world to ask what human life means to him. I think this story is Graham's autobiography, his notebook about himself, in which he sees himself as an angel, an innocent. He's interested in purity. That's where the humor is in the story, as well as the pathos. It comes from his subjective perspective. Casting Hugh made all that tacit. Suddenly, you put the film in a fairy-tale mold that it wouldn't have had if he were more like the real Graham. They sold the film as a kind of knowing piece of black comedy, but that's not what it is, at least not to my mind. I think Hugh's performance and the way he looks elevates it to a form of poetry. He has a beautiful, medieval face. It's like Peter Lorre's face, an exquisite face.

You wanted someone that the audience could connect with?

I wanted an experience totally from the inside, that gave the viewer emotional and visual empathy with the character and his world, with no moral distance. That's what I think cinema can do very well. The really good filmmaker is going to engage you on the subconscious level so you can empathize. You find yourself in situations where you identify with a character or a feeling you never thought possible. All of a sudden, there you are, inhabiting a total other universe. Film can do that because of the clever manipulation of space, color, and time. That's partly what we wanted to do with Graham. To render an emotion or an experience from the inside is more truthful than to render it from the outside. That was the basic principle. The question of where to put the camera in a scene is answered by who the scene is about, and what he or she is feeling.

Did Hugh understand what you were after?

Totally, without even really needing to talk about it. He's very literate and cine-literate. Rare for a twenty-two year-old, certainly. He's an unusually intelligent person. We were both film enthusiasts on a number of levels.

How did you work together on the characterization?

I tend to think of actions for the character, but I won't necessarily tell the actor what they are. I try to reduce the scene to a series of actions, or a singular action, to trace the focus of his or her actions. So, I have verbs in red ink, in case the actor loses focus. It's something that we learned in film school studying the Stanislavsky basics, which is to reduce acting to a single point of focus based on a verb, rather than an adjective or a noun.

Did you work differently with Hugh than, say, Antony Sher, who has much more training?

Yes! They demand totally different things from you. Sher was completely different, and he was interested in the idea of working with someone like me who has no notion of the theater. I like Sher; I've seen him on stage, and I thought he was great in *Richard III*. But when we met and talked for the first time, I admitted to him that I knew little about the theater and I only understood film acting in terms of actions. I think he was very interested in that because it's very precise. He wanted to experiment and do something different. I found his performance to be very controlled.

You didn't have to give him very much?

Almost nothing, once we'd discussed the character and the pitch and seriousness of his character. It was very important to me that there was something sympathetic about his character. That increases the complexity of the piece because he's the first character who could be Graham's salvation, who could love him and bring some depth to his life. Of course, he gets it totally wrong. It's the asshole prefect who runs the place, the dictatorial autocratic one, who gets it right. It's like Polonius having all the wise sentiments in *Hamlet*.

Was there a lot of rehearsal?

No, none. We didn't have time or money for it. In fact, the first time Sher and Hugh saw each other was when they met on camera for the first time, as characters, which was useful and fun. Either you spend three weeks in full rehearsal or you just do it by the seat of your pants and throw yourself into the deep end, because you can get something very immediate in those circumstances. That's why I plan so well, because when you've got so much that is unplanned, you have to be ready with a very intricate safety net to catch these moments.

Describe the shooting. How long did it take?

We had forty-three days, splitting between shooting in London and Munich because of this German public money, which we had to spend over there. We wound up having to construct the interior of Graham's house in a big hangar over there with a corrugated iron roof that resounded every time it rained. There was no air conditioning and it was 120 degrees. We worked under these circumstances for three or four weeks. We had a very tight schedule and it was quite hard switching to German, because we had a largely German crew.

Was the shooting difficult?

For me, it's always difficult. Shooting is difficult, but it was more difficult in Germany because of the language difference and because the crew really weren't up to speed. It was a cultural chasm, really. We came from England, making an English film with English crew members. We were a very tight unit after five weeks of shooting in England, and then we got transplanted. But we got through it okay.

What about the editing? Did that give you any trouble?

No. I love it. That's the part I can enjoy, because you've got your material and then you're really making the picture. You can make decisions and, if it's not right, you can undo it and try something else. But it's not like that on the set. You've got to get it right.

What was the budget on *Young Poisoner*?

£1.4 million. I insisted on a proper shooting schedule because I knew that what we needed was complex, and would involve cranes and difficult camera moves. I knew that was essential to the feel of the film and that it wouldn't work as a grabby five-week shoot. It needed that kind of attention to design. It was important that Graham's interior universe be properly rendered.

I think that one of the key things in the film is the music and sound. Had you chosen all the source music in advance?

I had planned music for the film, including where the cues were, because I like to know where the music is, even if I don't know specifically what the music is. I like to be aware of it while I'm shooting. I had a wish-list which changed according to the rights and the money situation. It was touch-and-go, but we managed to get a deal with Durham records, a sub-label of Polygram. They gave us a bunch of their songs relatively cheaply. It's all that crap of the mind, that wall-to-wall shit that goes on the radio that people listen to all the time. I wanted it to be insistent and grating and to really bother you.

Can you talk about your working methods with the cinematographer and production designer?

My cinematographer I met when I was at film school. His name is Hubert Taczanowski. He was trained at the Lodz Film School in Poland, the best place in Europe for training cinematographers. We met in 1988 and became friends immediately. I think he was happy to find another European. We both felt quite happy but stranded and we liked all the same films. I love Wajda's films from the 1950s, and I'm very interested in Poland and World War II anyway. My family's half Polish, and I've always felt an affinity for things Slavic.

Were those camera moves written into the script?

Yes, I drew them all. They were totally specific.

Did the cinematographer contribute ideas?

He lights and creates feeling. Actually, he operates and has his own conception of visual grammar. That's his business, and sometimes other directors I know want more input. I feel I have to control the frame; it's absolutely my job. I read that Welles said that's the whole art of film directing: You take the camera and whip it through your shoot or throw it across the set. Don't respect it; it's just a piece of dirty metal. Don't be intimidated by the thing. It's a fight and you need to quash the camera. So, I wrestle for control of it. I like it to accommodate me. Then, once that's settled, everything else falls into place.

And the production design?

To the frame. Yes, I was very much in it. It's very solipsistic. *My Little Eye* was very different. I went through all sorts of ideas. We had five days to shoot. I didn't get half the shots I wanted, but somehow the film that came out was still true. Who can explain? The funny thing is that people look at that and think, oh, God, is it only ten minutes! It somehow convinces people because of its simplicity.

Is it the same thing with the editing?

Well, I like to choose every cut. Anne Sopel, the editor of *Poisoner*, handles the film, but yes, for me it's all the same thing. The editing is the most fun. That's the bit I wouldn't miss. I would gladly avoid shooting if I could. Some people really love planning, and dreaming of the shots and designing. I used to like it, but I'm finding it more and more tense and scary.

It's interesting that you said that you wanted the film to be a representation of Graham's mind and the world inside him. Would we really associate this almost pop-arty world with this fellow? He probably comes from a very drab part of London.

Sure, but he was very creative and very alive, at least the way I conceived of him. He was very innocent, an artist or a sorcerer's apprentice, something romantic. That's very important to me; I didn't want it to be a drab vision. I wanted it to be an electric vision of a drab world transformed by creativity. People want to see it as a grim kitchen-sink story or a black comedy, but it wasn't any of those things. There was also a whole other element to the script at one point, revolving around Graham's Nazi sympathies, which he had in real life. I wanted them much more pronounced in the script. I wanted Graham to take Sue to a screening of a documentary about Nazism. I remember Jeff arguing vehemently that this was wrong, that I was imposing my interest on the character. We had to constantly remind ourselves of the limits of Graham's cultural world and his available language. This was a guy who had nothing except what his intellectual curiosity brought to him. For somebody like that, creating something in a test tube is like filmmaking. It's the equivalent of any tactile physical thing. It's sexual, it's fetishistic and creative. It's everything for him, his whole medium for relating to life and dealing with people in the world, for understanding power relationships, and loving and hating people. I felt Graham was a naif who only related to the world through this craft, and that if we gave him too many cultural options, if the world around him was too resonant, it would give him a way out. That's where the pop stuff comes from. Out of this detritus, something almost beautiful but deadly and sad emerges.

The film starts and the first thing you hear is a reference to *A Clockwork Orange*.

Why hide it? I just thought, get it out of the way. And people were very put off. I look at the Internet now and they say, "Oh well, it's a rip-off of *A Clockwork Orange*." Actually, the film stands quite well on its own. I just thought, we're in the third or fourth generation of filmmakers now and they've been doing this in other arts for a long time. John Coltrane can start with "My Favorite Things," here's the first verse, now we're off on our own. I think filmmakers can do the same. I want my films consciously to have a dialogue with other films.

But why *A Clockwork Orange*?

Because there were a lot of similarities in the story anyway. Graham was like Alex. His journey seemed symbolic, like Alex's. It was taking place at the same time as Alex's story, in 1971-72. Graham was released into *A Clockwork Orange* land. He probably went to see it, and I personally love *A Clockwork Orange*.

The film seems very apocalyptic.

Yes, it was integral to Graham's story that his ambitions be apocalyptic. It wasn't enough that his search for the ultimate poison be an interior search; it also had to be metaphysical. He should be looking for something that's alchemical, a reflection of himself and somehow an abstraction of his personality. And it should mean something global and apocalyptic to him. This is an artist whose ambitions are high.

You said in an interview that Graham is a character full of love.

I think it's blocked love, misplaced energy, fetishized. It's sex too, an unhealthy, repressed sex drive.

Do you think we understand why he does what he does?

No, because I don't know why. I'm interested in the why, but as a filmmaker, you sometimes have to put that aside. You have to be more interested in the how, in how the world feels from that perspective, the actual feel of what the world is like inside that mind. That to me, on some level, is more truthful.

Do you think Graham's an amoral character?

He's not able to feel any love or empathy for another human being. He's totally cut off from human warmth. If he has feeling, it's for things and processes, colors and objects. It seemed interesting to explore the question of empathy from the point of view of somebody who has none. I don't know if it's helpful to call that moral or amoral. It's a slightly different conception.

What is interesting about him dramatically is that he is an extreme version of a very common human problem, which is the ease with which we lose touch with our feelings and how it can be supplanted by something else, in Graham's case by a substance. It could also be a philosophy or a political ideology. There are many ways people lose sight of one another's humanity. It is a key human problem and Graham is a farcical version of it taken to an extreme.

Do you think Graham's voice-over is a reliable narrative device?

No. It's deliberately ironic, and facetious at times. It's also a very useful bit of narrative thread.

Do you think that audiences should sympathize with this character?

I think they shouldn't be allowed to feel any other way, if the filmmaking is strong enough. I wanted to involve the audience in his experience, to place them inside the experience, however awful what he was doing became.

Did you struggle with the tone of the film?

It was a delicate balance between apparently discordant elements. It may have been instinctive, like a musical thing. Like certain types of music played at the top and bottom end of the scale, like Schoenberg rather than Bach, it's discordant and ugly. I was interested in opposing extreme thoughts and extreme horror, and seeing what you got.

The latter part of the film seems to have more first-person narrative devices, like POV shots and slow motion shots. Why was that?

It wasn't a conscious thing. I can see how the point of view might have needed to be stronger there. There are key moments of pathos in the latter half of the story, like when he gets ejected from his sister's house at Christmas and his general isolation at work, the sense that he was an apparently reconstructed person trying to find a way back in and he had a detachment from everyday life. How do you feel if you're that sort of person, sitting in a pub watching people drinking and playing darts? What do they look like to you? How far away do they seem? It seems to me that they feel a long way away, so you shoot them with a telephoto lens from the other side of the room because even though they're close, they're not really close.

Is it really possible to get inside a screen character?

I've always believed you can. I've always thought you should be looking for the balance that you have in dreams, between being a participant and looking at the world as if it were through a clean point-of-view shot, where you're not a part of the universe but simply watching it. If you're talking about camera placement, whose scene is it? Where is the action from? Often in a film, your protagonist is just looking. Certainly in *Apocalypse Now*, you've got a protagonist, Willard, who does practically nothing but look, and in extreme close-ups. If you analyze Martin Sheen's performance, it's just eyes right, eyes left. It's incredible how much that does to signify the presence of a protagonist in a film. As the audience, you suppose you're looking at the film through his eyes. That's what Scorsese does in *Taxi Driver*, and in all his pictures, to encourage identification, a very clever manipulation of camera and space and image, which carries an identification with a character where you're both observing and inhabiting their interior. It's in that balance where the real tension of the film can be located. You're close enough to feel the world from inside his head and you can also see him desperately going wrong, and bumping into things and smashing people. It's the fact that you're just on the edge of it, you're in the dream, but you're looking at him in the dream too.

Can you talk a bit about the final structure and shape of the film?

There were three separate arenas: childhood, institution-workplace, and adulthood. We went through a whole color design before we shot anything. We were looking not only at the period, but at films from the period, the way film stock changed, the way the period photographed itself. We wanted it to be like a progression of English film stock so that it would have a historicity. It goes from the Ealing Studios look of the late 1950s, through to *A Clockwork Orange*, bleached Eastman, of the early seventies.

You obviously had very specific ideas about your aesthetic choices?

Yes, in terms of the look and the feel of the thing, which really goes from innocence. It was a kind of weird innocence-to-experience. It was Graham's sentimental journey, from the sixties to the seventies. Because we were so far removed, and in the nineties, it was a retrospective look. I wanted ways of making that interesting and relating it to the central emotional arc of the story. So what's colorful and rich and buoyant in Ealing becomes something rather grim and hand-held, or more location-based, in the last half of the picture. The music goes through that change as well, from pre-Beatles. We wanted to get on either of side of what everybody likes. Everybody likes the great explosion in the sixties, Dylan, The Stones, The Beatles. We wanted to get the shit, the real dross at either end of that. To me, it was more interesting. Everybody knows the classic rock.

It's also a physical film in the sense that we're very aware of people's bodies. People are throwing up, getting slapped, a lot of physicality in the film. You obviously worked on that.

Again, it comes out of the story. We didn't realize until we were shooting it. And then every day we'd say, "Well, what are we going to do? We're going to hit Hugh with rolled-up magazines. Okay, now we're going to hit you on the right side of the face, now on the left side of the face. Now, we're going to put Hugh naked in the bath. We're going to scrub him till he's raw. We're going to stand him shivering in the garden." Every day, it was another torture for Hugh, basically. When that became apparent, I realized that we were probably doing something right. This is how to get the performance out of him. We were filming his martyrdom without realizing it. Scorsese does that: He makes his metaphysical world very physical. *Raging Bull* is a martyrdom, but you're looking at the flesh and blood and water for real.

Although the film has a relentless pace, it also has moments of intimacy where the narrative slows down.

The problem is to take stuff that will play to anybody, and not be patronizing to your audience, who may have a different attention span or a different range of cultural references. How do you make your work accessible? I really wanted every shot of *Poisoner* to do its job and entertain thoroughly, to reach out and grab you. The question you have to keep asking yourself as a director is whether the shot is interesting? Is it a ballet? Is each shot a piece of choreography, the perfect minute expression, in movement, of what the character is about at that given time? That's a very intense and focused thing to come up with. It has to be about economy and compression. Any big canvas that engages the subconscious immediately has to be fantastically dense. Life honestly lived is constantly in flux, so the great movies are actually symphonies of continual motion. Tarkovsky does that, as does Polanski. Even when the shots are static, they're moving. It'll be still, but then movement will come in within the frame. It won't cut arbitrarily; the cut will mean something.

The film did well, didn't it?

It got critically lauded everywhere and won a lot of prizes. It has enabled me to at least establish my name as a filmmaker. It hasn't made a great deal of money, I'm sorry to say. I wish it had, but I guess that was never really in the cards. It's a pretty flaky film. I didn't personally see any money. I feel that it's a good picture. I hope it'll make sense in thirty or fifty years. I wasn't happy with the way it was marketed in this country. It was sold very badly on the heels of *Shallow Grave*, as a kind of youth-market, black comedy thing, which it really had nothing to do with. It was a much more personal film than that. It wasn't winking knowingly at its audience. It was asking them to come and take part in this horrible, magical world. It's attitude was less cynical than that. In America, it was given a much better poster and a much better airing. People didn't go to it with the same prejudices. More people know about it there. It seems to have some sort of cult life. To keep the poison metaphor going, it's a little ball of mercury tough enough to stay in the bloodstream for quite some time. That's my hope for it.

I thought that the character was sufficiently ingenuous and alienated, and sufficiently attractive in his good qualities, that young people would feel for him and identify with him. I identify with him in a lot of ways and I thought that other people would. He's a very solipsistic character, and I think that people are scared of admitting to the solipsism in themselves. They like visions of youth which are communal, which are about gangs, and community and togetherness, and about groups and tribes. The isolation of what Graham is and does is very scary to people. It's very modern, the loneliness and solipsism. It's not a fashionable portrait of youth. I was very concerned to make it unhip and nerdy.

Do you feel well prepared for the next film because of this experience?

No, not at all! Not in any way. I've been writing something that is totally left-field for me. I decided I would try and do something totally different. I felt that I knew nothing when I started, and we're about to start shooting, and I still feel like I know nothing. [Laughs]

Do you feel a part of the British film industry?

No! I feel totally left out. [Laughs] There are always magazine articles on new British filmmakers. They never ask me: They ask people like Danny Boyle and Antonia Bird. I have to say that I feel I have nothing in common with those people. I mean, I'm very happy for what they do, but Antonia Bird directs other people's scripts. She's a working director. I think it's a very good thing to be. I don't feel confident enough to do that. It's about as much as I can do to direct my own script. I was offered scripts to direct in Hollywood after *Poisoner*, so I had the opportunity to be a Hollywood filmmaker, and I would like to, one day. But if I had gone there now, I would wind up doing crap that I have no control over. I'd have made a million dollars, and that would've been great, and it would've been the last million dollars I would have earned, which would be enough for a lot of people. But I'm much greedier than that. I would much rather have a life making films I want to make, and if I can make a living doing that, what a joy, a privilege. But it's longer between films, and you have to fight. You have to get people to believe in you. Channel Four has been very good to me.

What's the hardest part of being a director?

[Sighs] Well, it changes. Up to the point of making *Poisoner* was a great time for me. After *Poisoner* came out, it all became very hard. My attitude to films and the filmmaking community changed. I spent six months going to festivals with *Poisoner* and meeting other filmmakers. I never want to do that again.

Did you feel jaded?

Certainly I felt jaded by the world of filmmaking and film marketing and independent filmmaking and all that stuff. We were told before we went to Sundance that it would be the place where everything went on and young people came along with their films. I've always been a very cynical person, I never really believed that. It was such a jolt in terms of the hype and artifice of everything. Even when you're at the center of that stuff and it's going well for you, it seemed a disillusioning experience. I can't say I enjoyed it. You go to film festivals and you're there on your own, or with a couple of other people from your crew, and there are other people there from other films, and naturally you're competitive with them. I didn't feel any great fellowship between young filmmakers. I think people are scared and like to hang around and get off to parties and be in photo shoots and all that crap. I didn't see any community. I still don't.

You don't think it's as pure as it's made out to be?

I don't think it's pure at all. I think that what they call independent filmmaking now is really the experimental part of Hollywood. All the kids want to go to Hollywood and make big films. And who can blame them? I would too. You want to make sure you're yourself when you go, though, that you don't get totally swallowed, digested, and spat out, that you go on your own terms, if possible.

What qualities do you need to succeed as a filmmaker, apart from tenaciousness?

I think you're in competition with everyone else and, finally, you're in competition with yourself, your aspirations, your ambitions, and how hard you're prepared to fight and where you're prepared to cave in. I haven't been on a set for three years. I've been writing for two of those years. I've written something from scratch. Luckily, I've had Channel Four paying my rent while I'm doing it, but that's very lucky. It's not a great living, but it's good enough. It's not a safe thing to do. I go from film to film and each one is different. Each one changes you totally as a person. Each one puts you in a different circumstance, a different challenge. I never anticipated that it would be so hard.

ALAN RUDOLPH

Alan Rudolph is perhaps best known as the maker of small, stylish films often featuring characters endlessly discussing love and the joys and pain of intimate relationships. Rudolph began his career in the early 1970s, working with Robert Altman on such key films as *Nashville* and *The Long Goodbye*. This apprenticeship was crucial in shaping the nonconformist sentiment of much of Rudolph's work, and the critical place Rudolph's films give to the actor, no doubt helping to form such distinguishing stylistic features as the long take and moving camera.

Rudolph's first real directorial effort, the stylish *Welcome to L.A.*, was anchored to an intriguing song cycle about that city that featured melancholy music and introspective lyrics by Richard Baskin. The film had its admirers, but some detractors lamented the fact that the composer made the aesthetic decision to perform the songs structuring the film's narrative. *Welcome to L.A.* set the pattern that has come to characterize most of Rudolph's subsequent films: the central role performance plays in his work; intimate discussions among his characters; great attention to visual style and narrative experimentation; and a lively music score that often carries great narrative import. Although this film and Rudolph's subsequent film, the little seen but highly inventive *Remember My Name*, were reasonably well received by critics and audiences, Rudolph has had a bumpy career. He is not a populist filmmaker and has always had difficulty raising funds to make his films.

Despite these difficulties, however, Rudolph has made over fifteen films in a career that now spans almost twenty-five years. He is best known for such romantic films as *Choose Me*, starring Genevieve Bujold and Rudolph regular Keith Carradine; *Trouble in Mind* with Kris Kristofferson, a film set in some distant future or perhaps some imagined past; *Equinox*, the lushly romantic and darkly troubling tale of twins separated at birth, both played by Matthew Modine in a superb performance; and more recently, *Afterglow*, a four-character romantic farce that ends in a cathartic, harrowingly tragic scene with Julie Christie and Nick Nolte sobbing on a bed, and for which Christie received an Academy Award nomination as Best Actress. Rudolph's films may be laced with a romantic sheen, but they are also highly ironic, self-aware and consciously play with generic convention. They also veer wildly in tone, sometimes within the same scene.

Rudolph has drawn inspiration from historical reality in such films as *Mrs. Parker and the Vicious Circle* and *The Moderns*, while offering his highly idiosyncratic take on such material. As he mentions in our interview, *The Moderns* was never about the artists of the mid-1920s, but rather about the American tourists "at the other tables." *Mrs. Parker* examines the difficult relationship between Dorothy Parker and Robert Benchley, played by Jennifer Jason Leigh and Campbell Scott in two fine performances. This relationship is the dramatic center of the film and the only real aspect of the film that could not be corroborated by historical fact.

Rudolph's films always mix humor and drama with gleeful abandon that makes some viewers no doubt uncomfortable. It is often difficult to know how one is meant to take the material. This mix is never so apparent as in Rudolph's most challengingly experimental narrative, his adaptation of Kurt Vonnegut's *Breakfast of Champions*, featuring superb performances from such highly acclaimed actors as Nick Nolte and Albert Finney, and a totally surprising one from Bruce Willis. Audiences have never seen Willis be so thoughtful or funny and give such a risky performance. Willis not only appears in the film, but was basically responsible for its financing and distribution through the sheer force of his power within the Hollywood establishment. I spoke to Alan Rudolph in Toronto.

Rudoph

Could you talk about your formative years, growing up in the fifties and sixties in Los Angeles?

The fact that my father, Oscar Rudolph, was very much involved with the movie business and television in its early days in some ways left me unaffected. He passed away a few years ago, but he was at the birth of, or near the birth of, the movie business and played in silent movies as a kid star with people like Mary Pickford. He became Cecil B. DeMille's assistant director, and then was an AD at Paramount in the 1940s. He became a director in 1950s television. He did everything from sitcoms with Ann Southern and Donna Reed to *Playhouse 90*. We moved to New York for a while and then back to L.A. By the time I started to get "formed," I realized I didn't care very much about the movie business, because it was really the dying end of the studio system in the fifties and early sixties. Nothing was terribly stimulating. Just terrible.

Did you see your father at work?

Oh, yeah, all the time. I watched him make *The Lone Ranger*. I thought it was the greatest thing. I remember he'd finish one at lunch and start the next episode after lunch; same rocks, just change the bad guy, give him a different hat and so on. But I was versed in the elements of TV and moviemaking. I knew what cameras looked like, that it was all manufactured. That was the most important part: the illusion.

You weren't a movie fanatic?

No, I was. The films that my father and I watched together influenced me, whether on television or at the movies. He just loved the Ealing Studio films, *The Lavender Hill Mob*, etc. I remember seeing *Dead of Night*, which was the scariest thing I'd ever seen in my life. My father made half a dozen or more low-budget feature films. One of them was a children's film called *The Rocket Man*, written by Lenny Bruce. I had a small part in it, a couple of days' work. The most important influence of my entire life, I think, in terms of film, was that there was this one scene in *Rocket Man* where a runaway car is going down the highway, and the plot has something about a ray gun which can stop time. I was supposed to run across the street and trip, and this car was coming down the road, and a kid shot the ray gun at it and stopped it right before it hit me. So they film this, me running across the street and falling over. I'm okay. I'm lying on the street. They bring the car right up to me and cut. Then they make the car move backward and film it. In the movie, it would go forward. Now, for a kid of age nine in the fifties, it was the most amazing thing, that you could manipulate images like that.

As you got older, were there other filmmakers?

In the early 1960s I went to college but I didn't know what I was doing. My late brother, who was in the Naval Air, bought me one of the earliest Super-8 movie cameras. He became a pilot in photo reconnaissance and was ultimately shot down. Of course, that was the turning point of my life. Even before he died, I was making these little films. I didn't go to a film school, I'm not a "necro-filmiac." The film schools were just starting anyway, and I didn't know what to make of them. But I would go out and shoot what is the equivalent now of music videos. I would make these little movies with my friends, edit them myself, and get a song, then start a projector and tape recorder, and hope it would stay in sync. I got really hooked by it.

So your love of music goes way back?

Yes, I'm not musically trained, but I think it approaches your senses in a proper, invisible, emotional way. In my late teens and early twenties, I would go to the movies a lot. I was starting to see most foreign films, the great formulators, without knowing that these were the most impressive films of the time, because I didn't really have any historical knowledge. There was Fellini, Bergman, Truffaut, Kurosawa. I would come out of the cinema six feet off the ground. Of course, I can barely watch a film without being influenced by it, even if it's awful. I don't mean influenced in terms of "I want to imitate that," but I can't get it out of my mind. I can go see *Dumbo* and have nightmares. I'm a sponge that way.

How did you decide to go to the Directors Guild Training Program?

I was making films for people in film school. I'd say, "Okay, I'll make you a film, but you'll buy me film stock," and I got wonderful grades for some of these people. [Laughs] Then this Directors Guild Training Program started. I wanted to get into the film business and I had an edge. My father was a director and the whole business was based on nepotism, so I wanted to take advantage. Of course, when I wanted to get in, they created a program to train assistant directors and producers in a more objective, less nepotistic way. They let college graduates get on-set experience and hopefully, by the end, they'd be better assistants than the ones that they had around, mostly old drunks and the dumb son. Somehow I managed to get into the training program. I didn't have any practical experience as an AD, but I understood what it was about. When I started, I was at the absolute bottom of the Hollywood system. Studios were being sold; they weren't making any profits. It was the pre-*Easy Rider* era, 1966-67. I wanted to make my own films, so I quit being an AD and wrote scripts for myself.

Did you know what you were doing when you wrote those scripts, in terms of rules of structure or character formation?

No. But I haven't changed my filmmaking instincts nor my scriptwriting instincts from those days. I still don't know the rules. Around that time, I got a call asking if I wanted to work as an assistant for Robert Altman. I didn't know much about him. I thought he was a young Canadian guy because he'd done *That Cold Day in the Park*. I hadn't seen *M*A*S*H*. I met him and we talked. Bob's a very magnetic and impressive human being. He has always been so much ahead of his time, and my first impression was "Wow," especially after working for a couple of years in the studio system, and with some extremely untalented people.

Previously, I'd made a couple of little 16mm movies. I had my own filmmaking instincts but I couldn't find anyone to connect with. So now I met Altman, and he said, "Do you want to be on this next film we're making?" I said, "No, I don't want to be an AD anymore." The producer said, "We've got a new film opening tonight. Why don't you see that, come back Monday and give us your answer?" It was *McCabe and Mrs. Miller*. I'd never seen anything like that in my life. I came in Monday and said, "Anything. I'll do anything."

What was the film you were to work on?

The Long Goodbye. It was such an awakening to be exposed to Altman's skills and his way of thinking. Bob is one of those people who, if he likes you and thinks that you know something and can help him, will encourage you and ask you to do more and more. One of the first big thrills I ever had was on the set of *The Long Goodbye*, on the first day, and suggesting something and hearing, "That's good," and actually seeing professionals incorporate an idea I had. It was amazing.

You weren't a typical first assistant director?

No, even when I was working in television. I was on an early *Movie of the Week*. The director was a nervous guy, and he was very much afraid of the studio production people, who liked me very much. I remember saying to him, "Look, I'll make this happen on schedule," because I could see he didn't know what he was doing. I said, "Take your time, don't worry, I'll make us stay on schedule. I just want you to get what you want." At lunch, he went to the head of production of the studio and said that I was working against him and that I should get fired. Of course, they were shocked at this. I told them what really happened, and they said, "Well, this guy is nuts." But that was the studio system to me. It was perfect in a way because I realized they weren't interested in what I was interested in, and I had no colleagues. I had friends, but none of them were trying to make films on their own. I remember working one day on Kazan's set [*The Arrangement*], filling in for a third AD who was ill. Kirk Douglas was in it, and I watched Kazan do sixty-two takes and realized, I'll never know that. I mean, this was obviously the great Elia Kazan. "I'll never know the difference between take eighteen and take fifty-eight." I realized he didn't either. It was a shot of Kirk Douglas getting up off a couch, probably thirty seconds long. I thought there were mysteries out there that I could never get, standing as far back as I was. Even if I was right next to the camera I wouldn't know. I also know now that you should quit at take six. [Laughs] Take fifty-eight certainly didn't improve that film.

This period with Altman lasted about five years or so?

Well, it hasn't stopped.

I mean, up to your first film *Welcome to L.A.*, that was four years or so?

Yes. Bob produced that. After *The Long Goodbye* they asked me to do *Thieves Like Us*, and I said: "No, I want to make my own films." And Bob said, "Okay." Later he called me again—Bob does not take "no" easily—but I really stood by it. I really wanted to make a film. I'd written a script that somebody bought for $500 and thought I was going to get to make a movie. A year later, when I was flat broke and depressed, but still sticking to my guns, I got a call from Bob who said, "Alan, listen, I'm making a film. You cannot say no, you have to do this. I need your help on this film." It was *California Split*. He said, "I've invented a new 24-track sound system and I want to try it out on this film. I want you to take the background and put mikes on the extras. I'll take the foreground. I don't know how much of yours I'll use." After that experience, Bob said, "Okay, I am now making a film called *Nashville*. This is the one I've been wanting to do." He'd assign me actors in the background of scenes because there were so many of them.

Were you directing the actors?

I'm not going to say I directed anything on *Nashville* but as an extension of Bob and with his permission. He'd say, "Work something out with Keith [Carradine] or Ronee Blakley. You and Geraldine [Chaplin] do something around there," because some of the scenes would have fifteen actors, and he put mikes over everybody, and it was just terrific.

You contributed to the script, too.

Yeah, but Joan Tewkesberry wrote the script from Bob's thoughts. The last draft before we started shooting needed a production-minded person, and Bob had some new ideas. Joan is a great writer. It was with her blessing that I went through it and made it easier on everybody from a production standpoint, none of which mattered, because it was all just a starting point for Altman and the actors. All during this, I felt I had to make my own films, and Altman knew it. He said, "Find something to make. In the meantime I need you to write a script for me." One was *Buffalo Bill and the Indians, or Sitting Bull's History Lesson*, adapted from Arthur Kopit's play *Indians*. Bob's idea was to keep it all in a wild-west show. I thought it would be interesting to do research on these characters and make them real, to find out something about them from the pulp things that were written then. I'm not very good at research, but it worked out. The whole thing was wonderful and insane. Dino De Laurentiis was one of the producers, and here I was, some long-hair kid sitting in a room with Bob, Paul Newman, Burt Lancaster, Dino De Laurentiis, and David Susskind. The film itself was wonderfully mad.

It was a pretty experimental narrative.

The film could have taken any shape Bob wanted it to take. He and Dino were arguing back and forth about the film, but I thought it was great. It was released on July 4, 1976, the Bicentennial, and I remember the *Los Angeles Times* did an editorial—not on the movie page, but an editorial—that just tore it apart for being unpatriotic. Now, for me and Bob, it was about showbiz and the idea that there's no difference between Buffalo Bill and the icon of a movie star, and the symbolism of that and the fraudulence behind the false heroics. Newman, of course, got it instantly.

In terms of your own development as a director, were you consciously absorbing things from Altman?

I felt like you have to go with your instincts, your center, your inner voice, and what you see happening around you. I mean in life, not movies. Even if I had no experience in the movie business, no connection with my father, any of the exposure to it, I would have got there, or something relating to it. Altman sped up the process and set the highest standard.

Maybe your style would have been different if you hadn't had those years with Altman?

Without question. That experience with Altman in those early years got me to the next place that I wanted to go. Perhaps the most important awareness I learned from him was the respect and care for actors. I remember asking once, when we were finishing *The Long Goodbye*, "Do you always change the script this much?" And Bob looked at me and said, "This script is what a script is always supposed to be. It's a blueprint to get me and the actors to *here*." And that always stuck with me.

While I was working on *Nashville*, there was no rule book. It was all uncharted in both technique and content, just a day-to-day experience of living there and shooting. I felt completely protected because I knew the ship was heading somewhere, because I knew Bob knew. It wasn't chaotic at all; it was just brand new, and that accelerates your own inner experience more than anything. But Bob knew I had to make my own film. I'd written this screenplay, *Welcome to L.A.*, based on Richard Baskin's music. I was sitting in a hotel in Calgary the day before shooting *Buffalo Bill*, and I'd already asked a few of the actors if they'd be interested if I ever got to make it, and they'd said, "Yes." Bob told the United Artists people, who were all excited about *Buffalo Bill*, "The picture cost seven million dollars, but for eight million, I'll get you two movies. Alan's got a script. We'll get a cast of top-rate people and we'll do it for under a million dollars." The next thing I knew, I was making my first film.

What was it about this song cycle that interested you?

Well, not Richard's singing, that's for sure. It was the fact that I was born and raised in L.A. and I wanted to get out and not live there anymore, which I finally managed to do. I watched the place become something different, in the sense of smell and light, from what I had experienced as a kid. I felt very alienated from it, coming out to this sprawling place where people had really big houses but closed the front curtains, and life was very isolated. I wanted to make a film about this, stripping away the L.A. that people thought they knew. I knew internally that my style and my interests were much different from Bob's. We overlapped in some ways, but as a filmmaker, I knew I could never do what he did. I can imitate him. I think I can imitate Altman on camera, how he shoots. But what would that prove?

You don't have the same sensibilities.

We were really different. Part of it was that he looks at the bigger picture and works his way into the detail, and I would start at a detail, but wouldn't work my way too far out. I don't know what "regular" people talk about. I have no reality sense. Bob knows how to capture behavior, whereas my films are always intentionally artificial.

When you were directing *Welcome to L.A.*, because of your apprenticeship with Altman, did you feel comfortable working with actors?

Yes, I feel comfortable with actors because I respect them, and I know that they're the most important element. Although I've had no training whatsoever, I seem to know what it is they might respond to, or how to give them the support and the environment to do what they do. I don't use a monitor because I really like to see the actors and watch all of it. I'm an idea machine. I'll just throw stuff out at them. You have to understand it's the actors who are the most important element, because they are the characters or they become the characters. The characters are more important than anything else you do. One of the nice things about making *Welcome to L.A.* is that I got to meet Ingmar Bergman.

Ah, did you?

I had just finished the movie, and Bob kept asking, "When can I see something?" And I said, "Not yet." In the meantime, all the actors were telling their agents that this was the best work they had ever done. So there was a steady stream of directors who would come and ask to see film on people. John Boorman, Coppola, Ridley Scott, and all kinds of people would come through. I wouldn't show Altman a cut of the film until I was ready, and he kept getting impatient and saying, "When am I going to see it?" And I would say, "Pretty soon, next week, I think." I got a call from my then agent saying, "Listen, Ingmar Bergman is coming to Los Angeles for one day to meet some actors. He's doing his first English-language film in Germany [*The Serpent's Egg*] and he'd like to see film on Harvey Keitel and Keith Carradine. Would you show him some?" I said, "Ingmar Bergman? What about the day after tomorrow, because I've got to first show this film to Bob?" He said, "No. He's in town for only one day." So I go in to Bob and say, "Bob, we're going to look at the movie." He said, "Great." I said, "It's just going to be you, me, and Ingmar Bergman." [Laughs]

Bergman was so generous. He put his arm around me and said, "Now tell me about these people," and he understood all about this film. He was so supportive, and he just said, "I think they are too young for my cast, but they're very, very wonderful." When we met him, he had on a green fatigue T-shirt and some baggy pants, and your first instincts were you wanted to protect this guy. And yet, he was so strong. It was just a wonderful experience.

In many ways *Welcome to L.A.* is a very accomplished film, quite sophisticated.

I thought that as a film, *Welcome to L.A.* had a certain breakthrough quality. It's probably the most audacious film I've ever made. When we finished the film, United Artists didn't want it. Bob, bless his gambling heart, said, "We'll release it ourselves." So we started a company and had to release this movie at places that weren't geared to showing it, and it did all right. At least, it made its money.

Then I wanted to do *The Moderns*, and couldn't get it made. Bob called me up and said, "I think I can get another movie for you. Think of something." So, on my way over, I thought of two or three things. One of them was inspired by driving by a theater and seeing a "femme fatale" festival with Rita Hayworth and Ida Lupino or something. So we met and he said, "Tell me what you've got." I gave him a few ideas I was making up as we talked. One of them was a movie about a wronged woman, a parallel for the women's lib movement, but done in old movie terms [*Remember My Name*]. And he said, "That's it. Let's do it. It's great." I wrote it in a week or two; he put it in with a deal with Fox, which was for *A Wedding*, I think, and *Quintet*. Then Fox saw *Quintet* and canceled the deal. So we go back to L.A., and I've never been so depressed in my life. Nobody wanted to finance this thing, and I had picked the locations and had a crew and everything. And Bob said, "Let's just start shooting. There's two weeks before you'll have to pay any bill, and maybe we can pick up the financing in two weeks." So we started without money and somehow we got it picked up. We made the movie, showed it to Columbia, and they said, "Nice work but we don't want it." So I was 0 for 2. That movie never did get a general release, just a very limited one. I still consider it one of my best films. That's when I got lost. I thought it was light years in development from *Welcome*, because it was an actual story. It won prizes all over. Every time we tried to put it on video or on television, it reverted back to Columbia and nobody wanted to open up the legal questions, so they just said no to everything.

Was there a particular difference in terms of shooting that film from the previous one?

Yeah, I knew what I was doing a little more, plus there was more of a story and fewer characters. Also, I knew Geraldine now, and we could get into different places, and Alberta Hunter's music really brought it together. I was really pleased with that film, and I was shocked that it was so ignored, reviled.

It wasn't reviled by the critics.

Well, no, they barely saw it, but they didn't give me any points, either. I've never been a critic's favorite. Maybe that's healthy. No false goals.

But you started to work with genre in ways that you hadn't before.

Yes, but I couldn't take them seriously. Even during that time in the late seventies, you could see that life with Nixon and Vietnam and the coming of Reagan, made American society and the world in general a surreal, insane place.

Altman's take on genre is to really take it apart and subvert it. It's not quite the same thing in your films.

No, I respect the "movieness" of them. Movies were always the great indicators to me. Maybe it was my upbringing. Maybe it was the influence of all the great filmmakers. I remember seeing a Cocteau film where this guy comes to a big wall at night, and it's in black and white. The wall is bright white light, and he walks along, and Cocteau cuts or pans to this shadow walking. My God! This thing cost four cents to do and it's the most brilliant thing you could do for the sense of what he was after. When I made these movies, the budgets were so small that I had to figure out how to do something in no time with no money. I still do. Nothing much changes.

Altman produced a film of Robert Benton's called *The Late Show*, and I'd just finished *Remember* and was going to see it for the first time. Benton and I had just met. I didn't know much about him except that he'd written *Bonnie And Clyde*. He was a really smart, nice man. I didn't know at the time that he was very much into film analysis and had been a film critic. I said, "I'm watching my movie, would you like to see it?" He said, "Oh. I'd love to." When the picture was over, he said, "Oh, I love the style of it. You have these long takes." I said, "I don't know. I never look at it that way." He said, "What are you talking about?" Then he brought up French filmmakers. I said, "No, no. We only had 68,000 feet of film. We did these things with one take because we couldn't afford to shoot closeups or anything.

The style is completely dictated by the budget." "Oh, that's non-sense," he said.

But you can't give that explanation for your whole career.

No, but it started for me that way. I can make it look like a real film by not cutting, which, of course, is what kept the films from being popular. Except for *Breakfast*, the curse of my films for audience and critics is that they are, basically, in real time, but aren't reality. Even though they cut from place to place, the actors come in, sit down, talk and move around at a real pace, but the scene is never about what they are doing or what they are saying. My scenes are about emotions underneath. As soon as you start to skip the emotional steps, there's nothing to hold on to. But I got into the artifice right from the beginning on *Welcome*. It was a natural thing for me to do. During *Remember My Name*, I kidded myself that it was a realistic film, but I knew better.

After *Remember*, I was flat broke and totally depressed. A friend of mine was starting a film company and said, "We're going to make this crazy rock-n-roll movie. Do you wanna direct it?" It was *Roadie*, a fun experience, but a totally stupid movie, and I knew it. From there, the same company had a deal to do *Endangered Species*, which I really thought was an interesting idea. I said that I wanted a crack at the screenplay and I wanted Robert Mitchum or Lee Marvin. I had written something for Mitchum, met him, and had a good experience with him. The studio said no and gave us a list of two or three actors they had under contract, completely different from what I'd imagined. The infamous David Begelman was in charge. He saw our first week's dailies, which had minimum lighting and no makeup. We had lights for exposure but it didn't look like a movie. Begelman shut us down, fired everybody. I tried to quit. Contractually, I couldn't: I had to finish that movie.

Did you have any input into the script?

Yes. But, by that time, it was like somebody had ripped my guts out. The studio had changed two or three times. It was insanity, the worst experience. I turned to Carolyn Pfeiffer, the producer, and said, "Carolyn, I had the greatest beginning you could ever have as a director, working with Altman. And because of what the system does and my lack of being able to adapt to it or to change it, I've been led down the darkest path I can ever imagine, and I'll never do this again. If we are to make movies together, you've got to find some financing. We're going to start our own place." Out of that came Island Alive.

After *Endangered Species* I did a little documentary [*Return Engagement*] just to prove to the investors we could do something. I liked it very much, but nobody saw it. It was much better than people give it credit for, because the subjects [G. Gordon Liddy and Timothy Leary] were so off-putting. It was a great comment on celebrity and politics. And then the company said, "Can you do another documentary after this?" I said I wanted to make a real movie. And they said, "Well, we can only give you a couple hundred thousand dollars. What would a 'real' movie cost?" I figured it out and said, "$639,000." I made a production schedule first. I found out how many shooting days that amount of money would give me before I wrote a script. David Blocker, the producer, said, "How can we make a schedule and a budget if we don't know what the movie is?" I said, "Just assume it's two or three people in interiors talking all the time. And just assume that there are a couple of scenes with extras, and everything else is just regular stuff: people driving, walking, talking, nothing out of the ordinary. How many days would it be?" We figured it would be eighteen days. I said, "Okay, now I'll write a script." It was *Choose Me*.

I wrote the script in a week in a hurry, as always. I just didn't stop. I would write twenty-four hours straight. I loved it, not sleeping. The original story of *Choose Me* was about a guy who only told the truth and who is put in an asylum for being a pathological liar. That's what I thought I was going to make the movie about. Then, I was driving down the street and turned on the radio, and this lady was giving out intimate advice about relationships, and it was hilarious and scary and funny. I had just started writing that morning, so I headed back home and immediately inserted her character into the script. Then I knew what it was about.

So we finished *Choose Me*, and I went to France to do a few things, still trying to get *The Moderns* going. My assumption was that, like everything else I'd ever done, it was going to be a total commercial failure. All I ever cared about was getting the next one started. That's basically my formula. In a couple of weeks, I called and asked if the movie was still playing. People were saying to me, "Jesus Christ, where have you been? This picture is a success."

You called *Choose Me* an almost perfect experience in terms of working with the actors and crew, and making something the way you wanted to make it.

Yes, it was wonderful. There was a sense of direction, excitement, freedom. We were doing something I knew was working and I didn't care what anybody thought about it.

Did you have any cinematic models for it in mind?

Welcome to L.A. [Laughs] I wanted to take some very stereotypical characters and one brand new one, and, if there's any blip on the screen by *Choose Me* in our film culture, it was introducing the Dr. Nancy Love character, the public platformer of others' intimate secrets. Here was a person on the air that you never meet, never see, dispensing the most intimate, pivotal information to strangers, interrupted by radio ads.

Was the film always meant to have such an artificial style? It starts pretty much like a musical, it's so choreographed.

A lot of people talk about that opening. We were shooting at night and it was the one night we had a crane. It was a cheap little crane, but it was the only way to get above the EVE'S sign. We also had the extras for the scene, and I said, "Geez, let's do a title sequence." We did one, then two takes and that was it.

Do you generally have a rehearsal period with the actors?

If it was up to me, I wouldn't. If the actors want it, we will. There's always rehearsing before the shoot. I like it when you don't, when you get there and it's alive. In terms of filmmaking, I've always said,

"You can paint me into a corner, just give me the corner," because, to this day, every filmmaking instinct I have is based on how to economically do something without making it look cheap. One of the things I've realized is to preserve the spontaneity of the filmed event. The script is the rehearsed event. I did learn from Altman that the script gets you to that moment, but if you just shoot the script, which is basically what happened on *Endangered Species*, that's all there is. For me, it's not where the film is. I've always viewed any film I'm writing as a detective story for the audience. Let them guess along with you what's going to happen. I always thought they liked that, but they don't always, increasingly so, too. Audiences don't really know where to look for the clues if they're not used to looking.

Is *Choose Me* one of your most ambiguous films?

I don't know what that means. I do know that at the end of *Equinox* I used a song called "Ambiguity." [Laughs]

We don't know whether Mickey [Keith Carradine] is lying or telling the truth, even at the end.

But how does one know that in real life? You go by your own guts or the hard facts.

Or you know by some kind of contract between you and the film that these people aren't lying.

If you make a contract with the film, then you should expect the film to treat truth and reality in the way it comes to you in life. You have to trust yourself and your instincts. I think the reason why life keeps betraying us is that we don't understand that the nurturing part is the very part society tells you to avoid. If you say, "Life is really love played out," people say, "Oh, you're romantic, you're stupid, you're New Age," whatever. But I think, if it's going to boil down to something, it isn't hate that keeps people going. We wouldn't have civilization. If we turn the news on right now, and the news guy says, "Hey, it's chaos out there. Don't expect me to make sense of it for you." I'd say, "Wow. We have to watch this. He's really showing us something." Instead, it's "This happened, and this happened, buy this, then this happened." Life is about the eternal tensions caused by humans, love and hate.

Your films are often about the self-deceptions people have about themselves and the world.

The first line in my first film, *Welcome to L.A.*, is Geraldine Chaplin saying, "People deceive themselves." You see, I'm not interested in the pop stuff. I'm not like Tarantino. I could never make a movie where people talk about Big Macs while killing each other. I'm not interested in what's happening now, the junk culture, unless it's to expose it.

How did *Trouble in Mind* come about?

Trouble in Mind was the only script I could have sold, and if you read the script, it's pure Don Siegel. No embellishments whatsoever, no mention of place or time or any of the vanities that got projected into the movie, ultimately. It was about an ex-con, ex-cop and the villain, and somebody actually wanted to buy it. But I never pursued that end. When we started to do it, I said to Carolyn and Island Alive, "You know, I think I'll take this to some extreme place. I just can't see taking a gangster movie seriously." We started talking about casting, and I said, "Well, I like Divine as the bad guy. I don't think he's ever acted as a male in a movie." Carolyn said, "Divine? You mean the guy in the John Waters movies?" I also wanted to set it in some kind of future or future past.

   Trouble in Mind was a movie built out of old movie parts, on purpose, and then the idea was to have fun with them and yet to keep that romantic center, the romance of it, and all the sophomoric parables and metaphors. The attempt was to throw it totally out of time and place, so that you'd be relieved of having to deal with facts and just watch the story emotionally.

Kris Kristofferson's character [Hawk] is a very flawed character, yet he's artistic, romantic, and a criminal.

He is society's victim. He is, basically, a sacrificial lamb. He is the product of his time, his work, environment. All of his prejudices and his arrogance and his anger and violence are things he struggles with because it's all he knows. And he's a killer and a lover and a loner, and he needs companionship. He's a romantic, a realist, a fatalist. Yet he has faith of some kind. He's sinner and saint.

He's one of your most complex characters

Kris was so great. I had just worked with him on *Songwriter*, which was a hell of a fun experience. Then I cast this actress whose name I won't tell you. Her character was supposed to be like white trailer trash, and it was to be a very gritty, real thing. She came in, we met with her, I liked her. Suddenly, I envisioned the movie and I knew what I was going to do. Then her agent got in the way, and she wanted top billing and more money. The movie was only going to cost 2.5 million dollars, and she fell out. I didn't know what to do. Lesley Ann Warren suggested I meet Lori Singer. So Lori came in, totally the opposite of this other actress, with that flowing blonde hair, looked like an angel, acted like a hummingbird, moving about quickly, very enlightened and funny. So I asked her to be in the film but I had to completely rethink it.

I'd just seen *Brother From Another Planet*, and I thought Joe Morton was great. I asked him if he wanted to be in it. He wrote back to say yes, but he sent me a drawing of the way he thought he should look, with his hair out like this, and I thought, "Maybe that's the key to this film." That's when I suggested Divine and all kinds of casting. Little did I know that Joe Morton would be the most conservative-looking player in that piece. But I just loved where it led.

Was the mixing of tones difficult, finding the right balance?

Well, I may miss. Maybe I miss all the time, but for me it's the easiest thing to do. I never question it.

The ending of the film is very farcical.

Well, I didn't want a blood bath. It's all a dream. The film was in a couple of festivals, and I went to one in Europe. A critic interviewed me and said how much she liked the film. She'd already written the review, which I hadn't read but assumed was a good review. At the end of the interview she said, "I just want to tell you I wrote a negative review." I said, "You just told me you liked it." She said, "I liked it all the way to the end, but the end was so Hollywood. The happy ending when the two of them are getting together. It looked like the studio forced you to do that." I said, "First of all, there's no studio, and second of all, what are you talking about?" She said, "Well, you know, he winds up with the girl." I said, "Yeah, either that or he's dead. You took that as a reality? You see a guy who's been shot in the stomach sitting alone in a car, then the camera closes in to him and suddenly a woman puts her face next to his, and the next thing we show you is ten minutes of sunset. He's passed over." And she said, "Wow, I never thought of it that way."

Initially, the film was not going to be released. It was caught in a court battle while we were editing it. Island Alive went through a corporate split and takeover and we were caught in the middle. We opened the film for one week in L.A. without anybody's approval, just to have an audience, witnesses, and it was picked by the *Los Angeles Times* as one of their top ten films of the year. The court battle started, and the picture didn't come out until the following August, and by then nobody cared about it.

Is the film meant to be a comment on the greed of the 1980s?

Well, I'm not skilled enough to make a film like *Wall Street*, but I think it was about corruption of society and the lack of protection between the individual and a society that's gone all wrong.

And the seductiveness of wealth?

Seductiveness gone sour, the dream of this. These films are all dreams anyway. That's what annoys everybody so much about them. I'm surprised you didn't ask that about *Choose Me*, the dream moment when Genevieve [Bujold] is in the radio studio and suddenly she's in the same frame as Lesley Ann Warren in her apartment. People hate that so much. To me, it's wonderful.

It's a great moment.

But it was all about dreams. For all I know, in *Trouble*, Hawk [Kris Kristofferson] never got out of jail and the whole movie was his fantasy. The film was about freedom and being liberated and the price you have to pay. Can you ever really get what you're after, and do you need to get it to be released, rewarded? This guy paid for his mistakes and just wanted some moment of truth before it was over. It's about his destiny, I suppose, but you can't really say things like that in movies, because movies with any kind of poetic sense are generally ignored.

How did you come to make *Made in Heaven*?

I didn't really want to make *Made in Heaven*. I didn't write it, but they said I could interpret and embellish it. It was a very good script, but schmaltzy, and so I said, "Okay, here's my take. I don't want to do any visual effects. We're going to have a real corny love story, but you've got to let me add a dark edge to this. You've got to make the audience pay for the romantic reward." And they all went crazy. At my first screening of it, Keith [Carradine] said, "This is the best movie you've ever made." Unbeknownst to me the two writer-producers saw it that night and went to the studio basically and tried to get me fired. But I stayed on, and what followed was six months of battling for this thing. I had to give up all the darker elements to save the ending, which was the best part of the film, maybe one of the best things I ever did in my life. Then that got cut out too. To me, the picture has no point of view, yet many people think it's my best film. Is there a lesson to be learned here?

So why do you have those dream moments in almost every film?

I think it's reverence toward the illusion of film. I just can't buy film as reality, although I do believe it's as real as anything else, but by definition, I can't. Even Scorsese's films, despite their gritty reality, are very dreamlike. And the people who do reality, like Cassavetes, bring a poetry to it. My favorite films, I guess, are Laurel and Hardy. Talk about reality!

The Moderns **had a mixed response from the critics. Some people objected to your take on the 1920s, that the twenties were not really about art as much as they were about the buying and selling of art. They felt you trivialized the accomplishments of those people, made fun of them.**

What people?

The artists of the period.

First of all, *The Moderns* was a point of view. And if you've done any research on modern art, you know that the breakthrough happened way before the 1920s. Modern art wasn't born in the 1920s. I mean, *Demoiselles d'Avignon* was painted in 1906 or something. The twenties in Paris was when all the tourists were there, the time when the Americans discovered it. I said, "I'm going to have a scene where some guy doesn't buy a painting because it clashes with his wallpaper." It was about the commerce of painting. How can anyone take *The Moderns* as a document of the era? I always said the film was about the people at the other tables.

The Moderns is about Americans going to Paris. As filmmakers, we couldn't have respected the art of the period more. How many films do you see where somebody actually talks about Cézanne? And the main character is a forger, for crying out loud, and not a good painter. He says, "Cézanne is the master," which is the truth about Cézanne to all modern painters. To me, this was an anti-romantic version of modernism. In fact, if John Lone's character symbolized commerce, in the film studio way, then Keith's character represented the artist who sold out continuously to make the Hollywood movie just to stay alive. The film showed that the critics couldn't tell the difference. That's why critics didn't like the film, because it portrayed them all as fools and buffoons, which many of them are.

It's your most profound working out of the idea of the real versus the fake, which permeates your work in many ways.

It was a kind of meditation on a subject. We did this movie for pennies, totally out of passion, because of Jon Bradshaw who wrote the script with me. I wrote it myself, originally, and that's probably the one the critics would have liked. The first take on it went very much by the book. It was reverential. Then I got bored with that. Bradshaw was a friend of mine, a writer-journalist and an editor for *Esquire*. He read my draft and said, "I'm going to rewrite it with you. All you care about is this dream crap, the romance of Paris in the twenties. I want structure, structure." For ten years we just talked about it. Bradshaw died after I did *Made in Heaven*. I said to Carolyn [Pfeiffer], who was married to Bradshaw, "We've got to get *The Moderns* made for him. You've got to get whatever amount of money you can." She got three million dollars. We always thought we were going to Paris. I'd been there many times to scout. But you can't shoot Paris of the 1920s there any more; it doesn't exist. So we did it in Montreal, and said, "If we do it in Montreal, then the whole thing is like a dream. Forget the real. The only way I'll show the Eiffel Tower is if somebody's painting it or talking about it.

Do you think that you were acknowledging this fake aspect of what you were doing or adding to the confusion by shooting in Montreal?

Montreal was strictly an economic choice. But it turned out to be the most liberating thing because it played into the theme of what we were trying to do. I thought it was an anti-memoir, because everything I read about Paris in the 1920s was about third-rate people who went over there and wrote a book about it. It was all about seeing so-and-so in the café, doing this or that, and it had nothing to do with the struggle of the artists. I thought, "Jesus, there's maybe twenty famous artists that came out of that time, and thousands who didn't make it. Those are the ones I want to make the film about."

Were you happy with *The Moderns*?

I was very pleased with the film. I only wish we'd had a bit more money, but it probably wouldn't have made the film much better. It was a blur, making that film, although it was enjoyable. I was hurt that few cared about it when it was initially released. One problem with movies is that you get no credit for degree of difficulty. So *The Moderns* gets trashed while something like *Firestarter*, which was released at the same time, gets a good review because it "pinned you to the back of your seat and gave you a roller-coaster, jaw-dropping experience," *New York Times* or some such.

It's an ambitious piece.

One thing that did well from the movie was the soundtrack. Everybody regards it as a great soundtrack. It's a formative thing to be tempered and rejected early in your career because I've never looked for people's acceptance. I was blessed working early on with somebody [Altman] who truly is a visionary. I really make these films for me. Some of them I'm very pleased with, and I think I'm finally getting okay at it.

***Equinox* is one of your best films.**

And one of the least released films when it got rescued. It was actually on its way straight to video. It had a small release in the U.S., although it was very successful in England.

The film is very hermetic. It's about storytelling, about telling the tale, and I like that about it.

I do too. It was a tale that had been told many times before, the myth of the good brother and the evil brother. We played with it.

Did you think at all in Jungian terms when making this movie, with the idea of the double, the good and evil stuff, the circularity of the film's ending?

If I was versed in Jungian theory, I probably wouldn't have had so much fun with it, because I would respect what it was and be drawn to a more analytical, lasting psychological view of it. To me it's just characters.

The ending is very open. It can be taken as positive or negative. It's quite breathtaking as Matthew Modine stands on the cliff with the helicopter shots swirling around him.

Matthew's character can't get to the next point until he faces himself. This guy had instincts that he had suppressed because they made no sense to his life, because he wasn't told the truth that he was adopted. He had these royal instincts because he was the son of royalty, but he was living this working-class life, leading his whole life from this awkward, almost loser mentality, because he felt like an outcast. Meanwhile, his twin brother, who was an orphan, took his share of this powerful sense to dangerous, sometimes evil places. Finally, at the end, this guy sees his twin and finds out all the details of his life. He runs away and stares at the precipice, figuratively and literally. And he doesn't jump. That's the important part.

In Jungian terms, he sees what's not in himself, aspects missing in his life that he can potentially reintegrate into a more whole personality.

One of the key things for me is when Matthew finally says to Lara Flynn Boyle's character, "Let's go. Let's get away." That moment when she's at the window, but doesn't act. It's one of those moments in life when you must act, even if you don't understand why. He takes his moment, while she doesn't, and for the rest of her life, she'll probably be cursed by that moment of indecision. She stands on her own precipice.

Did you work with Matthew on his characterizations? It's a very physical performance.

Yes, he's a very physical actor. People wondered why I was interested in him for those two roles. It's because he's never played the darker part. I've never seen him do that. And he was great in it. I thought people were going to acknowledge this performance for years. Later, some people did.

All your films have this afterlife.

No, not really. Their afterlife is their real life. *The Moderns* has never been shown on television because of legal problems. *Remember My Name* has never been put on video, although it has been shown on television.

The source music is very good in *Equinox*.

It's all found music. I told David Blocker, the producer, "I'll find the most obscure music and it won't cost anything." I'd come in with a recording of a guitarist from Mali, a flute player from Iran, and a guitarist from Sweden. But anything recorded is owned by one of those big corporations, and, ultimately, it ended up costing us more than if we had hired a composer.

What is your relationship to Mark Isham, who has composed so many of your scores?

Oh, I love him. If I could play music, it would probably come out like his trumpet. Here's a story of my relationship to Isham, my views of existence, and my history as a filmmaker in one example: We do *Trouble in Mind*. I want the song "Trouble In Mind." I wanted blues, but I didn't want traditional blues. So we shot the film, and we're back in Los Angeles editing it. I go into David Blocker's [the producer] office on a Saturday and say, "I've just come from the record store, I bought twenty-eight albums, and they're all instrumental. I'm looking for a certain sound. And it's boiled down to this one guy, Mark Isham. Here's an album I found on some label in the New Age bin. It's a little soft for me, doesn't have quite the edge, but look at the back of this. This guy plays every instrument, and when he's on, he's really on. He composes everything, and he's got a real sense of music." Then the phone rings, on a Saturday, and Blocker picks it up. A Hollywood agent calls him, working on a Saturday, and says, "Oh, I'm so glad I got you there. I represent a composer who lives in San Francisco, who has recently moved to Los Angeles, and he gave me a list of directors he wants to work with, and Alan Rudolph is one of them. Have you hired a composer for your film?" And Blocker says, "Well, actually, we're discussing it right now." And he says, "Well, I'd like to throw a name in the mix. His name is Mark Isham." Blocker says to me, "You won't believe this phone call. Mark Isham's agent just called us." I said, "Hire him. No questions asked." I went to San Francisco and met Mark for the first time. He's such a great horn player, a jazz and classical musician. And he had all these old synthesizers. We sat for six hours in his basement. He'd invent music and then duplicate it. I think he's brilliant.

In the late 1980s, you also made *Love at Large*. How did you get involved with that?

Love at Large was the only film I'd ever written that was made by a studio, Orion, and they went out of business. It was only made because Tom Berenger was in it and they wanted to have him. I said to Mike Medavoy, the head of the studio, "Every time I make a film for a studio or any organization, they're never in business when it's finished. The guy who said 'Yes' is never around." He got angry at me. Of course, by the end of it, not only was he not there, the whole company had folded. A lot of that film's edges got rounded off, not because they imposed things on me, but because I was trying to be a good guy about it. Although I liked the film, I kept saying, "I'm making a murder mystery without a murder."

The story came out of two things: One was I had written a script about a lady private eye I couldn't get made, and I just borrowed the notion of the character; the other was a story I'd heard on the news about a guy who had two families. I wondered, how does he work *that* out?

Love at Large barely got released and nobody cared about the movie, and I thought, "God, more of the same." I knew it didn't have the edge to cut through anything, and that people really wouldn't see it as the romantic piece that it was, because they don't care about movies like that. I was still pleased with it.

That's when you did *Mortal Thoughts*?

Well, *Mortal Thoughts* was one of those calls. I was in New York with *Love at Large*. A company had a film that they had shot on for two weeks, shut down, and fired the director. They were going to trash the whole project. They sent me a script without an ending. Nobody could come up with an ending, and they were desperate. They asked if I'd be interested in directing it. I asked them when it started. They said, "Well, in thirty-four days every member of the cast has another job. So you have to shoot it in thirty-four days. And we have to start shooting the day after tomorrow." I said, "Okay, but I won't use any of the footage that has already been shot. I want to start over." And that was fine.

I met the producer. There were nine producers on this film. Taylor Hackford was sort of the company's guy. I said to him, "Look, this is what is going to happen with this film. I'll make it. You'll be worried for two weeks, maybe even a week, then you'll say 'This is working, everything is great.' And you'll let me alone. Then, when you and the studio feel completely confident about it, you'll start picking on me, nit picking." Which is what happened.

Your work in it is very good.

I was very pleased. I made up an ending. I didn't want the Polanski ending when she gets in the car and drives away and it just turns into an exercise. I wanted some sense of morality to it. They didn't like what I was going for. It was the hardest story to follow on a daily basis, because I couldn't get it clear in my head. And these actors were so sensational. I just love inventing stuff. I'd never done a film about bloody this and bloody that. It was an anti-love story. It was about people who don't love each other, and the price they pay. I was really proud of the work. It's the first film on which I felt like a true professional. Bruce Willis considered it his best work at the time.

So the studio had this screening that they call a "focus" screening. I call it "fuck-us" screening. They come out of the screening, and the guy who had taken over Columbia at the time said, "You did a fine job, fine job, but as you know, we have a huge commercial potential in this film because of the cast. We'd like you to reshoot. The picture cost six million dollars. We will give you twelve million dollars to reshoot several scenes and turn it into a romance between Demi and Bruce. We'd like the *Fatal Attraction* ending. She can kill him at the end, but we'd like them to go through a romantic period before that." Now here's a movie where Demi kills Bruce's character in self-defense because he's so hateful. I said, "I never saw *Fatal*

Attraction." He said, "You know, where you think he's dead but he comes back to life, and she kills him again." I said, "Look, I have no rights here, obviously. I'm going back home, and you guys do whatever you want." But Demi and Bruce stood by my version, and it stayed the way we made it.

It made money though.

Yes, because it cost six million dollars and they probably grossed, I don't know, twenty or thirty million dollars. But they held it up for six months. In the meantime, *Thelma And Louise*, which has a similar story, was shot, edited and released. *Mortal Thoughts* could have been out six months before *Thelma And Louise*. But ours was always a much darker piece.

Then you did *Mrs. Parker and the Vicious Circle*.

Mrs. Parker broke the pattern of my survival principle, which is to get something going before they've seen the evidence of the last accident. Altman produced it and introduced me to Jennifer [Jason Leigh]. It turned out she was a Dorothy Parker afficionado and wanted the role. There was a pause as we tried to get money for it, and, in the meantime, the Coen brothers started *Hudsucker Proxy* and wanted Jennifer for that. She borrowed our voice for it, which surprised me when I saw their film. I thought it was great, but I didn't realize that she had done that. So I had to wait nine months. The deal fell apart, and I was stranded. *Mortal Thoughts* had given me a certain amount of leverage, and nobody had seen *Equinox* yet, so I was waiting and waiting, and scared to death. Finally, we put something together—Altman called it "forced sex"—putting Miramax and Fine Line together to make a deal. We got six million dollars to make the movie. But we didn't put that deal together until four weeks into shooting. No one was paid for four weeks. We got by on credit, credit cards, and the financing was just coming in. That's the way these things get made.

Since Benchley and Parker are the focus of the film, did you feel you had too many other characters to orchestrate?

No. But I should never have signed a contract to deliver a film no more than 126 minutes. Maybe nobody would have liked it, but a two-and-a-half- or three-hour version of that movie would have been really quite great, because we did follow these characters. Each one had much more to do, and I think some of the actors felt a little disappointed that so much had to be cut out.

Stylistically, Mrs. Parker takes a more factual approach than The Moderns?

I wanted to play it as real as I could and stick with the biographical information. Unfortunately, the thing I was most interested in is the thing no one has any account of. When I look at Dorothy Parker's life, obviously the pivotal time was her years with Benchley. They were in love with each other, but they didn't know it. She started drinking in that period; she was getting out of the bad marriage. I wanted to recreate the reality of it. Then the critics came and dumped on it because they said it wasn't like that. *The New York Times*, which gave it a good review, had a follow-up piece about how I made up a movie based on her quotes, but I only used a handful of her sayings. They gave examples, the most obvious of which they said was when she meets Will Rogers and says, "I never liked a man I didn't meet." That was a line I made up. Alas, the power of the press.

It's an ambitious film in many ways.

Ambitious in terms of the subject, because we found that our speculations were true. I didn't think you could tell the story without getting into the personalities of that table. And we were very accurate with the research. Ultimately, it was about Parker's private moments. That's why I wanted to put in some poetry, and I also wanted the 1920s to be the vibrant-color time and the future to be black-and-white.

The performances are uniformly fine.

Yes, I was thrilled with Jennifer [Jason Leigh], Campbell [Scott], Matthew [Broderick], all of them. I think Campbell's performance is one of the best I've ever seen in my life. Peter Benchley, whom I had never met, contacted me when we were preparing the film and asked if he could visit the set. I said, "I'd love you to come. And, if you do come, see if you can make it one of these dates, because the whole table will be there. But be prepared to be put in the film." He said, "Well, Spielberg made me a reporter in *Jaws*, but I wasn't very good, I must admit." We put him in the film even though he was there only one day.

The turning point in American comedy for many people is Benchley's *Treasurer's Report*, because it was exactly as we showed it: they put on some show and it became a celebration. It was the funniest thing. Nobody had ever seen anything like this. It was the birth of modern contemporary humor. No jokes, humor without jokes. Behavioral humor, observational humor. Robin Williams wouldn't exist without Benchley. Certainly, Jerry Seinfield wouldn't. Peter Benchley said that Campbell's was the "second best" *Treasurer's Report* he'd ever heard, obviously referring to Robert's original. He came to Campbell and said, "I'm so overwhelmed by what you did. I can't believe it." Very few people gave Campbell his due for that amazing performance.

Jennifer Jason Leigh can be very good. But sometimes I think her performances rely too much on mimicry. In this film she gives a very emotional performance.

The truth of it is that Dorothy was a completely self-created person. She ran away from home at twelve, and she lied about most things. She created her own style and came up with that sort of mid-Atlantic accent. We had tapes of Dorothy Parker when she was older, and if I played them for you, next to Jennifer from the movie, you couldn't tell the difference. And, yes, imitation of a voice is one thing, but embodying is another. I felt that part of Dorothy Parker in life was a calculated performance. Or, at least, an affectation. She was very spontaneous in her wit, but she was also very affected in her daily performance, especially as she became more of an alcoholic.

The look of the film pushes all of your trademark stylistics: the long-take style, the moving camera, holding shots on people a long time,

and it's in widescreen as well. Did you feel that this material determined these stylistic choices?

I did. First of all, I loved what everybody was doing, so I wanted a wide screen to include them all. But I also knew that the movie needed big closeups, as big as I could get on Jennifer's face. The best landscape in the world is an actor's face. The film was selected for Cannes, which was a privilege. And you do get your fifteen minutes of fame when you're in competition, where all the schmos come out with the money.

I still wanted to do *Breakfast of Champions* which I'd completely rewritten without owning the book rights. I wrote the original draft in 1974 or 1975. Somehow it got to Bruce Willis, who called me up and said, "I'd love to be a part of this. What's going on with it?" I said, "I'm trying to get it made." So we went to Cannes with *Mrs. Parker*. Bruce was there with *Pulp Fiction*. For the first time in my life, I actually turned down things. I really wanted *Breakfast of Champions*. And I could say with some conviction that Bruce was interested in it, but agents got in the way and tore it apart, and then Cannes was over and *Mrs. Parker* made no difference. I was there, caught at the end of my tunnel, and there wasn't a light but an oncoming train. I had nothing ready that I had written. I had, as Dorothy Parker would say, put all my eggs in one bastard.

Mrs. Parker came out, and everybody said, "See, it proves this guy is not interested in anything that makes money. He is off on some esoteric path." Suddenly, I looked around my life and thought, "Wow, I'm on an island of one. I'm through, it's over. Nobody is ever going to call me with financing. I'm broke, and *Mrs. Parker* is out and gone." There were a few very good things that were sent to me by writers, but I could see that chasing other people's dreams was just as hard as chasing my own. So I sat down and wrote something for survival.

I'm absolutely madly in love with my wife and have been for decades. I feel she's just an amazing work of human art, and brand new every day. She's like a child and she's the most independent person you've ever met. I started thinking, "Where does this love reside?" It's not in the deeds, it's not in the actions, it's not in the memory of it, it's not in the words of it. It's all of that, but it's in the intangibles where love resides. It's like music; it comes to your senses and overwhelms you in ways that you can't put your finger on. As soon as you think you know what it is, it's not that. It's the most delicate thing there is. And where is it? Is it in the past? Is it in the future? Is it all of this? I thought, "Well, I'll just sit down and write some little opera and see what happens."

You didn't feel you had covered that material in *Choose Me*?

No, you can't ever cover it. I wanted to go back to where I started. I wanted to make this the grownup cousin to *Choose Me*. I felt a connection could be made from *Welcome* to *Choose Me* to *Afterglow*, the same way someone might make a connection from *The Moderns* to *Mrs. Parker* and a film that I was trying to get made about Man Ray and the Surrealists. It's not so awful to have things that are connected; people do it all the time. Scorsese's done it; Altman's done it. I'm not embarrassed by it. I learn from it. I wanted to put this film in a real place, but couldn't figure out where. I wanted a place where none of the characters was from. They were all disconnected from each other, from their past, in exile.

It's important to know they don't have an emotional connection to the place they live in.

The character that really led the charge for me was Jonny Lee Miller's. He's the most confused and ambiguous, and the most unlikeable for the audience because they didn't understand him, which was the point. I wanted him to be a complete product of his time, the young businessman who basically is controlling the world these days. I know these people but I avoid them. I really got into this character. I wanted him underneath to be confused about everything, because he'd been thrust into life thinking that everything he does is completely successful. These emotions that bubble up from within him, which he denies and tries to suppress, are what life is about.

Jonny was brilliant, but many critics were unkind to him. The young people hated this portrait of one of their own. This is when I really learned what audiences are like. I had one satisfaction at the Toronto Film Festival. A lady from one of those street magazines that think they know everything interviewed me live on radio. I'd read a review of the film, one sentence long, just trashing Jonny and Lara Flynn as shallow actors who were not able to hold the screen with Julie Christie and Nick Nolte. This woman interviewed me and I didn't connect the review to her. During the live radio interview, she said something that suggested she was the one who had written it. I said, "Oh, did you write that?" She said, "Yes, I did." I said, "You did something most critics do. You confused the actor with the character. Now, why would you think you know more about acting or developing a character than Julie Christie, who thought that Jonny was one of the most brilliant actors she'd ever worked with in her life, or me, or Jonny, or Lara? You don't like that character because he's your age and he didn't turn out the way you want."

It was easy to say, "Oh, Julie is so brilliant, and Nick is so great." Yet, I felt each of them was equally brilliant. Lara Flynn is amazing. She's like a throw-back to the classic comediennes in her way of working, like Lucille Ball's film work. Beautiful, perfect comic timing. And no jokes, just behavior.

Yes, but Lara's character puts people off.

Of course. Because she was written as a shallow person.

But what does this person want besides a baby? Does she have anything in her head?

What difference does it make? Everyone has something in their head. Lara Flynn read the script and said, "I'd like to play this as a combination "Stepford Wife" and "Holly Golightly" [Audrey Hepburn's character from *Breakfast At Tiffany's*]. This is a woman who fell in love with this handsome, enigmatic, powerful guy in college and married him. She just wants a family and sits around reading style magazines all day. She has the most shallow existence, and yet there's something else going on inside her that's not been cultivated."

Did you have Julie Christie in mind for the role?

Not when I wrote it, but she and Nick were the first choices. That's the power of Altman as a producer. He asked me who I wanted in the film. When I said Julie Christie and Nick Nolte, he said, "Well, I just saw Nick Nolte," and a few days later, Julie Christie called me up from London. I finished the script on Friday, and this was the following Wednesday. I thought we'd be shooting the next Monday. Then, almost everybody turned us down with the money. It only got made because of a really terrific guy who wanted to get into film production. He raised the five or six million dollars internationally. Nick did another two movies while we were waiting. The agents sent the script around, even though I told them not to, and we got comments back like "Nice script, but we don't want to make it. It's only about people" or "Who's Julie Christie?" and "Who cares about a movie about old people like that." I felt it was as accomplished a work as I'd ever done, that it explored certain truths and combined a certain spontaneity, and was exactly what I wanted. It was serious and humorous simultaneously.

The ending is quite a tragic, cathartic moment.

Well, it's cathartic. But it's a happy ending because they [Nick Nolte and Julie Christie] had to get beyond their pain. That's what their problem was. Nick is one the greatest actors. Not only is he a wonderful person and an inspiration but, on screen, he always looks like he just showed up as a real, dimensional person. He has the gift. He knows how to act "natural." He's one of the most prepared, studied actors, not in his performance, but he studies the role. We would go over the letters his character had written to Julie's character that, of course, never made it on the screen. Fantastic. I loved working with him.

I'm still waiting for Julie to agree to be in *Afterglow*. I don't think she ever said, "Okay, I'll be in it." She said, "Well, I have no sense of humor. I'm not one of these American actors that I've heard you like to work with who can invent. Please don't ask me to improvise. I don't do that." Of course, she was making up the best lines of the movie by the end of it.

It was one of the most exciting, wonderful, rewarding things I've ever done, and I was so proud of it. Julie cleaned up on a lot of awards, and Nick should have got much more attention, as the other two should have. But one speaks for all in a funny way, and collecting her awards, Julie always said, "This isn't for me, this is for the whole cast." After we made it, I said to myself, "That's the end of it. I finally turned the page and closed that volume. I wanted this to be in the family of *Welcome* and *Choose Me*, and that's the end of that whole chapter. I don't know if I'll ever work again, but I'm happy with that." While we were finishing *Afterglow*, *Breakfast* came up again. Bruce called me and said, "Listen, I want to make this." We started an absolutely revolutionary way to make a film. The star got it financed from foreign sales, and he owns it in North America. It has great actors in it and the script is really good, I think. Unconventional, unique, but good. Good enough, anyway, to assemble an extraordinary cast.

You have Albert Finney in it, don't you?

Bruce Willis, Nick Nolte, Albert Finney, Barbara Hershey, Glenne Headly, Lukas Haas, Omer Epps, Buck Henry.

What's the budget on the film?

It was under ten million dollars, and then it went a little higher. Bruce reached in his pocket for music rights and visual effects, the first time I'd ever used them. It's because of Bruce we finally made the film. He's a terrific collaborator, employer. I got complete control, with no studio, nothing.

Was this the first time you adapted a novel?

Yes. But more than that, for me, it's the sense of humor. It's the most complicated film and my biggest canvas yet. We did it in thirty-two days. I've never really had more than forty days. It was huge and small at the same time. It's *Hellzapoppin* for the first thirty minutes. You climb aboard this film and you have to go with it or walk out. There aren't any scenes that explain things. Talk about ambiguity. Yet it's different from the book, which is impossible to adapt, or impossible if you're trying to follow the story.

My first attempt at a *Breakfast* screenplay was back in the mid-1970s, as I said earlier, when Altman was thinking about doing it. I wrote it in a week, and before I realized it, I was meeting Kurt Vonnegut. At the time, the book was a complete satire—now it's just a reflection—and the humor was wild. Writing the script was really one of the most liberating experiences. I couldn't get it out of my system. But I also realized that I needed something to start my directing career with, and I went totally the other way with *Welcome to L.A.* I went into this very interior, emotionally realistic, surface artifice, which was comfortable for me. I had tried to get *Breakfast of Champions* made over the years, but couldn't.

On this new version, I added things that I'd learned and knew and observed over the years. The finished film is much closer to the book for a while, then it totally veers off. The book is like a rocket that never stops. How do you make a movie of it? So I just started taking it to other places. Albert Finney plays Kilgore Trout, a Vonnegut character who reappears in many novels, and is in Kurt's last book *Timequake*. It turns out that Vonnegut lives two blocks from where I live in New York. I've seen him on the street but never had enough nerve to talk to him because I met him only once, twenty-five years ago. Then I met him again through Nick at the *Mother Night* screening in Montreal, while we were shooting *Afterglow*. Kurt was at the table and said, "I'd have thought we'd be doing business by now." Twenty-five years later he remembered meeting me!

Do you think you got stuff out of Bruce that others haven't?

I hope so. I never worked with a guy who knows more about the entire process of filmmaking and acting. He's amazing. I think, and perhaps he does too, that this is his best acting to date.

Do you think you're at a point in your career where you're more bankable?

My friend, Tom Robbins, says I don't have a career. He says, "Guys like us don't have careers. We have careens."

You obviously have a career.

Look, the only calls I'll get after *Breakfast,* whether it's a huge smash hit or just smashed, will be people who have ten million dollars to make a movie, asking me if I can get Bruce for their movie. I decided really early that the tone of the film had to be breakaway, almost slapstick, with no jokes, just observational humor. The trick was to give it density. I wanted to make a movie that, for a half hour or so, you think is the darkest, funniest thing you've ever seen and, by the end, you're crying. That was my goal. I have no idea how anybody will respond to this movie.

What are your thoughts on the industry and making films in today's environment?

When I was a kid, my dad always said, "Everybody wants to be in the movie business." I gradually started to understand that the movies were not an escape for me. Man was predestined to make motion pictures. It's the quintessential human invention to duplicate a moving, dimensional representation of our own lives. Because we can't see ourselves, all we can do is watch other people. Somebody asks, "What is your definition of a movie?" And I say, "Their faces have to be bigger than yours." I've never seen a soap opera in my life, but I think all my movies are soap operas. They're street operas, I guess, these self-contained little stories that mean didley squat as stories but are something for the characters to pass through. Hopefully, it doesn't look like the story made them do it, but they made the story happen. The most interesting thing for me is to get into the nuances and emotions and the paradoxical qualities that are essential in all of our lives. In its cheapest form, I suppose, it's irony, but, in fact, it's the essence of humanity.

Film was always an entertainment, a way to go places you've never been or to lose yourself in the dark or to fall in love with people you'll never meet or sublimate all of your fantasies. Film became big-time currency relatively recently. *Jaws* started it. The turning point came when the economics of movies became like the business page, and movies were seen as an economic asset. Young audiences today, and for a generation or more, have had very little encouragement for self-exploration. It's just not there in our culture. So these kids, the target audience, go to movies not to be stimulated within. The stimulation is all physical, and people get offended by something that isn't working that way. This is something I've learned by seeing the screenings of my films. Audiences get angry with you for trying to do something beyond what they consider the requisites of a film, which is a certain amount of entertainment value, a certain amount of show, a certain amount of celebrity. If you're going to make a film in a different way, they won't go with you at all any more. Not all audiences, but most of them. It's an outgrowth of Hollywood's philosophy.

It's not just Hollywood. I think it has something to do with television, in terms of formula, repetitive forms, TV movies, etcetera.

You're probably right. But I think it's really simple. It's that movies are too valuable. You need the movie to get the lunch pail at McDonald's. Movies are too valuable as hard assets to their owners to mess with the formula.

I was speaking more in terms of audience expectations.

I'm talking mostly about young audiences. They view popular movies as their private portion of public art. "Yeah, I like that one. I like *Scream* because it's speaking to me about what I'm interested in on a pop cultural level," they say. They get offended if you give them something different, which is why it's so predictable.

Do you think that's really new, or have audiences always been like that?

What's new is that the vocabulary is already in place. People assign feelings to labels. In my opinion, we aren't living up to our potential as filmmakers. The audiences will follow because of their *need* for film. You have to see where your own personal art fits into the larger scheme of things. I've met more big-time filmmakers at film festivals who come up to me and say, "You know, you're doing what

I wish I could do." When I ask what, they say, "Well, I've had a lot of big hits. I've made a lot of money, but you get to do what you want." I say, "Because in Hollywood, if you're not a commercial success, you're a failure." For me, it's just the opposite. I'm a total success on one level, in that I keep working on what I want to do. But then again, I never had a call from anyone who had any money, asking, "What do you want to do next?" Never, never, never. I've always had to self-generate, start it, go out and do something. I've never had a deal where I know what I'm doing next. I couldn't even name the studios right now; I couldn't even tell you the heads of any of them. I would be very happy making my own films, financing them if I could, even distributing them, I suppose, if I could just continue. People say, "How does this guy keep going? He's never made a hit." I just know, from what my films cost, that somebody's making money. But, hopefully, they have more value than that, more value than money. I know they do to me. Life has more value than price.

LYNNE STOPKEWICH

Lynne Stopkewich is a young Canadian filmmaker who burst onto the International film scene with *Kissed*, one of the most controversial films of the decade. The film is a poetic narrative about a young, free-spirited woman who has a sexual predilection for corpses. But the film is more a character study and unsentimental black comedy than a horror film or Gothic tale, although it is unquestionably an erotic film. *Kissed* wants to say something truthful about the potential in all of us to achieve ecstasy. It is an unpretentious film with one of the more intriguing main characters in recent film history. The necrophilia that is at the film's center is addressed head on, and the film treats the main character's nonconformity in a direct, matter-of-fact manner that will, no doubt, shock some audiences. But the film's treatment of its female protagonist's problem is so sympathetic, and portrayed in such metaphorical terms, that most viewers end up strangely empathizing with the character. Somewhat surprisingly, this quirky, daring film has become one of the most commercially successful Canadian films released in the past decade.

Kissed has been grouped with some other recent films, such as Atom Egoyan's *Exotica* and David Cronenberg's *Crash*, as indicating a somewhat perverse direction in recent Canadian cinema, a troubling—possibly degraded—view of humanity. But what these and some other films indicate is not so much a perverted view of human behavior, but an acknowledgment of its complexity and the fact that old forms of art must continually be reinvented in the modern era. For many filmgoers, the extreme quality of some of these films is one of their attractive aspects. They can be compared to the best American independent films in that they are willing to eschew convention and formula, yet they also display something of a European sensibility and a deep knowledge of film history.

One of the main reasons I was interested in talking to Lynne, apart from having enormous respect for her film, was that she had been a former student in our university film program. To my mind, it is extremely important that younger filmmakers, especially women filmmakers, talk about their experiences in the film industry. Somewhat unusually, the fact that Lynne was a first-time woman director does not seem to have hindered her in the least in making *Kissed*. In fact, she argues that "being a woman was a huge advantage. The original material was written by a woman, the main character is a woman. It's all about female sexuality. There's a whole scene in the film centering around menstruation." It seems doubtful that a male director would have handled the same material with such sensitivity and feeling for its main character. Lynne seems sincerely interested in making films that explore what it means to be a woman at this moment in time. And for that we should be truly thankful, because *Kissed* is a remarkable first feature that indicates the arrival of an outstanding new filmmaker with a genuinely unique vision. Lynne is currently completing *Suspicious River*, her second feature. She spoke to me from Vancouver, British Columbia.

Stopkewich

When did you start making films?

I made my first film when I was about twelve. Then I took a film studies course before I went to university. I got completely blown away by watching my first European film. I had always loved film, but I'd never seen a film where you could combine an intellectual approach with the format of pure entertainment. At that point, I thought, "this is a really great medium of expression," and I did a Bachelor of Fine Arts in Film Production at Concordia University in Montreal. From there I did a Master of Fine Arts in Film at the University of British Columbia.

What was the training like at film school?

The initial undergraduate experience was very much about educating myself, in terms of film history and aesthetics and the fundamentals of filmmaking: how to work a camera, basic storytelling, and film theory. These were really important. It was also a very competitive environment. That, in some ways, was a good model for the real world, where you have to juggle a lot of different things and still produce a film which has some merit.

Did you make any films as an undergraduate?

I made a number of Super-8 movies in college, close to a dozen. When I got to university, I made two 16mm short films: *The Three Dollar Wash and Set* and *Flipped Wig*.

What about your experience at the University of British Columbia?

At that time, there were only two graduate programs in film production in Canada, and UBC offered one of them. They only took two students a year. You were allowed to create your own program of study, which I thought was great after the undergraduate experience, which had been fairly strict in terms of courses I had to take. Part of my decision to go to graduate school was to get a feature film off the ground. I had been watching the careers of Spike Lee, Susan Seidelman, and Jim Jarmusch, who had all come out of the New York University Film Program, and I thought a graduate program might be a great starting point for me.

You started working as a production designer while you were at graduate school, didn't you? What were some of the films you worked on?

The first feature that I designed was a film called *The Grocer's Wife,* which is a small, black-and-white, independent Canadian film made by John Pozer. It opened the Cannes Critics Week in 1992, so I was involved with a bit of a Cinderella story. Since I was both production designer and associate producer on the film, I saw how the film was put together. And because it had such a specific look and atmosphere, I was then given an opportunity to design a feature called *Tomcat,* with a budget ten times that of *The Grocer's Wife,* $1.5 million instead of $150,000. That was my platform for getting into design. Most of the films I designed were either Canadian features, or features produced under the Investment Tax Shelter, which would then go to video or foreign sales.

How did your work as a production designer help you to make your first film? Did it make you more attuned to the visual look of film?

I think so, but that was always a concern of mine. Even in my short films a decade before *Kissed,* there's a consistent sensibility and visual style. Designing was a great way for me to learn more about directing, because I was collaborating with the director and cinematographer. I learned more about lighting and about directing professional actors and the beast that a feature film shoot can be.

Because I was always working on low-budget movies, I became the low-budget production-design queen in Vancouver. [Laughs] There was a certain honor in trying to always stay under budget, which served me well when I made *Kissed*. I think that's part of the reason why *Kissed* looks as polished as it does.

What are some of the cultural and aesthetic influences on your film-making?

American popular culture. Television had a huge influence on my work. Cinematically, I'd say people like David Lynch and Fassbinder, who was the director of that first European film I ever saw. A lot of the classic American filmmakers like Hitchcock and Ford and people like Scorsese. Also a lot of the American Independents just because they did it, and you could also read about how they did it. I remember reading Spike Lee's book about the making of *She's Gotta Have It* at least three or four times. I thought "Wow, you really can do this. It is possible!" So, those were all really important.

What about other artists or writers?

Writers like Margaret Atwood and painters like Andy Warhol and Roy Liechtenstein have been important to me. Also, I went through a period where I was very influenced by feminist theory and writing. One thing I learned in film school is that everyone wants to make a film, but not everyone has something interesting to say. I'm interested in telling stories from a female perspective.

Where did the idea for *Kissed* come from?

The film is based on a short story by Toronto author Barbara Gowdy. I was actually in the middle of writing a completely different screenplay, which centered around a character exploring her sexuality, and I decided that I wanted to do a little more research into female erotica. As I was doing that research, I came across this book called *The Girl Wants To*. It was an anthology of prose, poetry, drawings, comic strips, and things like that. In it, I came across this story, *We So Seldom Look on Love*. I was completely floored by it. As I was continuing to write my other screenplay, this story and its main character just kept coming back to my mind.

How different is your film from that story?

That's a good question, because I think that it's very different in some ways, and very close in other ways. People who are fans of the author have told me they think that it does justice to the story. Yet, I know there are themes in the film that don't exist in the short story at all. I think the tone of the piece, or of the character, is different. The character in the story is a lot harder-edged and more Machiavellian in some ways.

Does the story also have a first-person narration?

Yeah. This is the thing that was the biggest challenge for me. From the perspective of a first-person narration, how do you externalize that internal world? How do you find dialogue and action that will translate? I didn't want the whole film to be voice-over. At the same time, it was great because I knew, as a first-time filmmaker, I wanted to maintain some of the lyricism and poetry of that voice. If I ran into problems in the shooting or the editing, I knew Barbara Gowdy's words were so powerful they would help ease me over the rough spots. In the end, all the voice-over written for the film was based on Barbara's writing, but it was rewritten and reworked because the film had become something different than the story. The words coming out of the character's mouth in the short story didn't seem to fit the mouth of the character we created in the movie. The voice-over was written to suit the character after the film was cut. That voice-over was a thorn in my side for months and months. It was ridiculous. [Laughs]

How personal is this material? I don't mean the necrophilia, but the themes that the film explores?

I think it's intensely personal in a lot of ways. One reason I got so excited about the material was that this character seemed like a life-filled, intelligent girl-next-door, but she is also obsessed with death and the dark side. I liked that contrast. In a lot of ways, that's been the dichotomy for me in terms of filmmaking. I really love to watch your classic blockbuster, and let myself escape into a film. Yet, I'm always looking for intellectual resonance. I like the fact that the character embodies those contrasts. She's someone who's completely unafraid, and driven forward by her curiosity. Part of the reason I took on the material was that my curiosity was stronger than my fear of the material.

How did the film come to be made and financed?

It took three years. Initially, it was private investment: my own savings as a production designer, my partner's savings from his work as a director, and family and friends. It got to the point where we decided, "Okay, how much will the film stock cost? How much will it cost to feed the crew? That's the bottom line. We'll work our way up from there." As long as there was money for that, then we could move forward. We had family and friends investing $500 here, $1,000 there, all the way along.

We tried to always use money that didn't have any editorial strings attached. Once we'd shot the movie, the National Film Board of Canada processed the rushes for us. And the Canada Council gave us a post-production grant. We got the film to the point where we tried to get into the Toronto Film Festival. And we still needed money to finish it. In the end, Telefilm Canada gave us a small grant which was well below what we'd asked for.

How much research did you do into things like necrophilia and embalming procedures?

Only as much as I had to. It was really difficult to get over my own fears and preconceived ideas about the material. At the time when I was writing the screenplay, the Internet really wasn't happening, and I was under the gun because we were shooting nine weeks after I got the rights to the story. I had a window of time where I had access to equipment for very little money, so I had to have the script ready. I wrote the first draft myself, and then I brought in a friend, Angus Fraser, who helped me with subsequent drafts. So, there wasn't a lot of time to do research. I only did the research that I needed to do. It was difficult to find any information at all, anywhere. When I found a textbook on embalming in the library, I would find that there was a three-month waiting list for it. [Laughs] And with necrophilia, forget it, there's nothing out there. You get a definition in the back of a medical textbook, and that's about it.

How prepared were you when you actually started shooting? Did you storyboard the film?

The first few days of the film were storyboarded and shot-listed, but after that, I threw it out the window. Our locations kept falling through, and I had to come up with something else on the spot. It's interesting for me when I look at the film now. Aesthetically, the structure of the movie is initially very montage-based, the camera is very static. As the film progresses, the camera work becomes looser.

Were you shooting in sequence?

Not totally in sequence, but pretty close. I wanted to shoot all the material with the little girl up front. And then, because of actors' availability, most of it was shot in sequence.

Did things develop on the set as you shot?

Yes, it got to the point where we would be shooting for twenty hours a day and the assistant director would say that we had X amount of time to get this scene shot. So, for a scene where I might have wanted nine setups, I would get three setups. And I'd have to cover a three-page scene with two shots. I tried with the cinematographer to make the right aesthetic choices, given all the limitations we faced at the time. The best scenes, for me, were the ones where I had some time—the scene where Sandra [Molly Parker] and Matt [Peter Outerbridge] make love for the first time, for example. Basically, the actors came in, and I gave them some general ideas of how I was thinking of blocking the scene. They ran through it, we sort of worked it out, fine-tuned some of it, and they would leave. Then I worked out the camera placement with the cinematographer. Then we would shoot the scene. That's how we did it.

Did you stick closely with the script you had written?

Yes. The actors often challenged the text. I was open to their collaboration and input. I wasn't really upset or nervous about the idea of changing lines of dialogue if it felt more comfortable for them. I would rewrite things, but somehow always end up with the original material. There were a couple of scenes that I was adamant about, like the scene where the character makes love on-camera to the dead guy. That scene was storyboarded a month before we shot.

The scene where she dances around him?

That's the one.

That's a key scene because it comes after she makes love with Matt for the first time.

Yes, exactly. There were a couple of key scenes in the film that I did not want to waver from. My partner would always say to me, "If you have at least five or six really interesting scenes in a film, you pretty much have a feature." [Laughs] The film would have fallen apart if a couple of key scenes hadn't worked. To me, that was the most important scene in the film.

What were you looking for when you cast the main roles?

This is going to sound really fundamental, but someone who could act. [Laughs]

And I was looking for someone who really wanted and needed the film. I knew the film was going to be grueling. That was the philosophy with the crew as well. We were in a situation where people were working completely on deferral, or nothing at all. And I wanted the same kind of spirit and energy that I was bringing to the project.

Do you have any training in acting?

I don't. Before I made this film, I took a course in theater performance, so I could feel what it was like to be in front of a camera and in front of an audience. My biggest fear was that the film, technically, would stand up but the performances would be horrendous. That was a really scary thing because you have to care about your characters. I walked a fine line, in terms of tone, between this self-reflexive feeling and earnestness, between the romance of this character and the harsh reality of necrophilia.

I had a huge fear of directing actors. My short films were very stylized. The characters and the actors were over-the-top, à la John Waters, and they were all non-actors. In this film, it was crucial that you cared about these characters, and that the performances were real. I really worked on that.

Did you have any trouble casting the two main roles, Matt and Sandra?

People kept telling me that it would be hard to find actors who'd want to play these roles. But, quite the opposite, I had actors crashing auditions. Especially young women who had gotten their hands on the script. And when we were shooting the movie, we had people sign statements of confidentiality. We weren't letting the script out. I knew that Gowdy had a huge following, and that particular story is quite infamous.

A lot of the Canadian actors working in Vancouver are working in the American service industry: American series, big features, and television movies-of-the-week. The Canadian actors get the walk-on parts, and, especially for women, the roles are limited. So, they were excited about it. Molly Parker was working on a movie-of-the-week with Glenn Close, and was supposedly unavailable. I was getting very frustrated that there didn't seem to be anyone at the auditions who captured the essence of the character.

Did you have a lot of rehearsal with the actors?

No, there was no rehearsal. With Molly [Parker], I sat down and went over the script with her in great detail as it was being revised. We talked a lot about the character, because I knew the set would probably be quite chaotic, and I wanted to do as much work as possible with her ahead of time. The character herself is very isolated and marginalised. She's alienated through her obsession. It kind of served the process by not having rehearsals. We did a read-through of the script about a week before we shot, which was a complete catastrophe. We had all the actors, except for Peter Outerbridge, just sitting around a table reading the script. Of course, the timing was completely wrong. Any actor who's been through this never gives you their performance in a dry reading. I remember the producer looking at me with a look of horror on his face, because it was either turning into a Mel Brooks movie or a very, very earnest art-house film. [Laughs]

Describe the shooting of the film. How long was the shoot? Was it difficult?

It was brutal. But it was also the best time I've had in my whole life. It was magical in a lot of ways. The days were extremely long. A twelve-hour day was a minimum. We shot for five weeks. Initially, we were going to be shooting six days a week, but, of course, it became seven days a week. Once we had a rough cut of the movie, I ended up reshooting some scenes. For many of the crew, it was their first feature, so things were out of focus and there were some technical errors here and there. That was really difficult, because when I shot pick-ups, it was a year later. So the two little girls who were twelve when we shot, were now thirteen or fourteen, and had shot up in height.

I lost a lot of material in the cut. Whole sections of the screenplay never made it to the screen. We got really ruthless in the editing, and cut it down to the best stuff. You've written these carefully constructed transitions, and suddenly your film is very bumpy and doesn't make sense. So, we went back and shot interim montage sequences to make the transitions smoother and clearer.

The visual style of the film is fairly striking. Things like the over-exposures, "going into the white light" effect. How did you work with your cinematographer on the look of the film?

I started working with him from the moment he read the short story. Even as I was writing, we started looking at other films, and I gave him an idea of the visual style I wanted. A lot of what you see in the film, such as the burn to white, is in the screenplay. I took some clues from the short story, and tried to find a cinematic representation for the states of mind. I wanted to experiment and try things, and see if they would work. So I would ask Greg Middleton, the cinematographer, how we could create these things. And he would come up with a solution.

Budget and schedule restraints also influenced the aesthetic, because I knew it would take a lot longer to shoot a moving camera than a static camera. So, most of the film is static camera, and I reserved the moments of moving camera for when the character is having a transcendent moment. I thought that would be an interesting way to represent her state of mind, and to help the audience understand her. That was the biggest challenge: How do you get into the head of this character and make her interesting, make her sympathetic enough that people wouldn't storm out of the theater on moral grounds?

Are you saying that if you'd had more time, money, and shooting days and shot a more elaborate script, you might have lost something?

Yes, I think so. A lot of things came together because of the constraints we faced. I think if I'd had more time to think about it, it would have become more self-conscious. In some ways, it became very instinctual. I just shot what I wanted to see on the screen, and I made the editorial choices based on my personal preferences.

What are the other reasons for choosing this style? It wasn't just because you didn't have enough time.

Well, it's partly choice, partly inexperience, partly not wanting to bite off more than I could chew. I've seen many people try to take on a really elaborate style, and I just wanted to get the bare bones on the screen and tell the story in as straight-forward a way as possible.

Do you think it's more intimate this way?

Yes, absolutely. I remember in my first film studies class as an undergraduate, all the students would sit in the back of the theater. The professor said, "You guys are trying to turn the film screen into a TV set by moving as far back as you can." The whole thing about film is that it fills your peripheral vision. I became a huge proponent of extreme closeups, being able to get right in there and see detail.

Was the film difficult to edit?

Yes. We shot it in 16mm, and we cut it on a Steenbeck [editing table] we'd set up in a friend's house. I was actually surprised that so much footage was usable, because there were so many first-timers on the technical end of things. I thought it was really important to try and make the most technically flawless film I could, because if there was a bump in a dolly move or something was out of focus or the camera wasn't quite right, people would be distracted from being able to enter into the character's world. That was really key.

The music and sound—the use of the female voice on the soundtrack and some of your selections for source music and the score of the film—are very effective. Were you particularly sensitive to this in postproduction?

Yes, that was crucial. Many low-budget films have thin sound. You can tell people are getting really tired, and they just want to rush through the sound. But we went back to the Godard adage that film is image *and* sound. Because I'm so strongly image-oriented, I wanted to go almost overboard on the sound. When we locked picture, we spent seven or eight months replacing a lot of the sound, because most of the location sound was unusable.

We released a soundtrack album that is really great. We wanted to use Canadian artists, and in the end, they were all Vancouver artists on a specific record label which my co-producer had worked with before. I went through mounds and mounds of their CDs to find the right songs for the film. The score was really interesting, because I had absolutely no idea which way to go with it. I found a composer

I thought I could communicate with. As it turned out, he was a choir director as well, and since there's such a female sensibility operating in the movie on every level, I thought it would be interesting to use female voices in the score. That's what we decided to do to get the ethereal feel.

Was Molly Parker clear about her character, and why her character was doing certain things?

I think there was a lot of fear and anxiety in general in dealing with this material. But, Molly's a very focused individual, as am I, so we were clear about what we didn't want to do. People gave me advice saying, "You have to know this character inside out, so when the actor asks questions about her motivation, you're going to know everything." In some ways, it was exactly the opposite. It was a journey of discovery for Molly and myself to figure this character out, because it's so outside of our own experience. So we tried to bring things from our own experience to bear on her character. In the end, that's why the character is so accessible. Yet, this character is still breaking major taboos. We said, "Okay, we accept that. Let's move on from there."

Did your sense of who Sandra was change as you made the film?

I think it changes every time I watch the film. She's always a shadowy figure out there, and I always see different things in her, different things in Molly's performance. Initially, Sandra was an enigma. The material was shocking. Both Molly and I had to become like her, to a degree. Molly's greatest fear as an actor was having to go to the place of being this character alone, and I promised her that I would go with her. So, we created our own little world in terms of how we would talk about the character.

What kinds of discussions did you have about this character?

We were interested in her emotional life and the reverberations and impact of the choices she had made. We believed that her behavior was something she couldn't really control. As she says in the film, "I need to do it, I have no choice." So we tried to think about things in our own lives we felt compelled to do, or were obsessive about. We tried to find other things we could plug into that could take the place of necrophilia. I don't think I understand the impulse behind necrophilia, but I understand the impulse behind obsession and that kind of intense focus to the exclusion of all else, and being reckless in terms of choices. My own moral stance was put aside.

There would be moments during the shoot when Molly and I would look at each other and say, "Wow, this is really intense stuff." There's a scene in the film where she's in the morgue, and she's touching this guy who's embalmed and dressed in a suit, and the scene ends by her unbuttoning her blouse. She grabs his hand, smells it, and starts rubbing it on her face. In the script, all it said was, "she comes into the room and wants to be near him." But now I had to create the scene with the actress. So, as the crew was lighting the scene, Molly and I stood there with the actor who was playing the corpse, and she said, "Well, what do you think she would do?" Molly had one of his hands, and I had his other hand, and I'm smelling this actor's hand and rubbing it on my neck. Suddenly, both of us realized that all the sound in the room had stopped—and the crew was standing, transfixed, somewhat horrified, watching us have our way with this actor who was playing a corpse! [Laughs]

Did being a woman director disadvantage you at any time?

No, I think it was the other way around. Given the material, being a woman was a huge advantage. The original material was written by a woman, the main character is a woman. It's all about female sexuality. There's a whole scene in the film centering around menstruation.

Do you think most audience members can sympathize or identify with Sandra?

Yes. That's been ninety-five percent of the feedback. Although, in Quebec, the response was completely different. They really couldn't identify with her at all, but they identified with Matt. And to a slight degree, the French press in France had a similar reaction, saying that he was more "evolved" than her because he sacrificed himself for her.

Whereas, when he commits suicide, a lot of the North American audiences just say, "Oh, that was a dumb move." [Laughs] It's been interesting, culturally, to see how people have responded. Across-the-board, people have liked her.

Can you talk a bit more about that first-person voice-over? It's very poetic, and also very literary. It's at those times when you see it for what it is: a narrative device. I wasn't sure whether you always wanted that literary quality.

It was a struggle. I don't feel unsatisfied with the voice-over. I think it works at times, and at other times it's too obvious. It was difficult to do because you're so close to the material that you don't know where other people are at with the film. And that was a real challenge, to think, "What is the audience thinking here, what is the audience thinking there?"

How do you understand Sandra's sexuality or compulsion? Did you see it as deviant, or simply an unconventional form of achieving ecstasy?

All those things at different times, depending on where I was at. When we were shooting the movie, I had to believe that she was completely "normal," that she behaved that way because that's who she was. But then I was forced to visit a funeral home before we shot the movie, even though I didn't want to. I saw a young dead guy in a suit lying in the prep room, and at that moment, fiction and reality came together. I thought, "Oh my God, this film is about a character who makes love to dead guys. How horrifying." I had to float in and out of reality in some ways with the film, in terms of my own perspective of who the character is and what her behavior is. I thought it was crucial in terms of the film's subversive edge to make her seem as normal as possible. I thought it was much more of a challenge not to make the film a stereotypical, dark, Gothic horror narrative, which is what you would assume it is, given the story. I wanted to fly in the face of those conventions and go completely in the other direction to create a different kind of stylization. That was really crucial. Otherwise, people in the suburbs wouldn't even enter the theater. And that was part of my interest in the material, to see how accessible I could make this completely inaccessible activity.

Did those people end up going to see this film?

Yes, absolutely. Obviously, it's not a universal kind of film. If people don't get it or don't enjoy it or whatever, that's a legitimate reaction. I enjoy that reaction as well, because at least it's a reaction. I get annoyed with films that I see, and walk out of, which just slide off. I don't remember them, and I don't care about them. I wouldn't be happy if people had no feeling for it whatsoever. Then I'd think it was a failure.

Were you satisfied with all the characterizations? For me, Matt is not fully drawn.

I completely agree with you. I know that his deterioration and their whole relationship needed more development. Especially for him to hold up his end of a two-character film. My resources as a film-maker and the time-frame and how we made the film was such that I had to give all my energy to Molly Parker's performance, to Sandra Larson's character. Everything had to serve her. It could certainly have addressed the issues of obsession, mortality, relationships, and sexuality more. I didn't want people to overly identify with him. In my mind it was her film and her story. It was a conscious decision to sacrifice his character for the sake of developing hers, because of our limitations.

I'm curious why you decided to inject these moments of black humor in the film. Did you do it because you felt that some things would make people uncomfortable?

It's partly that. It's also me letting the audience know "Hey, I'm still here, and I know what you're going through. I'm taking the material seriously, but not quite so seriously that it's in total earnest." I also took a cue from Barbara's work. In her short story, she writes about these characters who are basically freaks, but you care about them and can laugh with them. You're never really laughing at them. It's a matter of emotional engagement with the characters, and that was crucial. In general, that's crucial for me in film. I've been reading so many scripts where the story is really interesting, but I don't really care, because I don't find the characters compelling. Obviously, there's a huge suspension of disbelief in this film.

Do you expect audiences to be sexually stimulated by the film?

No, I don't, but I've had different responses. I think people relate to this film much more in an emotional way, and some have said in a spiritual way, but less so in a sexual way. I was really conscious about that in terms of how I represented the characters in sexual situations, and how I chose to shoot them. The scene where she makes love to the dead guy was very consciously shot in a specific style to try and alleviate the objectification of her presence on the screen. Her looking into the lens, her crawling toward the camera, things like that.

My biggest shock was when people saw the film and asked, "Well, how did she make love to him?" I'd say, "Well, I showed it in the film." And they'd say, "She keeps a towel on the whole time." And I'd say, "It's not about penetration. It's not phallocentric."

Structurally, when to show that scene must've been a key decision. If you show it too early, you risk losing sympathy with the audience.

You have to really build up to it. I think it was crucial because the first time you see her go through with it fully is right after she's had an unsatisfactory sexual episode with Matt, where she loses her virginity.

Your decision to shoot the scene with Matt in such a perfunctory way is such a contrast to the next scene, which is filmed with such exuberance.

It's one of the things that rang true with a lot of people, especially a lot of the women who I spoke to. They said, "Wow, when she loses her virginity with Matt, it really reminded me of me." The idea that there's got to be this whole romantic thing going on the first time you have sex. For the most part, that's not what happens at all. It was perfect for the film, because then we contrast that experience with this ritual that she's created over time, to the point where she does achieve a kind of ecstasy or transcendence.

Do you think Sandra's behavior can be analyzed or understood?

Yes, on a surface level. I don't think it goes much deeper than that. And I really didn't want to go much deeper than that.

You're very careful not to judge her behavior at all. Was there ever a moment where you wanted to comment on it more?

No. I was very careful to be as nonjudgmental as I could be. I think that's crucial in the film. Otherwise, it would be seen as my own manipulation of how to see the character. I had to manipulate the medium enough to allow people to get inside her head, to a degree at least. But I also wanted to pull back enough so that people could come to their own conclusions about the choices she makes and how she behaves.

Did your own ideas about death change in the course of making the film?

Completely. As soon as you start making a film, people assume you're really fascinated with the subject. Part of my interest in the story initially was that, at the time, I was terrified of dying. It was almost as though the story was challenging me to make it into a film—to see if I could handle the material and come through the other end. The largest taboo in the film is that it's so preoccupied with death, as opposed to the taboo of necrophilia. In doing research for the film, and talking to people about the film, bringing up the concept of death without it automatically lapsing into some morbid, Gothic, romantic discussion is virtually impossible in our culture. So, because I've had to talk about it so much, I have more perspective on it in my life.

What were the themes that you wanted most to develop through Sandra and her experiences?

The most basic one is the idea to remain true to yourself, no matter what, regardless of what society says, regardless of anyone or anything. In terms of societal standards, that can be very reckless, but the thing that drew me to this character was the fact that she did fly in the face of everything, and accepted herself. Her world isn't perfect. She's alienated and lonely. She has to create her own philosophy in order to justify her behavior. At the same time, she's a really strong character in that she accepts herself, and a lot of people spend their whole life trying to get to that place. She's more at peace with herself than most people, and I really admired that in her character. I thought that was really strong and brave, and I thought she was, ultimately, a very strong woman.

Did you accomplish what you wanted to accomplish with *Kissed*?

I think so. Yes. Even more.

How have audiences reacted to the film, and have there been different responses in different countries?

The shock for me is that it has been so embraced in such a mainstream way. It's not *Home Alone 2* or anything like that, but it's achieved its profile, it's been accepted. It's had a critical response far and away above anything I could have imagined. When you're making a film with such a risk of time and investment, you become obsessed, and you create a fantasy world of what this film is. And my fantasy world was that I'd just be able to make it. I didn't really consider anything that was going to happen afterwards. So it was a shock for me to come to a point where I had to actually talk about the film. And it had its own life. It hasn't been 100% positive across-the-board, of course. I don't think it ever could be. There's been a letter-writing campaign by the Christian Right to the government agencies that helped support the movie. There's been a bit of a negative response, but nothing compared to what I expected. I thought I was taking on a much more controversial subject. Overall, it's been really positive. I've had people who I never thought would understand the film, like my parents, [Laughs] and I've been really surprised.

What have you been doing since finishing *Kissed*?

I've been promoting it for the past year, traveling with it to festivals, and doing all the promotion in Canada and the U.S. Also, fielding a lot of offers and reading a lot of screenplays from people who are interested in what I'm doing and want to set up deals and things like that. Right now, I've had it with all that running around, and I'm just getting back to focusing on what I want to do, which is *Falling Angels*, Barbara Gowdy's second novel. I'm adapting it, and I'll be directing it. It's a story of three sisters growing up in a suburban neighborhood in Southern Ontario in the 1970s, and trying to survive what we would now call an extremely dysfunctional family. It's also done from a very black perspective.

How important is it to continue making films in Canada? Is there pressure on you to leave?

To go south? Oh, there's tons! Ultimately, my decision will be driven by where the material is. There are a couple of projects based in Los Angeles that are quite interesting, but this new project happens to be something written by a Canadian author, and the rights are owned by a Canadian production company, so it will be based in Canada to a degree. But it depends on where the financing comes from. If we get all our financing from an American company, it could easily be shot in the U.S.

What are some of the qualities one needs to succeed as a filmmaker?

An obsessive desire and an ability to understand what your vision is and to communicate it in a collaborative spirit. When I approach my films, I realize that they are collaborations. And that I also have to have some ideas and some vision of my own, but remain open enough to recognize all the creative contributions, and find my way through them.

Is it a struggle not to lose sight of your own ideas?

Not really. I like hearing people's opinions. I like hearing how others would approach something. Sometimes, I will turn to someone and ask, "Well, what do you think?" With the actors, more than anyone else.

Do you think that your experience on the next film will be different, that you'll handle yourself differently?

Absolutely. Especially since, for me, this filmmaking experience has been incredibly humbling. You come out of film school and say, "Oh, yes. I'm a hot-shot, and I'm going to do this film." Then you realize what it takes to get a film off the ground, and get it made. I had to sit in the editing room and watch and learn from all my mistakes. There were also many times when I did things right. You learn a lot. If I have any advice for first-time filmmakers, it would be to get really involved with the editing of their films. To see what they did right, and what they did wrong on the set. Especially when you're shooting without the benefit of seeing rushes, you have to really trust yourself to know that you got it, because you can't watch the footage the next day and make up for it with reshoots. I've learnt that my instincts are usually right.

MICHAEL TOLKIN

Writer-director Michael Tolkin is one of Hollywood's busiest screen-writers. He wrote the acclaimed script for *The Player*, Robert Altman's acerbic take on contemporary Hollywood that's based on Tolkin's own novel (for which he received an Oscar nomination). He has also worked on such commercial fare as *Mission: Impossible 2* and *Deep Impact* and several as-yet-unproduced screenplays for major Holly-wood studios. Apart from his extensive work as a screenwriter, Tolkin has directed several independent films. *The Rapture*, a highly unusual religious drama about the final apocalypse, was Tolkin's first film as a director. This was followed by *The New Age*, a drama of the search for spiritual and moral values in contemporary Los Angeles. This straddling of the independent film world and the major Hollywood studios places Tolkin in a unique position as a commentator on the state of the current American film industry. His career is also em-blematic of the difficult decisions continually faced by many highly intelligent, sincere artists who try to balance the needs of their own art with the commercial demands of an industry driven first and foremost by the bottom line.

Tolkin is unusual in Hollywood in that he clearly views the film medium as both an outlet for entertainment and an arena to explore troubling moral issues. How many films have dared to even broach the question of religion, let alone imagine an apocalypse in literal terms and a confrontation between the film's main character and God? *The Rapture* is one of the few films in contemporary cinema that dares to raise such troubling questions as how one can live a moral life in a spiritually barren world. Or how we can accept the existence of a God that allows such earthly horrors as have beset the twentieth century. And if having accepted the existence of such a God, can we then accept entry into Heaven when He allows such horrors? Certainly not typical dramatic film fare. Not only does *The Rapture* courageously tackle such heavyweight moral issues, it also features Mimi Rogers in one of the strongest, bravest female performances of the 1990s in the role of Sharon, the troubled protagonist who would rather spend all eternity outside of God's grace, and apart from her daughter, than submit to God's moral code.

The New Age also raised troubling questions about the search for meaning in the seemingly empty Southern California landscape with its New Age-obsessed characters, sharply played by Judy Davis and Peter Weller. Once again, Tolkin tackles uncomfortable subject matter, although here it is laced with comedy and acerbic social satire. Michael Tolkin is a man of uncommon integrity and strong moral beliefs, and a firm believer in a cinema of ideas—a rarity in these days of dumb comedies, superficial melodramas, and pointless action films that strain credibility. I spoke with Michael Tolkin in Los Angeles.

What's your background?

I was born in New York. My father, Mel Tolkin, was a pioneering writer in live television there. He was the head writer for *Show of Shows*, and worked on *Caesar's Hour*. When live television in New York died, he came out here [Los Angeles]. We came here in early 1960, and I grew up in Los Angeles. I went back east to Bard College in 1968 for two years, dropped out for a year, then transferred to Middlebury College in Vermont. I spent two and a half years at Middlebury, and got my B.A. there. Then I went to New York City, and sold an article about the race track to *The Village Voice*. I worked as a journalist in New York from late '75 till '78, and left in 1978 to come out to Los Angeles.

Then I worked in television. My father-in-law's partner was producing *The Delta House*, which was a spin-off of *Animal House*. We, my brother and partner at the time, worked on that as story editors, which really was my introduction to filmmaking. I was twenty-eight at the time. I worked on thirteen episodes. Through luck, there was a producer vacuum on the show, and we had a lot more authority than we should have had. So that was really my film school. I learned the language. I learned what editing rooms were. And I learned the politics.

What about cultural influences on your artistic formation—writers or filmmakers?

One of the things that was really central to me was a local television channel in the early '60s. It ran classic European films, and I'd watch them with my father. By the time I was thirteen or fourteen, I had seen *La Dolce Vita, The Seven Samurai, Seventh Seal,* and had a really good exposure to interesting European cinema. My father also took me to see English comedies.

In terms of American cinema, I guess I've always been more a Fordian than anything else. I've never been a Nicholas Ray intellectual. The films of Nicholas Ray and Sam Fuller, I appreciate, but they've never been at the center of my aesthetic. I'd rather watch *My Darling Clementine* than *Shock Corridor.*

Does that mean you're more interested in the classical model?

I don't know that I'm a complete modernist. I like the richness of the unsarcastic, uncynical classic model more than the modern model. I'm not as interested in sarcasm as I am in sincerity, which may not be evident from my work.

What about writers?

I go through periods. When I was a kid, Ray Bradbury was very important to me. So were Twain, Poe, and Conan-Doyle. Ian Fleming was very important to me. One of the great things about being fourteen is that you can go from reading Chekhov to James Bond without thinking twice about the rules of taste. I had an important binge of reading in my early thirties. I read James M. Cain, all of him, and all of Patricia Highsmith. That had a big influence on me. Certainly, I could not have written *The Player* without having done that.

Was it always your ambition to be a writer?

When I was eleven or twelve years old, we had a career day at school. We had to do a paper on a career, and I said that I wanted to be a director. My father was writing *The Danny Kaye Show,* and there was this director, I think his name was Robert Sheer, so I interviewed him. I did it in the control booth.

You had a sense of what a director did at such a young age?

My mother was a lawyer at MGM in the early '60s, and she would take me to the studio, where they would let me wander around. I could go on to any stage and watch things being filmed. I watched *Twilight Zones* being filmed. I saw some Sam Katzman rock-and-roll movies being shot. I saw Elvis in the commissary.

I'd like to ask a few questions about *The Player* before we move on to the films you've directed. In adapting the novel for the screen, what were some of the biggest challenges?

The surprise is always that if there is a story, it can be translated to the screen, and the challenge is the fear that a novel that is interior can't be translated because of its interiority. But if the character is moving through the world, and there's a lot of movement, that movement is what you're tracking. I think the biggest discovery was the idea that the story existed independently of the form. To say that the novel is the original, and that the movie is the copy misses the real experience. You look at the book, and then you think about the story. You're going to the story which the book manifests in written form, taking the story, and manifesting it in the film. I'm not sure it's really fair to compare one to the other.

When you look at the finished film, how much is you and how much is Robert Altman?

Well, it goes into the microwave, and everything gets melted together. I don't know that you can really separate them because a lot of it reflects things like politics and fighting in the editing room, tugging and pulling. There's a position that some writers want to take, and that position says that the director just keeps the actors from bumping into the furniture. As soon as the director thinks he's a storyteller, independent of the script, the director gets into trouble. The director can't improvise a story while he's shooting. He has to follow the structure of the script. Some directors let actors play with their characters to get into them, or allow them to improvise. Sometimes a director gets life, and sometimes he doesn't. But it's a director's game. Only over time, as writers build up a body of work, can one sense a writer's presence.

I did a piece for *Projections* a few years ago, and I talked about screenwriters who worked with Fellini and screenwriters who worked with

Kurosawa. Particularly with Fellini, you can see that each of his periods is directly connected to the writers he worked with. When you know those writers, and the work they did for other directors, you can see their power. You can really feel what the writers contributed, because you can feel their force. But then, I think European writers tend to have more of a specifically social voice than Americans. European screenwriters are writing social movies, so they have a perspective, and most American writers don't have a real perspective.

He's mentioned in an interview that there were some disagreements between the two of you, especially about the character of June.

It's inevitable. I've fought with every director I've worked with. Every director fights with the writer at some point. What was important to me about June Mercator was that she be indifferent to Hollywood, and in the end, she was indifferent to Hollywood. That was the intention of the character, so it didn't matter that we had different ideas about her.

In the film, as played by Greta Scacchi, she's a very opaque character. It's hard to get a handle on her.

Right. But what was important was her indifference to the business, that she did not care what Griffin [Tim Robbins] did for a living. That was all I cared about, and Altman worked with the actress and got a quality out of her that really fit the film.

In terms of the thrust of the novel and film, do you think they're different?

Some people come up to me and say that the book was better than the movie. I'm happy to hear that. It's flattering, but I don't know that it matters to me that much. They're different. There was studio interest in buying my second novel, *Among the Dead,* and turning it into a film. I refused because I didn't want to make the changes I knew I would have to make in order for that movie to be made. I didn't want to betray the book. I didn't mind changing *The Player* because the final point was almost the same. The sarcastic twist at the end, the implausible happy ending, was another way of saying what I said in the book. The book ends with Griffin still being plagued by guilt and fear. He's not clear of it, there's something hanging over him. In the movie, what he gets is not possible to get. He gets the total Hollywood ending. Yet, I think we were saying roughly the same thing. But with *Among the Dead*, what I think is important about that book, I doubt could survive into a film. So, if I was ever going to turn *Among the Dead* into a movie, I would have to write the script without selling it first. If I then had the control, and I felt it was right, I'd do it. But I don't want to return to it.

Do you think your view of Hollywood in the novel is the same view that comes through in the film?

That's for the viewer to answer, not me. Even if I had an opinion, I don't know that it's important. I think it's really dangerous to make experts of the viewers, and to give the viewer too much information. I think you have to be quiet. John Ford is a model. Ford never talked about his work as an intellectual activity.

Why is it dangerous to know more about the creative process?

Because you are no longer in it, you are now slightly above it. It gives you, as a viewer, an objective clarity, and I think you need to be mystified by the work. I think it's one thing for film students who really want to learn how something is made, so that they can find it in themselves, to know this. But having too much detailed knowledge can be dangerous. If a novel's successful, do you then go back and publish an edition of the novel with notes in the corner, or earlier drafts?

Let's talk about *The Rapture*. When did you write that script?

The earliest version of the script was twenty-two pages long—a script for a short. I think it was about 1984 or 1985 when I first wrote it. Someone told me to put it away and never show it to anyone else if I wanted any kind of career. Then Nick Wechsler read it and said, "Expand this to full length, and I'll help you turn it into a movie." That was about '89 or '90.

Where did the idea come from?

It partly came from discussions with my brother, when both of us had a fantasy about making a movie about the Book of Revelations. And there was an article somewhere about a mother who had thrown her children off a bridge and then jumped. A Japanese mother who jumped into the sea with her child, and drowned her. At the same time, there were also a couple of notorious child-abuse scandals. A father in New York tortured and killed his daughter.

I was thinking about how, in the complications of life, people could kill their children. That it was possible for one person to kill a child completely out of rage and evil, and someone else could kill out of a misguided love or a deep despair in which the murder did not complete a succession of violence. That a parent who'd never been abusive could kill a child, and a parent who was always abusive would finally kill a child. I started thinking about what it would take to kill a child out of love.

I'd written a script, and I was feeling insane. I took a drive in the desert, and got stopped by a cop in San Bernardino whose name was Foster. Then I went for a drive on a real back road in the Mojave Desert for hours and hours, and I really did see a bumper sticker that said "In Case of Rapture This Car Will Be Unmanned." All of those things came together and I got my story.

In terms of the subject matter itself, did you do much research?

I watched a lot of evangelical television in the early 1980s, and was appalled at how easily evangelical television was mocked by the media. I agreed with the Christian critique of the culture. I agreed with a main part of the diagnosis, that the culture was sick, that we live in an evil time. I'm not Christian, so I couldn't accept the Christian prescription. I also didn't think we were heading for their apocalypse. If I have an apocalyptic prophesy of my own, I don't see it coming, even symbolically, in their way. But I took them seriously. I read a number of Christian evangelical books. I read Hal Lindsey's book on the rapture.

When the film came out, Mimi [Rogers] and I went on a tour. We went to Atlanta, which was billed to us as the buckle on the Bible

Belt. There was a screening for evangelicals in a theater outside of town, and there was a Q-and-A afterward. There was a critic there who had been instrumental in leading the attack on Universal after *The Last Temptation of Christ,* and he liked the film. He said, "I'm going to recommend this movie." Partly, because he knew that I was knowledgeable about the terminology, and that I'd done my homework. That I could talk about it, and didn't mock their faith. Research has to be sympathetic.

Will you talk about directing your first film. How prepared were you? Did you have clear ideas about how each scene would be filmed?

I had a storyboard artist working with me, but I didn't know how to read storyboards, so they were useless. I didn't have any sense of how they were going to translate to the set. A couple of scenes were boarded, and it made absolutely no difference to me. I think we had three million dollars to make the movie, which was a fair budget in those days. We had maybe an eight-week prep, which is very fast. I was a baby to everything. As much as I thought I knew about film-making, I had no idea how exhausting it is to be a director. I didn't know what kind of authority I had, and the real process was discovering my authority. In terms of preparation, I spent a lot of time working with Mimi Rogers. Months.

How did she get cast?

We were looking for actors. Mimi read it and really loved it. I had lunch with her, and she said she wanted to do it. We got along really well, and we made a deal.

How did you work with her?

We spent a lot of time in rehearsal. We read over the script. I would play the other parts. We would talk about the emotion of each scene. Then we did some theater exercises together, just for trust. When we got to the set, we really knew each other. I knew how difficult it was going to be for her. I knew how far into herself she would have to go to pull out a performance.

Did she have different ideas about the character than you?

I think the scene where she had a clearly different idea is the scene where Foster [Will Patton] arrests her. I wrote the scene where she was going to pace back and forth like a prosecutor in front of a jury, accusing God. She said, "I just want to stand there. I don't want to tell you what I'm going to do. Just make sure that when I shout, the sound people are ready." She warned the boom operator, and the sound engineer that she was going to shout at a certain point, so they needed to be prepared for it. Then, I kind of blocked it without a performance, and cleared the set. And we shot it. She showed me in the performance what she had in mind. I think we shot it from two positions, two takes each time.

I think all you can hope for is that the actor will make the thing better than what you had in mind. That's the goal. The goal is not for the actor to do what you had in mind. The goal is for the actor to do something wonderful. The writer and the director don't always know what's best for the character. As a novelist, you know that the characters have their own life. They'll take you through the story. You may know roughly or even exactly where you want to go—but how you get there, what they think, how smart they are, changes. Usually, characters turn out to be much smarter than you thought they were going to be, because they have a life. The same thing holds for actors.

Were you comfortable with the acting process when you were preparing the actors?

I've learned from actors that writer-directors tend to talk a little too much, because they know the characters so well. What I want to strive for, as a director, is to give direction, or the note, as a kind of parable or koan, something the actor can take internally with a smile, that will enlighten them. Like a fortune cookie, I want to somehow say in seven words something that the actor would understand. In *The New Age*, there's a scene that didn't end up in the film, where Peter Weller was whining or talking a little too much, and Judy Davis had to listen to this and finally accept because she's already got a plan for something else. I went to her, and Judy's a mother, and said, "He's three years old. Give him permission to wet the bed." I was really happy with that because I knew that that was probably the best line of direction I've ever given anybody. It's all you need because then she can play the dialogue with this new attitude, with a sense of vitality.

Was there a long rehearsal period for *The Rapture*?

On *The Rapture*, we had a little more rehearsal than on *The New Age*, but it depends on the actors. Some actors don't want to rehearse because their agents say they should be getting paid for rehearsal time. On a low-budget film, you can let it slide. I don't know about big-budget films, yet. Peter Weller and I did the same thing I did with Mimi. I spent a few months with him in his kitchen. A few times a week, I'd go and stand there, make coffee, and just talk about the script, with some reading, and go over the lines. I like to be able to spend time with the actors, at least with the leads, and just get to know them. It's really important. Other directors just want to meet them on the set, and that's it. It's all idiosyncratic.

In the introduction to the published screenplay of *The Rapture*, you talk about a crisis of confidence at the beginning of the production.

Yes. For me, the worst day was not the first day of shooting, it was the morning of the second day. The first day was very exciting. We had the most extras that day, and a big crew. We were shooting the scene where the young prophet tells Mimi that her vision is her vision, alone, and that she can't take anybody else to the desert with her. I was exhilarated.

I woke up on the morning of the second day of shooting and I was terrified. My wife had to push me out of the house. I thought, "Maybe I should go to Mexico today." I got to the set, and parked in the crew lot. The van took me, alone, to the set. When I got to the set, there was a problem with the camera. While we waited around for two or three hours for this problem to resolve, I relaxed. The panic went away. Because I was impatient, my impatience and frustration took over from my panic. Since then, I've talked to other directors, and particularly at the beginning of a film, most directors get scared because they're just responsible for so much.

There were certain things I might've gotten that I didn't get because I didn't know how to articulate them. It's easy to blame an inexperienced crew, but I think it's important, if you want to grow as an artist, to assume that everything you don't like in the finished work is your own fault, and not blame anybody else. It's also important, at the same time, if you do blame somebody else, to know if it's right to blame them, and then think about how to avoid being in that situation again. Avoid hiring certain kinds of people if something in their character reminds you of the kind of character that gets you into trouble.

On *The Rapture*, what stylistic ideas did you start with?

Well, I worked with Robin Standefer, who was my production designer, as she was on *The New Age*. I think more than anything else, the style was determined by the budget. I also really liked Bojan Bazelli's cinematography. So, I had a sense of what I wanted. I wanted that clean, spooky feel that the movie has. I also like having silence around my scenes. It just seems to be something that I feel comfortable with as a filmmaker: That these scenes exist in their own bubble. That there may be nothing else but the thing you're looking at.

Many directors seem to have absorbed Hitchcock, and have a sense of how to build a scene in a Hitchcockian way. But they haven't studied John Ford. People have done gun fights, but the great thing about the gun fight in *My Darling Clementine*, at the O.K. Corral, is how slow the buildup is, and how fast it's over. One of the Clanton brothers gets an incredible closeup right before he dies, and you see a man. He's a terrible man, but you see a man. There's a moment of sympathy for him. That's Fordian. That's what Ford is. There's also the incredible angle and the dust and horses and the ballet of it, but what really makes it John Ford is the sympathetic closeup of that man. For me, that's where directorial influence comes in. It doesn't come in saying to yourself while looking at movies, "Oh, I see. The way to handle a scene with two characters is to have them stand up, one walks into a closeup, the other crosses the room. The camera moves halfway around the room to that other person." But it may be useful to occasionally think that way because it's good to get the vernacular. I think I read an interview with Clint Eastwood that said he always keeps a VCR going in his trailer, so he's always looking at movies when he's shooting. I don't think it's necessarily about, "Oh, I just got an idea. We'll frame it this way and this way." What's essential in preparing or thinking about a film, is really thinking about the tone that you want, and what's appropriate to the film you're making.

In terms of the current climate of filmmaking, the subject matter of *The Rapture* is unusual, and it's a subject that's avoided by most films. Have you thought about why it's a taboo subject?

I think that most filmmakers aren't religious, so it's hard to make religious movies. People tend to mock it. Then there's financing. Religion doesn't make a lot of money. There are a lot of religious scripts out there, but it's hard to get them financed. *The Apostle* had to be self-financed, and I think it's a masterpiece. It's a great movie, but he [Robert Duvall] had to pay for that himself. He couldn't get anybody to fund it. It's a perfect screenplay to me.

You mentioned earlier that *The Rapture* was a film that no one thought would get made.

Once I wrote the long version, Nick Wechsler and his producing partners, Laurie Parker and Nancy Tenenbaum fell completely in step with the film, and had faith in it. Everybody who worked on the movie had faith in it.

No one felt nervous about how the movie literally shows the end time?

I think they did, but one of the truths of filmmaking is that the things you get nervous about showing, because you think they're disturbing, are usually those things that are going to work.

Did you struggle with how to show that material, and whether to be literal about it? Were you worried about whether people would take a literal view seriously?

It's a hard question to answer because I knew I wanted to be as literal as possible. I was adamant about being literal. If there were certain things that I wanted to do, and couldn't quite explain how to do, it was because I wasn't clear enough about how to articulate them.

A writer may take up a paragraph after his book has been out for a while, read it and say, "Did I need that word? Did I need that line?" I think that's always the thing that makes you want to keep working. I suppose if you make something perfect, if you really exhaust yourself of everything in one piece, you create a vacuum in yourself and other imperfections would come in, and then you'd have to get them out and make them perfect. So, it's an unending process.

Your biggest ally in making a movie is your production designer, and then, the director of photography. There's not that much variation in how things are lit. You have to see the actors' faces. *The Godfather* was radical in its day because Gordon Willis changed cinematography. But what *The Godfather* did has become a huge cliché, with top-lighting, and that heavy look now is a cheap look. Paul Schrader was talking about DPs, and saying how they come out of film schools, and you can tell any DP the look you want. They'll give you a [Vittorio] "Storraro" look or someone else's look, and they all know how to give you that look and any look you ask for.

It's the production designer who really sets the way the film is going to look. How crowded is the set? What are the colors? How much room do you have? The space that's given you in the location, and how disturbed the eye gets by distraction, really determines what a film is. The advantage that black-and-white film has is that movement gets wonderfully exaggerated, so that you don't have to move that much, and you can really concentrate on the faces because you're not distracted by all the color. Color forces you to come in for closeups that you can't quite get in black-and-white. One thing Robin Standefer and I talked about in both movies was finding a palette that would allow me to get farther back, because I like medium shots. I don't think I'm crowded with closeups in my movies. I like the camera farther back.

Do you view Sharon as just a lost person who's grasping at anything? Is her anger at herself directed at God? Isn't she just as angry and frustrated at the end as she is at the beginning?

She's lost at the beginning, so you can't say that she's angry at God. She doesn't have a sense of that. When she starts taking the notion of the possibility of salvation as a reality, then she starts confronting the source of her unhappiness. As soon as she starts thinking about God, she starts judging herself. She starts coming to terms with herself, and stops running from her numbness. At the end, she's not where she was at the beginning because, at the end, she's fully conscious, whereas she's not conscious at the beginning. It could be that she's the most religious person in the universe. It could be that, at the end, by rejecting God, she's closer to Him than anybody else.

The final speech that you give Sharon, where she blames God for creating such a dreadful universe and the impossibility of loving such a God, is an interesting argument. But isn't the human race responsible for what we do with the universe?

I think if I were to make another film about faith, it'd be a different story. I think that I took one argument, and followed that argument all the way, without necessarily making it a two-character play. God never speaks. God reveals Himself in the movie, but He doesn't say anything.

Why does Sharon want to get to heaven so badly? She's such a desperate character.

To escape from this miserable life. I think that's the short and long answer. She wants to go to heaven, first of all, because she wants conclusive truth that all of this is just a preparation. She wants an answer to suffering; she wants her suffering ended. She views heaven as the end of separation, as the end of distance in her life. What she finds at the end is that the only way she can hold on to a shred of her dignity and integrity, and a shred of ethics, is by keeping her distance.

And to get some sense of meaning?

I would say that's the essence of meaning. Meaning is a sense of one's separate worth and then the recognition of another's separate worth. My individual worth in relation to God and my relationship to others. A triangular relationship.

In terms of your own feeling about this character and her arguments in the film, do you go along with her arguments?

You have to with every character in a film. When Randy says that God is just a drug, I'm with him. And that religion is just a drug, I believe that too. At least I am while he's saying it. You shouldn't load the dice in a story. The characters have to have their own integrity, and they and you have to believe what they're saying. If you look at literature and theater, the better the writer, the more you can see that even the worst characters are still making sense. Or that you understand some relationship between their evil and why they are evil.

You mean that their behavior is understandable?

Yes. Richard III is a hunchback. He's carrying something which makes him feel ugly, so he behaves ugly. Right away, you've got this person whose body is grotesque and who behaves in a grotesque way. His body's grotesque, so you look at him and say, "I know why he is that way, even if he doesn't."

The film seems structured in terms of acts, but not the classical three-act structure, some other sort of structure. What did you have in mind?

I don't know. You write a script that has a certain balance, and then you go to the editing room and start cutting. One of the things that always happens in films is that in order for the screenplays to satisfy the studio, elements have to be established: actors, characters, scenes. Things have to be set up. In a movie, you discover that you usually don't need the setup, and you certainly don't need to introduce characters as richly as you do in a screenplay. In a movie, with the face or the eyes of a good actor, or even a bad actor, a look, a smirk, a snicker, a bit of longing—you've got the whole story there.

Did the low budget hurt the film?

A budget always hurts a movie. I'm sure James Cameron didn't have enough money for *Titanic*. It would've been a better movie if he had 250 million. I'm sure he'd say that. From the point of view of the filmmaker, no filmmaker would say, "Oh, I had too much money." Yes. I would've liked having more money, but I didn't.

What do you think the biggest challenge was in making that film? Just the making of it?

Yes, just making the thing, and pacing myself. The biggest challenge in that movie really was that I'd never directed anything and had so little experience of the theater, and I was thirty-nine and not a twenty-five-year-old with a ton of self-confidence. The biggest challenge had to do with time and authority as much as with camera placement. What's the day? Do I have time to do this? Making decisions correctly. That's also the great part about it.

Do you feel that you achieved what you wanted to achieve with *The Rapture?*

I think the movie is going to be remembered for a long time.

Where did the idea for *The New Age* come from?

Nick Wechsler and I wanted to make an Italian movie. At the time I was writing the movie, the economy was bad and looked like it was getting worse. I lived a few blocks away from Melrose Avenue, a smart shopping street that was going into decline. It was the cool Rodeo Drive in the 1980s, with a lot of interesting shops, designers, interesting shoe stores, clothing stores, galleries, and they started closing down. I saw the pattern, particularly in the clothing stores. You'd see a ten-percent-off sign, and it would be up a little too long. Then twenty, thirty, then seventy percent. At seventy, you knew they were dead. I think that was the genesis of the film.

There was, in particular, a guy I had seen who had been a salesman in a clothing store. Sometimes, in a city, you realize that you've been watching somebody for twenty years, and you've never said a word to him, but you see him around. I had that connection to him. He'd been the floor manager of a very successful clothing store, and then he opened up his own store, which he over-designed. Instead of having windows, he had bad window displays, so you couldn't really see into the store. It was a very forbidding, sealed-off entrance. He was out of business in about five months. You could see the panic. The next time I saw him, he was working in a department store. I saw his life story, and that became the genesis of the film.

The film came from a lot of places. It also came from watching people floundering spiritually, and sensing that people were looking for spiritual answers.

What about all those investigations into new-age ideas?

Well, that's in the air here.

Did you do much research for the film?

A bit less than *The Rapture*, because it's just all around. I went with Patrick Bachau to visit his guru, a yoga teacher, at a retreat in Santa Barbara. I spent five days there, which was really great.

Were there any structural problems writing the script?

That one actually came together fairly easily. I wrote it, and Oliver Stone read it. He had the money to produce it, and he produced. That one went very quickly.

What was your budget on that?

$7.5 million. Not enough to make that movie. When I look at it, it's troubling to me. I saw it again recently, and I was happy with it for the first time in a few years. Actually Neil Labute, before he made *In the Company of Men*, was writing criticism. He was writing for *Film Threat* magazine, and somebody showed me what he wrote about *The New Age* when it came out on video, and it was the best review

I've ever gotten for anything. He wrote a brilliant review of the film. So brilliant that it was as though it was everything I always wanted the film to be. The intentions got through to him so clearly that it allowed me to like the film in a way that I hadn't before. He liked things about it that I don't and things that I'd never been sure of. Still, I wish I'd had more money for it.

What would you have done?

Just taken more time. I felt rushed. I needed more time to make it work. I could have changed the scale. I think that there's a certain sense of claustrophobia in the film. The only reason to have a regret is to think about what you'd do differently the next time if presented with the same challenge, not to beat yourself up over how it could've been. I really regret not seeing the street more. I regret not having a sense of the whole block. I regret not having more people in some scenes. Not having more extras out in the desert. If we could have afforded a real retreat, different kinds of buildings.

Going into it, as your second film, you were probably more aware of the pitfalls of directing.

Yes, but I think I might have been perhaps too cocky and a little too sure of myself. Also, it was shot in the spring after *The Player* came out. So, we were shooting during Oscar and Writers Guild season. I got the Writers Guild Award, and I was nominated for an Oscar for *The Player*. Judy Davis and I were both nominated for Oscars, and we both lost. We both went to the Dorothy Chandler Pavilion, and I had to deal with a horrible hangover the next day on the set. I kept thinking about all those stories of John Ford out in Monument Valley drinking tequila until four in the morning, and then getting up with the roosters and spending the day shooting. But then I thought, who knows if he got anything good that day. I think my internal perspective may have been a bit healthier on *The Rapture*.

Stylistically, the film is reminiscent of Antonioni in a way.

Well, we had a very stark, modern house. We had people dressed a certain way. The real influence of the Italians was to say that nobody in America is making movies about American social reality, about the way people we know live. In that film, I was interested in the decay of the upper bourgeoisie. *The New Age* was telling a story of people who thought they were rich, but were like everybody else in America—two or three paychecks away from disaster.

But it does feel like a European art film.

I was in Italy last December, and *The New Age* had shown on TV in late November on the Italian TV network Rai Due, and the capsule review in the papers said it was like Antonioni. I was very happy to hear that. They said I was a very European filmmaker, and had a European sense of style. It was like a dream. The film worked there. Peter Weller has a house in Positano. He went out after the movie, and everybody had seen it and was very excited. I was thrilled to hear that.

Are people in Hollywood interested in the film of ideas?

When I'm clear, people are interested. I've been fortunate that way. Look, I got *The Rapture, The Player,* and *The New Age* made, and they are all fundamentally based on ideas.

In terms of the ideas in *The New Age*, where do you stand vis-a-vis the issues it raised?

Theologically?

Yes.

I'm a fairly serious Jew, and I wasn't when I made the movies. Aside from whatever my practice is, and it's much more complicated than I could say in an interview, I'm not so troubled by questions of faith. This isn't to say that I'm a person of faith. Whether or not there is a God, I think it's important to live as though there is one. It's important not to worship idols, and to look at the other, and see that the other is also made in the image of God, and that how you treat the other is how you're treating God. I think it's important to live as if that were true. It's not important, initially, to believe it.

How is that different than humanism or some other philosophy?

It's starting with the premise of God.

In essence, in *The New Age*, are you saying that California is spiritually bankrupt?

No. I actually think California is spiritually rich. I think it's bubbling with people who are trying to understand what a spiritual life would be. I don't know how effective that spirituality is, but I see religion everywhere.

In terms of *The New Age*, did any scenes prove difficult to stage or to shoot?

The suicide scene was hard to stage.

What about the party scene?

Yes, the party scene, I needed another three or four nights for both party scenes, the big swimming pool party and the other one. I was just jammed. I was shooting four and a half pages a night, which was too much. I would've liked moving the camera back. If I just moved the camera back a little on a couple of shots they would have been better. If I had let John Campbell put the camera on his shoulders and move around the characters. If we'd just done some handheld to break it up. If I'd made it a bit darker, because when you're shooting quickly, you have to light everything. That moment in the scene where Patrick is talking to Peter and the lights go down, and he looks over in the corner and sees Judy Davis, I thought that's what the lighting of the party should have been. That lighting was really beautiful, but that was very precise, careful lighting. It took a long time to do that, and we didn't have the time to do it all.

In terms of the film's attitude toward the two characters, do you think it's condescending to them?

I hope not. I don't think so.

How did you cast Peter Weller and Judy Davis?

Nick Wechsler gave it to Peter. Peter called me and wouldn't take no for an answer. His enthusiasm and energy just won me over. I'd wanted to work with Judy for a long time. Her agent gave her the script without my knowing it, and then called me and said, "Judy wants to do this."

In terms of the arc of those two characters, where are they at the end? Is Peter as shallow at the end of the film as he is at the beginning?

Peter's in hell at the end. Peter sent himself to hell. Judy has a job, she's decided to settle into life. But Peter couldn't, so Peter's in hell.

How important is casting to you?

As Robert Altman said, the job is really made when you cast your actors. The casting is the most important piece of directing you've done.

I worked with Spielberg on *Deep Impact,* and he said that his best directing is usually when he says "Speak it faster." A lot of directors will say that. The hardest thing of all is to get the actors to speak their lines quickly. They used to speak rapidly. Look at any film from the 1930s. I have the shooting script for *The Roaring Twenties,* and it's 163 pages long. A 163-page script now would be a three-and-a-half or four-hour movie. Directors don't know how to shoot quickly. They don't know how to pace the scene quickly. They take a long time getting into the scene and a long time getting out of it. The actors are slow. They take their pauses, and they move slowly. I think that in any work with any actor on a scene, it's almost never fast enough.

Why is it a virtue to speak quickly?

Most scripts wind up losing a lot of scenes in the editing room, partly because they didn't need to be there and partly because the movie gets too long. Maybe those scenes would have worked better had they been faster. Making a long, drawn-out aria of every scene, which is the way most people shoot and act, is a collaborative mistake. It then becomes hard to put the whole script in. The other solution is to cut the script down to what you think it's going to be after the editing, cut it to the bone, and keep the budget they were going to give you, and expand the number of days that you have to shoot the film. Shoot the real movie that you're making, not the movie that you're putting in the can, but the movie you're putting on the screen.

How specifically did you work with the actors?

The real preparation is the discussion with the actors, and casting. When I do a casting session, I give the actors the script. They do their scenes, and I go over it with them. The directing is often done right there in just getting the actors to see their way into the parts. I was at Telluride a few years ago when Shirley Maclaine was given an honor. She was talking about rehearsal time and said, "Either you get six weeks, or you get nothing." Two weeks rehearsal or six days rehearsal is bad because you get a little bit into it, but you don't get all the way into it, so sometimes it's better to have no rehearsal. She said that Billy Wilder started her first day on a closeup in a huge scene. She didn't even know what she was going to be acting there. That's a director's game, to break the actor down in a healthy way. There are all sorts of reasons for doing things. A director might do that because he's made so many films, he's tired of doing master-to-closeup shots. He just says, "I'm going to play around right now. Maybe it'll work, maybe it won't, but I'm loose enough now as an artist to try that."

Peter Weller really likes to be on the set. He likes to rehearse on the set, even before the set is dressed on location. Just to run the lines there, to play it out, to do business, to walk around. I think that's incredibly useful.

I was in Paris for the release of *The New Age* at the Deauville Film Festival. I had dinner with Roman Polanski. We're talking about work, and I said, "What do you do?" And he said, "Well, I go to the set in the morning, clear it of everybody, not even the DP is there. I get in there with the actors, and we rehearse the scene and block it. Then I bring in the DP. We look at it together, and we decide what we want to see and where we're going to put the camera." I said, "That's what I do!" He smiled.

It's the rare director who really gets to rehearse a long time. Kubrick took fourteen or sixteen months to make a film, actually two years of really working with the actors, because there are four or five months of rehearsal, and then the shooting. Weeks and weeks on the same scenes, and what he did is equivalent to a staged theatrical rehearsal for each scene, breaking the actors' wills, and making them extensions of what he wanted or deep collaborators in something. It's almost like a meditation. They ascend to a level of concentration that you can't get otherwise. Now, when you look at his movies, you can see sometimes, particularly in something like the first forty minutes of *Full Metal Jacket,* at the Marine base, that only by working that way can you get that power. If you look at *The Shining,* there are plenty of scenes in that where you say, "Yes, the only way you can get that out of those actors is working for weeks." And then you look and say, "Did he need to take that many hours? Why did he need to do it?" That's how he worked. It's mutual. The actors and everybody knew what they were getting into.

The New Age **seems more complex, in some ways, in terms of directorial ambition than** *The Rapture.*

Yes. That's where time and money made a difference. More time to move the camera, more understanding of what that means. One of the shots I really love in the film is the scene where the camera starts on the Clemente paintings, and then moves into the living room and goes on this very long crane over the furniture to Peter and his girlfriend at the piano, and he makes love to her on the piano. I just love the way the camera comes in. It took a while to get that shot. That was work. We didn't have that kind of time on *The Rapture.*

You haven't worked in any particular genre in your first two films.

Well, when *The Rapture* came out, somebody said, "I hate that kind of movie." I wanted to say, "What kind? I want to see the other ones!" You know, "Not another movie where a mother kills her child to send it to God! If I see that again this week . . . "

Is there any reason that you didn't choose to direct a genre film?

I actually don't like genre that much. It isn't what drives me. It doesn't really appeal to me. I have no abiding interest in doing, you know, my cop film. I think the closest I've come to genre is *The Player*.

A lot of your work seems to involve characters who are faced with some kind of moral dilemma. Why is that?

Because that's my version of a shark.

You don't think that moral dilemmas can come out of a movie about a shark?

One of the things I liked about *Deep Impact*, as I worked on it with the producers and the director, was that it was a story about the whole world being told it has a death sentence. That's a moral dilemma. When we realized that the disaster is not the comet hitting the ground, but the announcement to the world, we had a movie. That's why I like it. It's a big action movie, but, for me, that's the foundation of that film, the moral dilemma that follows a disaster announcement.

Is it still possible to make great films?

Even though the Golden Age of Hollywood may have passed, it doesn't mean great work can't be made. I don't want to make a hard argument about this, but in some ways, *Apocalypse Now* was the last great American movie, at least a certain kind of great work. It was the end of something that started with Griffith. That was the final statement because the war gutted something in America. We are not the country we were before Vietnam. The post-Vietnam, post-assassinations America is a different country than before. A crummier country, a less intelligent country, a country that's too sophisticated and too cynical.

Remember what I was saying earlier about the shot Ford has in *My Darling Clementine*, of Clanton [Walter Brennan], right before he dies? Tragedy is not just about how the movie ends. Tragedy is also where you put the camera, and your decision to cut to a particular shot. What is the person doing when you're looking at him? How sympathetic are you to a villain's impending death? How much are you allowed to see his humanity at that point? The Nietzschian notion that only an optimistic time is capable of tragedy is probably true. If the movies are lacking a depth of tragedy, it's because we live in a pessimistic time.

What did you do after *The New Age*?

After *The New Age*, I didn't know what film I wanted to make next, so I took some writing jobs for hire, three in a row. I did *Harold and the Purple Crown*. I wrote a script for Dream Works called *Innocence Lost*, and then I did the rewrite on *Deep Impact*. *Harold and the Purple Crown*, is based on a children's book. It's a great script that Universal owns now. I don't know if they are going to make it because it's a $50-million children's movie, which is a lot of money for a children's movie. The second one, I am trying to get to direct. The third one was a straight rewrite. I guess there were four jobs because I did a rewrite on *Mission: Impossible 2*. During all that time, I was also working on a script called *20 Billion*, which Sidney Pollack is producing. The film is in limbo.

It took a while for me to figure out what I wanted to do next, and having been away from the set for a while, I had to think about how I have to reinvent myself as a director to get up in the morning and go to the set. I understand why some directors don't make movies very often. I also understand why a director would want to make a movie every year. Directors as different in their approach as Oliver Stone and Joel Schumacher make a movie every other year. Sidney Lumet makes a movie every year, and so does Woody Allen. I think that sometimes you just find that time has passed and things have fallen apart.

Sometimes you take on a project because you know it's going to lead to something else. You say, "I'll make this movie, and give over two years of my life to this, but I'm really doing it because, as a result of this movie, my next dream, the next film that I really want to make will be possible." It was Gary Cooper who said that one out of every three pictures keeps the bicycle wheel turning. And John Ford said that you make two for them and one for yourself, at a time when you're making two or three movies a year. So, every two years you might make a picture that you really want to make out of three or four. And those aren't always the ones that work, either. Hollywood or popular culture is strange that way. I haven't been able to work that way.

Are you comfortable working in Hollywood, in terms of independence.

Not really, but this is where I live.

Are you comfortable with the state of the film industry, the kinds of films being made, and what it takes to get a movie made?

In the last couple of years, there have been enough good movies to make being in the movies seem like a noble endeavor. Both *The Rapture* and *The New Age* were at Telluride, and last year I went to Telluride just as a filmgoer, which was tremendous because I saw seventeen movies in three and a half days. Great movies. It was like going to Mecca. It's not like Sundance, where it's just a huge market. Telluride is a very idiosyncratic festival, and in some ways, very challenging. There are old movies, there are odd movies, there are very hard films that are never going to get a distributor, but there are enough movies to revive my love of film and my wanting to do serious work to earn the right to be back there with a movie.

Are there films that still need to be made?

The human story always needs to be told.